Giles Tremlett is the *Guardian*'s Madrid correspondent. He has lived in, and written extensively about, Spain almost continuously since graduating from Oxford twenty years ago. His first book was *Ghosts of Spain: Travels Through a Country's Hidden Past*.

Praise for *Catherine of Aragon*:

'Anyone interested in Tudor history will enjoy the splendid portrait on show in *Catherine of Aragon*.' Miranda Seymour, *Daily Telegraph* Books of the Year

'This absorbing biography of Catherine breathes life into a woman too easily reduced to an immovable object meeting the irresistible force of Henry's lust for Anne.' Helen Castor, *Sunday Times*

'Tremlett's fluid, effortless prose brings to life a woman of formidable intelligence, character and conviction.' *Beautiful Britain*

'Tremlett's well-researched portrayal reads easily, and while recognising Catherine's flaws, he restores the lustre to a popular queen whose image was later reduced to a piously dour castoff. Tudor-era fans as well as scholars will appreciate this account.' *Publishers Weekly*

'A humanising picture of this formidable woman.' *Library Journal*

'Tremlett deftly takes the reader through all the twists and turns, and shows us a woman who, rather than being a passive victim, was fully the equal of her husband in conviction and determination.' *Booklist*

CATHERINE OF ARAGON
Henry's Spanish Queen
A Biography

GILES TREMLETT

faber and faber

First published in 2010
by Faber and Faber Limited
Bloomsbury House
74–77 Great Russell Street
London WC1B 3DA
This paperback edition first published in 2011

Typeset by Faber and Faber Limited
Printed and bound by CPI Group (UK) Ltd, Croydon, CRO 4YY

A CIP record for this book
is available from the British Library

ISBN 978–0–571–23512–4

FSC
www.fsc.org
MIX
Paper from
responsible sources
FSC® C013604

For Edward and Berenice Tremlett, my parents

Contents

List of Illustrations

Portrait of an Infanta. Catherine of Aragon? c.1496. by Juan de Flandes. Thyssen-Bornemisza Museum, Madrid. Photo: Album/Oronoz/akg-images.

Portrait of Arthur, Prince of Wales, c.1499 by English School, (15th century). Private Collection, Courtesy of Philip Mould/Philip Mould Ltd, London/The Bridgeman Art Library.

Queen Isabel I, the Catholic. Portrait by Juan de Flandes. Patrimonio Nacional, Madrid. Copyright © Patrimonio Nacional.

King Ferdinand V of Spain, King of Aragon (1452–1516). Spanish School, 15th century. c.1470–1520. The Royal Collection © 2010 Her Majesty Queen Elizabeth II.

King Henry VII by Unknown artist © National Portrait Gallery, London.

Elizabeth of York by Unknown artist © National Portrait Gallery, London.

Portrait of a woman, possibly Catherine of Aragon (1485–1536), c.1503/4 by Michel Sittow (1469–1525). Kunsthistorisches Museum, Vienna, Austria/The Bridgeman Art Library.

Catherine of Aragon as the Magdalene by Michel Sittow (1469–1525). Detroit Institute of Arts, USA/Founders Society purchase, General Membership Fund/The Bridgeman Art Library.

Laughing child, possibly Henry VIII, c.1498. Painted and gilded terracotta by Guido Mazzoni. The Royal Collection © 2010 Her Majesty Queen Elizabeth II.

Portrait of Henry VIII (1491–1547), c.1509 by English School, (16th century). © The Berger Collection at the Denver Art Museum, USA/The Bridgeman Art Library.

Portrait of Cardinal Thomas Wolsey (c.1475–1530) by English School, (16th century). National Portrait Gallery, London, UK/The Bridgeman Art Library.

Lord Cromwell, Wearing the Order of St George by Hans Holbein (1497/8–1543) (school of) © The Trustees of the Weston Park Foundation, UK/The Bridgeman Art Library.

Portrait of John Fisher, Bishop of Rochester, mid-16th century by Hans Holbein the Younger (1497/8–1543) (follower of). Private Collection/ © Philip Mould Ltd, London/The Bridgeman Art Library.

Juan Luis Vives. Spanish humanist and philsosopher (1492–1540.) Portrait. Photo: Album/Oronoz/akg-images.

Emperor Charles V (1500–58) c.1515 by Flemish School, (16th century) Fitzwilliam Museum, University of Cambridge, UK/The Bridgeman Art Library.

Queen Mary I attributed to Lucas Horenbout © National Portrait Gallery, London.

Catherine of Aragon attributed to Lucas Horenbout © National Portrait Gallery, London.

Henry VIII, c.1525–27 by Lucas Horenbout (fl.1534–44). Fitzwilliam Museum, University of Cambridge, UK/The Bridgeman Art Library.

Catherine of Aragon (with marmoset) by Lucas Horenbout. Duke of Buccleuch and Queensberry Collection.

Anne Boleyn, 1534 by English School, (16th century). Hever Castle, Kent, UK/The Bridgeman Art Library.

King Henry VIII by Hans Holbein the Younger (1497/8–1543). Thyssen-Bornemisza Collection, Madrid, Spain/The Bridgeman Art Library.

Iberia: kingdoms and territories, late fifteenth century

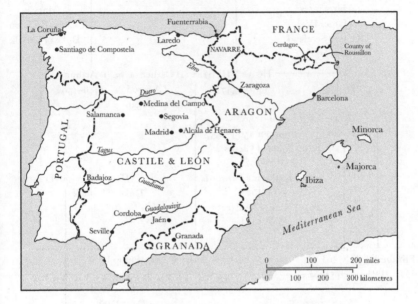

THE TUDORS

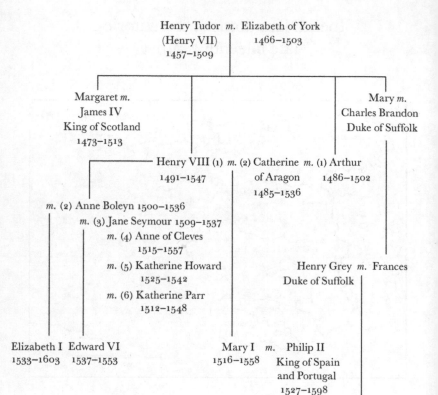

Henry Tudor *m.* Elizabeth of York
(Henry VII)   1466–1503
1457–1509

Margaret *m.*
James IV
King of Scotland
1473–1513

Mary *m.*
Charles Brandon
Duke of Suffolk

Henry VIII (1) *m.* (2) Catherine *m.* (1) Arthur
1491–1547   of Aragon   1486–1502
                 1485–1536

m. (2) Anne Boleyn 1500–1536
m. (3) Jane Seymour 1509–1537
m. (4) Anne of Cleves
1515–1557
m. (5) Katherine Howard
1525–1542
m. (6) Katherine Parr
1512–1548

Henry Grey *m.* Frances
Duke of Suffolk

Elizabeth I   Edward VI
1533–1603   1537–1553

Mary I *m.* Philip II
1516–1558   King of Spain
              and Portugal
              1527–1598

Jane
(Lady Jane Grey)
1537–1554

Dates refer to years of birth and death

SPAIN'S ROYAL FAMILY, CASTILE AND ARAGON

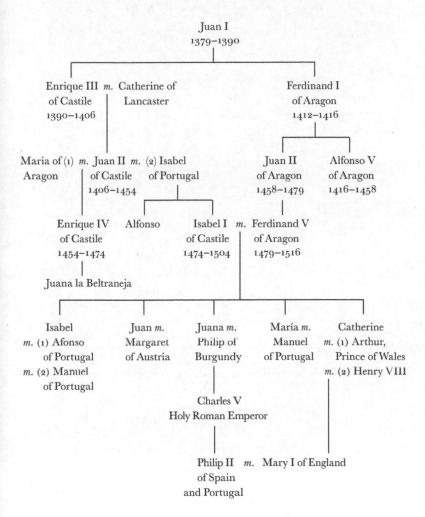

Juan I
1379–1390

Enrique III *m.* Catherine of
of Castile   Lancaster
1390–1406

Ferdinand I
of Aragon
1412–1416

Maria of (1) *m.* Juan II *m.* (2) Isabel
Aragon   of Castile   of Portugal
             1406–1454

Juan II
of Aragon
1458–1479

Alfonso V
of Aragon
1416–1458

Enrique IV   Alfonso   Isabel I   *m.* Ferdinand V
of Castile   of Castile   of Aragon
1454–1474   1474–1504   1479–1516

Juana la Beltraneja

Isabel
m. (1) Afonso
of Portugal
m. (2) Manuel
of Portugal

Juan *m.*
Margaret
of Austria

Juana *m.*
Philip of
Burgundy

María *m.*
Manuel
of Portugal

Catherine
m. (1) Arthur,
Prince of Wales
m. (2) Henry VIII

Charles V
Holy Roman Emperor

Philip II *m.* Mary I of England
of Spain
and Portugal

Dates refer to years of rule

The poetry of history lies in the quasi-miraculous fact that once, on this earth, once, on this familiar spot of ground, walked other men and women, as actual as we are today, thinking their own thoughts, swayed by their own passions, but now all gone, one generation vanishing into another, gone as utterly as we ourselves shall shortly be gone, like ghosts at cockcrow.

G. M. TREVELYAN, *An Autobiography and Other Essays* (1949)

Introduction

Salvador Felipe stood at the doors of the great cathedral in Zaragoza and began to read aloud. It was mid-June, 1531, and the infernal summer heat that replaces the biting winter winds of Spain's central Ebro Plain must have been settling in. The cathedral had been packed for Sunday morning mass and Felipe should have had a good crowd when he raised his voice to name the king of England, Henry VIII. The English king, Felipe announced, was being summoned before a tribunal in the city. If he wanted to hear what others were saying about him, then Henry must appear at the cathedral cloisters on the following Wednesday. If the king did not wish to come himself, he could send a legal representative.

The summons was extraordinary. Monarchs were not the kind of people to be dragged against their will before the ecclesiastical courts. Even this far away, though, many people would have known that England's king was proving to be anything but ordinary. His name was already well known to people here in the capital city of the kingdom of Aragon. He was, after all, married to the woman who introduced the kingdom's name into English history – Catherine of Aragon. She had left her native land long ago, but people had not forgotten she was the daughter of two great Spanish monarchs – Ferdinand of Aragon and Isabel of Castile.

Catherine was now at the centre of one of the greatest scandals being gossiped about across Europe. Henry no longer wanted his wife of twenty-two years. He wanted, instead, a clever and ambitious young Englishwoman called Anne Boleyn. Henry was

1

doing all he could to get rid of Catherine, but his wife was proving a formidable opponent. Catherine had dug in her heels. She was fighting for her marital rights with intelligence and, above all, rock-like obstinacy.

This was why Miguel Jiménez de Embum, abbot of the powerful Cistercian abbey at Veruela, fifty miles away at the foot of the imposing Mount Moncayo, had called the tribunal. He was acting at the request of Paulo di Capisuchi – dean of the Vatican appeal court of the Rota – and, so, ultimately, of the pope. His task was to gather evidence for and give his opinion on what in England was already known as 'the great matter'. This was not a divorce, as it is understood today, though many people used that word to describe it. It was, rather, an attempt to have the pope declare Catherine's marriage illegitimate from the very beginning. Henry's determination to wriggle out of a marriage that was as much about European politics as anything else was felt keenly by some proud Spaniards. She had, after all, been a model wife and queen consort. Her husband had even left his kingdom in her hands while he fought in France. As queen regent in his absence, she had inflicted an historic defeat on his Scottish enemies.

Few people would have felt more deeply for Catherine than those listening to Felipe, who was the tribunal's herald, in Zaragoza. The cathedral's handsomely decorated walls, with their blue, turquoise and green ceramic tiling inlaid into elaborate patterns of *mudéjar* brickwork, were proof of the city's wealth and importance. Zaragoza sat on the bank of the broad, fast-running River Ebro and at the heart of the kingdom once ruled by her father. Catherine was of the most illustrious Spanish stock. Her mother, the mighty and pious Queen Isabel, had been ruler in her own right of the even greater kingdom of Castile. Her parents had conquered the last remnants of Moorish Spain and brought their kingdoms together to form a new and powerful country. Ferdinand and Isabel having died, this was now ruled by Catherine's nephew Charles, the grandly titled Holy Roman Emperor whose lands stretched across swathes of Europe. With this pedigree, Catherine was not a woman who could be cast aside lightly. Nor was she the kind to allow herself to be unceremoniously dumped onto the matrimonial rubbish heap. Her tenacious defence had already seen the case moved from a court in England to the Rota. She had, in fact, kept Henry from getting his 'divorce' for the past four years.

Salvador Felipe read out the citation in Latin. Then he read a translation in Spanish. He pinned the precious original document to the cathedral's door. After an hour, he took it down, replaced it with a copy and left. With this, the legal formalities were done. If the English king did not appear – and it was, in any case, impossible for him to do so at three days' notice – they would start without him. The evidence, inevitably, would be centred on the queen's sex life as a young bride. This was key to the whole question.

Zaragoza was not the only place where hearings into Catherine's marriage were being held. One had already, most famously and dramatically, been called at Blackfriars in London two years earlier. The English witnesses there backed their king against Catherine. They claimed she could not have remained a virgin during her previous, five-month marriage to Henry's elder brother Arthur – who left her a widow at just sixteen. The fact that his wife had slept with his brother was enough, by Henry's reckoning, to prove their own marriage unlawful in God's eyes. It was true that the pope had given written permission for them to wed. But the pope had been wrong. The Bible, Henry insisted, told him as much. It also left him free, or so he claimed, to marry again. His bride-to-be, Anne Boleyn, was waiting impatiently for her wedding day.

Something entirely different, however, was said in Zaragoza. The witnesses there included people who had travelled with the fifteen-year-old Catherine three decades earlier on her terrifying sea journey from northern Spain to Plymouth to join her future family. Their full testimony, transcribed into Latin and buried in a yellowing, parchment-covered manuscript that sat in the monastery's archive for centuries, has either been unavailable or largely ignored until now. The hundred-page original – or at least the copy held by the monastery – was moved to Madrid in the nineteenth century. It has sat in the archive of the Real Academia de la Historia ever since. It appears to be the only surviving record of what the witnesses for Catherine, who were heard in several other places, said during the 'divorce' proceedings.

The voices in the manuscript tell a different story from that narrated by the English witnesses. In their version of events, Catherine's first wedding night was a disaster. The robust young Arthur painted by the English as swaggering out of her bedroom in the morning, flushed with adolescent pride, is transformed into a sickly, traumatised fifteen-year-old. The Spaniards saw a young man overwhelmed by his failure to fulfil the mighty marital, sexual and dynastic obligations present in that big, formal, wedding-night bed.

It is, of course, possible that these Spaniards lied, or dressed up the truth, to protect their beloved princess. It is also possible that they did not. Either way, they were no more or less likely to be lying than the witnesses in England. That makes their testimony as valid as that of those who claimed to have met an ebullient Arthur demanding beer to quench the thirst of a night of hard love-making. Their words add, if not a definitive tilt, then some extra grains of sand to one side of the moral balance on which Catherine is habitually weighed. That balance measures whether she was the pious victim of a cruel, selfish husband or a consummate liar hiding behind an apparently saintly exterior. Judgements of her have swung backwards and forwards from one extreme to the other over the centuries – and still divide people today. A woman whose life and decisions were crucial to the murderous religious upheavals and revolutionary changes that swept through sixteenth-century England leaves few people indifferent.

The Spanish witnesses also add details to some other events in Catherine's life. Their voices have been included in this author's attempt to approach Catherine, at least initially, via her native Spain and her Spanish family rather than through her Tudor in-laws.

Catherine can, of course, be measured on many more scales than just that which deems her either truthful or deceiving. The most important traits of her character have, in fact, little to do with honesty or falsehood. What really matters about her is the strength of that character. A protected childhood amid a family of intense, self-demanding Spanish women does much to explain where this came from. Catherine grew up to become a woman of deep, even exaggerated, intensity. The complex and unhappy early English years, with their constant illnesses, eating problems and stern written instructions from the pope to avoid the self-harm of excessive fasting, give the first few clues to that nature. These were the reactions of a young, perfectionist woman who found herself lonely, lost and unloved in a foreign land.

That same intensity and perfectionism explain, too, both her success and popularity as a queen consort and her final embrace of potential martyrdom. Exactly how close Catherine got to execution and (in her terms) martyrdom, we cannot be sure. She was not alone in believing that a violent end awaited her and, of course, Henry showed few qualms about beheading later wives. What is abundantly clear, however, is that she was ready – even happy – to die for her own cause. That, by the measure of her time, is an example of extreme passion. For, in her day, passion was a matter of love, faith, suffering and, above all, of religious conviction. A woman of Catherine's convictions and education would have learned that the greatest example of unfettered love was that suffered by Jesus Christ before and during his own martyrdom. Christ's 'passion', indeed, was something she would have dwelt on during her own hours of devotion. To someone like Catherine, then, there was nothing more passionate or virtuous than dying for one's faith – even though, in the sixteenth century, most Christian martyrs belonged to a dark and distant past. Catherine also had the mettle that would have allowed her to take her peaceful defiance all the way to the executioner's block. Such people are, at most times in history, a rarity.

For this writer, who is not a Roman Catholic, it is Catherine's intensity of character that sets her apart. It makes her much more than a passive victim caught in the tumultuous river of history. Catherine of Aragon, in short, made her choices. She was fully aware of the extreme consequences these could bring both for her and for England. Her strength lay as much in what she did as in the knowledge of what may have happened as a result. Henry VIII, indeed, never met a tougher opponent on, or off, the battlefield.

Catherine's importance to English (and European) history is beyond doubt. It is not just that she lasted as long as Henry's five other wives put together. Her husband's reign introduced four remarkable women to England's story: Catherine of Aragon and her daughter 'Bloody' Queen Mary; and Anne Boleyn with her daughter, 'Good' Queen Elizabeth. 'From this contest, between two mothers and their daughters, was born the religious passion and violence that inflamed England for centuries,' says the historian David Starkey. Reformation, revolution and Tudor history would all have been vastly different without Catherine of Aragon. Without her, England might be a very different place today. As a shy Spanish teenage bride, awaiting her boyish groom in a large English 'bed of state' in 1501 – thirty years before the tribunal met in Zaragoza – Catherine could not have been aware of any of this. That moment, however, is where this story starts.

Giles Tremlett, Zaragoza, 20 September 2009

1 Bed

The Spanish girl with the long, light auburn hair lay in bed waiting. It had been an exhausting day. She had been on show, watched by thousands of pairs of foreign eyes, since she first stepped out of the Bishop's Palace and into the cold, early winter morning air of London. She had done what was bid, maintaining her composure during the interminable hours of wedding ceremony and mass. She, the bride, had walked elegantly across the raised walkways and stages in the cathedral, turning from one side to the other to show herself to the sea of staring faces below. Onlookers had gawked down from windows and rood-lofts to get a view of her in her white silk Spanish dress with its strange, hooped skirt. Cheering crowds had gathered on the streets and, inside, the tumult had been such that some found it hard to follow what was happening. Her new in-laws were delighted.

Her day, however, was by no means over. The bedroom at the Bishop's Palace bustled with activity. It had been busy, already, for the best part of two hours. A Spanish countess and an English duchess had, previously, fussed together over the making of the bed. An English earl had come to make sure they had done the job properly. He had even tested it out himself, trying out one side then the other to make sure it was comfortable enough and properly made. This, after all, was no ordinary bed. It was, as one chronicler of this most publicised of events put it, a 'bedde of estate'.

Watched by the assembled company of women, the girl stepped into the bed. There was no privacy. Her helpers made sure that she was 'reverently laid and reposed'. And, so reposed, she awaited the pale, thin-lipped and auburn-haired fifteen-year-old she had just married.

The young man with whom she had spent much of the day, but who she had barely ever spoken to, then entered the room. A train of ebullient friends, flunkies and officials entered with him. She could count on the fingers of one hand the number of times she had seen this serious, gentle-eyed youth before. His name, however, had been part of her life for as long as she could remember. He was 'Arturo', Arthur, a prince from the land that had given the world the exotic legends of Camelot. He was also, as eldest son of Henry VII, heir to the English throne. One day, it was assumed, she would be his queen.

Those with Arthur had spent the best part of the afternoon drinking, dancing and seeing to their own 'pleasure' and 'myrthe'. It is safe to assume that the young man had drunk his share of wine and ale as well. Arthur's younger brother – an energetic, excitable, robust and ruddy-cheeked ten-year-old prince called Henry – was probably deemed too young for this later stage of the proceedings. Young Henry had been the one who, earlier, had taken her hand and led her out of old St Paul's Cathedral along the raised platform above the 'tumult and multitude' of people packed inside. One of the company recalled that they found Catherine lying under the coverlet 'as the manner is of queens in that behalf' – whatever he meant by, or knew about, that. Then, with a gaggle of people still watching, Arthur climbed in beside her. The book of royal etiquette stipulated, admittedly for the slightly different circumstances of the marriage of an English princess, that the groom should be 'in his shirte, with a gowne cast about him'.

The couple would have rested their heads on a special sheet covering the pillows. Layers of straw, canvas, a feather mattress (all suitably rolled on and beaten to get rid of bumps) and tightly stretched sheets lay beneath them. More sheets, blankets, rugs and, perhaps, a coverlet of ermine were above. The bed itself should have been a tester bed, with its posts supporting a full or half canopy above their heads. There may also have been curtains.

Beside the girl's bed the bishops and prelates were reciting in Latin. This, at least, was a language she could understand. Much of the rest of the day's comings and goings outside the cathedral had been conducted in English – a language she was only just getting used to hearing. Most of the chatter in her chamber now would also have been in English – though a few would have known to address her in Latin or in French, a language which she could just about use herself. Few, excepting her own retainers, would have spoken the familiar Spanish of her home.

There must have been something comforting about the bishops' incantations. For the girl knew about prayer. Priests, as both tutors and confessors, were the men she had come to know best in her fifteen years. Now they were praying for her to remain safe, in this bed, from the demons of the dark, English night. The missal indicated the words they should use. '*Custodi famulos tuos in hoc lecto quiescentes ab omnibus phantasmaticis daemonum illusionibus: custodi eos vigilantes ut in praeceptis tuis meditentur dormientes, et te per soporem sentiant: ut hic et ubique defensionis tuae muniantur auxilio,*' they would have intoned. Abraham, Isaac and Jacob – familiar Old Testament spiritual war-horses – were called on to add their power to the blessing.

The bishops' presence here, sprinkling holy water on the princely bed, meant that the most important part of the day was due to begin. The young couple's duty, the priests were expected to remind them, was '*crescant et multiplicentur in longitudine dierum*' – to 'grow and multiply throughout the length of your days'. Soon the bishops withdrew. Fortified by a goodbye swig of wine and spiced sweetmeat, the noisy young men, the court functionaries, the bossy governess and all the rest left the newlyweds alone.

Catalina, still getting used to hearing the sharp consonants of her name softened to the English word 'Catherine', was one month off her sixteenth birthday. She was, or certainly should have been, a virgin. That, anyway, was what the ambassadors sent by her parents, Isabel and Ferdinand, the powerful *Reyes Católicos* – the 'Catholic Monarchs' – of Spain, had proclaimed to her father-in-law and his court just twenty-four hours earlier. Her husband, Arthur, prince of Wales and heir to the throne of England, may have been younger, but his fourteenth birthday was already thirteen months behind him. Catherine herself had been of a marriageable and (by presumption, at least) sexually mature age for even longer. The wedding treaty had stipulated a marriage after Arthur's fourteenth birthday. By the mores of their time, then, they were old enough for what should have happened next. Had not her father-in-law, King Henry, been conceived when his own mother, Margaret Beaufort, was still just a twelve-year-old girl?

This was, in fact, what it had all always been about. There had been years – most of her young lifetime – of waiting. Months of journeying across the mountains, valleys and sierras of her homeland had been followed by two attempts to get across the storm-battered sea to England. Weeks were spent processing through a strange, dark and damp land. Finally, with a display of pageantry never before seen in London, she had got married. All that had a single purpose. Her task was to join her native Spain to her newly adopted England. She was to do that by bearing children – preferably male – who would carry not just the blood of the Tudors but also that of the royal houses of Castile and Aragon. That task was meant to start in her very public wedding bed in the Bishop's Palace, just as soon as the onlookers had disappeared.

Did they or did they not set about the business of 'multiply-

ing' that night? Did lust, hope or simple duty bring their young
bodies – and, perhaps, their spirits – together? Or was it all too
much for a pair of exhausted, inexperienced, overwrought or
over-excited teenagers? Did they even know exactly how to
perform what was expected of them? Only Catherine and her
slight, serious-looking young husband ever knew what happened
next. Did she find him to be of 'good and sanguine complexion',
as one of his friends remembered him that night? Or was he,
underneath the gown and shirt, as startlingly 'weak' and 'thin' as
one Spaniard who travelled with Catherine later described him?
At the hearing years later in Zaragoza, Spanish witnesses who
served Catherine in England were firm about his impotence.
Arthur sneaked out of her room early, 'surprising everyone',
with Catherine later pointing to a young boy in her service and
muttering to her ladies that 'I wish my husband the prince was
as strong as that lad because I fear he will never be able to have
[sexual] relations with me.'

How, indeed, did they communicate their desires? Latin,
learned from primers and practised with tutors and priests, was
the only language they really had in common. How did that
Latin sound, now, in the intimacy of a shared bed?

Even Doña Elvira, the bossy and troublesome lady mistress
who Catherine had brought with her, seems not to have snooped
on them – though she would later claim to know exactly what
did, or did not, happen that night. Perhaps Elvira, who acted as
governess and iron-fisted ruler of her household, was the source
of later Spanish claims that there had been no virgin's blood left
staining the sheets.

The question of what took place here on top of straw, canvas
and feathers would become, a quarter of a century later, a battle-
ground around which changes of epic proportions occurred. For
the boy died before he could become king, leaving Catherine

of Aragon a childless, sixteen-year-old widow. She went on to become the first wife of his young brother, Henry VIII. Much later, Henry would ask the pope for permission to abandon her because of her sexual encounters with his brother. His chances of obtaining a successful annulment, then, hung on the idea that something had actually happened in that wedding bed.

Sex, royalty, power and European politics all met on the nuptial mattress. The essential ingredients of what her twenty-first-century countrymen would come to call a *culebrón*, a soap opera, were all here. Gossips and intellectuals from Bristol to Bologna all had their views on whether the girl and the boy had fulfilled what was meant to be their destiny and whether she had sinned by marrying her husband's brother. It was only then, as the supposed details of her sex life were aired in open court in London and Zaragoza, that Catherine gave her own version of that night. She insisted that nothing at all had happened. Catherine, who tried so insistently to be perfect, had failed in her marital duties. Her Spanish family, amongst others, had hoped for more.

2 Queen

Toros de Guisando. 19 September 1468

The four bulls of Guisando were lined up on an exposed esplanade where the foothills of the Gredos mountains fall south towards the vast plain of central Spain, the *meseta*. Huge granite beasts with long backs, they stood in obstinate, stony silence, as they had done for centuries. If the four *Toros de Guisando*, a first sculptural suggestion of the long and complex relationship of Catherine of Aragon's homeland with the ox and the bull, remain a mystery today, then they must have seemed supernaturally strange in the year 1468.

The potency of this image brought two groups of riders to this spot on a cool, clear September morning seventeen years before Catherine's birth. They had come, after all, to make peace. The bulls were to be silent notaries to an agreement, hammered out in advance, settling the future of Castile. A kingdom long racked by bloody internal squabbles was making yet another attempt at putting out the fires of civil war. The setting had been chosen carefully. Even in the late fifteenth century, politics and presentation went hand in hand.

The king arrived, as kings do, with as much pomp as could be summoned up in open countryside beside a small brook several miles from the nearest town or village. There were fanfares of trumpets as Enrique IV of Castile led a small army of some thirteen hundred men to the site where the stone bulls stood. Enrique was a striking man. Tall, blonde and well-built, he had broken his nose as child. The accident left him with an adult face that made him look, depending on who you listened to, like either a terrifying lion or a foolish monkey.

His rival was somewhat more low-key. She was, exceptionally, a woman. This was not a time when queens regnant, or those who aspired to the position, were either plentiful or particularly welcome in Europe. This unusually fair-haired and pale-skinned Spanish woman 'with eyes between green and blue' rode not a horse, but a mule. The animal, in turn, was led by a priest. There was, however, no attempt at humility here. The woman riding the handsomely and expensively harnessed mule was a king's daughter, Isabel de Trastámara. She was seventeen years and four months old and fast becoming wise beyond her age. She was both half-sister to Enrique and challenger for his crown. A train of some two hundred horsemen followed her. The man holding the mule's reins was Archbishop Carrillo of Toledo, primate of Spain – a formidable warrior priest and one of the wealthiest and most powerful political players in the land. He was also Isabel's chief ally. The records do not say whether he was wearing the same scarlet cloak with a white cross that he was said to wear over his armour when leading his men into battle. The evening before, late into the night, he had tried to change the princess's mind about making peace. That morning, after celebrating mass, Isabel had handed him a written pledge that she would make sure her brother and the strongmen who controlled him did not punish Carrillo for his loyalty to her. He, and his lands, would remain safe.

Isabel had chosen peace. The conditions were by no means all favourable to her, but they were worth it for the one major concession they included. She was to be proclaimed her half-brother's heir – the future queen of Castile. 'If I do have this right, give me the brains and energy to, with the help of Your arm, pursue and achieve it and bring peace to this kingdom,' she said, before setting out. The 'arm' she referred to was not the very worldly and occasionally sword-wielding arm of the archbishop but that of the entity who ultimately judged and decided everything in her world – God.

Isabel had become Enrique's challenger by chance. Her father, the weak and malleable Juan II, placed her well down the order of succession on his death in 1454. Above her were not just Enrique and her full brother Alfonso, but also the future children of both. Castile's violent nobility, headed by the *Grandes* or Grandees, had long played a terrible game with their monarchs in which it was those behind the throne who mattered as much, if not more, than whoever was sitting on it. Enrique was, in any case, one more in a line of monarchs who had long proved ineffectual. His nickname, 'The Impotent', was garnered from what appeared to be a complete inability to consummate his marriages – and the resulting cuckoldry to which he was submitted by his second wife, Queen Juana. The nickname could just as well, however, have referred to his inability to control his kingdom.

In one of the least dignified moments of his reign, an effigy of the king dressed in mourning had been placed on a mock throne on scaffolding erected outside the imposing, crenellated walls of Avila. There, on a summer's day in 1465, a group of the country's most powerful men – including the archbishop of Toledo – ritually humiliated the effigy in front of a crowd of jeering onlookers. A toy crown was torn off his head. The sceptre and sword were wrenched from his hands. The marshal of Castile, Diego López de Estúñiga, then knocked the dummy to the ground, hurling foul-mouthed abuse at it. The heavy-booted nobles had then set about this king substitute, kicking him and stamping on his limp body to angry cries of '*¡A tierra, puto!*', 'Down on the ground, you bastard!' They did not like this king. So they invented one of their own. Their pretender was Enrique's half-brother Alfonso – aged just eleven years old.

Amongst the many rumours circulated about Enrique (often by those chroniclers who Isabel paid to make sure her version of history was the one that survived) was that he was homosexual. That may have been what the chronicler Galíndez de Carvajal meant when he slyly reported that: '[The king] had around him men who followed his customs.' Medieval Spain was not, in this respect, a sexually tolerant place. True or false, the rumours did not help his standing as monarch. They might, however, have been overlooked had he shown himself a stronger ruler or managed that other essential job of medieval monarchs, the siring of a male heir. Women certainly formed part of his sexual universe. He had a formal mistress at court and boasted, perhaps too much, of his use of prostitutes. He only seemed capable of proper sexual excitement, however, in certain limited – and, possibly, fetishistic – circumstances. Whatever it was that satisfied him sexually, it was not his wives. When he and his first wife, Blanca de Navarra, were divorced after thirteen years of cohabitation, Enrique admitted they had never consummated the union. This, he suggested, was the result of bewitchment. His physicians certainly managed to provoke, by their own physical manipulation, a successful royal orgasm. The result was deemed disappointingly 'watery and sterile'. His other problem, according to a near contemporary, was that his penis was thin at the base but bulbous at the tip, making it difficult to maintain upright. Clumsy attempts at artificial insemination, which involved the queen using a thin golden tube to introduce the semen, failed.

Not surprisingly, Queen Juana's pregnancies were widely assumed to have nothing to do with Enrique. His daughter Juana, for example, was known as 'La Beltraneja' after her supposed father – the king's best friend, Don Beltrán de la Cueva. This had been the excuse used to mount the challenge against him in Alfonso's name. The heir to the crown was not of royal blood, the rebellious nobles argued, and the monarchy was in danger. Civil war ensued. Fifteen-year-old Isabel, forced to decide between her brothers, had chosen Alfonso. From the age of ten onwards, she had been obliged to live at Enrique's court. She and her brother Alfonso were, Isabel later said, 'forcibly and inhumanely wrenched from the arms' of her Portuguese mother 'when we were just children'.

It had not been so much Enrique that she disliked, but his wife. Her sister-in-law Juana was remembered by Isabel in later life as a wicked stepmother figure who destroyed her childhood happiness. Juana's jealous rages were infamous. A chronicler of the time recalled a particularly nasty attack on Enrique's mistress, Doña Guiomar, with a heavy, wooden-soled platform shoe, or *chapín*. 'When she saw her [the queen] swore with vile words and, grabbing her by the hair, hit her many times on the head and shoulders with a *chapín*,' he wrote.

The plague was sweeping through Castile. Isabel and Alfonso had spent a few months happily reunited with their mother in Arévalo. They had even had time to celebrate Alfonso's birthday with *momos*, mummery, in which a happy Isabel played the role of a classical muse. Alfonso may have been trying to escape the plague when he suddenly fell ill in Cardeñosa, north of Avila, in July 1468. He died quickly, provoking rumours that he had been poisoned. Alfonso left no children. Isabel, as a result, found herself immediately hailed as his successor and as Enrique's challenger.

The mantle of monarch-to-be may have been thrust upon her, but it fitted Isabel remarkably well. By refusing Carrillo's entreaties not to do a deal with Enrique at Guisando, she was already showing a streak of independence from the self-seeking nobles and bishops who backed her. Obstinate conviction, a family trait that would be passed on to her daughter Catherine of Aragon, was already showing through. If the rebellious nobles thought she would be easy to control and manipulate, they were wrong.

The peace she was about to agree with Enrique contained several elements. He would remain king. She would be his 'first legitimate heir', displacing the six-year-old Juana la Beltraneja.

The queen had 'used herself uncleanly for the past year' and would be packed off to Portugal. In fact, she was already several months pregnant by a new lover, Don Pedro de Castilla. This last humiliation – for, while kings were free to have mistresses, their wives were bound to be faithful – may have helped spur Enrique to reach a deal with his half-sister. Their agreement also supposed that the crucial decision about who Isabel should marry would be made jointly. In the meantime, Isabel would take the title, and rich estates, of princess of Asturias – a title equivalent in importance to the English monarchy's prince of Wales.

The meeting by the Guisando bulls was carefully stage-managed. Each side followed the script hammered out on previous days between their negotiators. First Antonio de Veneris, the papal legate, wiped the historical sheet clean by declaring all previous vows of allegiance to be invalid. Then Isabel and her followers declared their recognition of Enrique. She stooped to kiss her brother's ring, but he lifted her up and – in a piece of gallantry almost certainly written into the script – hugged her instead. An embittered Carrillo was allowed to be the last to declare his allegiance to the man against whom he had rebelled. Brother and sister trotted off together. The civil war was over – for the time being, at least.

Both sides later broke key parts of the agreement. Enrique did not even try to get the Cortes, Castile's parliament of nobles, clerics and city representatives, to ratify Isabel's status as heiress to the crown – despite his promise to do so. Isabel, in turn, ignored Enrique's right of veto over her marriage partner. She followed her 'free will' by secretly choosing her own husband, Ferdinand, heir to the crown of neighbouring Aragon. It was from him that their youngest daughter, Catherine of Aragon, would gain the second part of the name by which she went down in history. Enrique later backtracked completely, reaffirming Juana la Beltraneja's legitimacy and position as heiress. The troublesome, violent nobles, meanwhile, continued to foment chaos and jostle for position. None of this would change the outcome of events. For, when Enrique died six years later, it was the deal struck at Guisando that won through. The meeting before the bulls changed the destiny of Spain. It would, through the chain of events it helped unfold, also shape the destinies of Isabel and Ferdinand and, of course, of their daughter.

Catherine's parents married under precarious circumstances. Isabel had to flee the town of Ocaña, where she had been held as a virtual prisoner while Enrique tried to fix a marriage to some distant, non-threatening prince. England's Richard III was on his list of candidates. As she fled from Enrique's men, Ferdinand rode incognito from his father's kingdom in Aragon across the potentially dangerous open plains of Castile. The young couple who were so desperate to marry had never even set eyes upon one another before.

Both, however, knew the political value of marriage. Both knew, too, that their respective futures as monarchs of two nations covering most of the Iberian peninsula would be immensely bolstered by a partnership sealed with wedding vows. They met at Valladolid in October 1469. The only image Isabel had ever seen of Ferdinand was a roughly engraved medallion. It showed a young, bearded face and little more. Reports that Isabel identified him from her window amongst a group of eight approaching riders and gleefully shouted: 'That is he! That is he!' are too far-fetched to believe. Like many apocryphal stories, however, they hide an inner truth. For Isabel was to declare in her dying days that marrying the wayward and scheming Ferdinand – who Machiavelli admired – was the best thing she had ever done.

They were married on 19 October 1469 in a chapel at the palace of a local dignitary, Juan de Vivero. That same night the marriage was consummated. This time there were no doubts. Isabel and Ferdinand's first sexual intercourse was performed with a crowd of people waiting anxiously by their door. The sheets from the wedding bed, stained with a virgin's blood, were carried into the packed chamber next door and, to the sound of trumpets and drums, displayed for all to see.

When Enrique the Impotent died five years later, few mourned. His had been, by many measures, a miserable life. Even on his deathbed he was reportedly bullied by people asking him to reaffirm the name of his real heir. His emaciated body was unceremoniously carted off on wooden planks.

Isabel wore the black of mourning to the funeral mass that she presided over at San Martín's church in Segovia. When she stepped into the square outside, however, she removed her gown to reveal a brightly coloured and richly decorated costume. 'The queen suddenly appeared in a very rich outfit and adorned in resplendent jewels of gold and precious stone that enhanced her singular beauty,' the chronicler Alfonso de Palencia recalled.

This was an act not just of theatre, but of political intent. For the costume was, quite obviously to those who saw it, that of a queen. Isabel was in a hurry. A stage had been erected in the square outside the church. Trumpets sounded and drums rolled. There and then, in front of her own supporters, she had herself proclaimed Queen of Castile. There were rivals to see off – not least her own beloved husband, who was away in Aragon.

He was disturbed to hear that she had processed through the town preceded by her *maestresala*, Gutierre Cárdenas, 'holding a bared sword in his right hand, gripping it by the tip with the handle up – in the Spanish fashion – so that all, including those furthest away, could see that the person coming towards them was she who could punish the guilty with royal authority'. It was a gesture of power, backed by an overt threat of violence, that no one could remember a Spanish woman ever using before. Some in the crowd muttered their concern at the sight of it. Ferdinand also worried that it was unfitting for a woman. 'Tell me if, in the past, there has ever been an example of a queen who has had this symbol – a threat of punishment to her vassals – borne before her?' he asked Palencia and others who were with him when he was told about his wife's audacity. 'I have never heard of a queen who usurped this masculine attribute.'

The woman who has a good claim to be the most important monarch in Spanish history started her reign with characteristically bold gestures. The youngest of Isabel's four daughters, the as yet unborn Catherine of Aragon, would be described by a contemporary as 'the one who most resembled her mother'.

3 Birth

Alcalá de Henares. 15 or 16 December 1485

The town of Alcalá de Henares, set on a dusty, unprotected plain to the east of Madrid, is a place of extremes. In the summer it is baked dry by the unforgiving Castilian sun. In winter it freezes. A pale sun shines weakly from a clear pastel sky, losing its battle against the harsh, obstinate chill. The slightest breeze pierces all but the best-wrapped bodies.

The winter of 1485, the year of Catherine of Aragon's birth, was not just cold but unusually rainy. That may have made it slightly warmer than usual but the damp would have helped the cold settle into the bones. Alcalá, with its thick red brick and pale stone walls and its solid defensive towers, was a safe place for Isabel. It was close to the centre of her kingdom. This still needed the constant attention of a queen who had slowly strengthened her power over its previously unruly nobility. It was also a good place to give birth.

It had been an exhausting year. Isabel and Ferdinand had started it in Seville, comfortably installed in the Royal Alcazares – the Moorish palace complex enlarged a hundred years earlier by one of Isabel's predecessors, Pedro the Cruel. The Alcazares, with their patios and gardens, were one of the jewels in the Castilian crown. This had been immeasurably enriched by its encounter with the sophisticated tastes of the Muslim world. A hybrid architecture emerged in the parts of Spain conquered by the Christians – especially where a sizeable population of subjugated Muslims, known as *mudéjares*, remained. Christian patrons like Pedro and Isabel employed craftsmen of Moorish origin and a distinct *mudéjar* architecture had evolved in Christian Spain.

The delicate stucco lattice work, decorative masonry and colourful ceramic tiles that surrounded Isabel in Seville all owed their inspiration, if not their creation, to the Moors. Friezes on the walls, in both Gothic and Kufic script, were a reminder that Spain had been divided between Christian and Muslim kingdoms for the past seven centuries. The Patio de las Doncellas, or Courtyard of the Maidens, owed its name to a terrible legend claiming that the Moorish kings who lived here had once demanded an annual tribute of one hundred virgins from local Christians.

Isabel spent the winter before Catherine's birth preparing for the campaign against the last remaining Moorish kingdom, centred on Granada. This Muslim-ruled territory covered almost all of the southern Mediterranean coast of the Iberian peninsula, including the ports of Malaga and Almeria. The queen enjoyed planning her wars and had recently become a convert to the use of artillery. She had ordered large quantities of gunpowder from Sicily, Flanders and Portugal. Foundries were turning out rudimentary cannons. Munitions were also being prepared for the new artillery pieces which her armies would use to besiege Moorish towns and castles.

There were reminders, too, that the Muslim territories of north Africa were only a hundred miles away from Seville across the Straits of Gibraltar. An embassy arrived from Fez, bringing her not just words of peace but also silks and perfumes. The world of Isabel, into which Catherine would shortly be born, was one in which the sophistication nurtured and conserved in the Muslim world was never far away. It was a light that had kept shining in Spain during Europe's harshest and most brutish medieval days.

Isabel and Ferdinand left Seville in a hurry in March 1485. The plague, that great medieval scourge, had arrived. The court – peripatetic as ever – moved with them to Cordoba, further up the River Guadalquivir. Here, again, there was plenty to remind Isabel of Spain's Moorish past. The vast bulk of Cordoba's huge mosque still dominated the city. The monarchs lived close by in another *mudéjar* building, the Alcázar de los Reyes Cristianos, complete with Arab-style baths and gardens. Huge waterwheels creaked loudly as they raised water out of the river to irrigate the farmland. The city itself remained a melting pot of peoples, as Christians mixed with *mudéjar* Muslims and a thriving, long-standing Jewish community.

Isabel's determination to conquer the kingdom of Granada was far stronger than her husband's. In the summer of 1484 she had stubbornly set off to make war without him. Ferdinand wanted to do battle with the French, foes of his own family's kingdom of Aragon. A long-running squabble over ownership of the border regions of Roussillon and Cerdagne required their attention first, he argued. She had left him a few of her soldiers to help, but had taken the rest south. Eventually, however, he had come to join her and lead the troops into battle.

In this dual monarchy, where the two 'Catholic Monarchs' ruled together in Castile, Isabel's weakness was that she was a woman. That meant that, in Aragon, she was just a queen consort. Her strength was that she was the hereditary monarch of the bigger, richer and far more populous kingdom of Castile. Aragon had just a quarter of Castile's estimated population of between four and five million people. Isabel's husband may have ruled her heart, but she often helped rule his actions. 'The queen is king and the king is her servant,' commented one surprised foreign visitor, with a degree of exaggeration. 'He immediately does whatever it is that she decides.'

In fact, their relationship was a lot more subtle and finely balanced. In order to avoid a potentially violent battle over who should govern Castile, they struck a mutually beneficial deal. The agreement was summed up in a device which shares lin-

guistic origins with the English word tantamount. '*Tanto monta,
monta tanto, Fernando* [Ferdinand] *como Isabel, Isabel como Fernando.*'
This means either that they 'amounted to the same' or, simply,
that they did not care which of them gave the orders. All, in any
case, was to be done in both their names. In practical terms, she
weighed heavily in the internal affairs of Castile while he dominated absolutely in Aragon. She may have helped plot wars, but
he generally led the troops. He also carried the weight of foreign
policy – of which their daughters' marriages were a key part.

It was, in short, a form of shared sovereignty in which they
issued orders jointly but never formally, or administratively,
united their two kingdoms. That rankled, initially, with Ferdinand. His own kingdom of Aragon did not allow women to
rule. Those who did inherit the crown had to hand over power
to their husbands. The advantages of being joined to Castile,
however, were too great to ignore. He was not going to put
that at risk by challenging his wife's inherited right to rule. As
a result, Isabel's daughters were brought up by a mother who
was entirely exceptional for her times. She was, in fact, the most
powerful woman in Europe. A few decades after her death, a
Venetian enumerated the recent female monarchs in Europe.
They included Anne of Hungary, two Joans of Naples and 'others in diverse states' but none could match Isabel's importance.
Not until her granddaughter, Mary Tudor, was crowned in England or, more particularly, when the latter was succeeded by her
half-sister Elizabeth I, did Europe see any woman comparable
to her.

In 1484 Isabel had won the argument over what their dynamic
new dual kingdom's prime military target should be. Fighting the
Moors was better business than fighting the French. It kept the
meddlesome nobles busy, provided lands to reward them with
and increased her own wealth, patronage and strength. It was
also morally justifiable, indeed virtuous. For the Granada War

was a holy crusade explicitly backed by the pope. And Isabel, at least in her own mind, was nothing if not holy.

The thirty-four-year-old queen became pregnant early in 1485 but, despite a long history of miscarriages, was not about to give up on her crusade. So it was that, through the summer, she continued to drive the campaign against Granada forward.

Isabel was not the sword-wielding, front-line female warrior imagined by some. That story belongs to Joan of Arc. She was, however, a recognised mistress of some of the more important arts of war. Strategy, logistics, planning, even field medicine, were her specialities. She was her own army's quartermaster general, as well as its inspiration and morale-booster. During the late spring and summer of 1485 she moved from Cordoba to Baena and then Jaen, following the campaign closely. She fretted terribly at the defeat of an army that ventured into a Moorish ambush in the valley of Velillas. To her great satisfaction, however, her engineers with new artillery and stocks of gunpowder then proceeded to batter the fortress at Ronda into submission and take more than ninety other Moorish castles and settlements. The decade-long war for Granada was only in its third year, but already it looked as though a final victory might be achieved.

The season's warring came to a close with celebrations in Jaen in September. The fighting could wait, now, until the weather cleared again in the spring. The court made its slow, cumbersome way north past the last few olive groves of Andalucia and on to the plains of La Mancha in October. The royal family installed itself in the great fortified palace in Alcalá de Henares that had been recently reformed by Cardinal Mendoza. There, ten days before Christmas 1485, Catherine of Aragon was born – the last of five children.

Isabel, it is to be presumed, remained as courageous and self-controlled as ever during childbirth. 'I have been informed by the ladies who serve her in her chamber that, neither when in pain through illness nor during the pains of childbirth . . . did they ever see her complain, and that, rather, she suffered them with marvellous fortitude,' one visitor to her court reported later. The child herself was a welcome, if hardly unique, addition to a family with just one male heir and three other girls. She was given the same name as her English great-grandmother, Catherine of Lancaster.

Isabel and Ferdinand's chroniclers, who sometimes had to present their work for royal approval or correction, dutifully reported the event, but showed little excitement. This was, after all, a fifth child and a girl. She hardly looked set to play a part in settling any future succession to the crowns of Castile or Aragon. 'The monarchs would have been happier with a boy, because having just one male heir was a worry to them,' noted a chronicler.

The one person to pay more than just passing reference to the infant Catherine's arrival was Gonzalo de Baeza, Isabel's *tesorero*, her treasurer. More than any chronicler, it was Baeza who kept a steady eye on Catherine as she grew up. Infantas, as Spanish princesses are known, cost money from the day they were born, or even earlier. And Baeza kept track of it all. It is from his carefully kept accounts books that we learn she was baptised by the bishop of Palencia and that her christening gown was made of white brocade, lined with green velvet and trimmed with gold lace. It was Baeza who paid for the *varas* (a length of about two and half feet) of fine *olanda* linen from Holland that was used for her nightshirts, bibs, sheets and pillowcases and for the thicker *naval* linen from Brittany from which sheets were also made. There was scarlet Florentine cloth to make little tunics and cummerbunds. The newborn child got two pounds of fresh cotton to stuff a newly-made mattress for her crib. The latter does not appear in the accounts, probably making it a hand-me-down. A little brass basin was bought to wash her in and, in a court which cared about smell, a small perfume sprinkler became one of her first possessions. There was a new bed for the maid who watched over her – though the latter, Elena de Carmona, fell ill and had to be sent home to her southern town almost immediately. There was also a wet nurse. These traditionally played a key role not just in feeding children but, once weaned, in bringing them up. It was an important job and the wet nurse was meant to be 'good looking and of good stock, with plentiful milk'. Catherine's brother Juan became so attached to his that he considered her 'like a mother' and, more confusingly, once wrote asking to marry her.

Baeza gives us a tiny glimpse into Catherine's start in life. Her birth was a happy, if largely unremarkable, event at an otherwise unremarkable time. The celebrations coincided with the Christmas festivities. The cardinal of Spain gave a party for the nobles and ladies of the court. There was jousting and more partying in the chilly, muddy streets of Alcalá. There would be more warring to be done the following year but the monarchs took their Christmases, and their leisure, seriously. Catherine of Aragon spent her first Christmas in the warmth of a court, and a monarchy, at rest.

4 Betrothed

Medina del Campo. 14 March 1489

The English ambassadors Thomas Savage and Richard Nanfan had never seen anything quite like it, or certainly not in the
receptions given to their foreign counterparts at home. It was a
March evening in the Castilian town of Medina del Campo –
a time of year when bright but chilly days merge quickly into
icily cold nights. The ambassadors were here to meet the royal
couple who headed what was rapidly becoming one of Europe's
most powerful monarchies. It was not just Isabel and Ferdinand
they wanted to see, however. They were also here to cast their
eyes over a tiny princess, their daughter Catherine.

The ambassadors had spent two days at their comfortable
lodgings, hung with fine tapestries, in the town. They had finally
recovered from an arduous trip that started two months earlier
in the port of Southampton and had twice seen them driven
back to English ports by unruly winds and fierce storms. There
had been much crying 'to God and to all the saints in Paradise'
when they came close to drowning in the Bay of Biscay. In the
dead of night their ship was blown over sideways by a gust of
wind, taking in 'so much water that she was quite under water
and all on one side for a while, and the great sail almost entirely
steeped in the sea'. On land things had scarcely been any better.
For a week they took refuge from a snow storm in the northern
Spanish port town of Laredo. Finally they scaled the exposed
slopes of the Cantabrian cordillera on the road towards Burgos
and Medina del Campo. Along the way they braved the wrath
of a feisty Spanish landlady who at first ordered them off her
premises and into the cold for being 'so bold as to come into

her house without her leave'. They were, she told them in no uncertain terms, 'great devils' and 'bawdy villains'. She took their money, however, and, after a miserable night, they 'rose very early' and fled.

Now, finally, they were in one of the main wool and textile centres of the *meseta*. Medina del Campo was the great trading town of Castile, with fairs that attracted goods and people from across Europe. In the comfort of this small walled city, overlooked by an imposing castle, they were due to meet the Spanish king and queen. Fifteen years after Isabel assumed the throne and a decade after her husband inherited his father's crown in Aragon, news of the couple's expanding kingdoms and growing strength had spread across the whole of Europe. The dual nature of the Spanish monarchy, nevertheless, still intrigued the English visitors.

'Perhaps some may blame me that I speak of "kings" (in plural), and some people may be astonished, and say, "How! Are there two kings in Castile?"' observed the herald Roger Machado, one of the English ambassadors' party, when he wrote down his impressions of that journey. 'No [I say], but I write "kings" because the king is king on account of the queen, by right of marriage, and because they call themselves "kings", and superscribe their letters "By the king and queen", for she is the heiress [of the throne].'

These were atypical monarchs for their – or almost any – time. They were also, however, people who had to be taken into consideration by any other self-respecting European king. England's Henry VII, another monarch to have emerged from the confusion of a violently fractious kingdom, already rated them so highly that he was eager to make one of the strongest sorts of alliance that could be formed outside warfare. The founder of the Tudor dynasty would betroth his eldest son and heir, Arthur, to the Spanish royal family's fourth daughter, Catherine. It did not matter that the former was just two years old or that the latter was three. Alliances were sealed by such promises. These could always be broken, as they often were, but this was the best sort of promise to offer. It was why Dr Savage, a future arch-bishop of York, and Sir Richard Nanfan were here. The Span-iards were not so needy of an alliance with an apparently shaky new dynasty like the Tudors, but they had a surfeit of daughters and were determined to put them to good use. 'If your highness gives us two or three more daughters in twenty years' time you will have the pleasure of seeing your children and grandchildren on all the thrones of Europe,' a prescient Fernando del Pulgar, who went on to become an official chronicler of her reign, had told Isabel many years before. With four healthy daughters, there were now enough to include the English in their plans.

At seven o'clock in the evening, as dusk fell, the messengers from the king and queen arrived at their quarters. Two bishops, a count, the *comendador* of an order of knights involved in the bat-tle for Granada and a string of other nobles, officials and 'great persons' appeared. These were no ordinary messengers, but this was no ordinary meeting. The same queen who had shed the black of mourning and dazzled the people of Segovia with her brilliant, regal robes had not lost her knack for turning on the powerful resources of political theatre. Her visitors, quite simply, had to go home impressed. They were to be given a dizzying ini-tiation into the dramatic ostentation which, as chroniclers of the time repeatedly found, the Castilian court turned on so suddenly and explosively when called upon to overawe important guests.

A torch-lit procession took them to the doors of the royal pal-ace where the monarchs, restless and peripatetic as ever, had established their movable court. The modest palace in Medina del Campo, where Isabel would die fifteen years later, was a compact network of halls, courtyards and galleries. They were conducted into a 'great room' where, as Machado breathlessly reported, 'they found the kings . . . seated under a rich cloth of gold'. In the centre of 'this great cloth of state' was an escutcheon quartered with the arms of Castile and Aragon. The monarchs both wore robes 'woven entirely of gold'. The king's was lined with the finest sable fur. It was the queen, however, who provoked a literary gasp of awe from Machado. The spectacular clothes and jewels she wore that evening – and the other outfits worn over the following days as the ambassadors were entertained with feasts, jousts, bull-fights and dances – were worthy, in his mind, of minutely detailed reporting.

Over her robe of cloth of gold Isabel wore 'a riding hood of black velvet, all slashed in large holes, so as to show under the said velvet the cloth of gold in which she was dressed'. The hood itself was decorated with a broken line of finger-sized, oblong-shaped blocks of gold thread encrusted with jewels 'so rich that no one has ever seen the like'. A white leather girdle with a pouch, which seemed somewhat masculine to Machado, was decorated with a 'balass ruby [from Persia] the size of a tennis ball, five rich diamonds and other precious stones the size of a bean'.

The queen's heavy jewellery dazzled as much as her dress.

She wore on her neck a rich gold necklace composed entirely of white and red roses, each rose being adorned with a large jewel. Besides this she had two ribbons suspended on each side of her breast, adorned with large diamonds, balass and other rubies, pearls, and various other jewels of great value to the number of a hundred or more. Over all this dress she wore a short cloak of fine crimson satin furred with ermine, very handsome in appearance and very brilliant. It was thrown on [negligently] cross-wise over her left side. Her head was uncovered, excepting only a little *coiffe de plaisance* at the back of her head without anything else.

Machado, a man with a keen eye for the monetary worth of clothing and jewellery, estimated that the queen was wearing some two hundred thousand crowns' worth of gold.

This was blatant power-dressing. Each ruby, each diamond and every stretch of rich cloth or fur reinforced the idea of Isabel's absolute superiority over all those who surrounded her. In fact, in the strictly defined society of Isabel's Castile, sumptuary laws prevented others from outdoing her in her glory. These laws regulated everything from the use of silk and brocades to the gold- or silver-plating of swords and spurs. No one was to outshine the royal family.

The formal hand-kissing and speech-making that followed was slightly spoilt by the fact that the man appointed to speak on behalf of the Spanish monarchs, the ancient Diego de Muros, bishop of Ciudad Rodrigo, had lost most of his teeth. The English visitors strained their ears, but failed to understand the Latin words that babbled past his toothless gums and out between his lips. This was, in any case, a minor inconvenience compared to that suffered by a previous English ambassador, Thomas Langton. He had been sent to see the monarchs in Madrid in 1477. They were, at the time, still establishing themselves and battling for supremacy in a civil war against supporters of Isabel's challenger for the crown – Juana la Beltraneja. On that occasion a special scaffold had been erected for the ambassador. It collapsed mid-speech, catapulting Langton to the ground. The dutiful ambassador picked himself up, dusted himself off and carried on as if nothing had happened.

Such diplomatic faux pas were now unthinkable in the Castilian court. Nothing was to be left to chance with the new embassy. The next twelve days of negotiating and entertainment were planned with absolute precision. The ambassadors were alternately charmed, amused, overwhelmed and conducted to the negotiating table. They also got their first glimpse of the young girl who Machado would refer to as either 'the princess of England' or the 'princess of Wales', Catherine of Aragon.

The three-year-old had missed out on the jousting and

banquets, though her elder siblings Juan and Isabel had danced for the ambassadors with their Portuguese teachers. At the jousting, Machado found Queen Isabel wearing a Spanish mantilla 'all spangled with lozenges of crimson and black velvet, and on each lozenge was a large pearl . . . [and] a rich balass ruby the size of a beechnut'. It was, he sighed, so impressive that 'no man ever saw anything equal to it'. Two rubies, 'the size of pigeon's eggs', and a large pearl deemed worth twelve thousand crowns hung as pendants from her head-dress. Such was the display of jewels on necklaces, mantilla and clothes that Machado's normally acute sense of pricing was defeated. 'So rich was the dress she wore that day that there is no man who can well imagine what could be the value of it,' he wrote.

The ambassadors' first meeting with Donna Catherine, as Machado also called her, appears to have been stage-managed to look like a simple family affair. The 'richly dressed' queen (an overwhelmed Machado had exhausted his powers of description by this stage) and Ferdinand, together with the elder three children, led them into a gallery hung with fine tapestries. Here they found little Catherine and her sister María, then aged six, both as lavishly dressed as their mother. They had with them their junior court of fourteen maidens (aged fourteen or younger) 'all of them dressed in cloth of gold, and all of them daughters of noblemen'. Catherine was still too young to dance for her visitors, but little María gamely took the floor with 'a young lady of her age and size, and led her to dance'.

This brief encounter is one of only a handful of childhood sightings of Catherine in the chronicles of the time, excepting Treasurer Baeza's financial accounts. She was, like the rest of her family, on display. Like any three-year-old, however, she had little of import to say for herself. Machado himself made no attempt to describe the future queen of England. The Spanish ambassadors who had been sent to London the previous year were more fulsome when taken to view the tiny Arthur both asleep and naked. 'He appeared to us so admirable that whatever praise, commendation, or flattery anyone might be capable of speaking or writing would only be truth in this case,' they wrote.

The following day the ambassadors caught another glimpse of Catherine, this time in a less formal atmosphere. It was a day of fun and games, with the visitors being introduced to that most Spanish of activities, the bull-fight. This already rated alongside jousting and other games of chivalrous mock-warfare – especially a game called *cañas* inherited from the Moors in which sticks replaced arrows and lances – as entertainment for the country's nobility. The bull-fight of the time was more like a mounted version of the bull-run (of the kind still practised, on foot, in Pamplona or, on horseback, in the Castilian town of Tordesillas) than the cape-waving affair of today. The riders attacked the bulls with lances. This could be particularly gory and Isabel was so upset by one bull-fight, where two men and three horses died, that she changed the rules. She demanded that upside-down cow-horns be glued over the points of the bulls' horns, so that they curled harmlessly backwards. On this day the bull-fighting was combined with mock skirmishes and running with dogs 'in the way they fought with the Saracens [i.e. the Moors]'. Isabel brought Catherine with her to watch and, it seems, she showed herself an affectionate and attentive mother. Machado certainly thought he had witnessed a new and different side to the Castilian queen. 'It was beautiful to see how the queen held up her youngest daughter,' he recalled.

Two days later, after a hard final session of bargaining, the Treaty of Medina del Campo was signed. England and Spain sealed their alliance. France, which had backed La Beltraneja in the battle for the Castilian crown, was effectively discarded as a Spanish ally. Both the English and Spanish monarchies had reasons for quarrelling with France. England and Aragon had territorial squabbles with her. Isabel, for her part, had long ago declared France to be a place that was 'abhorrent to our Castilian nation'.

The ambassadors said their goodbyes to the monarchs and little Catherine later that day, though it was the Spanish royal family who left Medina del Campo first. They were off, once more, to wander their kingdoms, though their first stop was to be a visit to Catherine's maternal grandmother – whom Isabel visited regularly – at nearby Arévalo.

The ambassadors went off laden with gifts. These included a Spanish war-horse, a smaller Moorish jennet, a couple of mules, yards of silk and sixty marks of silver each. 'People speak of the honour done to ambassadors in England; certainly it is not to be compared to the honour which is done to the ambassadors in the kingdom of Castile, and especially in the time of this noble king and queen,' concluded Machado, perhaps displaying the Iberian pride, and blood, that his surname suggests. Henry VII, it is to be presumed, was informed that his son's future parents-in-law were suitably impressive and powerful. Spain was a great ally to have against the age-old enemy of France. Catherine of Aragon was a good catch. The three-year-old princess's future path was set.

5 Infanta

Burgos. 18 March 1497

Catherine stood on the stage in the great hall at the palace in Burgos, dressed like a little queen. She was now eleven years old and, like her mother and elder sister María, was wearing a brocaded cloth-of-gold gown and a gold-decorated crimson scarf set off by a black mantilla. For as long as she could remember she had been, at least in theory, not just a Spanish infanta but the princess of somewhere called *Gales*, or Wales. The agreements made in Medina del Campo still stood. Later in the year they would be reaffirmed, a two-hundred-thousand-*scudos* dowry agreed on and her departure set for the day when her betrothed finally came of age – by turning fourteen. One day, just three years off, she was due to travel to a foreign land and be received as the bride-to-be of a crown prince.

Now, though, it was her turn to do the receiving. Her eighteen-year-old brother Juan, heir to his parents' crowns, was to marry Margaret of Austria. In a court as given over to ritual and formal ostentation as that of Isabel and Ferdinand, the arrival of a daughter-in-law – a future queen consort – was inevitably going to be a pomp-laden affair. The Spanish monarchs liked the natural drama of dusk. Night was falling as Margaret's cavalcade was ushered into Burgos. Welcoming candles burned in the windows of houses. More than a thousand torches, mounted on stands, lit the streets.

The ambassadors from the other European kingdoms and principalities had been called in. One of them, the Venetian ambassador, spotted Catherine on the tiered stage set up in the palace's grand hall. The royal family was carefully arranged in order of importance. Catherine was one step down from her sisters María and Isabel, but one up from her illegitimate half-sister, also called Juana. The latter was daughter to one of Ferdinand's mistresses and seems to have been born before his marriage (though more illegitimate children would be born later). Around this time the artist Juan de Flandes painted what is thought to be Catherine's portrait. His stylised painting shows a serious-looking young Catherine holding a rose in her hand. Reflected light glistens brightly on her most striking feature – the coppery hair that is pulled tightly back from a neat centre parting.

Margaret climbed the steps to the palace to meet the waiting Isabel. She attempted to kneel but was lifted up by her mother-in-law. The choreographed pomp, with sixty of Isabel's ladies in their full finery queuing up to kiss the new princess's hand, certainly impressed the Venetian – who went into raptures over the queen's maidens. We do not know what Catherine made of it. She certainly knew, by then, that she too would eventually go through something similar. Did she imagine herself in Margaret's shoes? Perhaps she only had eyes for Margaret's glamorous French-style clothes. Her sister-in-law had appeared in a dress of gold brocade and crimson lined in ermine, topped off by a black felt hat and accompanied by some very large pearls.

Margaret's arrival formed part of a wider master-plan of dynastic alliances. Isabel and Ferdinand used their abundant stock of children to cement these alliances. Their eldest daughter Isabel had already wed the heir to the Portuguese throne, Afonso. By the time of Margaret's arrival, however, she was a widow. Isabel's children, like the queen herself, were passionate and dramatic about their marriages. They added a charge of emotional intensity which superseded the artificial and theatrical norms of courtly love or the more pragmatic expectations of political wedlock. The younger Isabel had thrown herself into mourning after her husband died in a riding accident. She cut her hair off and vowed to mourn him for the rest of her life. 'She does not want to know another man,' reported the Italian humanist Peter Martyr. An excess of fasting and vigils (a common reaction to bad times amongst Isabel's daughters) had left her 'thinner than a dried-out tree'. Her parents had other plans for her, however, and seven years later she would marry her late husband's cousin, another future Portuguese king, Manuel. She died soon after that, while doing her ultimate duty – giving birth to a male heir. For now, however, she continued to wear 'a widow's habit', making a striking contrast at Margaret's reception to her sisters in their bright clothes. Margaret's father, Maximilian, was the Holy Roman Emperor. With another sister, Juana, already married to Maximilian's heir, Philip of Burgundy, and Catherine pledged to the English heir, Ferdinand's European network was firmly laid out.

Juan's relationship with Margaret fitted the pattern of marriages in Catherine's Trastámara family. It was a political alliance, but the newly-weds threw themselves into it with unexpected ardour. The amount of time they spent in bed together worried the court physicians. They fretted that the prince was too young and weak for such exertions. The lust he felt for his wife worried even Juan himself, who had to be told by his confessor not to feel guilty about it. Fun-loving Margaret had an acute sense of humour. She had been brought up at the French court, where she had been temporarily betrothed to Charles VIII. Her second betrothal, to Juan, also looked as though it might come to nothing when the ship carrying her to Spain hit a storm in the troublesome Bay of Biscay. Margaret used the occasion to coin her own wry epitaph, should she fail to make it to Spain alive.

> Here lies Margot, the willing bride,
> Twice married – but a virgin when she died.

Although, by this time, Juan had his own court, the family to which Margaret – who was to be a loyal friend to Catherine in years to come – was attaching herself remained constantly on the move. Catherine's childhood, as a result, was that of a wanderer. The sixteen Christmases she spent in Spain were celebrated in thirteen different cities.

Catherine's development over these years of continuous travel is best traced through Baeza's punctilious accounts. Mostly these contain the orders of material for her clothes. Amongst all the dress-making and materials, however, there are small, occasionally endearing, snapshots of Catherine as she grows up. Thus it was that, some time during her first year of life, Baeza paid for 'a bust [or statue] made of wax of the infanta's weight, using thirty pounds of wax' and for 'the work making it and the paint for the face'. He did not, unfortunately, say whether the wax figure was meant to be a life-sized toy or a gift, perhaps to some church. The following year Catherine took her first steps and was given 'a little push-cart, to show the infanta how to walk'. She also began to have a sweet tooth, with Baeza marking down regular orders both for quince jelly and for the sugar and rose-water needed to make a syrupy drink known as *azúcar rosado*, or 'rose honey'. By the age of five she was getting cloth to make doll's clothes and received a *ducado* coin to give on Easter Friday. Gold jewellery, including a head-band and four bracelets, arrived the following year. By nine she had a chess set and her first high heels (the wooden stacked *chapines* that kept young ladies' feet out of the mud). Her second lot of *chapines*, received two years later, were of two different heights – recorded as being 'three fingers' or 'a hand'.

Catherine's retinue of servants and ladies-in-waiting grew year by year. As an infant she already had her own maid, bed-maker and doorman. She had slaves, too. One appeared in the 1491 accounts, with three lengths of woollen cloth ordered up to clothe her. A slave from the recently colonised Canary Islands, probably a native Guanche, needed dressing the following year.

Slaves were by no means uncommon in fifteenth-century Spain. The Flemish illustrator Christoph Weiditz, visiting Spain two decades later, drew pictures of Moorish slaves with iron chains attached to their waists and legs. Two slave girls, including a Moorish girl known as Catalina, would eventually accompany Catherine to England. The slave girl Catalina, in fact, became such a close part of her world that she would be treated as a vital eyewitness to later events in Catherine's life.

As Catherine grew, the little 'infantas' chamber' she shared with her sister María became increasingly sophisticated. María was the sister Catherine must have been closest to, and they often appeared in Baeza's books as a single lot. The two infantas also began to accumulate chambermaids and uniformed footmen. The former were ruled over by her governess, Ynes de Vanegas. By the age of eleven Catherine had half a dozen young *damas*, or ladies-in-waiting, of her own. Vanegas's own daughter, who would become a loyal companion and friend to Catherine during her English adventure, would have been one of them. A year before Catherine was due to travel to England to marry she was given her own almoner, a priest to oversee her charitable giving. He was an Englishman, John Reveles. Baeza recorded her giving him a mule.

In between came expenses for the *acémilas*, the pack beasts used by Catherine and her sister María. The beasts plodded along, criss-crossing Spain from Valladolid to Jaen, Seville to Cordoba, Madrid to Burgos or Cavia to Tortosa. Catherine, too, plodded with them.

Travel was by no means comfortable. The royal family moved on horses and mules, or were carried on platforms borne by animals or men. Attempts to introduce four-wheeled carriages, which Margaret of Austria brought with her, fell foul of the steep mountains, rugged tracks and thoroughly battered remains of Spain's Roman roads. 'They are for flat terrain,' one senior royal servant remarked with evident disdain. Isabel and Ferdinand's court moved so often that a quarter of its spending went on transport. The *acémilas* trudged along in great trains behind them carrying their goods in bundles and chests.

Isabel's accounts books show that Catherine started riding – or at least balancing on top of – her own mule at the age of six. A large, padded mule saddle held together with golden nails and covered in silk cushions and blankets was ordered for her then. The saddle had crossed poles attached to it, presumably so that she, and it, could be lifted on and off or so that she could simply be carried along by bearers. These trips were not always easy. Spain is chopped up by mountain ranges and long, broad rivers. There were dangerous moments as they scrambled through mountain passes or waded through fast-flowing water. The mule ridden by her elder sister Juana stumbled and was washed downstream as the family waded across the River Tagus at Aranjuez in 1494. Juana clung bravely to her saddle and, when rescued by a stable-boy, was 'red as a rose' and 'with great spirit'.

Travelling like this, it would have been impossible for Catherine not to have noticed the great variety of peoples in her parents' lands. Regional dress was so pronounced – especially amongst women – that Isabel herself reputedly sent ahead for clothes in order to look the part in each region. 'One day she would appear in Galicia as a Galician and the next in Vizcaya as a Vizcayan,' a Spanish historian wrote a century later.

Amongst other things, Catherine must have seen members of Spain's large population of *mudéjar* Muslims and of the smaller, but equally well established, population of Jews. Did she notice, one wonders, when the latter disappeared after their mass expulsion on three months' notice in 1492? 'About their number there is no agreement, but, after many enquiries, I found that the most generally accepted estimate is fifty thousand families, or, as others say, fifty-three thousand. They had houses, fields, vineyards and cattle, and most of them were artisans,' an Italian Jew wrote a few years later. 'They sold their houses, their landed estates and their cattle for very small prices, to save themselves. The king did not allow them to carry silver and gold out of his country, so that they were compelled to exchange their silver and gold for merchandise of cloths and skins and other things.' Perhaps Isabel explained it to Catherine using the words that, according to the same source, she used to the Jewish negotiators who tried to get the expulsion edict overthrown. 'Do you believe that this comes upon you from us? The Lord hath put this thing into the heart of the king,' she supposedly said, unloading the responsibility onto her husband and, ultimately, God. In fact it was probably Isabel, or the priests close to her, who lobbied most vigorously for the expulsion. One legend has Torquemada, prior of the convent of Santa Cruz, stepping in to prevent Spain's Jewish community from being allowed to buy its way out of the edict by paying a large tribute. 'Judas Iscariot sold his master for thirty pieces of silver,' he allegedly raged at the monarchs as he waved a crucifix at them. 'Your highness would sell him anew for thirty thousand. Here he is, take him, and barter him away.' Anti-semitism and ethnic cleansing, then, were both part of Catherine's early experience of an intensely intolerant and unforgiving world.

Isabel, like nearly all European monarchs of her time, squabbled with the church about temporal powers. The queen was, however, a great reformer. She did much to rid the Spanish church of the corruption and venality that was leading people to question the clergy's authority elsewhere in Europe. She accepted absolutely, however, the spiritual authority of priests like Torquemada. The first time Isabel confessed to Friar Hernando de Talavera, for example, she was shocked that he remained seated rather than kneeling in front of her as previous confessors had done. 'We should both be on our knees,' the queen told him. 'No *señora*, I must be seated while your highness kneels, because this is God's tribunal and I am his representative,' Talavera replied. 'This is the confessor that I have been looking for,' Isabel said afterwards. The stricter her religion was, the better she liked it – even if that meant rooting out and burning heretics or chasing away Spaniards of other faiths. This was the religion that Catherine, who received her first breviary aged ten, learned at her mother's knee.

Catherine must also have known about the work of the Spanish Inquisition, whose autos-da-fé – with their colourful processions of the guilty attended by both clergy and nobles – were public spectacles. In fact, the Inquisition was hard to avoid. Shortly before she arrived in Zaragoza in June 1498, for instance, three heretics were burnt at the stake on the orders of an Inquisitor who held up to six autos-da-fé in the city every year. An infanta led a protected existence but court chatter must have passed on some of what was going on beyond the boundaries of the royal household. Even those who had direct contact with the royal family could fall foul of the Inquisitor. One of Ferdinand's doctors, Maestre Ribas Altas, was reputedly burnt at the stake for sketching himself onto a tiny picture of the crucifixion 'in such a way that it seemed the *santa Imagen*, holy image, was kissing his bottom'. The barbarity of punishments – burnings at the stake included – was standard for the time.

The queen's children drank deeply of her anti-semitism and zealous hatred of heresy. Before marrying her second husband, Manuel of Portugal, Catherine's sister Isabel demanded – apparently without consulting her mother or father – that he cleansed his country of 'heretics'. She would not travel to Portugal until he had done so. Manuel promptly signed an edict of expulsion and, after the forced conversion of most of them, the Portuguese Jews (who included many Spanish refugees) officially ceased to exist. Would Catherine have done the same? We do not know, not least because Edward I had expelled England's own Jews two centuries earlier.

Muslims had their own ghettos, the *morerías*, in many of the cities that had long been Christian. In eastern areas such as Aragon and Valencia they were essential to local agriculture, with Muslim farmers paying a quarter of their crops to the local Christian lords. 'He who has no Moors, has no money,' was a popular saying recorded by the German traveller Hieronymus Münzer. Christoph Weiditz sketched them in the first half of the sixteenth century, the women's legs wrapped in strips of cloth and their faces half-hidden, at least in public, by veils.

Catherine must also have seen some of the least pleasant sights of a country where justice was often rough and vengeful. Did she, like Münzer during his five-month trip in 1494 and 1495, ever come across a group of men hanging from the tall stone posts that stood at the gates to many Spanish towns? 'On leaving Almeria we saw a column made of stones, with six Italian Christians hung from it by their feet, for sodomy,' wrote Münzer. He saw the same thing, for the same reason, outside Madrid. 'Two men were hanging, with their testicles tied to their necks,' he said.

Movement was constant. The family slept in up to a dozen different towns, cities or monasteries in a month as Catherine's parents used their travels to assert authority over their lands. That meant listening to petitions and administering justice wherever they went. Palaces, monasteries, the houses of nobles or army camps were all part of the nomadic experience. In one camp, just outside Granada, Catherine and the entire family had to flee after a maid slipped with a candle and fire swept through their tents. With so many people travelling with the court, provisions could be difficult to find. Even the most basic logistics could go wrong in a country where the land was not always productive and water could be scarce. A black slave and two yeomen died from, of all things, thirst on one trip when eight-year-old

Catherine was travelling to visit her maternal grandmother at Arévalo.

The court had, of course, an intimate life as well. In fact, the magnificence and pomp recorded by others was the exception rather than the rule, at least for Catherine. These were state occasions, grand shows put on in the hope that others would remember or record them. They were, in other words, royal propaganda. Everyday life was not like that.

Isabel was a surprisingly attentive mother. Her daughters, especially, were kept close. The queen jokingly referred to her stern eldest daughter, also called Isabel, as 'my mother-in-law', but when the two met for the first time after her second marriage they threw protocol to the wind. Mother and daughter hugged so hard that they fell to the ground. Her beloved son Juan, meanwhile, was addressed affectionately as 'My Angel!', even when being reprimanded. With Juana (whose erratic behaviour gained her the unfortunate nickname of 'La Loca', or 'The Mad') Isabel was at her most possessive. She certainly tried to keep her in Castile after she had returned from Flanders with her husband in 1502. This provoked one of those scenes for which Juana became sadly famous, when she stood out on the open ramparts of the La Mota fortress 'like an African lioness in a fit of rage' until 2 a.m., shocking all who saw her. Isabel's relationship with Catherine was less troubled but equally close, with Isabel constantly putting off her youngest daughter's departure for England. The similarities in their characters suggest a warm and, from Catherine's side, admiring relationship. They shared an intensity and rock-like obstinacy that some people, to their later chagrin, failed to spot behind an apparently sweet and calm facade.

That same intensity had a darker, self-destructive side. Sometimes it turned against them. Catherine's mother fell into deep depressions and suffered terrible bouts of jealousy when her husband strayed. 'She loved after such a fashion, so solicitous and vigilant in jealousy, that if she felt that he looked on any lady of court with a betrayal of desire, she would very discreetly procure ways and means to dismiss that person from the household,' said a contemporary humanist, Lucio Marineo. Her daughters were aware of Isabel's battle to rein in her jealous feelings. They, too, would struggle with similar demons. 'This passion is not found only in me,' Juana said later. 'My lady the queen . . . was equally jealous. But time cured her highness of it, as I hope to God it will for me.'

Isabel worked especially hard on Catherine's schooling. The little girl seems to have started learning to read and write at six, when she received her first letter-case. This may have arrived early, for seven was the accepted age at which the crucial skills of reading, writing and Latin started being learnt in a household where the education of daughters was taken with an unusual and remarkable degree of seriousness.

Queen Isabel had had little formal education herself but, in typically determined fashion, she had taught herself Latin as an adult. Her children learnt it young with the help of the same talented woman Latinist, Beatriz Galindo, 'La Latina', who had taught Isabel. Catherine learned the language well enough to converse in it. For a long time after her arrival in England, indeed, she appears to have felt more comfortable with Latin than English. Isabel embraced the new humanist learning arriving from Italy, and hired Italian tutors for her children, with Alessandro Geraldini – who would accompany her to England – overseeing Catherine's education. She and her sisters became, as a result, four of the most learned women in Europe. Her learning certainly impressed those, like the Dutch humanist Erasmus, who met her later in England. Though well-known as a serial flatterer of potential patrons, he offered the highest sort of praise – by putting her on the same level as men. 'The queen is well instructed – not merely in comparison with her own sex,' he commented, 'and is no less to be respected for her piety than her erudition.' Courtly skills were balanced alongside the Latin and a 'domestic studies' programme of sewing and needlework. These included falconry, horse-riding and hunting. Music, and learning to play instruments, formed a crucial part of that programme. So, too, did dancing lessons. She and María had Portuguese dance teachers and the dancing at Isabel's fiestas could go on until the small hours of the morning.

Surprisingly, considering that her spouse had been decided on when she was three, no attempt was made to teach Catherine English. A full three years before her departure Catherine's future mother-in-law, Elizabeth of York, suggested she make the most of Margaret's presence to learn some French. Latin would be of limited use in England and Spanish of no use at all, she warned. The twelve-year-old Catherine should also get used to drinking wine, Elizabeth suggested, as English water was undrinkable. Quite what Isabel, a noted teetotaller, made of the advice, we do not know. Three years later Elizabeth let it be known that she was glad Catherine had learnt some French. There was no mention of how the wine-drinking was going.

Isabel was highly preoccupied with her daughters' moral and religious education and, if her library is a guide, they would have spent time studying the lives of saints and other devotional works. The *Carro de las donas*, by the Franciscan monk Francesc Eiximenis, was one of a number of 'how to raise your daughters' manuals that sat on the royal bookshelf.

Eiximenis was relatively progressive in that he did not consider women intrinsically – or even in imminent danger of becoming – envious, greedy or gossipy. That did not prevent him from displaying many of the prejudices of the time. He firmly believed, for example, that sparing the rod was spoiling the child. Bad girls should be beaten. 'Punish them and wound them on the back with some switch rather than on the head,' he advised, in an attempt to minimise the damage. Girls should carry rosaries and spend a part of each day praying. Contact with boys, Jews or Moors was bad for them, and they must refuse food offered by non-Christians. Girls, the manuals generally agreed, were to be discreet and contained, and exercise self-control. Weaving, sewing and prayer were appropriate pastimes. Their greatest enemy was 'the madness of love'.

Catherine learned little, therefore, about the opposite sex. Her mother was a stickler for decorous behaviour. The queen was determined to protect both her own reputation and that of Catherine, her other daughters and her ladies. Isabel's former sister-in-law, the scandalous Queen Juana, was held up as the model of all that a woman should not be. Apart from her own marital infidelities, Juana had also been infamous for her bawdy ladies-in-waiting. These carried daggers, displayed deep cleavages and had a tendency to 'accidentally' stumble when dismounting their horses, thus exposing large amounts of thigh painted with fashionable white make-up.

In Isabel's fastidious court, men and women stayed apart. Catherine slept in Isabel's chamber, along with her sisters. Doctors and other men were not allowed into the quarters until all of them, and the ladies-in-waiting who also slept there, were up and dressed. The women also ate apart in the intimacy of Isabel's chambers. The infantas and their mother only emerged from this feminine bunker to eat with others when there were important visitors, in which case the full spectacle of the public court went into action.

Even then, the sexes ate at separate tables. Catherine got a glimpse of how things could be different when honoured visitors arrived from other, less segregated, courts. Isabel was happy to drop the rules, for example, when a French embassy visited in 1492, though she got a reprimand from her stern old confessor, Friar Hernando de Talavera, for doing so. Isabel reminded him that she had done the same for embassies from England, Portugal and Burgundy. 'We weren't doing anything new,' she retorted. Talavera also complained of excessive dancing at another reception. His complaints do, at least, suggest that the court knew how to have a good time, if only when his back was turned. On Margaret's arrival, however, Isabel issued instructions to avoid the 'familiarity, common treatment and informal communication used by queens and princesses in Austria, Burgundy and France'. There would, instead, be 'gravity . . . as was the [common] usage in Spain'.

Segregation was not restricted to the royal table. Roger Machado noted that, as guests at a house in Plasencia, his party had to eat on their own. Their host preferred his wife's company. 'It is not the custom in this country that women ever come and eat in company with strangers,' Machado explained.

A Burgundian who passed through the Castilian court asked one woman why she showed such apparently cruel indifference to three would-be lovers who hung on her every word and gesture. 'We do as we want while we are waiting to marry, treating them like this,' she explained, 'because once we are married they lock us up in a room in a castle. That is how they get their revenge on us for having such a good time when we were single.' Some Spaniards who went to Burgundy when Catherine's sister Juana married were shocked by the loose morals and wasteful extravagance. Burgundians, the word came back, 'honour drinking well more than living well'.

Segregation did not mean that there was no fun to be had at her mother's side. Tales of chivalry were told or sung after dinner with Isabel herself sighing at the tragic bits. Amongst other things, Catherine would have heard the retelling of old battles from the war in Granada. She must also have heard the famous romantic legends of the land she was destined to travel to. Arthur, the Round Table, the Holy Grail, Lancelot and Merlin were all characters in the rich chivalrous imagination of the Spanish court. They were there in Isabel's books and on her tapestries too.

Sterner members of the court disapproved of the racy romantic adventure stories contained in the so-called Books of Chivalry. One court official damned them as 'useless, fabulous, full of lies and based on lust, love and boasting . . . causing weak-breasted women to fall into libidinous errors and commit sins they would not otherwise commit'. They were the same books that later helped drive the fictional Don Quixote mad. Isabel also had a copy of the archpriest of Hita's earthy and occasionally profane *Libro del Buen Amor*, 'The Book of Good Love'. Board games, chess, word games and cards were played. There was music, too, at the table. This may have been devoted to chivalry or courtly love when Isabel was there, but did Catherine ever hear the bawdy '*Dale si le das*' from the *Cancionero de Palacio*, the extensive 'Palace Songbook', with its sly references to pubic hairs and the sexual organs of man and woman, *carajo* and *coño*? Musicians were always on hand. They were, indeed, amongst the best paid people at court. Spain already boasted a long tradition of troubadours and popular songs coming especially from north-west Galicia and the Muslim territories of al-Andalus.

Music was by no means the only contact the young Catherine had with Islamic culture. Centuries of living side by side left Christian Spaniards with a taste for certain luxuries more readily associated with the East than with a comparatively backward medieval Europe. Even Isabel occasionally wore clothes with Moorish decorations, and her husband sometimes carried a Moorish sword. Catherine herself was ordered a *medio sayo morisco*, a sort of Moorish waistcoat, to wear when she was two. A royal penchant for silk cushions, for pillows and rugs was another piece of the court's Moorish inheritance.

Apart from anything else – and despite the exhortations of Eiximenis – Catherine would have been in regular contact with Moorish slaves and servants. The court's own Moors were amongst the first to be converted to Christianity after the conquest of Granada. Catherine and her sisters held on to their slave girls when they moved away to marry. Juana's Moorish girls reportedly bathed her and washed her head so much that her husband worried for her health.

Hygiene was a preoccupation of Spain's Arab-influenced communities, which included those Christians and Jews who had lived under Muslim rule. Castile produced one of the most prized soaps in Europe, known in England as Castell soap. Hard and white, like many modern soaps, it was made from olive oil and was, in origin, another Arab gift to Spain. The Spanish hygiene manuals of the time were full of advice on everything from hair-washing and nose-blowing to tooth-brushing and avoiding the curse of bad breath. Isabel's court even had a specialist *alimpiador de dientes*, or tooth-scrubber. It is impossible to say, however, to what extent the royal family took advantage of the impressive bath-houses in the palaces captured from the Moors.

Smell was another major concern. The court's *perfumadores* made sure it was as sweetly scented as possible. Again, the Moorish influence was evident. Their bottles and jars contained rose-water, amber, musk, balsam, scented clays and woods and the scent of orange or lemon blossom. The court also kept a civet cat. The *perfumadores* extracted a sticky, white, acrid-smelling musk-like substance from the apocrine gland by its anus.

If Catherine's daily life was infused with the subtle influence of al-Andalus, there can be little doubt that her most vivid memories of home would be of that most Moorish of cities, Granada. This was the last, if not the only, place in Spain that she could really call home. For here, in the red-walled oriental magnificence of the city's Alhambra complex of palaces, Catherine spent the final years before she embarked on her English adventure.

6 Alhambra Princess

Granada. 2 July 1499 – 21 May 1501

They reached Granada from the north, after a month traipsing across the flat, ferrous-soiled plain of La Mancha and through the first rugged sierras of Andalucia. The first thing that thirteen-year-old Catherine would have seen was the Sierra Nevada mountain range rearing up in the distance through the hazy July heat. Only as they closed in on the city would she have spied the rust-red walls and towers of the Alhambra, perched on their rocky spur. Catherine may not have known it, but her life as a wanderer was over. There would only be one more major journey to make from here and that would take her far away to England.

The young infanta reached Granada in the summer of 1499 with a family that, in recent years, had been struck repeatedly by tragedy. A curse hung over them, delivering blow after blow. Both her brother Juan and eldest sister Isabel had died in the previous three years. Isabel had been a victim of childbirth, leaving behind her newborn baby son Miguel. Juan had died shortly after marrying Margaret. Sexual over-exertion, too much for a sickly youth of eighteen, was said to have finished him off – though consumption seems a more likely cause. His faithful dog, a lurcher called Bruto, had stayed on at the court (having originally taken up station beside his coffin during the vigil in Salamanca's main church) as a constant reminder of a missing prince who should have become the physical embodiment of his parents' newly united Spain. Juan's posthumous child then died at birth, adding to the accumulation of grief and pain.

Isabel and Ferdinand then placed their hopes for handing their kingdoms to a direct male heir on their surviving tiny grandson, Miguel. He was sworn in, still little more than a baby, as heir to the crowns of both Aragon and Castile. The boy's father was Manuel, the Portuguese king. Portugal was also his to inherit. The dream of a united Iberia rested, briefly, on his tiny shoulders. Catherine's infant nephew was brought up in the Castilian court, his grandmother watching over him. His teenage aunts Catherine and María gained, in effect, a baby brother. The wheel of family tragedy, however, kept on turning. Little Miguel died at the Alhambra, in Isabel's arms, shortly after the court had settled there in 1500. Catherine's nephew was not yet two years old. It was, wrote the chronicler Andrés Bernáldez, 'the third stab of pain to pierce the queen's heart'. Peter Martyr, who ran a school for the children of nobles at Isabel's court, noted that the princeling's death 'has profoundly affected his grandparents. They have evidently been unable to bear with equanimity so many strokes of fate.'

A different kind of family tragedy was unfurling in Flanders. News began to reach Spain of Juana's unhappy life with her cruel, philandering husband Philip the Handsome of Burgundy. The one piece of good news they received from her was the birth of another grandson – Charles. After so many tragic deaths in the family, La Loca was now heiress to the crown of Castile. Charles was next in line. He also stood to inherit his grandfather Ferdinand's crown in Aragon – thus keeping Spain together as a whole. But that was not all he stood to inherit. He was also due to receive the northern European lands of his other grandfather, Emperor Maximilian. This tiny nephew, on whom Catherine would pin her hopes in her troubled later life, would grow up to rule over one of the greatest empires Europe had ever seen.

Isabel became increasingly ill and slid into depression. 'From then on, she lived without joy,' recorded one chronicler. She often retired to her bed. Although she never became unstable (unlike her mother, Isabel of Portugal, or her daughter Juana) the dark abyss of depression and mental illness remained a dangerous legacy for her descendants for generations to come.

Catherine was no longer living in a joyous court. The bleak events of the past years impinged directly on her life. The lengths of velvet, of woollen cloth and Arabic silk, of cotton and linen from London, Flanders and Florence, that were ordered for her clothes were increasingly of a single colour – the black of mourning. In earlier years there had been a wealth of colours: the green favoured by Spanish princesses, or purples, scarlet, blues and yellows. These rich and happy colours had been present on caps and the full array of decorated skirts, tunics, dresses, leggings, jackets and ermine or rabbit-lined cloaks that Spanish women wore in layers. Now, as the monarchs struggled with private grief while trying to maintain their regal calm in public, a black brush had been swept across the royal wardrobe.

If Catherine spent her last few years at home in an increasingly tragic and troubled family she did, at least, spend them in a magical place. At least one image of Granada stayed with Catherine for the rest of her life. Its symbol, the pomegranate fruit (with its purple flesh bursting suggestively out of a gash in the skin), remained hers until her dying day.

Isabel and Ferdinand had conquered opulent Granada, the city of two hundred mosques, early in 1492. That conquest brought an end to more than seven centuries of Muslim kingdoms on Spanish soil. The north African tribesmen who invaded Spain in 711 had swept quickly through the Iberian peninsula, conquering almost all of it. The Christian *reconquista* took centuries. Granada itself had been ruled by Muslims for almost eight hundred years. Legend has it that Boabdil, the last king, wept as he left the city. 'You should not weep like a woman for what you could not defend as a man,' his mother allegedly spat.

After the conquest of Granada, however, the monarchs had hurried off to do other things. Ferdinand had been away from

Aragon for too long and the rest of Castile also needed attention. Spain's new overseas territories, too, had to be divided up and administered. A sailor called Christopher Columbus, meanwhile, had set off on a voyage of discovery in 1492 and returned the following year with his painted Indians, parrots, gold and news of strange and exciting new lands that would be theirs. Catherine, aged seven, was probably there to see his triumphal procession of New World exotica through Barcelona. With so many things to do, the wandering court that had gone north from Granada in 1492 did not return until the summer of 1499.

Her parents had fallen in love with the Alhambra, however, even before it became theirs. Before the conquest they had made special trips to gaze from afar upon its warm, rust-tinted walls. Once conquered, it became the jewel in their crown – and something on which they spent a considerable amount of money. They saw it both as a gift from the God who had guided their crusade and as a symbol of their success in the morally uplifting, if practically cruel, endeavour of turning Spain into an entirely Christian country. Just as they had expelled the Jews, so they began the ethnic and religious cleansing of the city. The kingdom of Granada's eighty thousand Muslims, initially able to live and worship freely, were gradually converted or driven out. 'None of them was forced in any way to convert to Christianity,' Isabel and Ferdinand insisted, in an attempt to placate the Muslims of north Africa, later. The Moors remembered it differently. 'We were converted to Christianity with severity and by force, burning our books and sullying us; and even though every book spoke of our religion, they were tossed onto the fire with disdain and mockery,' said one who fled to the court of the Turkish emperor, Bayazid II.

Catherine probably noticed little of this from inside the enclosed paradise of the Alhambra. Her view of the city was from its walls and gardens or from that belvedere known as the Ayn dar Aisha – the eye of the house of Aisha. The smoke and smell of burning sacred literature would not have reached so high. The sweet perfume of *azahar* – orange and lemon blossom – was more likely to become fixed in her memory.

For the first time in her itinerant life, Catherine attained considerable stability after she reached Granada in 1499. Over almost two years she moved only twice and that was to go backwards and forwards along the same 130 miles that separated Granada from Seville. The Alhambra became home.

Peter Martyr, the Italian humanist who set up Isabel's school for noble children, considered Granada Spain's most beautiful city. 'The atmosphere is pure and healthy; it boasts not just mountains but also an extensive plain; it has wonderful orchards, and its gardens compete with those of the Hesperides,' he said. With the snow-capped Sierra Nevada looming in the distance and the fertile land full of market gardens below it, Granada and its plain were as good as the Elysian Fields. Martyr, who became the first historian of Spain's empire-builders (as well as being, although he never went, the first abbot of Jamaica), eventually died in this, his earthly paradise.

Hieronymus Münzer visited the city in 1494, when Muslims still outnumbered Christians by at least four to one. 'I believe there is no bigger city in Europe,' he said. This, for a northern European like Münzer, was an exotic world of figs, saffron, cherries, artichokes, almonds, raisins, wild palms, olives, pomegranates, oranges, lemons, apples, pears and plentiful trout. Goats, sheep and oxen provided abundant meat, along with wild boar, deer and partridge.

On Fridays the call to prayer still reverberated around the city. 'The shouting from the towers of the mosques was hard to believe,' he wrote. He counted more than two thousand people at prayer in the main mosque. He also recalled the early morning calls to prayers – 'for they are truly devout' – and the veiled women in long white robes of silk, cotton or wool.

Münzer estimated the population of the city at a little over fifty thousand people, its narrow streets packed with small homes. 'They almost all have [running] water and cisterns,' he said.

Pipes and aqueducts are of two types: one for clear drinking water; the other to take away dirt, excrement, etc. . . . There are channels in every street for dirty water, so that those houses which, because of the difficulties of their place, do not have pipes, can throw their dirt into the channels at night.

Around the main mosque he found – apart from the standard washing facilities – urinals and blocks of squatting toilets that fed straight into an underground sewer.

What really amazed Münzer, like generations of travellers both before and after him, were the palaces of the Alhambra. 'I don't think there is anything to equal it in the whole of Europe,' he wrote. 'Everything is so superb, magnificent and exquisitely built that one might think oneself in paradise.'

The Alhambra that Catherine encountered, and which Münzer saw, was considerably bigger and even more elaborately decorated than it is today. 'We saw innumerable palaces, paved with brilliant white marble; beautiful gardens, adorned with lemon trees and myrtles, with pools and tanks of marble,' wrote Münzer. The bedrooms were 'sumptuous' and there were white marble basins of crystal-clear running water in every palace. Glistening marble was everywhere, inside and outside, in columns and on the floors in great big fifteen-foot slabs. Water moved gently through the gardens and into the rooms through a system of pipes and channels the likes of which the well-travelled Münzer had never seen before. 'And a bath – oh what a marvel! – with a vaulted roof.' The baths had rooms for hot, warm and cold water. They were far superior to anything planned for the ill-fitting Renaissance palace commissioned for the Alhambra site by Charles V later in the sixteenth century.

In Catherine's time the palace ceilings and stucco work

were still painted in vivid colours. 'All the palaces and rooms have superb coffered ceilings made of gold, lapis lazuli, ivory and cypress, in such a variety of styles that one cannot begin to explain or write about them,' said Münzer. Even the famous stone creatures in the Court of the Lions were brightly painted. The Court of the Myrtles, on the other hand, was paved in white marble. It glowed at night, radiating a soft, white, dream-like light. This, along with the sharper light of moon and stars, was mirrored and amplified by the glassy surfaces of pools of clear water. It would have been impossible not to have been enchanted by such a place.

The Alhambra was a royal playground, a city of palaces, parks and gardens meant for the delight of whichever royal fam-ily ruled over Granada. Over the last two years of Catherine's lifetime in Spain, that meant her parents, her sister María and herself. The Generalife, the garden and palace complex above the Alhambra, was counted amongst the monarchs' favourite places. Münzer remembered it as 'a truly royal and famous gar-den, with springs, pools and charming little channels of water'. The Venetian Andrea Navagero saw a gushing waterfall that fell ten *brazas*, or arm-lengths, into a tank of water, splashing those who came close with droplets of cooling water. Rabbits hopped amongst the myrtles and water was everywhere, distributed by yet more pipes and channels.

All the Generalife needed, said Navagero, was someone who knew how to fully 'enjoy a life, in repose and tranquillity, given over to study'. This, after all, was a place of contemplation. 'Enter with composure, speak thoughtfully, be short on words and leave in peace,' read one piece of Arabic script in the north pavilion of the Patio of the Acequia. 'Respect those whose words are beautiful,' read another. Catherine – who, as far as we can tell, was both studious and tranquil – was one of the last to live in the Alhambra as it was intended.

Her idyll, if that was what it was, came to an end in the late spring of 1501. The future princess of Wales had been expected in England eight months earlier (when her husband-to-be turned fourteen), but Isabel procrastinated. An Italian visitor who reached Granada late in 1500 reported that Catherine had been ill, though she was well enough to receive him on New Year's Day 1501. It still, however, took her several months to set off for England.

Isabel was, perhaps, unwilling to part with her last child. Catherine was younger than her sisters had been when they left. Eight months earlier she and her parents had gathered at the old royal encampment of Santa Fe – near to Granada – to say goodbye to María. The sister she was closest to, the one she had grown up with, went off to marry the king of neighbouring Portugal. She was a replacement for her deceased elder sister Isabel.

Maybe it was Ferdinand who was not so keen to say goodbye to Catherine. His earlier anxiety to get her on the boat as fast as possible, fuelled by rumours of manoeuvres at Henry's court to prevent the marriage in favour of a Flanders bride who would bring better trading opportunities, had abated. An outbreak of the plague in England further dampened his urgency. Then, early in 1501, Ferdinand suddenly had to leave Granada to put down a rebellion in Ronda.

Did Catherine's father have last-minute misgivings about losing his only remaining daughter? He certainly did not stop Isabel from coming up with her various excuses for delay. Ferdinand later told Catherine that 'of all my daughters you are the one I love best'. His casual disregard of her needs and wants over the coming years does not bear that out, although a small episode in her childhood suggests he held his youngest daughter in a certain esteem. He once tried to persuade the Aragonese parliament of nobles – the Cortes – to allow Catherine to stand in for him at one of their infrequent meetings in the town of Calatayud. The meeting never happened, partly because the nobles found the idea of the child Catherine presiding over them so strange, but it was not the only time that the wily Ferdinand was to ask her to be an ambassador.

One Spanish chronicler reported that English ambassadors arrived early in 1501 to find out when she would be travelling. It is tempting to think of them being entertained in the luxurious surroundings of Generalife gardens, though there seem to be no other reports confirming either the sending or the reception of an embassy.

This, then, was the charmed world that Catherine left behind. When she finally set off on 21 May 1501, on a long, slow journey northwards towards England, she did so as one of the last princesses of the Alhambra.

7 Adios

Alhambra–Laredo. 21 May–27 September 1501

Catherine rode out of the Alhambra early one May morning on the start of her journey to a new life. It must have been an emotional parting for her parents, who had finally run out of excuses for keeping her with them. As they got older, however, the Spanish monarchs became less grandiose about their daughters' departures. Just five years earlier Catherine had seen Juana go off to Flanders accompanied by 133 ships bearing an army of fifteen thousand men – most of whom died of cold, malnutrition and Burgundian unkindness. The entire family had traipsed across Spain to wave her off from the port of Laredo. María, on the other hand, had been taken as far as Santa Fe, just a few miles from Granada – where the royal family stayed with her for a week before she set off for Portugal. By the time Catherine left, their energies had been sapped almost completely. Isabel and Ferdinand simply rode with her as far as Santa Fe and waved her on. She was late already, they explained. Her parents would just slow her down.

The excitement, on this occasion, was mainly on the English side. Isabel had even let Henry VII know that she thought he was overdoing the wedding plans. 'Demonstrations of joy at the reception of my daughter are naturally agreeable to me. Nevertheless it would be more in accordance with my feelings . . . that the expenses should be moderate,' she wrote to her ambassador in London, Rodrigo de Puebla. 'We do not wish our daughter to be the cause of any loss to England. On the contrary, we desire that she should be the source of all kinds of happiness.' If he wanted to be generous to her daughter, the queen said, she would rather it was with his love.

Isabel had originally planned to accompany Catherine to the port at La Coruña. Given the time it took her daughter to reach the north coast, her protestations that she would slow her daughter down sound feeble. Perhaps, once more, the fifty-year-old queen was not feeling well. So, instead, Catherine was placed in the care of Elvira Manuel, her bossy new lady mistress, and her husband, Pedro Manrique – the overbearingly proud lord of the northern town of Ezcaray. An archbishop, a bishop and a count accompanied her to England. These were to return after the wedding while, to Catherine's long-term dismay, the haughty Elvira Manuel and her pompous husband stayed on. The English had also asked her to bring ladies who were 'of gentle birth and beautiful or, at the least, by no means ugly'. Six young Spanish girls, who seem to have met the requirements, set out with her.

Catherine's party was in no hurry, despite the anxiousness of those awaiting her in England. Henry VII had wanted her there almost from the day of her engagement in Medina del Campo, arguing that pre-pubescent brides-to-be were commonly sent to the country where they were due to be married. The date of her arrival had been a constant preoccupation. A special papal dispensation had been asked for so that the couple could marry, if necessary, before Arthur reached fourteen. Henry became increasingly impatient after the original September 1500 deadline went by. Isabel pleaded various illnesses (her fever, Catherine's ague) to put him off but that did not stop Henry issuing invitations for a May wedding. Perhaps the king's formidable mother, Margaret Beaufort, was the force pushing his own concerns. She had been through two weddings and borne a child before her own fifteenth birthday. Catherine was probably aware by this stage that, according to De Puebla's despatches, 'the king is much influenced by his mother . . . in affairs of personal interest and in others'. She may also have heard that Margaret was an archetypically hellish mother-in-law for Elizabeth of York. 'The queen, as is generally the case, does not like it,' De Puebla added.

The trip north to La Coruña took an unusually lengthy three months. It involved, amongst other things, a diversion to Santiago de Compostela. Catherine, already showing a strong religious streak, wanted to make the pilgrimage to the supposed burial site of St James. This was a jubilee year and pilgrims arriving there gained a plenary indulgence − a remission of all the time to be spent in purgatory. The searing heat of the Castilian summer slowed her party down further, requiring further days of rest at the monastery in Guadalupe. There were many other stop-offs along the way, as cities honoured her with bull-fights, banquets and visits to view the bones of local saints. The northern city of Zamora, for example, slaughtered ten calves, three fighting bulls and twelve dozen fowl while also providing eight large casks of wine. She may have passed though Salamanca, where her brother once rode down streets carpeted with sweet-smelling aromatic herbs. Her parents' claim that 'we ordered those with her to go as fast as possible' does not survive close study.

The long trip gave Catherine plenty of time to think about what awaited her. Although the marriage was political, Henry VII and Elizabeth of York were genuinely excited about their eldest son's bride. On one occasion, when Catherine sent two copies of a letter to them, her future in-laws squabbled over who got to keep the one that remained after they forwarded the other to Prince Arthur. 'The king argued obstinately with the queen about keeping one of the letters for himself to carry around with him,' De Puebla reported. 'She fought hard before giving it to him.' Henry, the son of an iron-willed mother, was fascinated by the strength of character shown by the Spanish royal women. He told one visitor that he would give up half of his kingdom if Catherine was like her mother. In later life this fascination would be extended to her sister Juana, who fired up an old man's ardour and became something of an obsession.

Catherine had exchanged love letters with her fiancé during her time at the Alhambra. He wrote from what, for her, must have been the mysterious-sounding castle of Ludlow. 'I have read the most sweet letters of your highness lately given to me, from which I have easily perceived your most entire love to me,' he wrote in October 1499.

Truly those your letters, traced by your own hand, have so delighted me, and have rendered me so cheerful and jocund, that I fancied I beheld your highness and conversed with and embraced my dearest wife. I cannot tell you what an earnest desire I feel to see your highness, and how vexatious to me is this procrastination about your coming. I owe eternal thanks to your excellence that you so lovingly correspond to this my so ardent love. Let it continue, I entreat, as it has begun; and, like as I cherish your sweet remembrance night and day, so do you preserve my name ever fresh in your breast.

Both Arthur and Catherine were thirteen at the time. The love expressed in their letters, and written in Latin, was a game. Their elaborate and repetitive protestations of devotion dripped with passion but stayed firmly within the baroque boundaries of courtly love. They already knew, however, that this love game was intensely serious. That was clear from the way Arthur closed his letter. 'Let your coming to me be hastened, that instead of being absent we may be present with each other, and the love conceived between us and the wished-for joys may reap their proper fruit,' he wrote. The fruit he referred to would have to come from Catherine's womb. It was her job, after all, to prolong the Tudor dynasty.

Catherine had been thoroughly drilled in the history of Europe's royal houses. She knew that Henry VII had emerged triumphant from the Wars of the Roses – the wily Tudor being the eventual victor in the long-running fight between Lancastrians and Yorkists. As the founder of a new dynasty the continuity of his line via Arthur was of vital importance to Henry.

Catherine's job was to produce grandchildren, and male grand-children at that, to keep the Tudor line going.

Catherine's parents, having also emerged from a period of tur-moil and civil war, were permanently anxious to know whether the Tudor newcomers were really in control. The impostor Per-kin Warbeck was a particular obsession. He had written to Isabel directly claiming to be one of the Princes in the Tower, Edward IV's two missing sons. These tragic boys were never seen again after being locked up in the Tower of London by Richard III in 1483. Warbeck, who was probably Flemish, told Isabel he had been saved by a man who had been ordered to kill him and that his identity had been kept a secret.

De Puebla kept Catherine's parents thoroughly up to date on the whole Warbeck affair. Henry realised the Spaniards were wor-ried and when Warbeck, who had been arrested, tried to flee in 1498 he informed De Puebla the minute he was recaptured. 'The same hour that he was arrested, the king of England sent one of his gentlemen of the bedchamber to bring me the news,' he said in an urgent despatch. De Puebla was able to reassure them later that Perkin 'is kept with the greatest care in a tower, where he sees neither sun nor moon'. Later on, Henry VII interrogated War-beck in person in front of De Puebla. 'I, and other persons here, believe his life will be very short,' he reported afterwards. The pre-diction proved correct. In January 1500, following the executions of Warbeck and the simple-minded young earl of Warwick – a more genuine claimant to the throne – he triumphantly informed Isabel and Ferdinand that there no longer remained 'a drop of doubtful royal blood' in England. The main pretenders had been killed, in part, to calm Spanish concerns. The blood-letting, Cath-erine would be told later, had been for her.

Catherine had probably also heard of Henry VII's unpopu-larity and reputation for greed. The gold coin that entered his safe boxes rarely, if ever, came out again, De Puebla wrote in one letter. Henry's servants possessed 'a wonderful dexterity in getting hold of other people's money', the ambassador reported with obvious admiration. Another Spanish envoy, Pedro de Ayala, believed that a downturn in trade in England was partly due to 'the impoverishment of the people by the great taxes laid on them'. Henry was not unduly upset by this idea. 'The king himself said to me that he is happy to keep them low, because riches would only make them haughty,' he said.

While Henry was unpopular, Elizabeth of York was much loved. De Puebla put this down, cynically if accurately, to the fact that she was powerless. Another Spanish visitor thought that the 'very noble' Elizabeth was kept in subjection by her mother-in-law. Elizabeth had written warmly to Isabel, hoping they might pass on their news – and that of their children – regularly.

Arthur, De Puebla said, was loved by the people mainly because, through his mother, he was Edward IV's grandson. With his Yorkist blood, Catherine's fiancé embodied the new 'union' of the old warring roses of England. De Puebla added, apparently as an afterthought, that those who knew the prince in person found him to be most virtuous. Catherine's only way of judging that had been through his tender, if formulaic, written professions of love.

De Puebla's despatches were a rare window through which Catherine could peer into England. The picture of the English that emerges from his pen turns the national stereotypes of today on their heads. For while the Castilians come across as stiff-upper-lipped and serious, the English were seen as flighty, untrustworthy and impetuous. Amongst other things, he complained, the English were continually changing their minds. That was something that Catherine, eventually, found especially hard to cope with. She may, however, have been reassured to hear that, like the Spanish themselves, the English were enemies of the king of France.

Catherine's direct experience of the English was mostly limited to her almoner, John Reveles, and occasional meetings with ambassadors. She may also have exchanged words with a few of the other Englishmen at Isabel and Ferdinand's court. These included a singer called Porris and a painter, known as the Maestre Anthony. She would probably also have been told of that gallant crusading English knight known as the Conde d'Escalas (Lord Scales) who won over Ferdinand and Isabel's hearts when he appeared as a volunteer in the Granada War accompanied by a hundred archers and foot-soldiers armed with axes and lances. Scales was said to have turned the battle at Loja with his men. He had two teeth knocked out by a stone, however, and worried that his looks would be spoilt for ever. Ferdinand assured him that this was the virtuous injury of a crusader which, as a result, made him 'more beautiful than deformed'.

We do not know how fearful Catherine was when, having been driven back to Laredo after a storm caught her first ship, she boarded the vessel that would finally take her to England. Did she recall coming to this port five years earlier to bid goodbye to her elder sister Juana? Did she compare her comparatively meagre expedition to the vast fleet that awaited Juana and her army of followers?

Perhaps her mind was more on the sea itself. Henry had sent one of England's best captains, Stephen Brett, to steer her vessel after the failure of her first attempt to get to England. The Bay of Biscay, however, routinely terrified all those who ventured into it.

The vessel set off from Laredo at five o'clock in the afternoon on Monday 27 September 1501. That dusk she would have got her final glimpse of Spain – possibly the towering Picos de Europa where they fall almost straight into the Cantabrian Sea. More than a dozen years after the English ambassadors had arrived at Medina del Campo, Catherine was finally on her way. She would never see her homeland again.

8 Land

Plymouth. 2 October 1501

The Bay of Biscay, for once, remained calm. Trouble came, however, as soon as they passed the island of Ushant and rounded Brittany. A fierce southerly wind threw lightning, thunder and huge waves at them as storms rolled in every four or five hours. 'It was impossible not to be frightened,' wrote one of those on board.

News of Catherine's departure from Laredo reached England before her. Margaret Beaufort, readying her own London house for a reception party, marked the date of 27 September down in her Book of Hours – a place where only the most important of events were registered. Catherine's long-awaited arrival was also marked on 2 October. There was much relief. Henry VII had fretted that storms and hurricanes might have sunk the ship in which she first set off from La Coruña, drowning his eagerly awaited daughter-in-law before she had even caught sight of England.

At three o'clock in the afternoon her ship finally entered the harbour at Plymouth. She had been meant to arrive at Southampton, but by this stage any form of dry land must have seemed a godsend. Plymouth was a prosperous enough port, though not well enough known for the Spaniards with her to recall its name when questioned about the journey years later. A crowd of Devonians awaited her anxiously and joyously at the quay. 'She could not have been received with greater rejoicings, if she had been the Saviour of the world,' her doctor, the Licentiate Alcaraz, wrote to Isabel two days later.

More than four months after leaving the Alhambra, Catherine finally set foot on English soil. She then did what any daughter of Isabel could be expected to do under the circumstances and processed straight to church. Presumably she gave thanks for surviving what an English chronicler called 'the outrageous blasts' that had nearly ripped the 'masts out of their sockets'. In his letter home, Alcaraz added a wish that God might have greeted her in that Plymouth church by promising her an enjoyable life in England and assuring her that she would leave heirs to the throne.

The arrival of a daughter-in-law, and a foreign one at that, was a major event for Henry VII. Catherine was not just a guarantee that the Tudor line would be continued. She also provided the stamp of international approval. Her presence in England said that the Tudors were more than good enough for the powerful monarchs of Spain. Sixteen years earlier Henry had defeated Richard III at Bosworth Field. Richard, his horse dead, was reportedly 'killed fighting manfully in the press of his enemies'. The battle was a test of God's will. His victory proved – by right of *Dei judicium* – that God himself recognised Henry's right to be king. Few people would have confidently predicted that this somewhat obscure pretender who had landed on Welsh shores just two weeks earlier, after spending much of his life as an exile in Brittany, would grab the throne or hold on to it so successfully. Catherine's arrival was such an important event that it warranted a specially commissioned account. The task of describing her journey into England appears to have fallen to the poet Stephen Hawes, with the commission almost certainly coming from Henry VII himself. He wrote his chronicle in the style of a medieval romance and gave it the title *The Receyt of the Ladie Kateryne*.

Her coming set the West Country's nobility into a flurry of activity. 'With goodly manner and haste [they] sped themself with right honourable gifts to repair to that noble princesse,' the *Receyt* reports. The news soon reached London. Chroniclers

there heaved a sigh of relief that, after several false starts in previous weeks, the 'flying rumours' of her arrival were finally right.
The king's council despatched four heralds 'to serve the princess'. King Henry sent Catherine a welcoming letter telling her
of his pleasure, joy and relief at 'your noble presence, which we
have often desired'. The first words she heard from her father-
in-law may have been delivered, as he originally wrote them, in
French. 'It may please you to regard us henceforward as your
good and [loving] father, as familiarly as you would do the king
and queen your parents, for on our part we are determined to
treat, receive, and favour you like our own daughter, and in no
wise more [or less dearly] than any of our own children,' Henry
told her. He could not help mentioning, however, that she had
appeared somewhat later than expected.

Her trip towards London barely went any faster than that
across Spain. In thirty-three days she managed only to get as
far as Dogmersfield, in Hampshire. What did she make of this
foreign land that, suddenly, was her home? Seen through foreign eyes, England could seem like an endless stretch of wood-
land and marshes. It was alternately green or wet (or both) but
abundant in livestock and with peasants who fared better than in
other countries. Hedges, oaks and other trees provided a canopy
of vegetation that, according to one Frenchman, was such that
'in travelling you think you are in a continuous wood'. The wild-
life, according to another traveller, included 'bears and hogs,
besides the wolf and the fox; and of graminivorous animals,
stags and hares, and others of the same sort'.

Along the way there were innumerable encounters with the
great and the good of each county they passed through. How did
these foreigners, only a tiny handful of whom she could converse
with, seem to Catherine? The English were considered handsome
but, apart from that, did not enjoy a good reputation amongst her
fellow southern Europeans. They had, for example, far too high

an opinion of themselves. 'The English are a proud race without any respect, and claim a superiority over all other nations,' one Italian observed. 'The English think there are no people like themselves,' said another. 'If they see a handsome foreigner they say he looks like an Englishman.' They also had a reputation for being restless and slippery to deal with. 'In the morning they are as devout as angels, but after dinner they are like devils,' said one Milanese ambassador who particularly disliked them.

Then, of course, there was the weather. 'In England it is always windy and, however warm the weather, the natives invariably wear furs,' reported a recent arrival from the warm Mediterranean basin. 'The summers are never very hot.'

The same writer, the Venetian Nicolo di Favri, noticed many of the peculiarities of English dress and behaviour that would have jumped out at Catherine. Women, for example, seemed both unusually good-natured and to enjoy remarkable freedom in their public behaviour. He noted that:

Their usual vesture is a cloth petticoat over the shift, lined with grey squirrel's or some other fur. Over the petticoat they wear a long gown lined with some choice fur. The gentlewomen carry the train of their gown under their arm; the commonality pin it behind or before, or at one side. The sleeves of the gowns sit as close as possible; are long and unslashed throughout, the cuffs being lined with choice fur. Their head gear is of various sorts of velvet, cap fashion, with lappets hanging down behind their shoulders like two hoods and in front they have two others lined with some other silk . . . Others wear on their heads muslins which are distended and hang at their backs, but not far down. Some draw their hair from under a kerchief and wear over their hair a cap, for the most part white, round and seemly; others again wear a kerchief in folds over the head; but be the fashion as it may, the hair is never seen. The stockings are black and their shoes doubly-soled, of various colours, but no one wears *chapines* [the stacked heels that Catherine had sometimes used in Spain], as they are not in use in England.

The men, too, had their peculiarly English fashions, as the Venetian reported.

The men are well-made, tall and stout: well-clad, wearing gowns called doublets plaited on the shoulders, reaching half-way down the leg, and lined with several sorts of very fine fur; on their heads they wear caps with one or two ornaments: with short hair like the priests in Venice, the hair over the forehead being cut away.

It was English women's public behaviour, however, that was strangest. 'When they meet friends in the street they shake hands and kiss on the mouth and go to some tavern to regale, their relatives not taking this amiss, as such is the custom,' said the Venetian. 'One may see in the markets and streets of the city married women and damsels employed in arts, and barterings and affairs of trade, undisguisedly,' said another visitor. 'They display great simplicity and lack of jealousy in their usages towards females.' It could hardly have been more different from the strict and segregated world that Machado and the other English ambassadors saw when they had visited Catherine more than a decade earlier.

The first full clash of customs came when Catherine and her party arrived at Dogmersfield on 6 November. The Spaniards had happily installed themselves in the big house there and were greatly impressed by its 'handsome park', which included a large pond that provided fresh fish for the table. Henry VII was fed up with waiting for his daughter-in-law. He set off to find her himself, meeting up with Prince Arthur on the way. They were intercepted, however, in open countryside by a worried prothonotary of Spain. Henry was informed that his wish to see the princess could not be fulfilled. The rigid precepts of Castilian formality clashed with what must have seemed to the Spaniards like the coarse norms of England. A Spanish infanta could not possibly entertain either her future husband or father-in-law before the full marriage ceremony had been completed. Her virtue, protected for so long, would be under threat. Isabel and Ferdinand had issued strict orders. Henry VII's chronicler explained:

They had received by strict injunction and commandment of their sovereign lord of their land that they should in no manner or wise permit or suffer their lady and princess of Spain . . . to have any meeting nor any manner of communication or company until the start of the very day of the solemnisation of the marriage.

The king was not pleased. After the long months of waiting, he wanted to see what he was getting out of his deal with the Spanish monarchs. There and then, out in the open, he called an impromptu meeting of his counsellors. Bishops and nobles gathered around him. What should he do? This was England, they said, and he was the king. He could do what he wanted. The 'pleasure and commandment' of Catherine now lay in the hands of 'our noble king of England'. That was enough for Henry. He left Arthur behind him and spurred his horse on into Dogmersfield, where Catherine had arrived a few hours earlier.

The Spaniards were still determined to block his passage. The archbishop of Santiago, the bishop of Malaga and the count of Cabra all tried to persuade him not to see her. The princess, they claimed, was already resting. Henry had had enough. He did not care if she had retired to bed. He threatened, if necessary, to walk straight into her bedchamber and meet her there. 'That was the mind and the intent of his coming.' His words must have struck panic into the Spanish party. If meeting the king before the wedding was dishonourable, to do so in her own bedchamber would have been unspeakable. Catherine, however, appears to have reacted calmly. She asked for some time to get ready. This was not going to be the grandiose Castilian-style reception she might have hoped for, but she had been taught to dissimulate and knew how to be gracious.

The king was still in his riding clothes, and probably looking dishevelled after his trip, but 'she gave him an honourable meeting'. Catherine received him in one of her outer chambers. This first encounter with her father-in-law appears to have been somewhat confused, if full of good intentions. Neither, after all, could speak the other's language. Henry probably spoke to her in the fluent French learnt during his exile in Brittany. Catherine, meanwhile, stuck to Spanish. Her English almoner, Reveles, might have been called in to bridge the language gap. William Hollybrand, a Spanish-speaker who later served as Catherine's treasurer, may also have been in attendance. 'Goodly words' were uttered in both languages as Catherine and Henry tried to get across the 'great joy and gladness' they were feeling.

Henry appears to have left happy. There is no record of how Catherine or her fellow Spaniards felt about having their precious formality so thoroughly trampled over by a king in riding boots. When Henry went off to change his clothes, Catherine and her party had to start thinking on their feet. By now Prince Arthur had made it to Dogmersfield. He and his father were due back soon. After years of letter-writing and a lifetime spent living with his name, Catherine was finally going to meet her husband, the fifteen-year-old prince of Wales.

The surviving portraits of Arthur show a long, thin, delicate-boned face. He bears some resemblance to his younger brother Henry at a similar age, but a thin-lipped mouth and narrow frame both add to an impression of delicacy that contrasts with his brother's robustness. There is also a hint of warmth and humour in his face as he sits for one portrait with a white, carnation-like gillyflower – the symbol of betrothal and purity – in his hand.

One can judge little of Arthur's character from the love letters he wrote to Catherine. They are in such neat, upright handwriting – with no crossings out – that either a scribe must have helped him or the composition and copying out of the letters formed part of his homework. They contrast strongly with the swirling, energetic and sometimes illegible handwriting of

Catherine whose later letters – which often start with a bold 'from my own hand' – occasionally give the impression that her hand is struggling to control the torrent of words and emotions she wishes to get down on paper. Arthur had, in the prophets of the new humanist learning like the poet Bernard André and the physician and scholar Thomas Linacre, exacting and brilliant tutors. He had already 'either committed to memory or read with his own eyes and leafed with his own fingers' works by Homer, Virgil, Ovid, Cicero, Caesar, Livy and Tacitus. With the coaching of such men, Arthur was one of the few who had no need to feel intellectually intimidated by his well-schooled Spanish bride. In some ways, indeed, these two young, obedient perfectionists were very alike.

This, then, was the youth who appeared with his father in Catherine's chambers at Dogmersfield later that afternoon. This time things went a bit more smoothly. Latin was used. This meant not only that Catherine could understand what was going on, but that Arthur could too. The bishops were on hand, in any case, to do further translating so that 'the speeches of both countries by the means of Latin were understood'. A betrothal that had already been through several proxy ceremonies – mostly with a coy and somewhat overwhelmed De Puebla pretending to be Catherine – received a further blessing from the churchmen present. As a result they were now deemed to have become 'spousally ensured'. That was good enough for the Spaniards, who thought of her as properly married from this moment on. There was no wedding night, though. That had been planned for after the big ceremony in London a few days later. Catherine, instead, threw an impromptu party that evening. She called in her minstrels and danced with her ladies. Arthur also danced 'right pleasant and honourably', but without touching his wife. He took the wife of one of his father's officials, Lady Guildford, as partner.

The next morning Catherine set off on the final stage of her journey towards London, stopping at Chertsey. She then rode towards Lambeth. At Kingston upon Thames a party of some three to four hundred horsemen in red and black livery rode up to accompany her. At their head was the dashing Edward Stafford, duke of Buckingham and England's wealthiest and proudest aristocrat – a man who might most closely have fitted the princess's idea of a proper noble, a real grandee. The next day the duke delivered her to lodgings in Lambeth, where she was to await the start of a fortnight of pageantry, wedding ceremonies, jousting and partying. Henry was determined to celebrate her arrival as flamboyantly as possible.

9 On Show

Southwark, St George's Field. 12 November 1501

It was time for Catherine to show herself off. Her wedding was just two days away but first, on this Friday, she had to make her formal entry into London. That, at least, was something she was prepared for. She had seen her parents make such entries dozens of times in Spanish cities. Catherine could not know, however, quite how much effort London had put into turning her arrival into one of the great events of Henry VII's reign. Weeks of work had gone into preparing a spectacle the like of which London had rarely, if ever, seen. The city had been transformed into a stage. The long-awaited star of the show was the Spanish princess.

The infanta dressed to impress and English observers were suitably admiring. They praised the richness of her clothes and found her choice of head-dress especially noteworthy. 'Upon her head [was] a little hat, fashioned like a cardinal's hat,' one reported. This was held on by gold lace and underneath it sat a carnation-coloured undercap from which her long, light auburn hair fell freely out over her shoulders 'so as men might well see all her hair from the middle part of her head downwards'. That hair, portraits based on Catherine suggest, would have cascaded in rich, glossy and luxuriant waves down her neck and back.

Catherine's entry had been carefully thought out. Her party of Spaniards lined up on St George's Field, Southwark. Each was partnered with an English person of equal status. So they set off towards London Bridge, everybody neatly paired except for the Spanish count, archbishop and bishop, who rode together. Catherine herself rode a richly harnessed mule and was accompanied by the papal legate and Henry, duke of York, her husband's ten-year-old brother. It is her first recorded meeting with the small, energetic and ruddy-faced child who would become Henry VIII. She did not know it, but the boy beside her was to shape most of her future years.

The king's heralds led the way, forcing gawking bystanders to the sides as the cavalcade progressed. Catherine was unlikely to have noticed the seamy side of Southwark, famous for the dozen stews — or brothels — that provided a rich income to the local landlord, the bishop of Winchester. This disreputable stretch of the Thames's south bank would later also become famous for its bear-baiting arenas, theatres and other entertainments. Ostrich feathers and tinkling silver bells adorned the horses and uniforms of the English nobles who followed Catherine. Her own band of wind musicians — with their trumpets, sackbuts and oboe-like shalmewes — led the Spanish contingent. The paired riders followed neatly along, two by two, behind them. A touch of farce was added by the fact that, while both English women and Spanish women rode side-saddle, the latter did so on what the *Receyt*'s author called 'the wronge side'. This meant that the paired women actually rode back to back — the English pointing to the left and the Spaniards to the right. All but one of the Spanish women, careful not to outshine their princess, wore black dresses with long black mantilla-like head-dresses. Here, again, the culture clash showed, for their English counterparts glittered extravagantly beside — or, rather, behind — them in cloth of gold. The lesser Spanish women were left near the end, carried along on wagons. They wore rougher clothes and 'were not the fairest women of the company'. The liveried yeomanry of the duke of Buckingham and the earl of Northumberland provided the necessary colour and bulk for the tail end of the procession.

London was a great European trading centre, so Spaniards were hardly a novelty. But the crowds of 'common people' — who perched dangerously on 'high places, windows and houses' to get a good view of the procession – had never seen such a display of Castilian pride. Reactions were mixed. The *Receyt*'s author found the Spanish women strange, partly because they rode the wrong way around on saddles with peculiar crossed staves on them and partly because they wore black. The humanist scholar Sir Thomas More, in one of his less saintly moments, was positively cruel. 'Except for three, or at the most four, of them, they were just too much to look at: hunchbacked, undersized, barefoot pygmies from Ethiopia. If you had been there you would have thought they were refugees from hell,' he wrote to a friend. He might have been more generous had he known that, thirty-four years later, his loyalty to the principles he shared with the pygmies' princess would cost him his life.

Catherine passed under one of the capital's most gruesome spots as she rode out onto London Bridge. For there, on top of the southern gatehouse, the heads of England's traitors, stuck on pikes and tarred to preserve them, were traditionally displayed. Ever since the execution of Scottish hero Sir William Wallace in 1305, those entering London across the river risked catching sight of a wrinkled head. Although there is no record of traitors' remains being on display that day, Catherine would have done well to shiver at the thought. Several of those who later embraced her cause – including More – would eventually have their own parboiled heads displayed there.

Six elaborate and colourful 'pageant' stages had been set up around the City of London, often beside the fountains or watering houses where piped running water reached the streets. Catherine encountered the first of these in the middle of London Bridge, as her party squeezed its way through the narrow, tunnel-like street between the shops on either side. The pageant stages and the shows performed on them were meant to impress the 'common people' as much as the Spanish visitors. The latter, in fact, would not have understood a word, for the actors spoke only in English. Catherine's educated mind was easily capable of understanding many of the religious and astrological symbols employed. The girl holding the toothed wheel in her hands on the two-tier stage on London Bridge, for example, was clearly identifiable as her namesake, St Catherine. For the most part, however, Catherine was the uncomprehending recipient of the actors' paeans to her husband, to England and to herself.

The mayor of London, wearing crimson satin and accompanied by his sword-bearer, led them from pageant to pageant. He was followed by the Recorder in black velvet and two dozen sheriffs and aldermen with their servants all dressed in scarlet. Up Gracechurch Street, round into Cornhill and then onto Cheapside they went, stopping at each pageant as they headed towards old St Paul's Cathedral. The pageants themselves were extravagant and colourfully decorated stage sets – some with more than one floor – adorned with lions, dragons, giant roses, horses, fish, serpents, bulls, virgins, rams and mermaids. Staircases, lanterns, planets and man-driven machines added to the splendour while the speeches of actors provided the narrative for her journey across this Tudor dreamworld. More prosaically, she was making her way through England's great city to its most important place of worship, St Paul's.

There were reminders, too, of why she was here. 'Blessed be the fruit of your belly/ Your sustenance and fruit shall increase and multiply,' one actor declaimed. Catherine might have preferred, had she understood them, the words offered on London Bridge. There she was told that she would have two spouses. This was not a prescient reference to the boy riding on her right-hand side. The other husband was Christ.

> Love your first spouse chiefly, then your new
> And these rewards thereof shall ensue:
> With the second, honour temporal
> And, with the first, glory perpetual.

In Catherine's mind, perpetual glory always sounded better than temporary honour – whatever the price to be paid.

We do not know how impressed Catherine was by London. She had swapped Granada, with its two hundred minarets, for the city with the most churches in Europe – its skyline bristling with a hundred steeples, church towers and spires. London was also the fast-expanding home to some fifty thousand people, and its population would triple over the century. It was, however, much dirtier than Granada. Great open drains and sewers ran down the sides or the middle of many streets. Its wood-framed houses grew wider on each of up to four floors and occupants of the upper floors were known for tipping their rubbish out of the overhanging windows directly onto the street below. The streets were busy and dark and often stank – even though rakers and night-soil men daily carried refuse out of the city. 'Houses block out from us I know not how large a measure of light, and do not permit us to see the heavens. And the round horizon does not limit the air but the lofty roofs,' More complained. He once saw someone squatting by a wall 'to ease himself in the open street'. Pigs wandered freely, scoffing on the waste. Ravens and kites were also encouraged to feast on the filth. The Dutch scholar Erasmus was appalled, wanting people 'appointed to see the streets cleaned from mud and urine'. The Thames itself was insalubrious and smelly. The city's waste ran into it and the banks were piled up with mounds of human and animal excrement waiting to be carried away by dung boats. A German visitor, arriving later in the century, remarked that Londoners' habit of washing their clothes in Thames water meant that everybody carried the stench of the city's filth.

'In the city what is there to move one to live well? but rather, when a man is straining in his own power to climb the steep path to virtue, it turns him back by a thousand devices and sucks him back by its thousand enticements,' More wrote when describing the city to his fellow London humanist John Colet. 'Wherever you turn your eyes, what else will you see but confectioners, fishmongers, butchers, cooks, poulterers, fishermen, fowlers, who supply the materials for gluttony and the world and the world's lord, the devil?'

For now, though, London was showing its brightest face. Tapestries, silks, satins and gold and silver cloth had been hung from the buildings in some streets. Catherine's musical ear would have caught what one later English chronicler called the 'goodly ballads, [and] sweet harmony [of] the musical instruments, which sounded with hearty noise on every side of the street'. She may also have appreciated 'the beauty of the English ladies, the goodly demeanour of the young damsels, the amorous countenance of the lusty bachelors'.

Londoners had put on their best finery. Catherine would have noticed 'the costly furs of the citizens standing on scaffolds' to catch a glimpse of her. She must also have spotted, at the pageant beside the stone water fountain known as the Standard, the large party of nobles, uniformed retainers and yeomanry who packed both sides of the street and perched on window ledges, gutters and battlements. These were the king's men. Henry VII had sneaked surreptitiously into the house of a merchant called Whiting to watch the procession. She was also being watched by her fiancé Arthur, her mother-in-law Elizabeth of York and the king's mother, Margaret Beaufort.

Londoners appear to have been impressed by what they saw. Even More could not help praising Catherine herself. 'Ah, but the lady! Take my word for it. She thrilled the hearts of everyone: she possesses all those qualities that make for beauty in a very charming young girl,' he wrote. 'Everywhere she receives the highest of praises; but even that is most inadequate. I do hope this highly publicised union will prove a happy omen for England.'

The procession began to run late and Catherine was hurried away from at least one pageant while the actors were still saying their lines. Eventually she arrived at the last pageant stage at the gates to St Paul's churchyard. Here the mayor and city officials presented their gifts. These included 'much treasure' and, after a collection amongst merchants and guilds, 'basins and pots filled with coin to a great sum'.

Catherine was a gracious recipient. She was amiable and full of goodness as she thanked them, in a 'most-learned manner', for their gifts and kind words. She did not know that the same men had threatened to take some of their money back when told they would also have to foot the bill for one pageant. From here she was led into St Paul's by the archbishop of Canterbury and a gaggle of other clergy. This was where she was to be married on the Sunday. Here, as the choir sang, she made her offering at the shrine of St Erkenwald – the seventh-century bishop of London whose tomb was renowned for miracles.

By this stage the author of the *Receyt* was breathing a deep sigh of relief. The day had gone off without mishap. No one had fallen to their death from a window or been kicked unconscious by the 'cruel' and 'stern' horses that processed through the packed streets of London. There had been 'no mischance . . . to man, woman or child'.

After making her offering to St Erkenwald, Catherine was led out of the west door, through the cathedral's carved stone gate, with its brass pillar and iron leaves, and past the Lollards' Tower (where the bishops locked up heretics) to her lodgings at the Bishop's Palace. The show, at least for the day, was over. Catherine, if later events are anything to go by, had already started to win over the people of London.

10 Wedding

Old St Paul's Cathedral. 14 November 1501

The inside of St Paul's had been transformed. A wooden stage had been erected along the nave of the long, cavernous building with the high wooden roof and soaring, 489-foot spire. The size of the stage was impressive. This was twelve feet across and ran, like a vast ramp, the entire 350 feet from the west door to where a dozen broad steps rose up to the choir door. It stood proudly on four-foot-high timber struts and the railings along each side were hung with a fine wool or silk twill cloth known as 'say'. A raised round dais had a carpet of red cloth tacked to its floor with sparkling gilt nails. Cloth of Arras tapestries – the best of the royal collection – clothed the stone walls with their rich textures and flamboyant scenes.

The closing act of Catherine's wedding show was to be performed here, within sight of as many people as could be packed into the church. The king wanted Arthur and Catherine to hold centre stage. An enclosed, latticed closet was built on one side, opposite where the ceremony was to take place. Discreetly hidden from view, Henry and his queen would watch from there. They did not want their presence to distract from the main event. This day belonged to their son and to his new bride.

Catherine had arrived back at the Bishop's Palace late the previous night. The afternoon and evening had been spent at the recently rebuilt royal residence of Baynard's Castle, on the riverside, getting to know her mother-in-law. Her encounter with the kindly Elizabeth of York went well and the dancing carried on until late. A great torch-lit procession took her back to the Bishop's Palace after dark.

That morning, dressed in her white satin wedding gown, she was met at the palace door by the ten-year-old Henry, whose task it was to lead her to the cathedral door. His maternal aunt, Lady Cecily, carried the train. Already the trumpeters positioned high up in the vaults above the west door were blaring out their welcome.

Crowds had been gathering both inside and outside the church for a while. The *Receyt*'s author, in an apparent swipe at the peacock outfits of some, spoke damningly of those 'rude and unlearned people' who had come either to show off or gawk. They certainly found something to gawk at, because Catherine's dress gave them their first ever glimpse of what would later become a staple of Tudor fashion, the farthingale. The great hoops that pushed out her voluminous skirt were probably made from a kind of flexible green bamboo. Her ladies followed suit, wearing 'beneath their waists certain round hoops bearing out their gowns from their bodies after their country's manner'.

A large white silk veil, bordered in gold, pearls and precious stones, covered much of Catherine's face and hung down as far as her waist. Her wedding gown was also surprising to the English eye. It was described as 'very large, both [in] the sleeves and also the body with many pleats'. That, one English observer said, made it 'much like men's clothing'.

The first part of the wedding ceremony was about politics and money. The agreements between England and Spain were read out, with Catherine's dowry announced to all and sundry. Catherine was then handed letters patent from both the king and Arthur detailing her endowment and surety.

With the temporal paperwork done, it was time for the spiritual. The long rigmarole of a wedding attended by eighteen mitred bishops and abbots commenced. The young prince – who had arrived earlier to await his bride – was also dressed in white satin. Together, Catherine and Arthur made their solemn vows. This, however, was only Act One. After the marriage rites the bride and groom moved further along the stage, hand in hand, to the high altar. At the choir door they turned this way and that, first to the north side of the stage and then to the south so 'the present multitude of people might see and behold their persons'. Certain present-day wedding traditions were observed. Arthur's grandmother, Lady Margaret, for example, wept copiously. 'Either she was in sorrow,' observed her friend John Fisher, 'or else when she was in prosperity she was in dread of the adversity for to come.' There followed a mass at the high altar. Then Catherine walked out of the church without her husband, who had slipped off to welcome her at her chamber door. She was led out by young Henry. The trumpets rang out again. She was now a properly married woman in all but one thing – the marriage had to be consummated.

Outside, the people were already celebrating. A pageant stood near the west door. It was another overpopulated pastiche replete with mountains, rocks of jet, amber and coral and a strange collection of plants and trees. A greyhound seemed to have grown out of a rose, while roses themselves sprouted from a tree. Three kings, a red dragon, a lion and a white hart were also squeezed on as the royal symbols of England, Spain and France fought for space. The most important part for many of those present, however, was the fountain. This was running with wine. A little gate in front of the pageant opened and closed as people filled their cups.

The banquet was held in the great hall of the Bishop's Palace. Catherine sat at the highest table with her Spanish archbishop. For most of the guests it was the start of two straight weeks of partying. Over the next fortnight there would be disguisings, banquets and jousting. Gravel and sand were put down to make a special tiltyard at Westminster, where three hundred ladies accompanied Catherine and the queen to one joust. London's private palaces vied with each other to produce sumptuous entertainment. From Lady Margaret Beaufort's house at Cold-harbour to the earl of Derby's house, the banquets were lavish and the food and wine unending. At one party Catherine danced with one of her ladies, while Arthur danced with his aunt, Lady Cecily. The show, however, was stolen by the rumbustious young Henry, who danced with his eleven-year-old sister Margaret and, in a fit of boyish enthusiasm, 'suddenly cast off his gown and danced in his jacket with the said Lady Margaret' while his parents looked on with indulgent amusement. When the king called a temporary halt to the partying for a thanksgiving mass, more than five hundred nobles – some, perhaps, nursing hang-overs – packed into St Paul's. This time it was Catherine who sat behind the lattice screen to spy on them.

A later chronicler said the wedding-day feast, with the royal plate of gold and silver on prominent display, was so marvellous that it defied description. The Scottish humanist Walter Ogilvie, who was a guest, described the displays of gold and silver ware on the sideboards like this: 'You might have seen jewel-encrusted goblets, dishes of purest gold, and whatever finery goldsmiths and engravers or even the famous Mentor knew how to devise.' The *Receyt*'s author, in turn, praised the king's cooks for their 'cunning preparations'. He thought the Spaniards fortunate. England, he claimed grandiosely, led the world in gastronomy. English food routinely won 'praise and commendation amongst all other countries or nations in the world'.

So, in the wake of all this partying, was the marriage consummated? The question remains the essential mystery of Catherine's life. For this was where the story of her life began to divide. Many years later she would insist that consummation never happened. Juan de Gamarra, then a twelve-year-old boy in Catherine's service, told the hearing in Zaragoza that he had remained in her antechamber on the wedding night. 'Prince Arthur got up very early, which surprised everyone a lot,' he said. When Gamarra went into Catherine's room, the atmosphere amongst her ladies was of concern for Catherine and disappointment with Arthur. 'Francisca de Cáceres, who was in charge of dressing and undressing the queen and whom she liked and confided in a lot, was looking sad and telling the other ladies that nothing had passed between Prince Arthur and his wife, which surprised everyone and made them laugh at him.'

Did Gamarra, who recalled the name of Catherine's spiky lady-in-waiting Francisca de Cáceres perfectly, make that up just to protect her? Did other witnesses in Zaragoza do the same? And was Catherine, a woman praised for her piety, a liar? A later English chronicler was amongst those convinced that she was. This is how he put it:

Every day endeth and night ensues, so when night was come, this lusty prince and his beautiful bride were brought and joined together in one bed naked, and there did that act, which to the performance and full consummation of matrimony was most requisite and expedient . . . in the morning he called for drink, which he before times was not accustomed to do. At which thing one of his chamberlains, marvelling, inquired the cause of his drought [thirst]. To whom he answered merely saying: 'I have this Night been in the midst of Spain, which is a hot region, and that journey maketh me so dry, and if thou hadst been under that hot climate, thou wouldst have been drier than I.'

11 Silence and Sadness

London, the Bishop's Palace. 15 November 1501

If Arthur swaggered boastfully out of his bride's bedroom demanding beer the following morning, Catherine appears to have had an opposite reaction to the night's events. Her chamber, that day, became a Spanish bunker. Silence reigned in the Bishop's Palace. Only her closest ladies were allowed in. 'No access utterly was suffered to be had,' said the *Receyt*. The only person to gain access to her, outside her most intimate circle, was the earl of Oxford. As the Great Chamberlain of England, the earl was sent to see how she was, bringing a gift from the king. One assumes that, regardless of how she was feeling, she replied graciously. If Gamarra was right, the mood was sombre. Was this the moment when Doña Elvira, who acted as Queen Isabel's eyes and ears, also decided that Catherine was still a virgin? The proper Spanish test would have been to inspect the sheets and display them as public proof of a virgin's blood. Elvira was the sort of woman to grill the slave girl Catalina, whose job it was to make Catherine's bed, about exactly what the sheets showed. Did her doctor, the Licentiate Alcaraz, write again to Isabel to report on the latest events? A nephew who travelled with him to England told the Zaragoza hearing that his uncle was shocked by Arthur's physical condition. 'He said his limbs were so weak that he had never seen a man whose legs and other bits of his body were so thin.'

Catherine may simply have been observing etiquette by keeping herself to herself. The court rules handed down from generation to generation in what was known as the 'Royal Book' stated that, at this stage, an English princess would be expected to 'keep her chamber all day . . . and no man to come there'. In any case, a failure to have full sex on her wedding night (if that was the problem) hardly ruled out success at a later date. Time, after all, is usually on the side of fifteen-year-olds.

The new princess of Wales seems to have recovered her spirits quickly. She was now one of the highest-ranking women in England. She enjoyed herself in the partying that followed over the next fortnight, joining in the dancing (though, again, only with her own ladies) and watching the jousts. There are no more signs of intimacy between her and Arthur, however, with the two of them being seated at separate tables in at least one banquet.

Her transformation from a Spanish infanta to an English princess was not complete with the wedding. She still had to learn the customs and etiquette of her new home. Two days later she began learning to eat like an English princess. 'Whereas she ever tofore was served after the guise and manner of Spain, now unto her was used the accustomed service of the realm of England,' the *Receyt* noted. This involved learning the tiresome rules of how, when, what – and by whom – she was served among people famed as big eaters and even bigger drinkers. The English, one foreigner said, were 'flesh-eaters, and insatiable for animal' as well as being 'sottish and unrestrained in their appetites'. Whether her training in English table manners also meant getting used to 'the great silence that is used at the tables of the honourable and wiser sort' noted by a later Tudor or to the fact that people 'belch at table without any reserve or shame, even in the presence of persons of the greatest dignity', as a visiting Frenchman later observed, we cannot tell.

The partying transferred to the River Thames. A flotilla of brightly decorated barges took them all upriver to Westminster. A floating orchestra of reedy shalmewes, brassy sackbuts, tabor drums, recorders, clarions and trumpets provided the music. It was, the *Receyt*'s author claimed with his usual hyperbole, the greatest and most colourful thing the river had ever seen. Here again, though, the friction between city and king shone through. The Mercers' Company – the guild of London's fabric traders – was fined ten pounds because its barge was 'not garnished . . . so well as others'.

As the celebrations drew to a close, the party moved further upstream, out of London to the recently rebuilt riverside palace at Richmond that was Henry VII's pride and joy. The trip was yet another water-borne musical festival. As they rowed upstream Catherine was moving ever further into her new life and floating away from the old. For Richmond was where she would wave goodbye to most of those who had accompanied her to England.

It would have been hard not to be impressed by the elegant grey stone towers and galleried garden walls of Richmond Palace when they appeared around a bend in the river. The builders had only just finished in time for Henry to show it off to his daughter-in-law and Spanish guests. The great hall had recently been glazed and completed along with the 'pleasant dancing chambers', 'secret closets' and the 'goodly chambers' set aside for Catherine and Arthur. This was not the Alhambra, but Richmond boasted a fountain running in a marble-paved inner courtyard and had 'most fair and pleasant gardens'. Her fellow Spaniards certainly enjoyed themselves in England's most modern, comfortable and playful palace. Richmond also had fine hunting. A Spanish guest, probably the count of Cabra, shot a deer with his cross-bow and there was 'great slaughter . . . of venison'. They were also invited to use the bowling alley and tennis facilities that Henry had built, as well as the archery butts and the tables set up for chess, dice and cards. A tight-rope was stretched between two high posts and a Spanish acrobat who had travelled with Catherine entertained everyone. His daring act included not just juggling with tennis balls, bells and swords but also dancing, jumping and hanging by his toes. The high point came when he managed to hang 'by the teeth, most marvellously'. On their last day the Spaniards were showered with presents. The archbishop, the bishop, the count and the count's brother each carried away more than three hundred marks' worth of gold and silver plate. The visiting Spaniards finally left for Spain on 29 November, two weeks after the wedding. Some fifty-six people, including both slaves and servants, had been detailed to stay on with her. But the links with home were being cut. It was hard for Catherine to say goodbye. She suffered their parting with 'great heaviness' and 'painfully' and her mood was described as 'partly annoyed and pensive'.

Henry soon realised that his daughter-in-law was feeling sad and moody. He called Catherine and her remaining Spanish ladies, along with a group of English ladies, to the brand-new library he had built at Richmond. It was an appropriate meeting place for his bookish daughter-in-law. The Spanish court may have been more advanced in its humanism and learning, but here were some of the finest manuscripts and books of the period under the curatorship of England's first ever 'royal librarian'. Henry was able to show her books that were 'sage, merry and also right cunning, both in Latin and in English'. We do not know how much the sight of so many written words lightened Catherine's heavy heart. In case that did not work, the king had prepared a surprise. He had recently spent freely with a Flemish jeweller. In order to 'increase gladness, mitigate sorrow, refresh and comfort the spirits', the jewels were now displayed before Catherine. There were rings set with precious stones, fat diamonds and other pieces of jewellery. Catherine was told she could pick whichever one she liked best. Then her ladies were invited to follow suit. With this, the *Receyt*'s author optimistically stated, Catherine 'assuaged her heaviness and drew herself into the manner, guise and usages of England'.

If only it was that simple. In fact, trouble was already brewing between Catherine's Spaniards and Henry. She was soon drawn into the series of rows and misunderstandings which helped shape the next stage of her life. Within a fortnight, a bewildered Catherine found herself standing before a furious King Henry as she struggled to understand his anger. The Spanish ambassador Rodrigo de Puebla, the king complained, had made him look like a fool. Henry claimed that the ambassador had tricked him into asking for immediate payment of the final instalment of her dowry – made up of pearls, jewels, tapestry, gold and silver plate – even though it was not due for another year. Catherine's officials had then refused to hand it over. This, he explained, was an unpardonable humiliation. 'I am exceedingly sorry that I have asked for the jewels,' he said angrily.

I should not like to be held for a person who asks what is due to me before the time. God be praised, I am not in want, and, if it were necessary, I could, for love of them and of you, my lady daughter, spend a million of gold without contracting a debt.

With that, Henry stalked off, but he was not satisfied. Gold had been dangled in front of his nose. He had reached out for it. Then it had been snatched away. The insult was too much to bear. He wanted those jewels now.

'With respect to the jewels,' a second Spanish ambassador in England, Pedro de Ayala, reported, 'the king would like that, as they were offered to him, they be given and delivered to him.' Henry was ready, in fact, to do anything to get his hands on them, he said. As the bad blood between the king and Catherine's remaining Spaniards grew daily, Ayala urged Queen Isabel to approve the payment. His request was ignored. It was the first time, but by no means the last, that Catherine would find herself caught in a row between Henry and her parents over money.

Catherine had good reason to be perplexed by Henry's line of reasoning. On the one hand he claimed to be embarrassed about asking for the jewels. On the other, he insisted that he should have them. She was beginning to learn that her father-in-law did not always play a straight game.

Henry already had a reputation for miserliness. De Puebla, whose long experience in England meant he generally continued to act in parallel to the other Spanish ambassadors (like Ayala) who came and went, had long ago warned Catherine's parents about this. England's king was, he told them, a man who 'spends all the time he is not in public, or in his council, in writing accounts of his expenses with his own hand'. The splendour of the wedding ceremony had served a purpose – to display his wealth and power to his countrymen and make sure the Spaniards went home singing his praises. The gifts of jewellery had been a rare moment of munificence. Catherine, certainly, would never experience anything similar from him again.

In the meantime, she found herself enmeshed in yet another web of intrigue as Henry once more tried to get his own way while blaming someone else for his decision. In this case Catherine was also the innocent victim of the growing divisions amongst her own self-serving, proud Spanish courtiers. At the root of the problem was a dilemma about whether she should accompany Arthur to his home at Ludlow Castle or remain at Henry's court. He had to return in order to discharge his duties as prince of Wales. But what about his wife? There were several reasons why this might be an issue. First there was Catherine herself. Ludlow was a large, exposed castle in a damp, cold corner of England. She had already seemed sad and homesick amongst the relative luxuries of Richmond. How would a princess from the Alhambra cope with the rigours of Ludlow, especially when her husband might spend his time away, roaming his lands? Then, of course, there was Arthur. There was a latent fear that two lovers of such tender age might, literally, waste themselves away in each other's arms. If sexual exertion was deemed to have hastened the premature journey to the grave of Catherine's eighteen-year-old brother Juan, then how much more of a mortal danger might it be for a young man of fifteen?

Henry decided to confront Catherine with the problem, asking her directly what she herself would prefer. Unable or unwilling either to read Henry's mind or impose her own will, Catherine astutely avoided answering him. She 'did not have any will but his' and would 'be content with what he decided'. Henry, hiding his own intentions, claimed he would 'do only what she wished'. Soon Catherine found Arthur himself trying to persuade her to accompany him, apparently on his father's instructions. Henry was not being straight with his new daughter-in-law but his trust in Arthur's powers of persuasion does, at least, point to some intimacy between the young newly-weds.

In the end, Catherine was instructed to go. Henry, 'making show of great sorrow', claimed he regretted having to send her away. De Puebla, the regal kicking horse whenever there was a row over Catherine, was usefully at hand. It was all De Puebla's fault, Henry insisted. He had sent Catherine's confessor, the Italian humanist priest Alessandro Geraldini, to tell him that Catherine would have been 'in despair' if she had been left behind.

Doña Elvira, who had lobbied for Catherine to stay, fumed and plotted revenge. Catherine's little court of Spaniards had sunken into a state of sullen, fractious discontent. 'You should without delay provide and order that all we who are here, men as well as woman, act in unison . . . now everyone reads, and asks, and speaks what he like, and thus causes more disadvantages than advantages,' Ayala wrote to her parents.

Elvira and her husband, Pedro Manrique, were at the centre of the trouble. They had already rowed with Henry over their wages. Henry, angry about the jewels, was in no mood for a round of salary negotiations. He was, or feigned to be, scandalised, claiming that he had never heard of such a request before.

Did they not know that his son would look after them? Who were they to question, let alone negotiate?

It is impossible to tell who cast the first stone in this battle between the English and Catherine's Spaniards. Manrique and Elvira stood on their pride. In Spain, they were important people – Henry, surely, would realise that. In England, however, that meant very little. Both her *maestresala* or master of the hall, Alfonso de Esquivel, and Juan de Cuero, the man who refused to hand over the jewels, were downgraded to the status of usher. As for Manrique, he was simply informed that his Spanish position as Lord High Steward did not exist in an English princess's household. The Spanish monarchs were aware of how badly such a slight, and the accompanying loss of face, would be taken. They immediately wrote to De Puebla ordering him to avoid 'that the said Pedro Manrique be subjected to any kind of humiliation or affront of any kind'. The damage, however, was already done.

Catherine was incapable of imposing order. She tried, instead, to get Ayala to sort out the arguments between her staff and her father-in-law. 'The *señora* princess has several times ordered me to enter into negotiations about such similar subjects, but I have not obeyed her orders in this, because I have no power from your highness,' Ayala reasoned in a letter to her mother. Catherine felt powerless to act for herself. Her marriage was only a few weeks old and things were already going badly. In that unhappy state, a few days before Christmas, she and her party set out west for Ludlow.

12 Married Life

Ludlow Castle. Late December 1501–April 1502

Catherine's new home perched dramatically on a hilltop above a bend in the River Teme, its vast bulk looming over a good-sized walled town dominated by a large church tower. Built to withstand the attacks of rebellious Welshmen, Ludlow Castle was at once menacing and impressive. When Catherine arrived the castle was at its most intimidating, the heavy grey towers and high battlements exuding an oppressive message of royal might and authority. This was the castle from which the English kings controlled the Welsh Marches and where Arthur and Catherine were being sent, in the words of a chronicler of the time, 'to keep liberal hospitality and to minister to the rude Welshmen indifferent justice'.

We can only imagine how – in the damp, dark days of an English winter – this monochrome, rugged castle might have appeared to a homesick girl used to the delicate luxuries and colourful environment of the Alhambra. She lived in one of the buildings erected against its north wall, looking out above the river. Here a Great Hall was flanked by a Great Chamber block on one side and another residential block on the other. These, in turn, gave on to towers that rose still higher above the river and surrounding country. The chutes of the *garderobe* latrines in these towers emptied out by the castle walls dozens of feet below. Water was pulled up from a well sunk more than a hundred feet down to river level. A small, delightful circular chapel dedicated to St Mary Magdalene sat in the middle of the inner bailey. This tiny jewel of Norman architecture was a likely refuge for Catherine and her confessor, Geraldini. Candles, smoke, furnishings and the gleam of the chalice combined with the sights and sounds of the liturgy – with or without music, incense or other additions – to make chapels like this home to some of the richest sensual experiences of the time. Catherine would have found here an escape from the grey, chilly world beyond the round walls of the chapel's small, intimate nave. Perhaps she also prayed, as her doctor apparently recommended, for her husband to regain his youthful strength.

We know very little about Catherine and Arthur's stay in Ludlow. It was here that she started a long-term friendship with Margaret Pole, sister of the earl of Warwick who had been killed in 1499 to clear the way for Catherine's marriage. Her husband, Sir Richard Pole, was Arthur's chamberlain and, years later, Margaret would become governess to Catherine's daughter Mary. The guilt she felt at Warwick's death weighed heavily on her, or so the Pole family thought. Catherine felt 'very much bound to recompense and requite us for the detriment we had received on her account', the Poles' son, Reginald, recalled later. The affection was mutual. Like many of Catherine's closest supporters, Margaret Pole would later die on the executioner's block. It is difficult to imagine that late winter and early spring as a happy time. Catherine experienced little more than tragedy, grief, sickness and solitude during the four months she spent here. She and her husband never gave up their attempts to procreate. Arthur was an occasional night-time visitor to Catherine's bedchamber. This may have happened, as she later claimed, only seven times or he may have gone 'in his nightgown unto the princess's bedchamber door often and sundry times', as one of Arthur's privy chamber grooms claimed almost three decades later when their sex life suddenly became of interest to the world.

They celebrated Maundy Thursday, when Arthur seems to have washed the feet of twelve or fifteen poor men (though only after his almoner had given them a preliminary scrub) and given them alms. Catherine, presumably, would also have taken part. In her case, tradition dictated that she wash the feet of poor women.

Arthur had been 'furnished with men and money' by his father before they set off. The senior Spanish officials not only lost rank but also became subordinate to Pole, as well as to Arthur's household comptroller Sir William Ovedall and his steward Sir Richard Croft. Their sense of humiliation only grew and when Catherine's courtiers were unhappy, they usually found ways to make her life miserable too.

If Catherine knew anything at all about the Welsh before she arrived in Ludlow it would have been what Ayala had written to her parents a few years before she set sail. He warned that the Welsh were renowned fortune-tellers. He drew comparisons with Spain's own, supposedly Celtic, north-western region of Galicia. 'You must know that there are many in the province of Wales who tell the future as they do in Galicia when they read a man's back, while here they read various other things and have their own practices.' The English were also very superstitious. 'They follow prophecies, affirming that they are true,' he reported. Catherine may have known that her own father-in-law turned to a Welsh priest, famed for foretelling the deaths of previous English kings, when he wanted to divine his own future.

Catherine stayed through to a spring during which, when it drew to a fateful close, the weather was so awful that one visitor to these parts recalled 'the foulest cold windy and rainy day and the worst way [road] that I have seen'. There were huge stone fireplaces on both floors of the wood-floored central hall, whose windows – either glazed or simply shuttered against the wind – looked out across the river. Foreigners sometimes found even the greatest English houses, their floors covered by rushes, unbearably dirty. 'I really do not know how I can go on living in England,' wrote one Italian, Andrew Ammonius, in English royal service before he died of the terrifying illness known as the sweat. 'The dirt of these people, of which I have had experience enough, is altogether hateful.' Ludlow was possibly somewhat cleaner than the kind of English house described as having floor rushes 'harbouring expectorations, vomitings, the leakage of dogs and men, ale-droppings, scraps of fish, and other abominations'. The letters sent home by Catherine, Elvira and the others with her were, however, filled with complaints. Queen Isabel, back in Spain, would later refer to Ludlow as 'that unhealthy place'.

Insanitary conditions encouraged the spread of disease. Sweating sickness, which Catherine would learn to fear, raged around the area at this time. It seems to have been a deadly flu pandemic, which had flared up several times since the early days of Henry's reign. One chronicler described it as amongst the most painful and lethal diseases anyone could recall. 'Suddenly a deadly and burning sweat invaded their bodies,' he wrote. Blood boiled from 'a most ardent heat' which 'infested the stomach and head grievously'. The raging fever caused sufferers to tear off their sheets and clothes and cry out in desperation for cold water to quench 'their importune heat and insatiable thirst'. 'Others that could . . . abide the heat and stench (for, indeed, the sweat had a great and strong savour) caused cloths to be laid upon them as much as they could bear, to drive out the sweat.' The sweat either killed you within forty-eight hours or released you, though many people went on to suffer a second or third bout. Survival rates were low. The chronicler probably exaggerated when he claimed that all but one in a hundred victims 'yielded up their ghost', but the virulence with which it swept through whole populations was enough to account for two London mayors and six aldermen in just eight days. The best way to survive, it was thought, was to take to bed, drink lukewarm liquids, keep moderately warm and make sure, whatever you did, that you never stuck a hand or foot out from under the sheets and blankets to cool yourself down 'the which to do is no less pain than short death'.

Catherine herself was struck down by illness in Ludlow. So, too, was Arthur. Whatever the causes – and testicular cancer has been given as another possibility in Arthur's case – Catherine proved more resilient. Her own doctor apparently diagnosed Arthur as suffering *tisis*, a Spanish catch-all word covering everything from pulmonary tuberculosis to any wasting, feverish disease that produced ulceration of some bodily organ. 'He [the doctor] often said that the prince had been denied the strength necessary to know a woman, as if he was a cold piece of stone ... because he was in the final stages of *tisis*,' the doctor's nephew claimed when called on in Zaragoza to explain Catherine's supposedly intact virginity. Arthur certainly struggled against a 'most pitiful disease and sickness'. On the second day of April 1502 the sickness 'did utterly vanquish and overcome the pure and friendly blood' that flowed so weakly through the prince's veins. Arthur, still aged just fifteen, died.

Some blamed Catherine. They whispered that it must have been her Spanish sex drive, and Arthur's inability to keep away from her, that drained him of his strength. 'Woe worth [was] the time that ever the lady Catherine came into this realm,' one gentleman was reported as saying. 'For she was the cause of the death of the most noble prince.'

Messengers were hurriedly despatched to London. The king's counsellors did not dare break the news to him immediately. His confessor, an Observant Friar, waited until early the next morning before tapping on the king's chamber's door. He ordered everyone else out. The friar turned to the Book of Job to explain what had happened. '*Si bona de manu dei suscipimus mala autem quare non sustineamus,*' he said. 'If we have received good things at the hand of God, why should we not receive evil?' A stricken Henry sent for Elizabeth of York and broke the terrible news to her. Seeing him so pained, Elizabeth contained her own grief and tried to comfort him. He should remember how, compared to his own mother, they were fortunate. He had been a single child, but she reminded Henry they had another 'fair, goodly' son and two more daughters. What was more, she said, they themselves were 'both young enough' to have more children. After comforting her husband, she set off back to her chambers. There she collapsed and the contained grief spilled out. 'That great loss smote her,' the *Receyt* records. The king was sent for and now it was his turn to comfort her. 'He for his part would thank God,' said the *Receyt*, 'and would that she should do likewise.'

Arthur's body was disembowelled, embalmed and filled with spices before being laid out in his chamber at Ludlow. Some of the same poor people who had received Maundy alms now stood there holding torches. Eventually the carriage bearing his body was dragged through torrential rain and down roads thick with mud by horses and oxen to Worcester Cathedral. There he was buried. His weeping Officer of Arms tore off his coat of arms and threw it onto the coffin as a sign that he was now a man without a master. Ovedall, Croft and his ushers followed suit, breaking their staffs of office and their rods over their heads and dropping them into the grave. Although two of Catherine's gentleman courtiers were there when the body was taken into Ludlow's parish church on the first leg of its gloomy journey to Worcester, she herself was absent. She stayed at home as the rain lashed down and the wind screamed around that grey, lonely castle.

Catherine's short marriage to the heir to the English crown was over. There was some speculation about whether she was pregnant, but this soon evaporated. Catherine's destiny, for as long as she had known it, was to become queen of England. Now, for the first time in her life, she did not know what future awaited her.

13 My Husband's Brother

Durham House, the Strand, London. May 1502

A litter covered in the black velvet of mourning drew up inside the high walls of Ludlow Castle. Into it stepped Catherine, a sixteen-year-old in widow's clothes. Her marriage had proved short, painful and barren. A sick Catherine and her court of unhappy Spaniards spent the weeks after Arthur's death writing letters to Spain complaining about the 'unhealthy' and doom-laden castle. She lay on her sick-bed breathing out bad-smelling fumes, Spanish officials were told many years later. 'On Arthur's death, the lady . . . became very ill and pained,' they wrote. 'From her mouth issued many humours.' Her mother-in-law, Elizabeth of York, finally sent the 'litter of black velvet with black cloth, wherein the princess was brought from Ludlow to London, fringed about with black valance and the two head-pieces of the same bounden about with black ribbon and fringed about with black valance'. Catherine's return to London – and an uncertain future – in this gloomy contraption could not have contrasted more starkly with her glorious, colourful entry into the city just six months earlier.

It must have been with some relief that Catherine settled into the new riverside home that King Henry set aside for her. Durham House was a grand, solid-looking bishop's palace in the smartest part of suburban London. It was one of half a dozen large, noble houses with extensive gardens strung along the River Thames by the Strand. Maps from later in the century show a short drive leading down to a two-storey palace whose broad facade, punctuated by a pair of three-storey towers, lay directly on the river. The main house sat around a courtyard.

A walled garden looked out over the Thames towards Lambeth and its marshes. The river here was busy with the lighter craft that operated above London Bridge, including barges, barks and swift rowing boats ferrying people along the city's main thoroughfare. Amongst her riverside neighbours were the most palatial houses of London's grandest suburb, including York House and the Savoy palace. Most had originally been built by powerful bishops as their Westminster homes. Catherine had her own landing stage or, at least, steps from which to make barge trips towards Henry VII's court when it was based at Richmond or Greenwich. Westminster was a short barge ride away. Her residence was idyllic compared to the dark, stinking streets of the city itself – whose gates lay less than a mile to the east. The palace was easily large enough for her court of sixty people, whose members now recovered their old positions, titles, honour and, unfortunately, their pomposity. Catherine had no husband to welcome into her bed. She did not, however, sleep alone. María de Rojas, her favourite lady-in-waiting, crawled into her huge bed to stop her feeling lonely.

Doña Elvira had recovered her old power and soon submitted her acquiescent charge to the strictures of formal mourning and Spanish sobriety. Elvira's dark, grim presence was hardly likely to help Catherine as she tried to overcome the sadness and frustrations of teenage widowhood. A gloomy, claustrophobic atmosphere was imposed while Catherine or, rather, others pondered her future.

Unknown to Catherine, that future was already being hotly debated. Her parents mourned their lost son-in-law but wasted no time in seeking a new one. Even before Isabel and Ferdinand had penned a letter to Henry expressing their condolences they had ordered a new special envoy, Hernán Estrada, to set off for England. Estrada carried secret instructions. These told him to do two, apparently contradictory, things. First he was to tell Henry VII that her distraught parents wanted their beloved, grieving daughter back with them and that he was to send her home immediately. He was ordered to remind the English king of the sad life of her eldest sister, Isabel, who had taken young widowhood so badly that (inspired, perhaps, by reading too many medieval romances) she immediately cut off her hair. He was also to demand repayment of her dowry from the notoriously stingy Henry. This was, however, just an opening gambit. What they really wanted was a new marriage. Catherine's destiny was still, they believed, to be the English queen. Her future husband would have to be the new heir – Arthur's younger brother, Prince Henry. It did not matter that the ten-year-old prince was six years younger than Catherine. She would just have to wait for him to grow up.

So it was that, as Catherine settled into Durham House, a complex game of chess began. Henry and Ferdinand – who was the real player on the Spanish side – moved their pieces slowly, deliberately and, on occasion, with duplicitous delight. They were tough, stubborn negotiators. With Prince Henry still so young, they were in no hurry. Catherine was a powerless pawn on their board, albeit one with the potential to transform herself into a queen. Regal pride, the shifting politics of Europe and the tight-fistedness of both men all came into play as the pawn was moved this way and that over the next seven years. Catherine's own feelings and desires were rarely taken into account. She was to become the archetypical poor little princess, locked up in the ivory towers of Durham House.

Before any of this could really start, however, there was a serious question to answer. Might she be pregnant? A pregnancy, with the possibility that Catherine might be carrying a new heir to the crown in her womb, would have changed everything. The English held off pronouncing Prince Henry as the new prince of Wales 'for a month and more . . . in the which season the truth might . . . easily appear'. Even the royal doctors could not always work out if a woman was pregnant. A Genoese doctor had mistakenly declared Elizabeth of York pregnant a year earlier on the basis of 'much *embonpoint* and large breasts'. The confusion surrounding Catherine's sex life did not help. Her fractured, inward-looking court of Spaniards could not even agree as to whether she was still a virgin.

Doña Elvira, on the one hand, insisted on virginity. This, on the face of it, was a foolish thing to claim – even if it was true. If her marriage had not been consummated then it could be argued that it was not, in canon law, a marriage at all. To put it simply, it could now be said that she never had been the princess of Wales and had no rights to what, in theory, was a considerable dower.

Non-consummation might, however, allow a lady mistress like Elvira to step back into her life. It might also allow her parents to demand the return of the dowry money they had paid over. Elvira's certainty in proclaiming Catherine's virginity may, however, have been based on an intimate knowledge of her charge's bed. The bedchamber and, at its centre, the bed itself, had long been key elements in the internal protocol of most royal households – be they English or Spanish. Whatever else Arthur did in Catherine's bed, he was entering Elvira's territory. Her job description, after all, included that of 'First Lady of the Bedchamber'. She may have been the original source of a later Spanish claim that the wedding sheets were unstained by Catherine's blood.

Whatever her reasons, Elvira may have secretly enjoyed pinning the damaging label 'impotent' onto the king of England's son. She was already bitter about her husband's earlier demotion. Was this revenge, icily served? It would have been a risky lie. Virginity was checkable, though the tests were not always reliable. These varied from inspection of the hymen, to washing a woman's clothes in rose-water or waving a chicken wing over her abdomen. The one person who could have cleared things up was Catherine herself. She, however, remained publicly silent on the issue. It was not until almost three decades later that she declared 'she had never carnally known the said Arthur'.

Isabel and Ferdinand, however, already had their doubts. In mid-June they wrote to Estrada demanding to know for sure whether Catherine was still a virgin. They even suspected a plot to cover up the truth. He was to use 'false flattery', if necessary, 'so they do not keep [the truth] from him'. Someone must have sown doubt into their minds. By mid-July they had their reply. Elvira wrote saying, as the monarchs themselves euphemistically put it, that Catherine 'remained as she was when she left here'.

The role of her Italian confessor, Alessandro Geraldini, in the affair is obscure. Someone, probably Elvira, was spying on him. The spy intercepted one of his letters and sent it to Isabel and Ferdinand. We do not know what the letter said, or who it was addressed to, but the monarchs ordered him straight home. Perhaps he claimed she was no longer a virgin. Catherine herself never forgave what she saw as a betrayal by the man who knew the secrets of the confessional. Fifteen years later, when he returned to England as a bishop and renowned man of letters, she angrily refused to see him. This was despite Pope Leo X's protestations that she should be considerate to an old teacher and 'great historian'.

Catherine's relationships with her confessors were as intense as her mother's, if not more so. They could even arouse suspicion and gossip. She could also be absolute and unbending in her judgement of people. In this case, she decided Geraldini was a traitor. His departure left the power structure within the entirely Spanish enclave of Durham House crystal clear. Elvira ruled supreme. Even her husband Pedro Manrique, nominally Catherine's major-domo and First Chamberlain, paled into insignificance.

Rodrigo De Puebla, who stepped forward again whenever the more senior envoys from Spain returned home, watched with concern as Elvira took control. The words he used to describe Catherine's life in Durham House were 'rule', 'obedience' and 'seclusion'. These are the words of a convent, not those of a palace. Durham House, in other words, was like a well-off, cloistered nunnery – with the iron-willed Elvira as mother superior.

One can picture Catherine and her six ladies, playing their games of cards and chess, reading and listening to stories and, perhaps, practising their *basse* dances and music. They could walk through the gardens in the summer and, in winter, peer out over a River Thames on which flocks of swans bobbed about amongst the barges, wherries and row-boats. We do not know how long Catherine dressed in mourning, but it is unlikely that she would have started wearing the gold gowns or sleeves of orange sarcenet silk that Elizabeth of York or her twelve-year-old sister-in-law Margaret were dressing in later that summer.

On Midsummer's Eve the smell of bonfire smoke and the sound of revelry must have drifted across to secluded Durham House as Londoners celebrated raucously late into the night. Catherine was missing out. Around the city, lamps were hung out and doors decorated with green birch, St John's wort, white lilies, fennel, orpin and garlands of flowers. Arthur's parents also lit bonfires that night and, a week later, on St Peter's Eve. Catherine probably missed, too, the colourful Corpus Christi processions when her mother-in-law donned a fur-lined gown of cloth of gold.

The king and Elizabeth of York were rarely far away – mostly at Westminster, Richmond or Greenwich. Elizabeth was a caring mother-in-law. In September she sent Catherine books. In October sixteen oarsmen rowed her barge to the Durham House steps. They took Catherine the short distance to Westminster, where she seems to have stayed several weeks. It was a

tantalising taste of life at a court of Henry VII that was showing the first signs of the brilliance it would attain under Henry
VIII. The disguisings put on at Christmas and other feast days
allowed a new breed of actors and theatrical authors to show off
their talents. Music, too, was entering a new and rich moment,
and this was one of Catherine's greatest passions. She does not
seem to have attended, however, the Christmas festivities. Perhaps Elvira declared them inappropriate.

The kindness offered by Elizabeth of York dried up abruptly
ten months after Arthur's death. True to her pledge that she
was still 'young enough', the queen had immediately got pregnant. The speed with which she achieved this speaks volumes
for the methods she used to space out previous pregnancies. The
baby was a girl, also called Catherine. Elizabeth never recovered
from childbirth. She died nine days later, on her thirty-seventh
birthday – another martyr to the cause of bearing heirs. The
baby Catherine followed soon after. His mother's death had a
profound effect on the boy Catherine of Aragon would eventually marry. Another death four years later reminded him, Prince
Henry wrote, of 'dearest mother . . . It seemed to tear open
again the wound to which time had brought insensibility.'

Henry VII soon started casting about for a new wife. This was
not a sign of disrespect towards Elizabeth but, rather, a recognition that, with only one male heir left, it would be valuable to
father more sons. He needed someone of both childbearing age
and political import. His thoughts turned, almost immediately,
to a young woman already close at hand. What, he suggested to
Catherine's parents, if he married her? Isabel was revolted. 'It
would be a very terrible thing – one never before seen, and the
mere mention of which offends the ears,' she proclaimed.

Elizabeth's death, however, allowed Isabel to insist that
Catherine come home. Her daughter's honour and reputation
would be at risk, she said, now that there was no mother-in-law

to look after her. It was, anyway, unacceptable for a Spanish infanta to remain in England looking as if she was begging for a betrothal. In mid-April 1503 Isabel sent instructions for Catherine to pack her bags. A fleet of Spanish merchants was on its way back from Flanders. It could pick her up at an English port. Catherine was told to be ready to board as soon as they dropped anchor.

If Catherine began dreaming about returning to the embrace of her mother and the delights of the Alhambra, the dream was soon cut short – for this was just a piece of brinkmanship. Isabel wanted to concentrate Henry's mind on a quick betrothal to his son. It worked. Terms were agreed in London on 23 June 1503. Catherine's pawn had, once more, been moved across the board.

Both sides agreed that a papal dispensation was needed. The couple had become, at least in theory, related in the first degree of affinity when Catherine married Arthur. The issue of Catherine's sex life raised its head again for, if she had stayed a virgin, there was no real affinity. The marriage treaty explicitly states that a dispensation was required because 'her marriage to Prince Arthur was solemnised according to the rites of the Catholic Church and afterwards consummated'. Two months later, however, Ferdinand was telling his ambassador at the Vatican, who had orders to seek the dispensation, that it was all a lie. 'The truth is that the marriage was not consummated and that the princess our daughter remained as whole as she was before she married,' he wrote. 'Even though this is true and known to be so where she is, the *mad* English . . . [believe] that the dispensation should say that the marriage was consummated.' This, he explained with startling prescience, was 'in order to get rid of any future doubt over the [rights of] succession of the children that, God willing, will be born of this new matrimony'. The English, he meant, wanted the pope to state clearly he had taken into account the idea of consummation with Arthur when giving Catherine a dispensation to marry and have legitimate children with Henry.

Popes in the sixteenth century were, however, smooth political operators. Julius II knew how to hedge his bets. The dispensation he eventually sent to England stated that the marriage had 'perhaps' been consummated. That single word meant the matter would be argued over for centuries.

Two days after the marriage terms were agreed in London, the seventeen-year-old Catherine travelled the short distance to the bishop of Salisbury's palace in Fleet Street. There she became formally betrothed to eleven-year-old Prince Henry. Spurred by fears that they might soon become embroiled in a war with France, her parents were increasingly desperate to put their signatures to the English marriage treaty. The terms would turn out to be unfavourable to Catherine. The price of the marriage (in terms of the two-hundred-thousand-*scudo* marriage portion, or dowry, Catherine should bring) was the same as with Arthur. Henry accepted that half of this, handed over as a first instalment of the money due for the marriage with Arthur, had been paid. Catherine, meanwhile, had to stay in England. She would simply have to depend on Henry VII for her maintenance. He was not about to hand over the one-third portion of the income due to her from Arthur's estates – and the fact that her own dowry had never been paid in full gave him the excuse he needed. Trouble, in other words, was being stored up.

Catherine's long-term future was, finally, secure. But she could not marry Henry – who had his twelfth birthday three days after the engagement – until he turned fourteen, by which time she would be nineteen. Obedient as ever, she slipped into passive acquiescence. It was as if her childhood had been forcibly, and artificially, prolonged for at least another two years.

14 Bleed Me

Durham House, London. August 1504

The Licentiate Juan searched for a vein on Catherine's body. She was pale, not eating and, once more, ill. It was time, therefore, to bleed her. He was skilled at this and Catherine wanted to be bled. She preferred it, anyway, to that other physicians' favourite – purging. Catherine was most likely used to being bled through a small incision in a vein in her arm, leg or neck – the flow of blood dripping down into a small bowl. English physicians worked with a handbook illustrated with a naked man who had twenty-four veins marked for blood-letting – each one deemed suitable for specific types of ailment. An early sixteenth-century Italian manuscript added twenty more bleeding points, ranging from the forehead, via the groin, to the feet. Licentiate Juan was, on this occasion, forced to attempt the operation twice – once on her arm and once on her ankle. The physician was a member of her household and had a reputation amongst his fellow Spaniards for 'doing this very well'. No blood, however, appeared. It was as if Catherine, abandoned and depressed, had already been bled dry.

This scene was just one of many dramatic episodes of illness that punctuated what would turn into seven long years as an anxious and immature widow. Her outbreaks of ague, 'derangement of the stomach', hot sweats, cold sweats, tertian fevers, summer colds and summer coughs baffled physicians – including the Genoese experts sent to her by King Henry. It is difficult, in fact, not to see them as emanating from the mind of an unhappy, lonely and intense girl at odds with the man meant to be looking after her, Henry VII. She ate little. 'Her complexion has changed entirely,' reported a worried Estrada in 1504. Although she was often sick, it was never from anything serious or life-threatening. Instead she would complain, on the same day, of 'suffering cold and heat'.

Bleeding aimed to restore the balance of the humours and was standard medical practice. It was especially recommended for fevers. 'We open a vein to breathe out that blood which is heated in vessels, and cooling the residue which remains behind,' explained the sixteenth-century French surgeon Ambroise Paré. The medical rituals of bleeding and purging, which combined both potentially strong or violent physical reactions with the symbolic potency of blood, vomit and excrement, had the added benefit of placing the patient centre-stage. For Catherine, uncared for in the wider world, illness at least generated the care and preoccupation of doctors and other attendants. She was quite capable, directly or indirectly, of inflicting this on herself.

If we are to accept Isabel's excuses about her daughter's late arrival in England, then Catherine's prolonged round of illnesses started much earlier – as a fifteen-year-old facing separation from family and friends in an unknown, distant land. Contemporaries believed she had an ability to make herself ill, often by not eating. 'Irregularity in her eating and the food which she takes makes her unwell which is why she does not menstruate well,' reported one intimate observer in 1510. Her 'disorderly eating' worried those about her. Catherine was displaying many of the classic symptoms of what today would be diagnosed as an eating disorder like anorexia nervosa. Henry VII was so concerned that he got his son to ask the pope, no less, to order her to eat. The missive sent back by Pope Julius is dated confusingly, but it leaves little doubt about the worry she caused those around her. It gave the prince of Wales power to prevent Catherine from overdoing the fasting, abstinence and praying which she conducted with such zeal that she was endangering her own health and ability to have children.

Julius said he had been told that the 'fervour of her devotion' was such that she 'holds to and observes holy oaths and prayers, fasting, abstinence and pilgrimage, and continues to strive after these even without your agreement'. Catherine was already showing the intensity and perfectionism which, for good or for bad, could make her both obstinate and determined. For the moment, it was simply making her ill.

'A wife does not have the full power of her own body,' the pope told the prince. 'And the devotions and fasting of the wife, if they are thought to stand in the way of her physical health and the procreation of children . . . can be revoked and annulled by men . . . Because the man is the leader of the woman, and because among the chief goods of marriage is included the upbringing of children, we . . . concede to you the authority to restrain and compel the aforesaid Catherine,' the pope decreed. 'She may not, without your permission, observe these devotions and prayers, and fasting and abstinence and pilgrimage, or any other project of hers that would stand in the way of the procreation of children.' The prince of Wales, he added, had the power 'to hinder and prevent her, if she attempts to go against your prohibition, from the observation of these things'.

Catherine's disorderly eating knocked her menstrual cycle off course. In her early twenties, for example, she went more than nine weeks without menstruating. Her eating problems may well have been one reason why she later had trouble producing heirs to the English throne. If sometimes she starved herself, other times she complained of starving – especially on fish days. 'When I am not feeling well and it is fish time, it would be impossible, even if I were dying, to get any meat to eat in the king's palace,' she complained in March 1509. 'They look upon anyone who eats it as a heretic.'

Illness and depression became an almost constant part of Catherine's life as she anxiously waited to see what the future held. She was overcome by a growing sensation that those who were meant to care for her – be they her parents or her father-in-law – had abandoned her. Catherine's Spanish physician diagnosed her as suffering one, almost interminable illness over half a dozen years. Not until April 1507 did he report that colour had finally returned to her face for the first time 'since she came to this kingdom' five and a half years earlier. Even he thought that the fundamental causes of her illness lay in her head and her heart. 'The only pains of which she now suffers are moral afflictions beyond the knowledge and ability of her physician,' he explained. The remedy he dared suggest to her father was simply 'paternal solicitude' – something which had been sadly lacking. This remedy, he insisted, was 'her only hope'. Her Spanish supporters later claimed, improbably, that a meeting of great doctors concluded 'that the cause of her sickness was that she was a virgin, having not [carnally] known Arthur, and that if she married someone who had *skills* with women, she would get better'. What she had needed, they meant, was a *real* man in her bed. They might have said that what she really craved was a little bit of love.

The psychological causes of Catherine's prolonged illness seem obvious. Widowed, abandoned and powerless, she was stuck in a foreign country where she did not speak the language. Her father and her father-in-law fell out over money and her planned marriage to Henry was an on–off affair, constantly being tossed around on the stormy, changing waters of European politics. She was naturally melodramatic and given to exaggerating her own difficulties. A stubborn personality, intensely preoccupied with her own dignity while also fretting about correct obedience to both God and her parents, could only have helped multiply her problems.

Catherine was a political bargaining chip of varying value. Her parents demanded absolute loyalty and, when needed, active service to their cause. In October 1503, for example, Isabel wrote with instructions. If the king of England did not respond to their demands for military help against France, Catherine herself was to raise two thousand infantry. Catherine was now seventeen – the same age Isabel had been when she made peace with her brother beside the stone bulls at Guisando. The instructions were a sharp reminder that she was now grown up. This was not, however, something she showed many signs of accepting.

Money was a problem from the start. Her mother had taught her that generosity was both a virtue and a sign of rank. It was her task to give away clothes to her ladies, make them gifts and ensure them healthy dowries so they could marry. She herself must also dress impressively when occasion demanded. Had she received the income from her deceased husband's estates, then the dowager princess – as she became known – could have done all this in style. She had become, instead, an item on the outgoings list in Henry VII's beloved, and tightly controlled, accounts books. This was a disaster in the making. Catherine had little idea of money. She spent freely. A worried De Puebla warned her parents more than once of her 'great liberality'. 'The princess is very liberal and there are many people who would like to strip her of her silver and jewels,' he wrote.

Isabel and Ferdinand expected the English king to look after their daughter properly. 'One cannot believe that the king would ever fail to meet his obligations to her, especially at a time of such hardship,' they wrote to De Puebla soon after Arthur's death. The latter, aware of Henry's mean streak, had warned early on of the dangers of abandoning her to the English king's mercy. He had been right to do so.

Her parents, however, commanded her to obey Henry. Above all, she should not take loans or raid the jewels or gold and silver plate she had with her. This they wanted to use for part-payment of the remainder of her dowry. If she wanted money, she would have to wheedle it out of Henry. 'Some persons have written to us from over there saying some people believed the princess of Wales should not accept what the king of England offers for her maintenance and that of her household and people,' they said soon after Arthur's death. 'They do not understand that she must accept whatever she is given.' Catherine, still passive and obedient, acquiesced.

In fact, Henry started off treating her well. His accounts show money going out to her almost as soon as she arrived in London. In the summer he sent £300 to cover three months' costs. (That gave her, in today's money, some £40,000 a month to spend). Any leftovers, he said, were 'to be delivered to the princess, to spend as she likes'. By November 1503 her budget had been set at £1,000 a year, or £83 6s 8d a month – with no leftovers. Henry also showed himself solicitous about her health, offering her the best doctors in England and claiming to love her as if she were his own daughter. Any length of time that passed without good news from her, he wrote in their common language of Latin, was too long.

Henry had probably not bargained on the fact that, by keeping Catherine on his own accounts, he would have to deal with her nightmarish household at Durham House. Catherine herself could not cope with their constant squabbling. Elvira, having evicted Geraldini, now rowed with Juan de Cuero – who had the key to Catherine's jewels and silver. Her husband Pedro Manrique rowed with just about everyone and clumsily got in the way of the marriage negotiations. Elvira was instructed from Spain to 'sort out the situation with her husband as best she can'. One can only imagine that she was as strict a wife as she was a lady mistress. Pedro Manrique, whom she once sued over her own dower money, disappears from the records soon afterwards.

Elvira and her aristocratic husband despised De Puebla – the man working hardest to bring Catherine's new marriage to a successful conclusion. De Puebla's problem was his blood-line. It was not a good time to be a Spanish *marrano*, from a family of converted Jews. While he was in England, his only daughter was arrested by the Inquisition in Seville. De Puebla begged Isabel to intervene on her behalf. The queen was also suspicious of De Puebla, however, and appears to have ignored his letters. Catherine shared the prejudice, though she was likely egged on by Elvira. She rather obviously, and unfairly, despised De Puebla too – as did more than one of the grander, aristocratic envoys who Isabel and Ferdinand kept sending from Spain.

Catherine had lost all control of her household. In August 1504 she asked Henry to step in, but he preferred to avoid the wasps' nest. He was sorry that the few servants she had could not live in peace with one another but he could not consent to her wish that he should settle their quarrels. Instead he sent expensive presents, including a head-dress and a gold St Peter, to Elvira, hoping this would inspire her to sort things out. He was eventually obliged to intervene, though he insisted Catherine should not find out. He rather obviously wished she would grow up and take charge of her own affairs.

Something else began to worry Catherine, however, later that year. With the wedding treaty signed, her parents had suddenly gone silent. She had heard that both were ill. Her sister Juana had written telling of her mother's ague and fevers. Catherine wrote to them both on 26 November 1504, demanding news. She had not heard from Ferdinand 'since a year ago', she said. Catherine told Isabel that she could not 'be satisfied or cheerful' until she saw a letter from her mother telling her that she had recovered. In Medina del Campo – where the English ambassadors had negotiated Catherine's betrothal to Arthur fifteen years earlier – Ferdinand also wrote a letter to his daughter on this fateful day. Her beloved mother had just died. 'Her death is for us the deepest grief that could ever happen to us in this life, for we have lost the best and most excellent wife that king ever had,' he said. 'The grief pierces our heart.'

It was a double blow. Catherine had lost a mother. She had also lost status, for she was no longer daughter to the powerful queen of Castile. Isabel's death, indeed, threatened to shake up the political alliances of Europe and the marriage treaties of its leading families. The new Castilian queen was her sister, Juana – even if both her husband and her father claimed she was too mad to rule. Catherine, as a result, now only derived her status from being the daughter of her father, the king of Aragon. Ferdinand was a relatively minor European monarch compared to the great Isabel.

In 1505, however, Ferdinand and Henry began discussions to renew and widen their alliance. Amongst other things, her father now made absolutely clear to Catherine that she must depend entirely on Henry for her maintenance. 'You may say from me to the princess my daughter that in all these things she should be very conformable and pay much respect and obedience to the king of England . . . by this means he will more love her and do more for her,' he wrote to De Puebla that June. Ferdinand was, in fact, indirectly scolding her here. The normally acquiescent Catherine, held on an ever tighter financial leash by Henry, was beginning to show signs of rebellion.

She had already ignored her father's instructions not to borrow money. 'I am in debt in London and this not for extravagant things, nor yet for relieving my own people, who greatly need it, but only for food,' she told Ferdinand. 'The king of England, my lord, will not cause them [the debts] to be satisfied, although I myself spoke to him, and all those of his council, and that with tears.' Henry was now showing anything but love.

He said that he is not obliged to give me anything, and that even the food he gives me is of his goodwill; because your highness has not kept promise with him in the money of my marriage portion. I told him that I believed that in time to come your highness would discharge it. He told me that that was yet to see.

This, for Catherine, was poverty. The only way she could get the money that she wanted was by selling things.

I have nothing for chemises; wherefore, by your highness's life, I have now sold some bracelets to get a dress of black velvet, for I was all but naked; for since I departed thence [from Spain] I have nothing except two new dresses, for till now those I brought from thence have lasted me, although now I have nothing but the dresses of brocade.

Having complained in the strongest language she dared use to her father, she instructed De Puebla to remind the king of the misery in which she lived. He was 'to tell him . . . in plain language, that it reflects dishonour on his name that his daughter lives in such need that she cannot pay for what she has eaten'. She may have been spending money on dresses, but she described her poverty in the most dramatic terms. Food was an obsessive source of complaint. 'The whole world knows that I have [debts] only in order to eat,' she claimed.

It was a typical overstatement but Catherine, at last, was showing that she had claws. There is even a hint in her letter that, if she wanted to escape from her rut, 'I should seek a solution myself'. Little could she imagine just how much, and how soon, she would need her newly found claws if she was going to do that. Visitors were on the way who would give her a rude awakening from her torpid passivity.

15 Deceived

Durham House. August 1505

Catherine did not like either of the two oil portraits, one painted on wood and the other on canvas, that had been brought to her at Durham House. They sparked, however, happy childhood memories, for they showed what Margaret, the fun-loving northern princess who briefly lit up the austere Spanish court during her marriage to Catherine's brother Juan, looked like eight years after returning home to the Netherlands as a widow. Margaret was now a candidate, though admittedly an unwilling one, to marry Henry VII. These portraits were meant to give him an idea of what she looked like. Catherine wished that her favourite court artist – 'Michel' – had been asked to do them, or so she told De Puebla. She was almost certainly referring to the errant Estonian painter Michel Sittow, who had previously worked at her mother's court. Catherine herself had recently sat for him in England. It must have been a joy to have someone at hand who, almost certainly, spoke Spanish and could tell her the goings-on in the court of Castile.

Sittow produced a tender, penetrating image of Catherine, his subject's eyes cast down as if lost in thought while warding off prying eyes with a shy, dissimulated smile. She has a pale, faintly rosy complexion and her face is already a bit fleshier than in the much earlier, more stylised childhood portrait (thought to be of her) by Juan de Flandes. The auburn hair, mostly covered in the English fashion, gleams a golden red where the light catches it above her forehead. Her eyebrows are finely plucked. Around her neck sits a thick gold collar threaded with the letter K (for this is how the English spelt her name) and alternating white and red flowers. The square neckline of her crimson velvet dress is decorated with small golden scallop shells – a subtle homage to the most revered saint in Spain, St James, whose shrine she visited before setting sail for England. Surprisingly, the artist gave Catherine a pencil-thin double halo. Sittow, perhaps seeing the same strong-willed servility, seems also to have used her portrait as the model for a pair of remarkably similar paintings of Mary Magdalene and the Virgin Mary. In both of these her hair is luxuriantly visible as it cascades in rich, coppery waves over her shoulders. In the Mary Magdalene painting she exudes erotic sensuality, hinting – if it is her – at a very different Catherine to the demure infanta she herself so carefully projected in public.

The portraits of Margaret were part of an exciting upheaval in her normally humdrum existence at Durham House in August 1505. They had been brought by visitors, men of rank who honoured and flattered her. These men were ambassadors from Margaret's family – which was still headed by her father Maximilian, the grandiose-sounding king of the Romans. They brought news and gossip from one of the most sophisticated courts in Europe, that of his son, the duke of Burgundy. Catherine did not bother to ask herself why the ambassadors kept visiting her. She assumed that the duke of Burgundy, her brother-in-law Philip the Handsome, simply wished to honour her. They brought news of his wife – her sister Juana. She was pregnant once more and due to go into confinement for the birth in the next few weeks. Soon she could travel with Philip from Flanders to claim her throne in Castile.

The dull house by the river had come out of mourning some time before. Catherine joined Henry VII's court the previous summer, following it on its wanderings from Richmond to Windsor, Westminster and Greenwich. The king was enjoying both his palaces and his hunting. Catherine loved to hunt – especially with falcons – and also seems to have enjoyed herself though, inevitably, she eventually fell ill. Catherine had also begun to see something of her sister-in-law, Princess Mary – who was, however, almost ten years younger – and other English ladies, but life at Durham House remained dreary. The emissaries from Philip the Handsome were a sudden and brilliant splash of colour in an otherwise grey place. They kissed her hands and knelt before her. Not since her marriage four years earlier had she been the focus of so much attention. They treated her not just as a grown-up princess and future English queen, but also as someone with influence. She was sufficiently important, they suggested, to be able to bring together some of the most power-ful people in Europe. If she wanted to see her sister – which she did – then, they suggested, she simply had to propose to Henry a meeting between himself, Juana and her husband Philip. She could accompany the English king and a happy family reunion would take place. Catherine liked the idea. They urged her to write to Philip proposing a meeting. Elvira also encouraged her, so Catherine sat down and wrote. She had, De Puebla noted with concern, been won over by them.

A reply came speeding back in Philip's own handwrit-ing. He praised her wonderful idea. He would love, with his 'whole heart', to meet Henry. How about a meeting somewhere between the English town of Calais and the Flemish town of St Omer? Catherine was thrilled, and vowed to write to Henry immediately.

Catherine did not know it, but she was being played for a fool. She was about to receive a violent push into adulthood from an unexpected quarter. There was a traitor in her house, none other than the woman she had long viewed as a surrogate mother, Elvira Manuel. Catherine was set to discover that Elvira had greater loyalties elsewhere. This episode was to prove a dra-matic turning point in her life. To begin with, though, it brought nothing but pain, humiliation and disbelief.

With Isabel dead, a battle for control of Castile – which meant control of Catherine's supposedly mad sister Juana – began between her husband Philip of Burgundy and her father Ferdinand. Catherine's interests clearly lay with her father Ferdinand in his battle against Philip the Handsome. It was much better for her marriage plans to be the daughter of the man who controlled Castile. Elvira's able and scheming brother, Juan Manuel, was a leader of the pro-Philip faction. Soon Elvira began to manipulate the still naïve Catherine to her own family's ends. King Henry himself declared his surprise at just how pro-Burgundian his daughter-in-law suddenly became.

Both Ferdinand and Philip needed to bolster their positions with alliances. Each wanted England's support. Juan Manuel thought, correctly, that the best way to tie up an alliance was for Philip and Henry to meet. Catherine, with Elvira's help, was chosen to be the unwitting intermediary. Philip, through his letters and his ambassadors, sweet-talked her. No one had flattered her quite so much in years. It is hardly surprising that she fell for his ruse.

Catherine was beside herself with joy when she received Philip's reply and sent immediately for De Puebla. She told him that she was going to write and beg the English king to meet Juana and Philip 'before the queen her sister gave birth'.

De Puebla, who remained loyal to Ferdinand, was horrified. He offered to deliver the letter himself, planning either to lose it along the way or explain to Henry why it had been sent. Catherine turned him down. In a moment of sudden imperiousness, she declared that one of her own servants would carry it to Richmond. Elvira, it seems, had already warned her against letting Ferdinand's ambassador have it. Catherine was still unaware of the web of intrigue being spun around her. When De Puebla asked her to wait a few moments while he consulted Elvira about 'household matters', she happily agreed. De Puebla then took

Elvira into another room and, screwing up the courage needed to confront such a formidable woman, had it out with her. Her brother Juan Manuel was a traitor, he told her. The messenger must not go. Backed into a corner, Elvira agreed.

She had no intention, however, of sticking to her word. As soon as De Puebla returned to his own lodgings, the messenger was despatched. The ambassador was tipped off and rushed back to Durham House. He burst in on a stunned Catherine. It was time, he insisted, that she found out the truth. De Puebla knew that Catherine considered him a lesser human being. Elvira had spent years poisoning his reputation. The aristocratic envoys who arrived from Spain – and then went back again – had also encouraged her to look down on the *marrano* lawyer. Now the little man with the Jewish blood stood before her with tears pouring down his cheeks. He asked her to swear not to repeat to Elvira a word of what he was about to say. Then he spelled out to her the whole sorry story of deceit.

Catherine was suddenly confronted with the most difficult decision of her life. She had to choose between the woman who had been her mother figure for the past four years and the little man whose blood-line and demeanour she so disdained. She may have been naïve, but she was not stupid. She had also been brought up to defend her parents' interests above all. 'She has an excellent heart and she loves her father more than herself,' De Puebla reported afterwards. She wrote immediately to Henry, begging him to ignore her earlier letter. She had been tricked, and so beseeched him 'to value the interests of her father, the King of Spain, beyond those of any other prince in the world'. She also entered into a secret pact with De Puebla. She would dissimulate in front of Elvira, pretending she was still in favour of the interview. The lady mistress was not to know that Catherine had seen through her. In the meantime she handed the ambassador a second letter which he was to deliver to Henry in person. 'I was the one who proposed the meeting . . . [and] now that I know what your highness knows, I beg you to think no more about it,' she wrote.

In the space of a few frantic hours, Catherine had come of age. She was nineteen and had finally learnt that blind obedience was not always best. Trust was a precious commodity to be used sparingly. It had been wasted on Elvira. Catherine's blind obedience and passivity had left her vulnerable. It was an invaluable lesson. Only she could look after her own interests.

Elvira's treachery must have made Catherine rethink an earlier episode at Durham House when she had tried to do her best for those she was closest to – her six *damas*. Catherine always became excited by the marriage plans of her ladies. Her own mother had been an inveterate match-maker, taking special care of the women who were nearest to her and overseeing the family alliances amongst her nobles. Now Catherine wanted to play the same game. This became impossible, however, as her position in England weakened, her finances wobbled and the two men responsible for her welfare paid less and less attention to her. Catherine had no means of contributing to her ladies' dowries. 'They should marry,' she sighed in one letter home. 'And I have nothing to give them.'

Her favourite lady-in-waiting, the same María de Rojas who shared her bed, was being courted by no less a personage than the future earl of Derby. Catherine considered him a fine match. He was, she said, 'a grandee of this country, and one of the most important'. The feelings were mutual. Marriage, Catherine excitedly wrote home late in 1504, was a distinct possibility. They both hoped that, after the wedding, María could continue living with her. Catherine asked her parents to give their permission for the match and guarantee payment of her *dama*'s dowry. She did not count, however, on Elvira. María was a good prize – the only child of, and heiress to, a wealthy Spanish landowner. Elvira adeptly nipped the English match in the bud, and arranged for María to marry her own son, Antonio.

Elvira's self-interest now overrode any sense of duty. She persuaded Catherine to raid her stock of silver and gold plate, even though this had been expressly forbidden by her father. It was, after all, part of the dowry he would pay Henry on her second marriage. Elvira was quick to show, however, that previously iron-cast rules could be bent. Soon Juan de Cuero – the man meant to guard her money – discovered that five major pieces of silver plate and some jewellery had gone missing. 'Doña Elvira and Don Pedro de Ayala have persuaded the princess to give certain persons a collar, a piece of brocade and some vessels of silver,' De Puebla reported in the same letter that told of the missing goods. He also gave the news of María de Rojas' betrothal to Elvira's son. 'I am amazed,' he commented. The gifts, it is reasonable to assume, went to the betrothed couple.

The affair of the proposed meeting with her sister Juana and Philip the Handsome finally shattered the cocoon in which Catherine had been living. This episode, together with her decision to raid her own plate, does at least show a woman ready to break the stifling mould of her life. Catherine was, albeit chaotically, finally showing spirit.

The unfortunate De Puebla was the first to feel these changes. He may have saved her from making a fool of herself over her sister, but Catherine still blamed him for almost everything else. The final straw was Henry's decision to move her out of Durham House. This happened soon after Elvira left Catherine, disappearing to Flanders. At least one household member recalled this as a 'horrible hour' in the lives of those at Durham House. Catherine claimed that she was now as good as penniless. 'Since I came to England I have not had a single *maravedi* [the currency unit used in Spain], except a certain sum which was given me for food, and this such a sum that it did not suffice without me having many debts in London,' Catherine complained in a letter to her father in December 1505. 'That which troubles me most is to see my servants and maidens so at a loss, and that they have not wherewith to get clothes.' She had tried to turn the 'rogue' De Puebla into a 'true man'. All he had done, however, was to get her thrown out of her home and moved into the royal palace at Richmond. It was his fault that, for the past two months, she had gone down with 'severe tertian fevers'. He should be sacked immediately and someone better sent to replace him, she insisted.

By pure chance, Catherine was to get that meeting with Juana. When her sister and Philip finally set off from Flanders for Spain in January 1506, the weather drove them into port at Melcombe Regis, near Weymouth, Dorset. Fate had intervened to ensure that what Catherine had first promoted – and then tried to stop – finally came to pass. Henry, naturally, took advantage of the situation to meet Philip – who ended up staying for almost three months. Unknown to Catherine, Henry signed the secret Treaty of Windsor in which he backed Philip against 'his enemies' – effectively backing him against Ferdinand in the tussle for control of Castile. For Catherine, however, the presence of the Burgundian fleet allowed her to see the sister whose face she had not looked upon for nine whole years. She was also to meet, for the first time, her sister's troublesome husband.

Within two hours of Philip arriving at Windsor, Catherine had also got there. Juana, however, was nowhere to be seen. Her husband had left her behind on the coast. Catherine and her sister-in-law Mary did their best to entertain a grumpy and arrogant Philip. The women were led into the king's dining chamber, 'where danced my lady princess, and a Spanish lady with her in Spanish array; and after she had danced two or three dances she left, and then danced my lady Mary and an English lady with her.' Catherine tried to engage her brother-in-law but he now remained steadfastly aloof. 'The lady princess desired the king of Castile [as Philip now considered himself] to dance, which, after that he had excused him once or twice, answered that he was a mariner, "And yet," said he, "you would cause me to dance" – and so he danced not.' Catherine's earlier enthusiasm for her brother-in-law, if any survived, must have died with that very public snub. She and Princess Mary sat together at 'the end of the carpet, which was under the cloth of estate', while Philip and Henry continued to chat about their own affairs, though Mary later impressed everyone with her lute-playing.

Juana arrived more than a week later, on 10 February, the day before Catherine was due to leave. Theirs was a strange and unsatisfactory meeting. Juana and her party 'entered by the little park, and secretly came to the back side of the castle, unto the king's new tower, where, at the stair foot, the king met with her, and kissed and embraced her'. Philip had told Henry not to go to so much trouble. There was no need, in his eyes, for the English king to give his wife such a dignified welcome. At last, however, the two sisters met. 'After the king had welcomed her, my lady princess her sister, my lady Mary the king's daughter, having many ladies and gentlewomen attending upon them, welcomed her.'

It was the first time in almost six years that Catherine had seen a member of her close family. It would also be the last. The meeting was all too brief and came to an awkward end. Since Catherine left the next day, she cannot have spent more than a few hours in her sister's company – for Juana cut their meeting short. Worst of all, the Juana who she met was a pale shadow of her former spirited self. She had suffered at the hands of a vain and impetuous husband, and it showed. Philip only tolerated her because she was now the queen of Castile. He wanted to control her kingdom, preferably without having to see her too much. A year and a half later Catherine was still brooding on that unsatisfactory meeting. She wrote to Juana, telling her of the 'great pleasure it gave me to see you and the great distress which filled my soul, a few hours afterwards, on account of your hasty and sudden departure'.

When Juana finally travelled on to Spain and arrived with Philip at her side, Ferdinand realised he had lost any chance of gaining control of Castile. The prince who Machiavelli so admired knew how to retire gracefully. He offered Philip some 'paternal advice' on how to rule Castile and starting making plans to leave Spain and attend to his Italian lands. They signed an agreement 'of most intimate friendship and alliance' in June 1506 which cemented Philip's power over Castile. (To cover his back, however, Ferdinand also immediately drew up a secret document claiming he had signed out of fear for his life.) Ferdinand and his son-in-law ruthlessly barred Juana herself from exercising her powers as queen as she, they alleged, would cause 'the total destruction and perdition of these kingdoms'. The queen, they claimed, had 'infirmities and sufferings' that made her unfit to reign. Juana, in other words, was now formally considered mad. Catherine's stock, meanwhile, hit rock bottom. Plans were now also afoot to betroth Henry VII's daughter Mary to Juana's son and heir, the future Holy Roman Emperor, Charles V. That would mean that the most important ties between England and Spain no longer ran through her. Catherine was becoming a second-rate princess.

Unknown to Catherine, a separate and potentially more devastating episode had taken place a year earlier before the bishop of Winchester on the eve of her fiancé's fourteenth birthday. Prince Henry, acting on his father's orders, solemnly denounced the marriage treaty reached while he was still a minor as being null and void. He would not ratify it. 'I the aforesaid Henry, prince of Wales, now nearly arrived to maturity of age, and being just at years of consent . . . do not consent to the said marriage contract, or receive the said Lady Catherine as my lawful spouse and wife,' he said. That did not actually rule out the marriage (especially as this denunciation was kept secret), but it did mean that King Henry could slip out of it whenever he liked. Catherine, in other words, was in limbo.

Prince Henry turned fourteen on 28 June 1505. The original marriage treaty said they could wed some time after this. It also, however, stipulated that there could be no wedding until the hundred thousand *scudos* still owed for her dowry were in the country. By the following summer Ferdinand had still not made the slightest effort to send the money.

Catherine's future was looking increasingly grim. The wheel of fortune continued to turn, however, and in September 1506 Philip the Handsome suddenly fell ill and died. Elvira's brother Juan Manuel, who 'governed King Philip at his will', had thrown a party for him in Burgos. Philip seems to have enjoyed himself too much and, on drinking some cold water to cool himself down, was struck ill. Womanising and partying, one chronicler said, were to blame. 'Through bad government [of himself] he passed from this lifetime to the next,' the chronicler noted. Ferdinand thus took control of Juana – and of her kingdoms. Catherine's stock rose again accordingly.

Juana, meanwhile, threw herself into eccentric, obstinate widowhood. She pushed her family's melodramatic fame to new and impossible limits. To start with, she refused to be separated from her husband's cadaver. This she carried around with her in its coffin, sometimes on night-time processions through the countryside, for years – possibly as a way of warding off future suitors. Her behaviour became more erratic as time went by. 'She urinates very often – more often than ever seen in any other person . . . Her face and everything else, they say, lack cleanliness. She eats on the floor, without a tablecloth or glassware,' her former confessor Diego Ramírez de Villaescusa reported.

While her sister wandered through Spain, a victim of both her own character and of their Machiavellian father, Catherine decided to do something to remedy her own situation. She had to see to the present – which meant her living expenses. She also had to see to the future by getting her father to pay her dowry. Most importantly of all, however, she looked to the long term, to eternity itself. She wanted to ensure the safety of her soul. For that, she needed to find a suitable confessor. So arose the issue which, for the first and only time in her life, saw Catherine at the centre of a romantic scandal. Ferdinand's deeply concerned ambassador warned that she was becoming dangerously attached to a young man who was now 'continually in the palace and amongst the women'.

16 Confessions

Richmond Palace. April 1507

Catherine was on her knees before a man who was beginning to arouse in her feelings of passionate, stubborn loyalty. She had been taught to obey – above all else – kings, husbands and priests. The first of these had become increasingly unreliable, while the second were proving either ephemeral or, for the moment, unattainable. Now, finally, she had a man of God in whom she could place her trust. The young Spanish friar, Fray Diego Fernández, listened to her confession. She would tell him her secrets. He would help her find, or stay on, the path to heaven.

Catherine had been pleading for a new Spanish confessor to be sent to her for a year or more. In April 1506, some four and half years after arriving in England, she wrote to her father from her new home under Henry VII's roof at Richmond saying that she needed a Spaniard because 'I do not understand the English language nor know how to speak it.' It was an astonishing sign of just how isolated she remained four years after her arrival. She wanted 'a friar from the Order of St Francis of Observance, who is a man of letters'. Soon after she found one herself.

No one knows where the forceful young friar Diego Fernández appeared from but by April 1507 he was firmly established at Catherine's side. He would become one of the most important men in her life, after her husbands and father. Appointing her own confessor was one of Catherine's first independent acts. It also generated one of her most passionate infatuations. Where Geraldini had been deemed a traitor, Fray Diego was 'the best that ever [a] woman of my position had'. The young friar, she insisted, was 'very faithful in his office as well as in giving good advice and a good example'. She was, people thought, besotted.

Diego may, indeed, have been a good confessor. He was also vain, arrogant and bullying. He was both a misogynist and a gossip. An English court of law later decided he was also a proven fornicator. The friar extracted full advantage from Catherine's desperate desire for a confessor who might live up to her family's demanding standards. Queen Isabel had been impressed by a confessor who made her kneel while he sat. Her daughter was more than happy to take instruction from a man whose high opinion of himself, and low opinion of women, made him a stern and capricious issuer of commands. She had not yet learned to rebel against her natural submissiveness to men and could still be blindly obedient where a man represented God. It was enough for Fray Diego to deem anything he disliked as sinful for her to obey and desist. The 'young chap', as one of Ferdinand's envoys, Gutierre Gómez de Fuensalida, called him after arriving in February 1508, 'makes a sin of all acts, if they displease him, and thus causes her to commit many faults'. He was, Fuensalida complained, 'young, light and haughty and scandalous in an extreme manner'. Later Spanish ambassadors agreed that the friar had an extraordinary hold on Catherine.

Diego's power was such that Catherine was prepared to snub even King Henry on his command, however much this went against her best interest. The English king, after all, both maintained her and held her future in his hands. On one occasion in March 1509, when Henry required her presence at Richmond, Fray Diego countermanded his instructions – telling her, at the last moment, that she was too ill to travel. 'I am well: I do not wish to stay here alone,' she protested. She had, indeed, spent part of the previous night vomiting but had woken up feeling fine. She had already been to mass and eaten. 'I tell you that, upon pain of mortal sin, you shall not go today,' Diego commanded. Catherine, 'not daring to displease him' and so commit mortal sin, chose to obey the friar and offend the king. Princess Mary and her party, who had already been waiting two hours and had seen Catherine at mass and at the breakfast table, set off without her. Henry was livid. When she arrived the following day with Fray Diego and a handful of her household members, the king ignored her. She then fell ill yet again. Henry did not dispense his usual sympathy. More than three weeks went by before he talked to her again. It was the first time, but by no means the last, that Catherine chose to obey God (or his representative) above a king.

Even Ferdinand's latest envoy, Fuensalida, took Henry's side in this falling out. 'I acquit the king of England of a great and very great portion of the blame . . . and do not wonder at what he has done but at that which he does not do,' he said. Scurrilous gossip suggested the relationship between friar and princess had crossed proper boundaries. Fuensalida never quite dared to spell it out in his letters to Ferdinand, but the suggestion was undoubtedly that they were having a furtive affair. It is easy to understand how the scandal blossomed. Royalty, religion and illicit relationships made for easy gossip. Diego was the only man to whom Catherine could get physically close and with whom she might be alone for any length of time. Confession is, by its nature, an intimate act. Clearly Catherine became, in some way, infatuated. She was not the kind, however, to indulge in a dangerous liaison with a confessor – however young, forceful or attractive he might be. She was far more likely to have poured suppressed passion into religion than into a torrid, prohibited and sinful romance. Religion was, in any case, their place of encounter – though Diego also gained considerable temporal power over her affairs. He would have been a foolish priest, indeed, to risk his life by laying a hand on a woman betrothed to the king's son.

Catherine's mother, however, had taught her that appearances counted for almost as much as reality. To be seen as pure was as important as being pure. King Henry thought the same way. He was furious. This thing 'was constantly brought before his eyes', said Fuensalida. 'The king of England, and all the English, abhor so much to see a friar . . . amongst the women,' he added. 'Nothing could be more detested by them.'

Catherine was called to see Henry. He remonstrated with her about Diego with 'very strong words'. She ignored him. Aware that there was nothing he could do, he eventually appeared ready to allow Catherine to hang herself on the yard-arm of gossip. For a man who liked to store up ways of wriggling out of his treaty agreements, Fray Diego was a potential gift. Henry was also learning that his daughter-in-law could be extremely obstinate.

Rather than remove the cause of the scandal, Catherine railed against those who spread the gossip. She leapt to her confessor's defence. The language in her letters, when talking about Fray Diego, was excitable and, at times, desperate. She worried that she could not pay him enough money. She could not bear to be without him and he, knowing this, threatened daily to leave her. Catherine even asked her father to tell Henry to be nicer to Diego. 'I do not consent that my confessor be treated in such a manner,' she says. 'Beg him that for the love of your highness he should order that he be very well treated and humoured.'

The friar himself was arrogantly, even vainly, contemptuous of his accusers. He confronted Fuensalida about them directly. 'In this house there are evil tongues, and they have cast slanderous imputations upon me, with respect not to the lowest in the house but to the highest [meaning Catherine herself], and this is no disgrace to me.' Fuensalida barely managed to stop himself from answering the friar with his fists.

One of the few areas of her life where Catherine could exercise power was in the choice of a confessor so this was a battle she could, and did, win. The major clashes described here did not come until 1509, two years after he was appointed, but Catherine seems to have become heavily dependent on Fray Diego from the very beginning. If she clung so firmly to her confessor, it was partly because the other men meant to be looking after her were not doing their part. Henry and Ferdinand continued to play their game of cat and mouse. Rather than send the hundred thousand *scudos*, her father constantly pleaded for more time to come up with the dowry money. Henry took his growing anger with Ferdinand out on Catherine herself. As things went wrong again, Catherine had slumped back into bouts of ill-health. Henry would respond to Ferdinand's manoeuvring by squeezing Catherine tighter. The louder she squealed, he hoped, the sooner her father might send the money. Otherwise, he would just have to marry his son and heir to someone else. There were plenty of other candidates around Europe.

Catherine was rarely allowed to see Prince Henry who, anyway, was kept on a tight lead. In April 1507, indeed, she complained that she had been kept away from him for four months. His father was paranoid about the safety of his only remaining male heir. Fuensalida thought he was being treated like an overprotected Spanish *dama*. The king restricted his movements and made sure he was accompanied wherever he went. 'No one, for their life, would be so forward as to speak to him and he is constantly in a chamber that has no entrance or exit except through the king's chamber,' Fuensalida reported a year later. There was no question of sending him off to Ludlow, as his elder brother had done, to govern Wales. Young Henry was 'so subjected that he does not speak a word except in response to what the king asks him', the envoy said. Henry VII, he added, was turning increasingly grumpy and giving his son violent tongue-lashings.

Something in Catherine had changed by the middle of 1507. She was physically well. She had grown up and was beginning to exercise her own will. Perhaps it was Fray Diego, whose advice she constantly sought, who made the difference. His arrogance extended not just to her, but to almost everyone. He was happy for her to challenge the authority of anyone except himself.

Catherine's room for manoeuvre was severely limited, not least because she was a woman. She complained to her father that she was fed up with De Puebla. Her cause needed a far better and more trustworthy advocate. That was about to come from a surprising place.

17 Ambassador

Richmond Palace. April 1507

Catherine stood before the king and listened as he tore her world apart. Henry had decided it was time to explain that her betrothal was off. Her father had not sent the dowry money, so there could be no wedding. 'The king said that the prince was free and he had no obligation towards the marriage,' she wrote to Ferdinand afterwards, begging him to send the money. Humiliation sat uneasily on Catherine's shoulders. It was like the shame of her poverty. She had been taught to be submissive, but also to be proud. She could not stop 'thinking that I am your highness's daughter', she wrote.

Catherine had already implored her father to send a new ambassador, someone who was straight-talking and, preferably, had experience of England. This, she explained, was a country 'remote from all others' and with such strange forms of behaviour that it needed special treatment. Soon the credentials naming the new ambassador chosen by Ferdinand arrived. Who could serve his interests better than a loyal, loving and noble subject already living in London and with excellent access to Henry VII? Catherine herself was to be his ambassador.

It was an extraordinary move on Ferdinand's part. Women, however high their status, were rare in the world of power and diplomacy. She was joining a select group of sixteenth-century women, most of whom owed their position or their power to blood ties or marriage. Perhaps Ferdinand, like others, saw something of her mother in Catherine. She was instructed to work in parallel with the increasingly sickly De Puebla – who had to be carried to court in a litter. Catherine presented her credentials to Henry VII early in the summer of 1507.

Her letters home had become increasingly distraught and dramatic. Her household, she claimed, wore rags and lived in complete misery. She continued to hawk her dowry plate and begged her father to send money. With her diplomatic credentials in her hand, however, she could at least try to do something to change her situation.

Immediately after Philip the Handsome's death in 1506, Henry had suddenly seemed kinder to Catherine, offering to give her the Fulham house reserved for the Flemish ambassadors or any other place she needed to recover from illness. Her stock had risen and she once again became a desirable bride for Henry's son. More importantly, Henry had developed an infatuation of his own. Like many men who met Catherine's sister Juana, he had been struck by her beauty. What some people saw as madness he found strangely exciting. Juana seems to have bewitched him during her short stay at Windsor. He even argued that, after Philip had taken control of her kingdom, 'she should be at liberty'. She was also, of course, the queen of Castile. If Henry were to marry her he would win a beautiful and interesting bride while also gaining in power. Ferdinand – whose consent was needed for the marriage – could continue being regent, he told De Puebla. All Henry wanted was Juana, her childbearing potential and the income that might come his way. It would have been a tremendous coup and Henry put considerable effort into pursuing her. Ferdinand told Henry that he had placed him top of the long list of those who wanted to marry her. The list, however, was just that. It had no purpose beyond keeping Henry quiet. Ferdinand had no intention of marrying his daughter off. While she remained a widow, and one obsessed by her dead husband, Castile was his to rule.

Catherine immediately spotted that Henry's infatuation offered her an opportunity. She played at go-between, passing on Henry's messages about Juana to Ferdinand. 'I bait the king with the hope of marrying Doña Juana and I flatter him and his councillors,' she told her father in a coded letter sent secretly in October 1507. She also wrote directly to Juana, saying that Henry had been pained by her departure and had not liked the way Philip treated her in England. He had been angry but was warned by his council 'not to interfere between a husband and wife'. Henry, she told her sister, is 'a very passionate king'. 'The great affection he has felt, and still feels, towards your royal highness from that time until now, is well known,' she added.

Diplomacy gave her a new lease of life. She found the verbal sparring with Henry VII stimulating. 'I spoke so well that I should rejoice to give an account of it,' she gushed to her father after one round with the English king. 'You speak cleverly,' Henry acknowledged at one of their meetings. 'But [I fear] your father the king, my brother, is too clever.' She applied herself to learning the tricks of the diplomatic trade with earnest enthusiasm. Letters, she knew, were routinely intercepted. King Henry's spies would love to know what she was saying to her father and, more importantly, what he was saying in reply. She began, therefore, to write in code. Her letters used the Spanish diplomatic ciphers of the time . Some of these codes, which Ferdinand sent to her, replaced individual letters with symbols that vaguely resemble Chinese figures. Others replaced key words – especially names – with Latin numerals or fanciful code-words. 'A messenger sent by the little duck to the falcon returned a short time ago much pleased with the answer of the falcon,' read one earlier message in Spanish code sent to De Puebla. 'The little duck and the *fuzarco* are so contented that they say nothing could better piebald than the fly with the falcon. Thus everything is going on well now, and it is in the mar-maid that it will be concluded in favour of the cuckoo and the young eagle.' We can picture Catherine sitting in her rooms in Greenwich or Richmond with her table of codes beside her, laboriously rewriting her letters in what, to anyone else, seemed gibberish. Sometimes the finished version looked so absurd that she worried no one would understand it. At other times she was so excited by the work of coding and decoding that she spent three or four days in 'unearthly' good spirits.

She was frustrated by her dealings with the English. 'Those in this kingdom are as dilatory as any in the world in negotiating,' she explained. She passed on diplomatic titbits, and used her new position to defend herself against threats to her future marriage. She even advised Ferdinand against a rumoured match between her sister Juana and the French count of Foix which would anger Henry and spoil her own wedding plans. 'I say it because, in this, I myself feel personally interested,' she admitted. By August 1507 she was telling her father that no woman, whatever their station in life, could have suffered more than she. 'I love you more than ever a father loved his daughter,' Ferdinand replied. Yet he did nothing to prove it.

Over the next year and a half, despite her best efforts, things slowly went from bad to worse. Catherine alternately pleaded for money, complained at Henry's ill-treatment of her, lambasted her father for his inaction and, as ever, blamed it all on the long-suffering De Puebla. She also became increasingly wily. Some letters she sent on circuitous routes via Flanders because 'it would have been dangerous, or at any rate might have been considered suspicious' to be seen sending too many couriers direct to Spain. She was happy, too, to let others think that she was still a passive, dumb victim. 'They fancy that I have no more in me than what appears outwardly, and that I shall not be able to fathom his designs,' she explained. 'I dissimulate.' It was a tactic that would serve her well. She also became convinced that the unfortunate De Puebla, whose alleged 'designs' she was referring to, was in cahoots with Henry.

With Henry she used both guile and obstinacy. When the English king suggested that her father was considering cancelling the marriage she insisted it 'could not be undone'. She also added a threat. 'I said that, even if this were not so, your highness knew what my wish was, namely, that I should not be taken out of the power of the king of England even if I were to die for it.' She would only leave England, she seemed to mean, in a coffin. If Ferdinand and Henry failed to sort her marriage out, she was saying, then she was not going to help them find a simple way out of their potentially dangerous stand-off. On one occasion when Henry suggested to her that both he and Ferdinand were still free to break the marriage treaty, she pretended not to understand. 'I told him that I could not comprehend him and that I did not like to take it in the sense which he meant.'

Ferdinand somehow persuaded Henry to stick by the marriage treaty and give him more time to come up with the missing money for his daughter's dowry. Early in 1508 he reassured Catherine that, as far as he was concerned, the marriage was still on. He also praised her work as his ambassador. She was proving so 'virtuous and prudent' in her handling of Henry that, from now on, he promised to treat her words 'as gospel'.

Catherine had noticed, however, that she was the real loser in this game. Whenever Ferdinand negotiated more time to pay, Henry's grip on Catherine increased. 'He does not lose anything thereby; on the contrary,' she told her father. 'He is the gainer. For, as he has told me, as long as he is not entirely paid, he regards me as bound and his son as free. He [his son] is not yet so old that delay is disagreeable. Thus mine is always the worst part.'

By July 1508 Ferdinand had still not produced the marriage money. A comically blustering Fuensalida, having arrived in February to help Catherine, made things worse by telling Henry that his regal honour obliged him to stick by a wedding agreement that Ferdinand kept breaking. Henry replied by quibbling over the dowry payment, claiming that Catherine's plate and jewels had lost value and that it must now all be paid in cash.

Fuensalida was shocked by the treatment she was receiving. 'The princess is not well. She is very thin and pale,' he reported. As negotiations dragged on and Henry became meaner, she began to lose hope. 'She is so cast down and disconsolate,' he reported. 'She shows a pleasant face to everyone, but she cannot hide what she feels from me.'

Henry VII, meanwhile, occasionally called Catherine in to complain angrily about her father. His son, on at least one of these occasions, was sent out of the room and he even started to keep his daughter Mary away from her. She was given shabby, smelly quarters and Fuensalida swore that even his servants got better food than the king sent her. The ambassador worked himself up into such a lather of righteous hatred of Henry and the English that he augured nothing but misery from a marriage to the young Prince Henry. 'The princess might one day become queen of England, but she is being offered the most hapless life a woman ever had,' he said.

The future of Juana's son and heir, Charles, had been organised, in the meantime, by his grandfather Maximilian. He had arranged a match between Charles, already known as the prince of Spain, and Henry VII's daughter Mary. Henry was delighted. He made sure Catherine was fully aware that the links between England and Spain no longer ran just through her.

When, in March 1509, the dowry money was still not in London Catherine began to give up hope. The men working with her only made things worse, she said. 'As Dr De Puebla conducted the affairs with too great gentleness in everything that regarded the interests of this king, so this other ambassador [Fuensalida] behaves with too great rigour towards him and his servants,' she told her father. 'I cannot make use of anything that is not done with moderation.'

Fray Diego, meanwhile, encouraged her to sell even more of her dowry plate. This she did, despite the tenacious resistance of Juan de Cuero – whom she soon also wanted sacked. 'The princess behaves towards him as though he had committed the greatest treason in the world and all because he hinders them every day from selling a piece of plate to satisfy the follies of the friar,' Fuensalida reported. Despite this, she managed to sell two hundred ducats' worth of gold over fifteen days. It was not 'known on what she spends it, except in books and the expenses of the friar'. Literature, it seems, was one of her few consolations. Fray Diego was another of them.

'What afflicts me most is that I cannot in any way remedy the hardships of my confessor,' she complained to her father. Fray Diego came up with some solutions of his own. He advised her, for example, to continue borrowing. Creditors – in particular a banker called Grimaldo (who had taken up with her gossipy lady Francisca de Cáceres, leading to yet another major falling out) – were knocking at her door. Diego, meanwhile, helped her to exercise her diplomatic influence. She even sent him to Henry to demand a copy of some articles of the marriage treaty. It was like waving a red rag at a bull. 'On account of this he [Henry] grew angry,' she indignantly informed Ferdinand. 'And [he] permitted himself to be led so far as to say things which are not fit to be written to your highness.' Henry took advantage of Diego's presence to confront him with the rumours that he was dallying with the princess. The English king, she complained, cast doubt on 'the honour of my house and said what is not true'.

Catherine was now an angry woman. 'Not only does her highness feign to be angry with me but shows herself to be in reality,' Fuensalida complained after receiving the sharp edge of her tongue. Catherine could no longer bear the sight of some of the most important people in her household. 'I would rather die than see what I have suffered and suffer from every day from this ambassador and from all my servants,' she wrote to her father.

Eight years had gone by since she arrived in England. Much of it had been misery. Now it was getting even worse. 'It is impossible for me any longer to endure what I have gone through and still am suffering from the unkindness of the king and the manner in which he treats me,' she told Ferdinand in the spring of 1509. Henry was now being deliberately vindictive. 'He tried to make me feel this by his want of love,' she complained after he had boasted that he no longer needed her father. 'He said he was not bound to give my servants food, or even my own self.'

Catherine felt she could sink no lower. Nothing she did as ambassador made any difference. She had sold so much of her jewels and plate that she could no longer pay for her 'high necessities'. Her father now also doubted that the wedding would take place and began making contingency plans to take her back home to Spain. Henry, he had decided, was 'little desirous to bring the affair to a conclusion'. Catherine was so distressed that she imagined herself at death's door. 'I fear my life will be short, owing to my troubles,' she told Ferdinand. Suicide seemed one of the few options left to her. 'I am afraid I might do something which neither the king of England nor your highness, who has much more weight, would be able to prevent, unless, and that is necessary, you send for me,' she told her father.

The melodramatic side of her nature was coming to the fore again. Whenever that happened, she instinctively reached for the refuge of religion. If she could not marry a man, she would become a bride of Christ. Ferdinand, she said, could ship her home and allow her to enter a convent 'so that I may conclude my few remaining days in serving God . . . That would be the greatest good I could have in this world.'

Within weeks, however, reality was to supersede even her own heightened sense of drama. It bounced her suddenly from one extreme to another. The stalemate of her marriage was broken by nature. Henry VII died on 21 April 1509 – probably from pulmonary tuberculosis. Henry had seen off the many plots against him and, despite the unpopularity of his rapacious ways, had successfully established his line on the throne. His seventeen-year-old son and heir quickly decided to marry Catherine. After all her sufferings, she would finally be queen.

18 Married Again

Greenwich. 11 June 1509

By the standards of her previous wedding, there was something almost clandestine about the way Catherine married her new husband. There was no grand stage at St Paul's. There was, in fact, no 'great church' at all. For this was a private, out-of-town affair with only a few selected guests. There was certainly no eager scribe at hand to record for posterity the details of how a twenty-three-year-old Catherine exchanged vows with King Henry VIII, who had not yet turned eighteen, at his waterside palace in Greenwich. The wedding was held in one of the Queen's Closets, possibly in the Chapel Royal, at what was to become the couple's favourite palace. We still do not know who presided.

The words, however, would have been agreed in advance. Catherine, after all, was marrying her former husband's brother. That was something that needed explaining, and excusing, in God's presence. That could be done by invoking the pope's dispensation.

They probably followed the pattern set when Catherine had first pledged to marry the eleven-year-old prince. 'Most illustrious princess is it your will . . . as the pope has issued a dispensation to allow this marriage, to take the prince who is here present for your lawful spouse?' Catherine was asked, in Latin, on that occasion. In reply, she repeated the word Henry had used a moment earlier when asked the same question. '*Volo* [I will],' she said.

The boyish man she married was already striking-looking. There was still something slightly feminine about his post-adolescent beauty, as yet unblemished by age or excess. An Italian visitor wrote a few years later:

The king is the handsomest potentate I ever set eyes upon; above the usual height, with an extremely fine calf to his leg, his complexion very fair and bright, with auburn hair combed straight and short, in the French fashion, and a round face so very beautiful that it would become a pretty woman, his throat being rather long and thick . . . He speaks French, English and Latin, and a little Italian; plays well on the lute and harpsichord, sings from book at sight, draws the bow with greater strength than any man in England and jousts marvellously.

Praise for the physical beauties of the tall, powerful-bodied and fresh-faced young king was universal. 'He is much handsomer than any sovereign in Christendom; a great deal handsomer than the king of France, very fair and his whole frame admirably proportioned,' said one Venetian a decade later. The hours spent in the saddle, day after day, burning off the frustration of his cosseted adolescence by practising for jousts in the tiltyard can only have improved his physique. His sporting prowess amazed many, especially his ability to ride up to ten horses into the ground on a single day's hunting. 'He is extremely fond of tennis, at which game it is the prettiest thing in the world to see him play, his fair skin glowing through a shirt of the finest texture,' swooned the same Venetian. 'Nature could not have done more for him.'

It is doubtful that Catherine cared much about how or where she married this time around. She was more probably glad – possibly amazed – to be married at all. The turnaround in her fortunes could not have been more complete. In the few weeks it took to renegotiate the marriage after Henry VII's death, the whole, sorry episode of her lonely, bitter, frantic wait disappeared into a suddenly remote past. Little in her upbringing had prepared her for those years. Her parents had, however, raised her to become England's queen consort. She had not known how to cope as a castaway princess – stranded, unloved and, even, unwanted at Henry VII's court – but she knew exactly how to be a queen.

Henry, who would get plenty of practice at weddings, did not like them to be flamboyant. The big occasion, in any case, was to come a fortnight later. For, while Catherine became a queen by marrying Henry on 11 June, she had not yet been crowned. Nor had Henry. The coronation was to be their big event.

The day before the coronation they processed through London to Westminster. Catherine followed Henry's retinue of scarlet- and crimson-clad nobles and officials – their chunky, 'massy and great' gold chains swinging around their necks – along many of the same streets she had travelled during her first triumphal procession through the city eight years earlier. These were, once more, railed off and draped with Arras tapestries. Priests stood by, smoke puffing from their silver censers. There were 'virgins in white' holding 'branches of white Waxe' along the route. The great difference this time was that she had a husband with her. Henry, she was just beginning to learn, loved to dress up. Her extrovert husband was a one-man festival of colour. He wore clothes of crimson velvet, ermine and raised gold decorated with diamonds, rubies, pearls and emeralds. A chunky baldric belt was slung diagonally across his body, studded with massive pink balass rubies. Catherine was swept up in the general excitement which marked the beginning of a new reign and the coronation of an English king and queen.

Catherine wore glistening white. She sat, dressed in embroidered satin, in a covered litter borne by two white palfreys. Even the horses were caparisoned in white cloth of gold. Her rich auburn locks – the same that Sittow's paintings hint at so suggestively – hung freely down her back. It was one of the rare occasions when an English queen, or any Englishwoman, might show her hair. It may have been the last time that any man, barring her husband, saw it. Edward Hall, the London boy who went on to chronicle Henry's reign, recalled that the queen's hair – set off by a coronet encrusted with jewels from the orient – was both 'of a very great length' and 'beautiful and goodly to behold'. She was followed by her own household, now mainly English, with six white palfreys and a 'chariot' bearing the senior members and ladies of her household, all dressed in cloth of gold. Even the draught harnesses were speckled with ermine and cloth of gold. A sudden summer shower dampened the occasion temporarily, however, with Catherine forced to halt and take cover under the drapers' stalls in Cornhill. It was not, some muttered, a good omen.

The following day was the midsummer festival. That morning, under canopies born by the barons of the Cinque Ports, Catherine and Henry walked the short distance from Westminster Palace to the abbey. A carpet of striped cloth had been laid out for them. As soon as they entered the abbey, the overexcited 'rude and common' onlookers fell on the carpet, tearing it to shreds as they fought to take home a coronation souvenir. Their behaviour was another sign of the enthusiasm generated by the coming of a new era. Catherine and Henry were anointed and crowned by the Archbishop of Canterbury, William Warham. Those present were asked whether they would 'receive, obey and take' Henry as their new king. 'Yeh! Yeh!' they cried. A simple woodcut from the time shows Catherine and the beardless Henry beaming at each other as smiling bishops hold crowns over their heads. And so Catherine, now properly a queen in God's eyes, processed back under her canopy to Westminster Hall across whatever remained of the ragged, striped carpet. The feasting then began. The first course was announced by a fanfare of trumpets and led into the echoing, ninety-two-foot-high hall by the ever-magnificent duke of Buckingham, mounted on a richly trapped courser, and the Lord Steward on a horse trapped in cloth of gold. The partying, a constant part of Catherine's early life with Henry, had only just begun.

Thomas More was amongst those dazzled by the new era. 'This day is the end of our slavery, the fount of our liberty; the end of sadness, the beginning of joy,' he wrote. It was time to 'cleanse every eye of tears and substitute praise for a long moaning'.

Henry obviously wanted to be crowned with a wife beside him. He was not bound by any treaty, but decided within days of his father's death that Catherine would be his bride. She certainly knew within little more than a fortnight, writing to Ferdinand on 6 May to tell him the news. It may have been one of those impulsive and absolute decisions for which – despite a more general disposition to procrastination – Henry VIII became famous in later life. It may also have been the result of judicious advice from his council. There was, in any case, also a hard and obvious logic to it. He had already demonstrated that he was in charge in as dramatic a way as possible by having two of his father's chief councillors arrested. Richard Empson and Edmund Dudley were taken to the Tower of London almost immediately after Henry VII's death in what some have seen as a dramatic internal coup. These were the men who had helped Henry amass the fortune now handed on to his son and whose 'unreasonable and extort doing noble men grudged, mean men kicked, poor men lamented, preachers openly at Paul's Cross and other places exclaimed, rebuked and detested'. The arrests were greeted by 'rejoicing of many persones, which by them were greved'. They were executed sixteen months later, fall-guys for Henry's father's sins – and for his deep unpopularity amongst his subjects. 'They do not cry much for the dead king,' Fuensalida noted. 'In fact they show so much pleasure that it is as if everyone had been let out of prison.' The young king, understandably, presented himself to his people as the opposite of Henry VII. He was a new king, with new ways, determined to impress the world not just with his own brilliance but with that of his nation. Chopping the heads off his father's enforcers was one way of proving that. A new queen and, with that, a new alliance, also signalled that he was determined to bring change.

Henry was young but, at heart, he was an old-fashioned romantic. In his dreams he harked back to a period of English military glory – of Henry V at Agincourt – almost a century earlier. It was a time when men knew both their natural rank in life and their natural foe. The latter, as every Englishman was expected to know, was France. Like any young romantic, Henry took his passions seriously. The king of France, he soon shouted at an ambassador sent from across the Channel, 'dare not look me in the face, still less make war on me!' His father had been shrewd, mistrustful and brooding. He kept out of foreign wars and built up power by, in part, removing it from the trouble-some, uppity nobility. He handed that power, instead, to grey, clever men – administrators who collected his money and owed their jobs to him rather than to their blood-line. His son, how-ever, was a dreamer. He wanted the romance and excitement of chivalry and sport, preferably the true sport of nobles and kings, which was war. He was in love with both splendour and prowess – be it in warfare, jousting, music or partying. The nobility, hav-ing been out of favour with his father, were delighted. Others, too, were entranced by the romance of a new age.

'Oh my Erasmus, if you could see how the world here is rejoic-ing in the possession of so great a prince. Avarice is expelled [from] the land. Liberality scatters riches with a bounteous hand, our king does not desire gold or silver, but virtue, glory, immortality,' the studious and cultured William, Baron Mount-joy wrote to the great Dutch humanist, who had first come across a precocious Henry as an eight-year-old child. Mountjoy, perhaps, had more reason to be pleased than others. He had just married Inés de Vanegas, daughter to Catherine's old nurse and one of those half-dozen Spanish *damas* who had made the stormy trip to England with her. Their luck, too, had improved dramatically. María de Salinas, another *dama*, became a particular favourite at court and also went on to marry well, becoming Lady Willoughby. She would remain a close friend of Catherine, literally until her dying day.

From her new position of strength, Catherine soon settled some old scores. Fuensalida was sent home in disgrace because he 'did me a disservice, by having said what he did, and by taking up the topics which he took up'. Fray Diego, it seems, got his revenge. Many of her quarrelling servants were also sent home. She told her father 'to chastise him [Fuensalida] and them; but afterwards . . . pardon them, commanding that they should be regarded as persons who have been in my house'.

Catherine never forgot betrayals. The Spanish lady who once dressed and undressed her, the same Francisca de Cáceres who abandoned her for the banker Grimaldo and was a sworn enemy of Fray Diego, received a stern refusal when she later asked for a recommendation. 'It is true that she was my woman before she was married, but now since she cast herself away I have no more charge of her,' Catherine replied. Cáceres was unworthy of a place in another court, she said imperiously, as 'she is so perilous a woman that it shall be dangerous'.

A valiant knight – which was how Henry saw himself – needed a lady to whom he could dedicate his conquests and around whom he could spin his romantic vision of his deeds. Although her parents had done much the same thing as Henry VII by employing university men, priests and lawyers to help both run their kingdoms and educate the nobility, Catherine was similarly old-fashioned. She may have been learned, and educated by religious humanists, as Henry was, but she had also drunk deeply of the romantic tales of chivalry. Even her formidable mother had known how to play the role of medieval damsel when required. Catherine also instinctively knew about projecting that most indefinable of qualities, majesty. She fitted, in other words, the part that Henry wanted filled. She would be his queen of romance, the damsel to whom he could dedicate his feats of arms and gallant demonstrations of courtly prowess.

More practically, of course, Catherine also brought Henry a major alliance that would serve him well against the enemy he was spoiling to fight in France. Her father Ferdinand was not just a natural ally against the French but had the added glamour of having fought, and won, a holy war – evicting the 'infidel' Moor from Spain. This was something Ferdinand himself never tired of reminding people. He was Europe's foremost crusader – and that made him every bit as glamorous as Henry V or England's other great hero, King Arthur. Some of that glamour rubbed off, too, on Catherine.

Further weight may have been added to Henry's choice of bride by the simple fact that he already knew Catherine. She had formed part of his world since he was a ten-year-old boy – when he had led her out of old St Paul's cathedral and had then danced at her wedding parties. As an over-protected and frustrated adolescent he had also known she was the woman he was most likely to marry and share a bed with.

Catherine may have had more of a role in fixing her own marriage than we know. Her father certainly trusted her to carry out her own negotiations. 'Shortly before the other king died you said that his death would ensure your marriage,' he reminded her. Now it was her task to prove those words true. 'You must use all your skill and prudence to show what you can do, telling my envoy what he should do to swiftly close the deal.'

His instructions were not needed. The deal had been struck even before he wrote to her. Ferdinand was impressed. His daughter's role in persuading Henry, he felt, must have been crucial. 'I trust so much in your virtue and prudence that I not only leave to you the direction of your own affairs but would entrust the salvation of my soul to you,' he told her. Now Ferdinand knew the moment was ripe, he stopped quibbling about money. If the new king wanted the remaining hundred-thousand-*scudo* dowry money in hard cash, he could have it. If he wanted Ferdinand and his daughter to renounce any claim to that money should Henry VIII die, he could have that too. He instructed his envoy Fuensalida to sign up to almost any treaty as long as a wedding happened instantly. If necessary, he was to grease the palms of the king's councillors with money.

He was still worried, too, that her previous marriage to Arthur might cause last minute problems. Someone had been telling Fuensalida that young Henry's 'conscience was troubled about marrying his brother's wife'. Ferdinand ordered Fuensalida to point out 'that there are [papal] dispensations for that'. Two of Catherine's sisters had married the same king of Portugal who, he pointed out, now lived cheerily 'with many children'. Edward Hall later claimed that 'this marriage of the brother's wife, was much murmured against, in the beginning'. In fact the only recorded murmuring came from the archbishop of Canterbury, William Warham, who was roundly ignored.

Catherine's own joy shines in her letters after the wedding. Night had become day. She loved her energetic, chivalrous young husband and continued to revere a father who had allowed her to be 'so well married'. As for her husband, 'amongst the reasons that oblige me to love him much more than myself, the one most strong, although he is my husband, is his being the so true son of your highness,' she told Ferdinand, 'with desire of greater obedience and love to serve you than ever son had to his father.' Ferdinand was just as pleased. 'To be well married is the greatest blessing in the world . . . and source of all other kinds of happiness,' he told her. 'God is good to good husbands and wives.'

Henry wrote to his Spanish father-in-law to say how in love he was. He had 'rejected all other ladies in the world that have been offered to us' in order to marry Catherine and had no regrets. Her 'eminent virtues daily more and more shine forth, blossom and increase'. After six weeks of marriage he could safely say that, if asked to choose again, 'her we would yet choose for wife before all other'. Henry was star-struck by Ferdinand, and it showed in the florid letters he began to send his father-in-law. The latter gruffly told him not to be so wordy, but to show his love in deeds. He also sent horse-mad Henry three magnificent horses – a Spanish jennet, a Sicilian and a Neapolitan – which, according to Catherine, 'he had asked me to beg your highness for'. If Henry had any doubts about Spanish matters, Ferdinand added, he could always negotiate directly with a personal representative who should be given 'all faith and credence, as if they were myself'. That representative would be easy to locate. She was his wife, Catherine.

19 Party Queen

Greenwich Palace. July 1509

'Our time is ever passed in continual feasts,' Catherine wrote to her father from Greenwich Palace, one of her many new homes, five weeks after her marriage. The partying that started with the duke of Buckingham riding into Westminster Hall on his courser was still going on. It would continue, to a greater or lesser extent, for much of the early period that Catherine was at her ebullient new husband's side. Splendour was a virtue, young Henry thought, and pleasure was a king's privilege. He began as he meant them to continue. The coronation feast, the chronicler Edward Hall said, was 'more honourable than [that of] the great Caesar'. Such was the variety and quantity of English dishes and food from 'beyond the sea' that, he apologised, it was beyond his powers to describe them. The quality of food may be explained by the appearance of 'Pero, French cook' in Henry's payments book – helping set a trend whereby later Tudor nobles could often boast of having 'musical-headed Frenchmen and strangers' as chefs.

Catherine, however, cannot have had much conversation at her coronation feast. There were only three people at the royal table. Henry sat in the middle with Catherine and the archbishop of Canterbury two yards away from him on either side. Two or more of her ladies appear to have sat, ready to serve her discreetly, at her feet 'under the table . . . and there continued, during that long and royal feast'. They may have occasionally held a large linen cloth around Catherine so that she could 'spit or do otherwise' without being seen. The newly crowned queen gazed out upon a vast, echoing hall full of noisy guests, scuttling servants, shouting heralds and trumpeters blasting out fanfares. There was ceremonial theatre to see, too. After the second course arrived another knight rode into the hall on a courser, 'armed at all points' with his helmet sprouting a plume of ostrich feathers. 'Sir knight, from whence come you and what is your pretence?' a herald cried out. 'Sir, the place I come from is not material,' came the reply. The knight's own herald then explained that this was Sir Robert Dimmock, the king's hereditary champion. 'If there be any person, of what estate or degree so-ever he be, that will say or prove that King Henry the Eighth is not the rightful inheritor and king of this realm, I Sir Robert Dimmock, here his Champion, offer my glove, to fight,' he proclaimed. Dimmock, horse and herald then wandered round the hall throwing down his gauntlet and daring anyone who thought Catherine had not married the true king of England to accept the challenge. Not surprisingly, no one took it up. At the end of the meal Henry and Catherine washed and walked off under their canopies to their chambers.

Catherine's place at the heart of this chivalric wonderland became clear when the jousting – an essential part of any major celebration for her sporting husband – began at Westminster Palace two days later. Two pageant cars had been drawn up. One boasted a fountain, set against a castle whose battlements were gilded with Tudor roses and with Catherine's own symbol, the pomegranate of Granada. The walls were decorated with green and white lozenges gilded with roses, pomegranates or the initials 'H' for Henry and 'K' for Catherine (whose name the English spelt 'Kateryne'). The castle and sheaf of arrows motifs of Spain were also present. Red wine, white wine and claret gurgled from the mouths of the castle's gargoyles.

Even the bards and trappers covering the horses ridden by the 'fresh young gallants' and 'gorgeously apparelled' noblemen taking part in the tournament were decorated with roses and pomegranates. As the two teams of eight jousters paraded out in their elaborate armour, the leader of one group approached Catherine and 'declared that his knights were come to do feats of arms for the love of ladies, wherefore he besought her grace to license those knights to prove themselves' against the others. 'The which request to them granted, the jousts began,' Hall noted. Catherine's role as the first lady of English chivalry was confirmed. Jousting and tournaments were a form of mock warfare. Her implicit role, therefore, was that of the lady for whom these men were ready to suffer death in battle. Over the two-day tournament the knights constantly dedicated their exploits to Catherine and her ladies. On the second day a new pageant car with a hunting park as its theme was drawn up before Catherine. Gates in it were opened to release live deer. 'Greyhounds were let slip and killed the deer,' Hall recorded. 'The which deer, so killed, were presented to the queen and the ladies.' The knights became so overheated in their enthusiasm for the fight that Henry imposed a limit on the number of blows they could strike on one another. The two sides, apparently now fighting a group tourney with swords, eventually had to be forcibly separated – 'which was not done without great pain'.

This constant partying was not just the flighty, royal excess of a teenage king. It was policy. Henry had called together his council at the Tower of London in the days after his father's death. They debated whether he 'should be brought up in worldly knowledge, or else in pleasure and liberty, leaving the care to his council'. The decision (as recalled many years later by one of those present) was to 'bring him up in all pleasure, for otherwise he should grow too hard among his subjects as the king his father did; and that agreement was kept'. Henry, in other words, should enjoy himself. Others would deal with the daily drudge of running the country, interpreting and carrying out his wishes. This did not prevent him from overseeing the grand designs of policy, but it did mean he could devote large parts of the day to – as one description of his activities during a summer progress in 1511 put it – 'shooting, singing, dancing, wrestling, casting of the bar, playing at the recorders, flute and virginals, and in setting of songs [and] making of ballads and . . . jousts and tourneys. The rest of the time was spent in hunting, hawking and shooting.' Tennis, star-gazing, gambling, dressing-up and other forms of revelry and tomfoolery should also be added to the list. The musically gifted Henry, in one of his most famous ballads, enumerates his pleasures like this:

> Pastime with good company
> I love, and shall until I die . . .
> Hunt, sing and dance, my heart is set
> All goodly sport to my comfort, who shall me let?

'Youth must have some dalliance,' Henry added in the same popular ballad, 'Pastime with Good Company', which he wrote in the early years of his marriage to Catherine. She must have heard it sung often. If idleness is a vice, her husband argued, then time spent in 'mirth and play' is virtuous – as long as it is done in the right company.

The company he attracted, however, was not always virtuous. At one stage, professional gamblers – Frenchmen and Lombards brought in 'by certain crafty persons' who found him an easy touch – had to be barred from court. They were, perhaps, men like Peter Roy, Peter le Negro and Bartholomew Costopolegrino who, when caught cheating at cards and dice in the English port of Calais claimed, in their own defence, to 'have played in the company of . . . [many noblemen] in England'. Henry's wife, though, was extremely virtuous company. There was also plenty of youth left in the twenty-three-year-old queen, if not quite as much as in her husband – who turned eighteen a few days after their coronation. Neither lacked time for dalliance. Where his father had fretted over the minutiae of the royal accounts,

Henry admitted that he even found the business of letter-writing 'somewhat tedious and painful'. He would read through his own correspondence during mass – which must have perplexed the more intensely religious Catherine. In her mother's chapel punishments were meted out to those who were untidy or inattentive or giggled during mass. Queen Isabel paid such close attention that she even jotted down her chaplains' mistakes when pronouncing their Latin and corrected them later. Her father, too, was a man who rarely took his eye off the detail of government. Ferdinand held daily audiences to hear 'all the matters and causes of this realm . . . be they of never so little substance'.

Catherine was expected to play her part in the king's pleasures. She and her husband were quite different in character. Where he was all fun-loving ebullience, she was good-humouredly serious. Fortunately she also shared many of his interests. From hunting to music, from their outwardly pious religious orthodoxy to their views on foreign affairs, they were more than compatible. Both were well read and well educated by humanist teachers. She could sew his shirts, but also discuss how to make war on France. He could spend all day hunting in the saddle. She was the daughter of a woman who employed 450 staff to keep her hunting estates ready and whose father took 120 falconers out on a single day's hunt. Her father even ignored those who worried about his health, preferring an early grave with hunting to a dull old age without it. Catherine herself liked to hunt with hawks – something that Henry also eventually came to enjoy.

The newly-weds matched, too, in bed. Henry had none of the sexual problems attributed to his brother – at least, not yet. The court went to bed late, often after midnight. A night-time procession padded its way with certain regularity from Henry's chambers to her bedchamber door. Henry, in his nightgown and, possibly, his russet satin or black velvet night-bonnet, followed his torch-bearing grooms down the spiral staircase of the canted tower on the corner of the Richmond donjon or through the courtyard galleries or corridors that connected their quarters at Greenwich and elsewhere. Nor, they soon discovered, did she have trouble conceiving. In the early, accident-prone days of Catherine's pregnancies, the spaces between them were as little as two months apart. Mirth and joy, then, were abundant. Love, indeed, seems to have blossomed beyond the artificial, if playful, norms of chivalric romance. 'Her highness is very healthy, and the most beautiful creature in the world, with the greatest gaiety and contentment that ever was,' Fray Diego, who remained firmly at her side, reported. 'The king my lord adores her, and her highness him.' Juan Vinyol, a Spaniard who travelled to the English court with one of Ferdinand's ambassadors the year after her marriage, recalled later (in evidence given to the Zaragoza divorce hearing) that 'King Henry loved the queen his wife greatly . . . stating publicly in French that his highness was happy because he was owner of such a beautiful angel and that he had found himself a flower.' They were, in short, a happy couple.

They celebrated that Christmas at Richmond where, once again, there were jousts in early January. Until now, Henry had held off participating. His councillors were worried that, given the mad enthusiasm with which he threw himself into his practice (by tilting at a ring), he might get badly hurt. He struggled, however, to rein in his passion. At Richmond he finally entered the jousts with his friend William Compton. Both gave false names and, hidden under his armour, Henry's identity remained a secret. An admiring crowd watched him shatter lance after lance on his opponents' armour. A good jouster was a man who could aim and support his lance firmly enough for it to unseat his opponent or, if not, shatter itself when it struck. Henry was amongst the best. His cover was blown, however, when Compton was seriously injured and looked as though he might die. Someone who knew the secret cried out 'God save the king!'

Henry was forced to reveal himself in order to assure the crowd that he was not the injured man. From this moment onwards Henry threw himself into jousting with wild abandon. This was entertainment not just for the king, but also for the people. The papal nuncio made a wildly exaggerated estimate of fifty thousand people at one tournament later in the reign in which Henry professed himself ready to take on all comers. The king and one of his favourite opponents, Charles Brandon, 'bore themselves so bravely that the spectators fancied themselves witnessing a joust between Hector and Achilles', the nuncio, Francesco Chieregato, wrote on that occasion. 'They began to joust, and continued this sport for three hours, to the constant sound of the trumpets and drums, the king excelling all the others, shivering many lances and unhorsing one of his opponents: so that the show was most beautiful,' said one foreign witness at another later joust. Henry's favourite pastime was genuinely dangerous. Catherine nearly became a sporting widow in 1524 after Henry suffered one of his more serious jousting accidents when he left his visor up on a new suit of armour.

When the court moved back to Westminster the new couple were still at play. One morning Catherine was sitting in her chambers with her ladies when a dozen outlaws carrying swords, bows and arrows burst in. The outlaws wore short, hooded coats of coarse green Kentish Kendal woollen cloth. They looked as if they could have come out of Sherwood Forest with Robin Hood at their head. That, indeed, was the impression they meant to give. This was an elaborate prank by Henry and the boisterous young nobles who were closest to him (for whom Robin Hood was a legendary hero). Catherine either was, or knew how to look, suitably surprised. She was 'abashed, as well [much] for the strange sight, as also for their sudden coming'. That did not , however, prevent her from throwing an impromptu party – with 'certain dances and pastime made'.

On almost a monthly basis through 1510 Catherine found herself presiding, at her husband's side, over major celebrations – be they jousts, tourneys, foot combats, running at the ring, entertainment for ambassadors, torch-light processions or May Day frolics. On one occasion she and her ladies were taken to the royal park at Greenwich to watch Henry and his men practise their axe-fighting, with the young king taking on a giant German called Gyot.

The latest Spanish envoy, Luis Caroz, noted in May that Henry 'amuses himself almost every day with running the ring, and with jousts and tournaments on foot'. The foot tournaments, in which two men threw lances with blunt iron heads at each other and then, separated by a barrier, exchanged blows with two-handed swords, were being held twice weekly. 'The best of them is the king himself, who is the liveliest and most assiduous participant,' said Caroz. Keeping up with the royal couple's party lifestyle was, he complained, enormously expensive for an ambassador. It was expensive, too, for Henry – who was already emptying the coffers so painstakingly built up by his father.

To Catherine, raised in an austere Castilian court given to occasional bouts of dramatic showing-off, the continual and lavish exuberance was a considerable change. After her miserable years of widowhood she was now able to spend and enjoy without a thought for tomorrow. Already in her first two months of marriage Henry had set aside £1,000 to pay off her debts, £200 for pocket money and another £860 for her impoverished Spanish staff. There were payments, too, for jewels, a palfrey to ride and her own, newly appointed wardrobe staff – presumably based, together with many of her new clothes, at Baynard's Castle. The orders of crimson and damask cloth of gold from a Spanish merchant and of silks and satins may also have been destined for Catherine's use.

By November the partying had paled in importance beside

some truly enormous news. Catherine was pregnant. A lucky star shone over the couple's head. Ferdinand sent congratulations from Spain. He noted how important the pregnancy seemed to her, Henry and England – and begged her to take special care of herself. 'With the first child it is requisite for women to take more care of themselves than in subsequent pregnancies,' he said. She should 'avoid all exertion'. He urged her, especially, not to indulge in the apparently draining activity of 'writing with your own hand'. Henry was beside himself with joy. He soon ordered up, for his 'most dearest wife, the queen', the materials needed to dress 'the cradle of estate within our nursery'. Over Christmas and the New Year the child voices of the royal choir sang 'Gloria in Excelsis', Catherine's own minstrels played and a Lord of Misrule oversaw the court's fun at Richmond.

Only two events spoiled Catherine's first year of marriage. She began to suspect that, however delighted her husband was with her, Henry had a wandering eye. One of her court favourites was the duke of Buckingham's sister, Elizabeth – a member of the wealthiest family in the land. A piece of court gossip turned nasty when both Elizabeth and the ever-proud duke became concerned about another sister, Anne, who was deemed to be carrying on a 'love intrigue' with Henry's jousting friend William Compton. It was said, however, that Compton was simply a front for the king, who was the man really involved. Anne, however, was married to someone else. The duke angrily confronted Compton and a furious king then leapt to his friend's defence. Buckingham stormed out of the palace and did not come back for several days. The wayward Anne was banished by her husband to a convent sixty miles away. An angry Henry then ejected the other sister, Catherine's favourite Elizabeth, from the palace and began to complain about Catherine's friends. 'Believing that there were other women [who] . . . go about the palace insidiously spying out every unwatched moment in order to tell the queen [stories], the king would have liked to turn them all out, only that it appeared too great a scandal,' Caroz claimed. Henry, in turn, discovered that his usually submissive bride was not a person to cross. 'Afterwards, almost all the court knew that the queen had been vexed with the king, and the king with her, and thus this storm went on between them,' said Caroz. Catherine knew that men, especially kings, strayed sexually but this was no protection against the stabs of jealousy that she felt. Adultery often occurred in the grey area where the game of courtly love – a respectable pastime, even for the already married – gave way to sexual temptation. Catherine must surely have hoped, however, that it would not rear its head so early in her marriage – especially when things were going so well. Her anger blazes through the documents of the time. 'She by no means conceals her ill-will toward Compton, and the king is very sorry for it,' said Caroz. Unlike her sister Juana, however, she mostly knew how to dissimulate, if not actually restrain, her natural jealousy. She was, in this, her mother's daughter.

The other blow to the happy start of her new marriage came on the last morning of January 1510. Catherine miscarried. Her self-appointed gatekeeper, Fray Diego, claimed that the miscarriage occurred 'without any other pain except that one knee pained her the night before'. There was then some confusion – aided considerably by Catherine's ignorance about how her own body worked – over whether she remained pregnant with a twin sibling. The royal physician, the friar explained, had then 'said that her highness remained pregnant of another child, and it was believed'. Both Catherine and Henry were desperate to crown their happiness with a child and heir – though the evidence that she might still be bearing one was slight. It may, in fact, have been their own enthusiasm and insistence – particularly, one suspects, that of the overwhelmingly optimistic Henry – that encouraged the doctor to misdiagnose. Even when Catherine began, however irregularly, to menstruate once more they still clung to the belief that she was pregnant. Caroz was amazed at the resultant shambles, with Catherine formally going into confinement at Greenwich to prepare for childbirth.

'Someone had told me that five months after the pregnancy was made public she was menstruating and, even though this occurs in a few pregnant women, these are so few that I was worried things were going wrong,' he said. Catherine's stop-start menstrual cycle, helped by her irregular eating habits, made things worse. Caroz suspected that, between them all, the young couple and the friar were clueless about human biology. 'After this thing that they call a miscarriage and after believing that she was still really pregnant with another child, God willed it that some time later the queen stopped menstruating and her stomach started to swell and they were then certain she was pregnant,' Caroz said. Her periods then returned once more and the swelling disappeared. Catherine's phantom pregnancy seems to have been provoked by wishful thinking and a perfectionist's desire always to do the right thing. 'She had desired to gladden the king and the people with a prince,' said the envoy.

With his reference to 'this thing they call a miscarriage', Caroz left open the idea that this was a phantom pregnancy from the beginning. That, surely, would have been taking things too far. The whole affair is made murkier, however, by the fact that Catherine finally wrote to her father in May claiming that she had only just miscarried. This was a straightforward lie – as Caroz and the friar's secret letters to Ferdinand reveal. It is a lie that takes the virtuous shine off the pure and pious Catherine of history (and which Spanish archivists, anxious to protect her reputation, at first hid from the Victorian historians who looked through Ferdinand's papers). 'It seems as though exceedingly few, if any, of the men and women who were mixed up with the public affairs of three or four hundred years ago can bear much close examination without their characters being more or less lowered in our estimation,' sniffed the historian Gustav Bergenroth after finally being shown the letters in 1868. 'Of this', he declared, Catherine had just furnished him 'with new evidence'.

It was, however, a white lie – designed to avoid the embarrassment of having to admit their mistakes. She and Henry had fretted about how to explain away a non-existent, but very public, pregnancy. A large amount of court ritual had accompanied Catherine's disappearance into confinement at Greenwich. The potential for looking idiotic was huge. In March 1510 Henry had even ordered red cloth, ribbon, gilt nails, hooks, linen and Holland cloth to dress the special silver baptismal font sent from Canterbury. Catherine was so distraught by their ignorant mistake, in fact, that she refused to re-emerge in public until the end of May. The font was sent back unused. Her feelings of guilt are apparent in her letter to Ferdinand. She begs him 'not to be upset' with her, 'for it was God's doing'. Would Ferdinand, himself a master of political deceit, really have cared about this kind of fib? He might even have admired her for it. It does reveal, however, a Catherine who was prepared to abandon the truth when it suited her.

It is possible that Catherine's fake pregnancy was a result of an infection. There can be no doubt, however, that – just as her daughter Mary did years later – Catherine also displayed some of the classic psychological and physiological traits that accompany what is now called pseudocyesis, but is generally known as a phantom pregnancy. It is a condition that, five centuries later, doctors are still unable to explain. Her womb certainly swelled without a child inside – to an extent 'never seen in a pregnant woman', according to Fray Diego. The accompanying traits often include irregular menstruation, strange eating habits (both of which Catherine had shown at varying times) and an intense desire to be pregnant. The latter was also true in the case of Catherine, a woman of powerful emotional intensity for whom an heir would be the ultimate gift to her husband and to England.

Her fears that the false pregnancy would provoke ridicule or gossip were well-founded. Rumours soon began to circulate that she was actually incapable of conceiving. The gossip, however, came to an abrupt end. By the end of May 1510, just to add to the confusion, she really was in the early stages of pregnancy – and probably had been since just before she went into confinement. What Catherine willed had finally come true. It was the perfect end to her first full year of married life.

20 An Heir

Richmond. December 1510

All the men had gone. Catherine would not see a single one of them for weeks. Only women now existed in the semi-secret, cocooned world of the royal birthing chamber. Not even her husband Henry would dare come through the door until a child was born – if that was what God willed. The rituals of childbirth required that things be this way.

Catherine had last seen a male face when she was ceremonially delivered to her door at the palace in Richmond after a special communion service preparing her to 'take her chamber'. All the official male roles – 'butlers, panters, sewers, kervers, cup bearers' – were now temporarily in the hands of women. Anything Catherine needed was to be left at 'the great chamber door, and the women officers to receive it'. The rule handed down in the 'Royal Book' was clear. 'No man after to come in,' it stated. Childbirth was the realm of midwives and other female attendants. The men could do nothing except pray that the mysterious goings-on behind the closed doors produced a healthy child.

Catherine's chamber had been transformed into a soft, warm chrysalis hung all over with tapestries, carpets and curtains. 'That chamber must be hanged . . . with rich cloth of Arras, roof, sides, and windows and all, except one window, whereby she must have light when it pleaseth her.' These were not meant to be too loud or elaborate as the visual overload was 'not convenient about Women in such case'. To complete the all-enveloping sensation of snug cosiness, the floor 'must be laid with carpets over and over'.

The focal point of this chamber was a queen-sized 'royal bed'. This was big enough for an entire family, measuring just over eight by eight feet. Special confinement counterpanes for the bed, one of 'rich purple tissue' and the other of 'crimson cloth of tissue', were found later amongst Catherine's goods. Both were 'furred with powdered ermine' and came with matching head pieces to cover the pillows. They were amongst the many treasures of childbirth that she hoarded away. The bed was where Catherine, possibly with one or more of her closer companions flopped beside her, could relax and sleep as she awaited childbirth.

A magnificent cradle, five and a half feet long, stood nearby. This 'cradle of estate' was built for a future king and, presumably, was where the baby could be displayed to visitors. A smaller cradle, just over three feet long, seems to have been set aside for the more mundane business of sleep. Amongst the treasures Catherine stored away in later years were a cradle's tester canopy, its long red and blue sarcenet curtains and a baby's counterpane of crimson velvet with yellow cloth of gold.

This time Catherine was being especially careful. The sadness and embarrassment over their 'lost' twins had been easily erased by their delight that the real thing was finally happening but she did not want to run unnecessary risks. Catherine's false, or semi-false, double pregnancy had at least provided a dry-run for the rituals of confinement and the preparations for birth. It also, however, exposed the couple's deep-seated anxiety. Over the summer Henry set out on a traditional progress around the south of England, wandering between country houses. Catherine stayed behind at Henry's childhood home in Eltham for part of the summer, however, carefully protecting the child now growing in her womb.

In the late autumn of 1510 the court moved to Richmond. Catherine's chambers here were on the first floor of the royal lodgings in the impressive, grey-walled main block, or donjon, rebuilt by her father-in-law. They looked south over a walled and galleried privy garden and, beyond that, the gently flowing River Thames.

When she went into labour on New Year's Eve Catherine had to choose between her royal bed and a separate 'pallet bed'. The latter, in this case, was not the usual straw-stuffed mattress but a luxuriously large and soft combination of wool and down mattress set under a crimson satin sparver, or tester canopy, in the same room. Three such pallet mattresses encased in Brussels cloth were later found in Catherine's personal wardrobe store at Baynard's Castle in London. Each was filled with feathers or down and, at around ten by eight feet, left plenty of room not just for a queen in labour but also for anyone else who may have been called in to help.

Catherine probably wore one of the two double petticoats or the three smocks of 'fine Holland cloth' decorated around the collar in gold or silk that were also kept in her wardrobe for 'whatte time she laye in child bedde'. A round mantle of crimson velvet furred with ermine was at hand to keep her both warm and regal.

A midwife was there to help and could expect handsome reward for a successful birth. Bandages or swaddling pads of linen and wool, known as 'roullers', were kept to hand for the moment of birth. Other experienced women were, if not in the chamber, then close at hand. These included Elizabeth Denton, the future child's Lady Governor who had looked after Henry as a young boy. There was also a well-born wet nurse called Elizabeth Poyntz – who was daughter-in-law to Catherine's vice-chamberlain and whose own husband already earned the considerable sum of around £1,000 a year. There was little the midwife could do to diminish the pain. There were no guarantees, either, of success. Whatever happened would be God's will. The Girdle of Our Lady, a relic held at Westminster Abbey that brought fortune in childbirth (and which Catherine later loaned to her pregnant sister-in-law Margaret Tudor, queen of Scotland), may also have been in the room. The rest was up to Catherine. The harsh realities and risks of childbirth were already accounted for. The 'rich font of Canterbury' had been sent back again by the prior of Christ Church, and clergymen put on standby, in case a sickly baby's soul had to be saved by a quick baptism. Representatives of the 'gossippes', or godparents, were also at Richmond. Catherine herself was also at considerable risk. Mothers by no means always survived childbirth. This she knew only too well after the deaths of her sister Isabel and mother-in-law Elizabeth of York. Henry knew all this, too, and set the gentlemen of his chapel 'praying for the queen's good deliverance'.

This, however, was the moment Catherine had been waiting for. From her earliest days she had been told that her appointed destiny was to bring England and Spain together through marriage and blood. The guarantee of all those laboriously crafted and bitterly discussed treaties – and of her own future – lay in her womb. As the year turned from 1510 to 1511 and the court prepared for New Year's Day, she laboured to bring the whole business to fruition. By 1.30 a.m. it was all done. Catherine had a son. England had an heir.

21 Motherhood

First came the hermit, trotting towards her on his horse, his face
and body partially hidden beneath a long, russet-coloured cape.
Then came the two pilgrims, dressed in black, wearing wide-
brimmed palmers' hats and bearing wooden Jacob's staffs. The
scallop shells on their cloaks were, Catherine saw, a sign that
they were on their way along the route of St James to the Spanish city of Santiago de Compostela. Now, though, they came to
pay homage to the wife of a king and the mother of a prince.

Catherine's status had never been so high. She was in the full-
ness of life. Her fecundity was not just a source of private satisfaction, but of public rejoicing. Bonfires blazed and wine flowed
in the streets of London when news of the birth reached the
capital. Cannons roared from the Tower of London, using up
more than two hundred pounds of gunpowder. Her husband
was beside himself with happiness. Henry set off on a pilgrimage of thanksgiving to the Shrine of Our Lady at Walsingham
in Norfolk, and sent Catherine two does as a present.

The new mother still had to be churched to purify her from
the stains of childbirth. A veiled Catherine would have knelt at
the chapel door waiting for a priest to take her in so that she
could give thanks to God for seeing her safely through the pain
and danger of childbirth. With the churching done, Catherine
and Henry left the baby behind and moved on to Westminster.
There, as Henry would, he organised a joust in his wife's honour.
It was no ordinary joust.

Contemporaries considered it the most extravagant and theatrical tournament ever seen in England. The 'exceeding cost'

made it the third most expensive spectacle of Henry's long reign, after his father's funeral and the deluge of ostentation that would later be known as the Field of Cloth of Gold. The hermit in the cape and the two pilgrims were characters in what was becoming the increasingly elaborate theatre of the joust. When the hermit threw off his cape to reveal a magnificent suit of armour, he turned out to be none less than Charles Brandon. He was one of the great English jousters of the time – along with Nicholas Carew, Sir Thomas Knyvet and Henry himself. (Brandon later married Henry's wilful sister, Mary.) The pilgrims, too, were jousters in disguise. One bore a surname that, for the moment, would have meant little to Catherine. He was Sir Thomas Boleyn, the father of two daughters called Mary and Anne.

A special gallery was built for Catherine and her ladies at the Westminster tiltyard. On 13 February the show began with a huge, heavy pageant being wheeled before them. This was one of the most ingenious pageants yet devised. It was 'made like a forest with rocks, hills and dales, with diverse sundry trees, flowers, hawthorns, fern and grass, with six foresters standing within the same forest, garnished in coats and hoods of green velvet. A gold castle rose from the centre, with a gentleman at the gate making a garland of roses.' The twenty-six-by-sixteen-foot pageant, drawn by a silver antelope and a golden lion, came to a halt in front of Catherine. The foresters blew their horns, the pageant device opened up 'on all sides' and out rode four armoured, spear-bearing knights with plumes of feathers rising from their helmets. Henry led the way. The words embroidered on his gold basse skirt and his horse's trapper were a public profession of love. Henry was *'Cure loial'*, Catherine's 'Loyal Heart'. Should anyone doubt exactly who the object of his affections was, Catherine's letter 'K' was embroidered all over his pavilion.

The day's jousting has been preserved for posterity in the Westminster Tournament Roll, which shows Catherine and her ladies watching from a temporary grandstand as 'Loyall' Henry, his horse's trapper decorated with gold hearts and 'K's, shatters a lance on a fellow competitor. John Blanke, a black trumpeter employed by both Henry and his father, is shown helping to blast out the fanfares. Henry's fellow knights also paid homage, the embroidery on their costumes expressing the joy that Catherine – who had been presented with a garland of six dozen silk roses – now spread almost wherever she went. They were *Bonespoir*, *Bon voloire* and *Valiaunt desire* – 'Good Hope', 'Good Will' and 'Valiant Desire'. A fifth knight called himself '*Joyous panser*', or 'Happy Thoughts'. Valiant Desire (the jousting champion Sir Thomas Knyvet) covered his costume with hundreds of gold pieces, one of which, suggestively, adorned his codpiece. The score-check for the tournament shows that Valiant Desire won the day, with Catherine awarding him the prize for 'best doer'. Horse-mad Henry ran twenty-five courses, far more than anyone else, and finished the day off with a virtuoso performance for his queen, pushing his mount through a series of acrobatic turns with much 'leaping, turning and exceeding flinging'. As a final trick he got the animal to beat its hooves against the wooden partition that ran down the length of the tiltyard to separate the riders. It sounded like 'the shot of the guns'. This he followed with a 'lowly obeisance' to Catherine before leaving the field and later being spotted in her tent 'kissing . . . her in a most loving manner'.

The celebrations did not end there. The joust merged, after evensong, into an evening of banqueting and entertainment. In the White Hall of Westminster Palace – with a crowd of ordinary Londoners looking on – there was singing and dancing. Henry slipped away and then, to the sound of fifteen trumpets, another bucolic pageant, covered in 'H's and 'K's, was wheeled in. A curtain (a newfangled pageant invention and precursor to the stage curtains of modern theatre) was pulled away to reveal Henry and his jousting friends wearing purple satin outfits also covered with the royal couple's letters made of 'fine gold in bullion'. Musicians and six ladies also appeared and, couple by couple, they descended and started to dance. The watchers became so excited by the goings-on that 'the rude people ran to the pageant, and rent, tore and spoiled' it. Two of the men in charge of it had 'their heads broken' during the scrap. Henry then inflamed the crowd further by encouraging the servants of the visiting ambassadors to tear the gold letters off his and the dancers' clothes. The onlookers took this as the go-ahead for a general free-for-all. They 'ran to the king and stripped him into his hose and doublet'. They then turned on the rest of the dancers. Knyvet sought refuge on a stage but was stripped almost bare, his codpiece gold presumably disappearing. As the over-excited mob began tearing at the ladies' clothes, the king's guard ran in and pushed them back. It must have been both chaotic and frightening for Catherine, her ladies or anyone else who got caught in the middle of the furore. The king, however, laughed it all off and the partying continued. The mob went home happy, having pockcted 225 ounces of gold. One sailor managed to pocket seven gold 'H's and 'K's which he later sold to a goldsmith for £3 9s 8d – a small fortune for a working man.

Catherine was not expected to see much of her newborn child. Four days after his birth he was taken off along a path strewn with rushes to the chapel of the Observant Friars against the garden wall at Richmond to be christened with the name of his father and grandfather, Henry. His mother, who had not yet been churched, could not attend. A procession of nobles bearing his gifts – including a weighty golden cup and salt from his French godfather, Louis XII – brought baby Henry back to her. When Catherine left for Westminster he was left with Elizabeth Poyntz and his other carers and staff. These were meant to include four 'rockers' for his cradle. The princeling had his own yeomen and grooms whose tasks included 'to see the [wet] nurse's meat and drink be ever assayed [tested, presumably for poison] while she giveth the child sucke'. A physician was also meant to 'stand over her every meal'.

While Catherine partied and received the adoration of her husband, these women did the work of looking after her child. Tragically that work soon came to an abrupt end. Just over a week after the celebrations at Westminster, little prince Henry died. He did not reach his ninth week of life. Catherine knew that infant deaths were common, but that did not make it any easier to bear. 'The queen, like a natural woman, made much lamentation,' said Hall. Henry hid his grief 'to comfort the queen', though Hall said this was no easy matter. Catherine, distraught, had lost her son. England had lost its heir.

22 Bedroom Politics

Westminster Abbey. Late February 1511

Three barges, dressed in black cloth, brought the funeral party downriver from Richmond at the end of February. The infant's body lay in its diminutive hearse at Westminster Abbey as the royal choristers sang and 974 pounds of wax candles flickered and melted around it. The tiny prince was finally laid to rest. Catherine's dream of uniting England and Spain through blood was, temporarily, buried with him. Henry might have hidden his pain from Catherine, but he was so upset by the reversal in his fortunes that one ambassador was advised not to offer his condolences 'as it would only revive the king's grief'. Catherine, however, was young and obviously fertile. He was even younger. They had plenty of time to make a new heir.

The intimacy between them was not broken by the baby's death. It may, indeed, have been heightened by the shared experience of tragedy. In Henry's eyes, Catherine's role was, anyway, by no means confined to that of royal childbearer. She was also, in effect, one of his most influential (if unofficial) advisers, as well as being the conduit to one of the most powerful men in Europe. Catherine remained her father's ambassador for most of her first year as queen. Even after a new envoy arrived, Ferdinand still used her as a way of communicating directly with Henry.

The young king, a man intent on war, considered himself fortunate. As soon as he came to power, the would-be warrior prince made it perfectly clear that his ambition was to attack France. He insulted Louis XII's envoys in public and when someone in his council wrote a conciliatory letter of friendship to him, Henry was furious. He knew, however, that it would be foolish to go it alone. Ferdinand was the key. Whenever Henry called his grooms and ordered them to take him to the queen's bedchamber, he was heading not just for his wife's bed but for his chief ally. His later relationships with women would become, to say the least, complex. As a younger man, however, he allowed himself to be swayed by those women he was closest to. Some would say, indeed, that he listened to them too much.

Catherine's position was ambiguous. Her father wrote soon after her marriage telling her that Spain and England now had 'identical' interests. This was not true. Ferdinand was, at least temporarily, then allied with France and always looked after himself first. Henry, however, was young and naïve. His father-in-law was a crusading, Moor-conquering legend, part of the romance that united him to Catherine. She naturally wanted their interests to be identical. The idea, after all, fitted perfectly with the meaning of her marriage and her life. Both chose to believe Ferdinand. It would take them time to realise their mistake.

The Spanish king was, by now, also taking Catherine seriously. The daughter who he once abandoned to her luck was now his voice whispering in the ear of the English crown. He pledged to keep her punctually informed of events in Venice, one of the key scenarios of European politics. Venice was a major Mediterranean maritime and trading power that controlled a swathe of Italy, where wars raged almost continuously. It was also gaining a reputation as one of the great centres of high culture on the continent. Henry, meanwhile, fell into line behind his father-in-law in puppyish fashion. He wrote gushing letters to Ferdinand, swearing to behave like a dutiful son.

Catherine began to receive instructions from her father, who empowered her to arrange a secret bilateral alliance with England. His letters were full of paternal advice to the young couple on the devious realities of statesmanship. She was to tell Henry to keep their ever closer alliance secret from France. 'Secrecy and circumspection are best for carrying out great enterprises,' he warned. Deception was also necessary. Henry, he advised, should feign friendship with the French king until he was ready for war 'to stop the French king doing something which, if he wishes to show his enmity later, could prejudice everyone'. They were to use 'secret messengers' to build a broad European alliance against France that would include the Emperor Maximilian. Spies, he warned, could intercept Henry's mail, so she must tell him to stop writing openly about his intentions. Delicate information should be sent by Catherine, in the codes that she had now mastered. Ferdinand himself would do the same and write in open letters only 'what the French should see'. In the meantime, they should forget fears of a French attack and rest easy about the security of England. 'While I live, the French will never dare do such a thing,' he boasted.

Catherine did, indeed, help negotiate a treaty. Ferdinand acknowledged receipt of it in a letter at the end of 1509. 'We received your letters . . . and with them the treaties that you sent,' he said. These may have been early drafts of a treaty signed the following year.

If Henry was champing at the bit for war, his council slowed him down. In March 1510 he followed his father-in-law's advice and signed a treaty of friendship with France. Politics and childbirth had, anyway, crossed paths again. Catherine's first pregnancy was heading towards its inglorious end. His councillors, some of whom were considered 'Frenchmen at heart' by suspicious Spaniards, told him it was too dangerous for the king to go to war without an heir. He should wait until he had a son.

With Catherine in confinement, the weight of negotiating a formal Spanish alliance with Henry fell on Ferdinand's latest envoy, Luis Caroz (who arrived some time between January and

May 1510). This should have been easy but, as Caroz observed, the playful king 'does not much like to occupy himself with business'. Catherine and her father, however, had prepared the ground well. When Caroz finally put it to Henry that it was time to sign the alliance, the young king reacted with 'great joy' and visible 'emotion' at being able 'to serve' Ferdinand. Henry did not like the detail of business, so he ordered his council to get on with it.

This was done by the end of May, but Henry somehow did not find the time or inclination to ratify it personally until November. By then Ferdinand had fallen out with France again. A French army was reported to be marching towards Italy and Ferdinand was beginning to get anxious that he would soon be embroiled in a war against France. It was one thing for Henry to feign friendship with the French king. It was quite another for him to fail to turn against France at the decisive moment. Catherine, once more, was the key. 'Should the king of England be disinclined to undertake anything to prevent the tyranny of France, then try to get the queen of England to persuade him,' he commanded Caroz. If Catherine was against war then he was to turn to Fray Diego and 'through him, get her to persuade the king'. Even then, another year passed before Henry signed up to war with France.

In the meantime, Ferdinand had mentioned a word that thrilled both Catherine and Henry to the bone: 'Africa'. That is where he wanted to take his war against the Moors – crossing the mouth of the Mediterranean to do battle on African soil. He had already had a few minor successes there, which the hot-headed and romantic English exaggerated wildly to themselves. 'The king and queen rejoice at the good tidings they have received respecting the victory in Africa,' Caroz wrote. They imagined he would soon conquer 'the whole of Africa'. Henry was so excited that he partially underwrote an expedition by

Lord Darcy, who set off for southern Spain with a thousand archers to help Ferdinand in his 'noble voyage with a great army against the Moors and Infidels, enemies of Christ's faith'. Henry's enthusiasm was such that he considered leading the expedition himself. When the archers got there, however, Ferdinand was nowhere to be seen. His African war had been postponed. The English troops did not behave well, getting drunk, molesting girls and killing some of the locals. The fiasco cost Henry £1,000. 'Thus the king's money goeth away in every corner,' commented one observer. It was a first sign that Henry's boyish enthusiasm could easily fall foul of Ferdinand's more devious mind.

Africa, however, was just a teaser for Henry's great dream of attacking France. Henry and Ferdinand eventually agreed to invade Aquitaine ('which province belongs by right to the king of England') together in the spring of 1512. Henry sent six thousand troops to Spain to join six thousand Spaniards in an attack over the French border.

This expedition, however, also turned into an expensive shambles. Henry sent his troops to wait at the Spanish border town of Fuenterrabia but Ferdinand then diverted his part of the army to carry out a surprise conquest of neighbouring Navarre. The poorly led, surly English troops missed some essential home comforts. 'The greatest lack of victuals here is of beer,' observed John Stile, Henry's ambassador to Ferdinand, 'for the hot wines doth harm them and the cider doth cast them in disease and sickness.' They eventually became mutinous and, once again, began fighting with the locals. With no sign of a Spanish army to back them, they forced their commanders to take them home. The Spanish king had tricked Henry, using his army to lull the Navarrese into thinking they were in no danger. Once there, he went no further. Aquitaine had never really been his target. Navarre was a major prize which allowed Ferdinand to set out the frontiers of modern-day Spain. To Henry and Catherine's undoubted embarrassment, however, the English had proved indisciplined and their commanders weak-willed. They had not just been tricked. Henry had also been humiliated before his father-in-law.

Ferdinand blamed the English for the failure to attack France. A young clergyman from Ipswich named Thomas Wolsey, who was starting a meteoric career in Henry's service, offered a different view. The fiasco was the fault of 'the king of Aragon's slackness', he said. Stile, watching Ferdinand close up, had also seen through him. 'By his policy and long drifts he attaineth many things to other men's pains,' he remarked.

Catherine began to feel the unaccustomed stirrings of rebellion against her own father. This was not the way it was meant to be and anger began to build slowly as she, too, woke up to Ferdinand's game. If she had to choose between a duplicitous father and an enthusiastic, naïve and humiliated husband, then she was clear about where her loyalties lay. In September 1512 she wrote a stirring letter to the English ambassador in Rome boasting that her husband had vowed to destroy 'the schismatic French king' even if Ferdinand abandoned him. Catherine may no longer have been working for her father – despite his instructions to his envoys to seek direct meetings with her – but she was still working against part of her husband's council by pushing Henry towards war. 'The king wants war, the council does not, the queen does,' a Venetian observed.

'The king says that in the spring he will attack the French,' another Venetian reported. 'The queen is very warm for this undertaking.' More than just warm for it, Catherine became positively hot for war. She also became actively involved in preparing for it. Like her mother, she was interested in the logistics of warfare. She shared her husband's passion for the navy (he had presumably named one of his largest new ships, the *Peter*

Pomegranate, after the pomegranate symbol she had adopted) and was worried about some of the vessels that were beginning to appear in the French fleet. Catherine 'wants four large galleasses [swift, well-armed, three-masters with both sails and up to seventy oars], and two wide, round-sterned "bastard" galleys [for transport] from the Signory [of Venice],' reported the Venetian envoy Andrea Badoer. 'She wants the Signory to send one, having heard that France is building two bastard galleys,' he added.

Henry liked to visit his new ships almost daily. Their launches were an opportunity to show off England's growing naval prowess to visitors and ambassadors. When the new fleet went to sea looking to harry the French in April 1513, the admiral Sir Edward Howard wrote from the *Mary Rose* to Wolsey: 'Sir, I pray you, recommend me to the queen's noble grace; and I know well I need not pray her to pray for our good speed.' Her prayers, in this case, did not work. Howard, who had jousted before Catherine after her coronation, died later that month as he tried to fight his way back out of a French ship that he had boarded. Other jousting stars who had been amongst Catherine's chivalrous loyal hearts, including Sir Thomas Knyvet, also died at sea as the country warmed up for an invasion of France that summer.

Henry was still delighted with his warlike wife, however. A Spanish delegation who met the couple in Winchester in 1512 saw him openly praising his wife and making a show of his love for her. 'He embraced her and kissed her in public, treating her with care and affection,' one member of the delegation, Hernan López, recalled later. 'All the nobles who were present, both bishops and knights, were amazed at the great love that the king professed towards the queen.' Another Spanish visitor, Juan de Lanuza, delivered a letter to Catherine from her father and found Henry positively bawdy in his adoration. 'When she saw that the letter came from her father she placed it between her dress and her breast,' Lanuza recalled years later. 'When the king of England saw that the letter was hidden by her breast, he said that he felt jealous of the letter, because it was in her breast.' Henry, by now in full red-blooded mode, even invited Lanuza to take a good look at the queen 'just to see how *bella* and beautiful she was'. Henry's gift to his wife over the Christmas and New Year holiday at the start of 1513 was 'a pair of great pots gilt' weighing 575 ounces. The goldsmith who worked on them, William Holland, complained he would go out of business if he had to devote himself continually to such a time-consuming task.

Ferdinand still sent his envoys to talk directly to Catherine but the honeymoon with Spain was coming to an end. Her father's behaviour was forcing Catherine to acknowledge that the interests of England and Spain were not the same. She was England's queen. If that meant she could no longer be a good daughter of Spain, then so be it. It was a decision the English soon came to value. For this was the year when Catherine proved just how well she loved, and could defend, her adopted country.

23 War

Dover. 30 June 1513

This, at last, was war. Catherine set out from Greenwich, with her husband and six hundred archers dressed in long, white, wide-sleeved gabardine coats and caps, on 15 June 1513. They travelled in small stages south towards Dover. There in the castle overlooking the sea, Catherine was formally appointed Queen Governor of the Realm. As soon as her husband set sail for the English port of Calais, from where he was finally to launch his campaign against the French, she was to rule in his place or, rather, in his name.

Catherine now became 'Regent and Governess of England, Wales and Ireland, during our absence . . . for the preservation of the Catholic religion, and recovery of our rights . . . and to issue warrants under her sign manual . . . for payment of such sums as she may require from our treasury.' She could raise armies, appoint sheriffs, approve most church appointments and spend money exactly as she wished. Henry declared that he was leaving the English people in the care of a woman whose 'honour, excellence, prudence, forethought and faithfulness' could not be doubted. They, in turn, were instructed to obey her every command. A small council was left behind to advise her.

With power now in her hands, it was time to say goodbye. Catherine and her ladies 'made such sorrow for the departing of their lords and husbands, that it was great dolor [pain] to behold'. Most of the army was already across the other side of the Channel. An armour-clad Henry reached Calais on 30 June, his large fleet filling the English Channel. He was greeted with so many salvoes of gunfire that, one observer said, it sounded as though the world was coming to an end. Henry had equipped himself with a dozen huge cannons, known as 'the twelve apostles'. 'They have as much artillery as would suffice for the taking of hell,' said one Venetian.

Catherine had pressed for war, but she was still worried that her glory-seeking husband would behave recklessly, placing himself in unnecessary danger. Shortly after he had sailed she wrote (using her by now fluent English) to his almoner, Thomas Wolsey, anxiously begging for weekly letters to reassure her that her hot-headed husband was safe.

Master Almoner, thinking that the king's departure from Calais shall cause that I shall not so often hear from his grace [Henry] for the great business in his journey that every day he shall have, I send now my servant to bring me . . . word of the King, and he shall tarry there until another cometh and this way I shall hear every week . . . write to me of the king's health and what he entendeth to do, for when ye be so near our enemies I shall be never in rest.

Some English clergymen had preached against war. She, however, wanted Henry to know that he still had her backing – especially since the pope had turned it into a holy war by joining the attack on Louis XII of France. Henry had been wanting war long before Louis fell out with the pope and threatened to call a schismatic General Council of the church to replace him. In her own mind, however, Catherine turned this excuse into the main reason for the war. It had been 'the cause of the church', she now claimed, that inspired them to invade France. The pope, for both Henry and Catherine, was the ultimate arbiter of right and wrong. Neither yet showed the slightest interest in challenging his authority.

Her letters now reveal exactly how far her personal allegiances had shifted. Agreements to attack France had been signed by Henry, the pope and Emperor Maximilian a few months before her husband set sail. Ferdinand's ambassador in London had pledged that he would join them. While his envoy in England was busy arranging for a two-pronged attack on France, however, Ferdinand signed a peace treaty with the French king. This he claimed to have done because 'while out hunting he caught a severe and highly dangerous cold which attacked the chest and brought on a fever'. With his life in danger, his confessor had 'pressed him to conclude the year's truce'. Or so he claimed. Then he tried to pin the blame on Henry, claiming that he had failed to keep a promise to pay him for joining the war. 'The king of England . . . neither gives help in the form of men or in money, nor does he offer to,' he complained. Henry had had enough. There had been 'a promise on your part to attack the French', he told Ferdinand, begging him as 'a good father' not to break his word. The Spanish king's fickleness soon became the talking point of London and Paris. 'When Henry was informed of Ferdinand's truce with Louis he fell into the most violent rage,' reported the Florentine ambassador in France.

Catherine's anger against her father also grew. This was the third time in a row that he had failed her husband. 'I trust to God that the king shall come home shortly with as great a victory as any prince in the world; and this I pray God send him without need of any other prince,' she wrote to Wolsey. The 'any other' was clearly a reference to her own father. Her loyalty was now to one man, her husband, and to one country, England.

Governing England in Henry's absence now occupied her days. There were felons to be pardoned, prebends, canons and bailiffs to be appointed, lands and annuities to be handed out, the estates of the recently deceased countess of Somerset to be dealt with and a long-running administrative spat between the archbishop of Canterbury and the bishop of Winchester to be resolved. She also, from a distance, dealt with the affairs of Calais, in Henry's rearguard. Letters, patents, grants and writs now carried *'teste Katerina Anglie Regina'* ('witnessed by

Catherine, Queen of England') rather than the '*Teste me ipso*' ('I have witnessed this') of Henry. She signed them 'Katherine [or Katherina] the Qwene'.

The queen regent continued to fret about her husband's safety. When Henry besieged the French town of Thérouanne, she wrote again to Wolsey saying that she had been severely 'troubled to hear [how] so near the king was to the siege'. She was 'very glad to hear so well the king passeth his dangerous passage' and wanted him, in the future, to 'avoid all manner of dangers'. She again begged Wolsey for a constant flow of letters to reassure her about Henry as she was 'without comfort or pleasure unless I hear from [you]'. The king's welfare, she said, was above everything else. If anything terrible happened, she warned, 'I can see no manner [of] good thing shall fall after it'. She also wrote to her former sister-in-law Margaret of Austria, who was now regent of the Netherlands, begging her to send a doctor to be at hand for her husband.

Catherine felt safer once Margaret's father, the Emperor Maximilian – basically serving as a paid mercenary but still a far more experienced fighter than Henry – appeared at the scene of battle. Her hope now, she told Wolsey, was that 'with his good counsel, his grace [Henry] shall not adventure himself so much as I was afraid of before'.

While Henry was enjoying his 'adventures' in France, Catherine soon had a more serious challenge of her own to deal with. Trouble was brewing on the borders with Scotland. She was, in fact, about to fight her own war. It would prove to be a far more bloody and serious affair than her husband's campaign. Some sort of reaction from the Scots – who were French allies – had been expected. Catherine almost seems to have welcomed it. In mid-August 1513 she wrote light-heartedly to Wolsey asking him to tell Henry that 'all his subjects be very glad, I thank God, to be busy with the Scots, for they take it for [a] pastime'. For someone so obviously enjoying the role of regent, the 'pastime' of war seemed to add to the fun. Catherine, after all, was her mother's daughter.

The powers Henry had passed to her as regent 'to fight and wage war against any of our enemies in our absence' were clear. These included:

full power to convoke and bring together, when it seems necessary and opportune to the queen, each and every one of our subjects who are most suitable and capable of defending and protecting our kingdom of England . . . to arm and equip them for war and to station, prepare and lead them.

She had, in fact, started preparing in July, as soon as news reached her that James IV of Scotland was mustering a large army. Early in August she demanded to know why the mayor and sheriffs of Gloucester had not responded to her letters asking how many men and horses they could supply. 'News from the Borders show that the king of Scots means war,' she said. There was no time for dallying. She ordered them to answer within fifteen days.

James IV's herald was, by then, already on his way to France to challenge Henry directly. French money had helped persuade the Scottish king that the time was ripe for war. So had an appeal to his chivalry from the French queen, who sent James her glove and turquoise ring, asked him to be her champion and promised to send fourteen thousand French crowns. The Scottish herald appeared at Henry's camp on 11 August and delivered his master's message, telling the English king that 'immediately you should return home'. He was sent back to Scotland with Henry's angry response ringing in his ears. 'It becometh ill a Scot to summon a king of England,' he said. Henry was confident that his wife and the earl of Surrey, who had stayed behind to watch the Scots, could see him off. 'Tell your master that I mistrust not so the realm of England but he shall have enough to do whensoever he beginneth,' he said. 'I provided for him right well, and that shall he well know.'

Catherine was not intimidated. She relished the challenge coming her way and had thrown herself fully into organising England's defence. 'My heart is very good to it,' she said excitedly in a letter to Wolsey signed nine days before James led his army of up to thirty thousand men across the River Tweed. One of his first actions was to attack and take Norham Castle, belonging to the bishop of Durham. The previous year, in one of her fits of enthusiasm for war, she had boasted that her husband 'would conquer and annihilate the kingdom of Scotland, according to the fashion in which the Catholic king [her father, Ferdinand] treated the king of Navarre'. Now it was up to her to mete out the promised treatment.

She was well prepared. Catherine had been busy and not just, as she coyly told Wolsey, 'making standards, banners and badges'. She sent ten thousand pounds, a considerable sum of money, north to be guarded (and, presumably, used for war expenses) by the Abbot of St Mary, near York. She also sent artillery, gunners and a fleet of eight ships, including the *Mary Rose*, which carried additional troops, towards the Scottish border. Grain, pipes of beer, rope, cables and suits of light armour were also shipped north. For her first line of defence she would rely on the earl of Surrey and the troops he was raising in the northern counties, together with those that had arrived by sea.

James had a large army, however, backed by some recently delivered and formidable modern French artillery. Catherine worried that he might defeat Surrey and break through, so she ordered a second army to be raised from across a swathe of counties from Nottinghamshire to Staffordshire, Rutland and Lincolnshire. Troops might also be needed from neighbouring shires, she warned, though these could only be raised 'subject to the commands of Queen Katharine, Regent'. Documents were drawn up, meanwhile, to declare Scotsmen living in England to be 'enemies'. They would 'have their goods seized and their persons banished under penalty of their lives'.

With all her attention concentrated on the Scots, Catherine was annoyed when Henry – flush from his minor triumphs in France – decided to send her one of his more illustrious captives, the duke of Longueville. She had better things to do than entertain a senior French noble. 'It shall be a great encumbrance to me,' she complained. Catherine was, anyway, about to set off northwards towards the Scottish threat herself. The duke and six others with him would just have to stay in the Tower of London for a few weeks, 'specially the Scots being so busy as they now be, and I looking for my departing every hour'. Perhaps, she suggested to Wolsey, those so busy in France – where campaigning included the odd break when Henry entertained his allies with his dancing and playing of the lute, gitteron pipe and cornet – might pray to God 'to send us as good luck against the Scots as the king hath there'.

In early September she wrote to the Great Wardrobe (the central store of royal clothing and equipment behind Baynard's Castle in London) demanding delivery of banners, standards and pennants for those who would march north with her. These included two 'standards of the lion crowned imperial according to my lord's [Henry's] standards and pattern'. If she was going to become personally involved in the war, however, she wanted her own symbols to hand, so she also asked for 'two banners with the arms . . . of England and Spain', along with banners bearing the cross of St George and images of the Virgin Mary, the Holy Trinity and St George himself. A herald and a pursuivant, dressed up in the coats of arms of England, were also to travel with her. It would be the herald's job to deliver any formal battle challenges or other messages she might care to send the Scottish king. Finally, so she might display a suitable amount of magnificence, six trumpeters with their trumpet banners were to accompany her and one hundred small pennons, or *penselles*, were needed 'to be set upon carriages'.

Catherine began to move north with a body of troops variously described as 'a great power' or a 'numerous force'. At this time she also ordered up a golden 'headpiece with crown', and had both a light sallet helmet and a rounded, broad-brimmed shapewe helmet (rather like an armoured sun hat) especially garnished – presumably with gold or jewels. There is no record of her being seen in armour, but there are ordnance records for guns which went 'northward with the queen's grace'. Catherine appears, in other words, to have been organising a third line of defence, with herself in command – or to have been heading north to join the army in the Midlands. That does not mean she was preparing to go, like Joan of Arc, into battle. She had field commanders for that. Her mother Isabel, however, had once set off to make war against the Moors without her husband. Catherine saw no reason why she should not do the same against the Scots. 'Our queen also took the field against the Scots with a numerous force one hundred miles from here,' reported a London-based Venetian who had obviously taken Catherine to his heart.

News of Catherine's exploits spread across Europe and into her native Spain, picking up colour as they travelled. Peter Martyr, in Valladolid, heard this version of her feats:

Queen Catherine, in imitation of her mother Isabel and imbued by the spirit of her father . . . made a splendid oration to the English captains, told them to be ready to defend their territory, that the Lord smiled upon those who stood in defence of their own, and they should remember English courage excelled that of all other nations.

England, she warned, 'was surrounded by enemies and, worse still, neighbours, who wanted to destroy it, trying to oppress us against all rights and justice'.

War, however, was not without its human moments. The king of Scotland was Catherine's brother-in-law. He had married Henry's eldest sister Margaret ten years earlier. Catherine herself sent the Girdle of Our Lady from Westminster Abbey to her when she was in confinement waiting to give birth. While Catherine remained childless, Margaret and her infant son James were first in line to the English throne. A pregnant Margaret, apparently racked by nightmarish visions of her husband falling off a precipice or her losing an eye, was said to have begged him not to invade England. He supposedly treated her warning as the stuff of dreams. 'It is no dream that ye are to fight a mighty people,' she said, according to the story as it was told more than a century later. Margaret knew those people well, and many of her childhood friends were on the other side. 'What a folly, what a blindness is it to make this war yours and to quench the fire in your neighbour's house of France to kindle and burn up your own in Scotland,' she warned.

Should the letters of the queen of France – a woman twice married (the first half in adultery, the last almost incest) whom ye did never nor shall ever see – prove more powerful with you than the cries of your little son and mine, than the tears, complaints [and] curses of the orphans and widows which ye are to make?

This version of the story, which may well be apocryphal, suggests that if the two sisters-in-law had been left to sort it out there might not have been any bloodshed. 'If ye will go suffer me to accompany you,' Margaret begged him.

It may be my countrymen prove more kind towards me than they will to you, and for my sake yield unto peace. I hear the queen my sister [Catherine] will be with the army in her husband's absence; if we shall meet, who knows what God by our means may bring to pass.

Catherine and Margaret never had the chance to talk sisterly peace in the dramatic fashion imagined later. Shortly after

Catherine had set out north, James IV's army was routed at Flodden Field, near the Northumberland village of Branxton. A battle that started out as a close-run thing turned into a devastating slaughter by Surrey's men. James fought to the death. It was one of the epic defeats of Scottish history, wiping out much of the country's nobility. It had been Catherine's stirring speech, Peter Martyr heard, that brought the English victory. 'Fired by these words, the nobles marched against the Scots . . . and defeated, humiliated and massacred them,' he said.

In fact, Catherine was nowhere near Flodden. She was still in Buckingham when news of the victory reached her. Surrey sent her part of the Scottish king's coat of armour as a trophy. She wrote a triumphant letter to Henry. 'This battle hath been to your grace and all your realm the greatest honour that could be, and more than ye should win all the crown of France,' she said. 'Your grace shall see how I can keep my promise, sending you for your banners a king's coat.' A gleeful and somewhat bloodthirsty Catherine had originally wanted to send more than just James's coat of armour. She would have liked to send his body (which had been suitably 'bowelled, embalmed and cered') as well. In this, it seems, she misjudged her adopted country because, she discovered, 'our Englishmen's hearts would not suffer it'.

She also sent Henry a document taken off a Scot showing 'such things as the French king sent to the said king of Scots to make war against you'. There was nothing squeamish about the way she expressed her joy at James's death. 'To me it is . . . the greatest honour that ever [a] prince had; [for] his subjects in his absence not only to have victory but also to slay the king and many of his noblemen,' she told Wolsey. She also nudged him towards reminding his master to give thanks to the real architect of the victory. 'This matter is so marvellous that it seemeth to be of God's doing alone. I trust the king shall remember to thank him for it.'

Catherine avoided rubbing in the fact that she had scored a greater victory than her war-hungry husband – who had won a brief cavalry battle in which the enemy ran away and had so far taken only the small the town of Thérouanne (though he would go on to get the more important town of Tournai, with its great walls, towers and bridges). Others, however, were deliciously – perhaps maliciously – aware of the irony. The Italian duke of Ferrara claimed that Catherine had written to her husband congratulating him on the victory and on his capture of the duke of Longueville but adding that 'it was no great thing for one armed man to capture another like that Frenchman he had sent, but that she was sending him three Scots who had been taken by one woman alone'.

It was not like Catherine, however, to boast quite so openly and there is no surviving letter written in such a bragging tone. The letter to her husband that does survive ends, instead, with her begging him to come home. In the meantime she would go on pilgrimage to the shrine at Walsingham. There was much to give thanks for.

24 And Peace

England and France. Autumn 1513

The island of Britain was, temporarily and for the first time, in the hands of two women. Catherine governed England as regent for her husband. It was her task to administer the victory. The newly widowed Margaret, her sister-in-law, ruled in Scotland as protector for her one-year-old son, James V. The infant king had been crowned shortly after his father's death at what, because of the tears shed for the dead left behind at Flodden, became known as the 'Mourning Coronation'.

Neither woman felt much like prolonging their war. Nor was Catherine as hard-hearted in victory as her initial jubilation might have indicated. She sent a message to Margaret, offering her consolation for a husband killed by her own soldiers. 'The queen of England, for the love she bears the queen of Scots, would gladly send a servant to comfort her,' it said. Soon one of those forthright friars of whom Catherine was so fond, Friar Langley, was on his way. Catherine's officers on the border, meanwhile, were ordered to 'advertise [advise] the queen of all occurrents [occurrences]'.

Within a fortnight of Flodden, the talk was already of a truce. Catherine's commanders in the north wrote recommending an end to the war. The bishop of Durham, despite his obvious upset over the damage to his castle at Norham, said there was little option. The weather was foul and the English army was running out of food. The captured Scottish beer, which the bishop said had been drunk 'by our folks to their great refreshing', had presumably run out. Punitive raids into Scotland to burn crops, steal sheep and harry farmers were being hampered by the rain.

Many of the remaining Scottish nobles, however, were hankering for revenge and Catherine was asked to decide whether troops should be permanently billeted at certain points near the border. The situation was by no means stable and war could have flared again at any time. Langley acted as an intermediary in the negotiations for a truce that was not finally signed until the following February.

Henry also did his bit to improve relations by begging the pope for permission to bury James IV at St Paul's, even though the latter had been excommunicated for breaking a papally sanctioned treaty of non-aggression with England. Scotland, left semi-barren of men, had its own problems. Royal proclamations had to be issued preventing looting and the molesting of women and children. The rape of widows and maidens was to be punishable by death and there was special mention of the ten thousand or more families of the Flodden dead whose 'wives are widows and desolate and their daughters maidens being heirs to them'.

Catherine oversaw the unwinding of the war machine, paying soldiers' and sailors' wages and signing off on the costs of artillery, shipping and transport. Even while at Walsingham, where she would have walked the last mile to the Virgin Mary's shrine barefoot, she still had to oversee the day-to-day running of a country where domestic worries began to take precedence. The plague, for example, was killing three or four hundred Londoners a day.

Catherine was probably the last queen of England to gaze upon the Walsingham shrine. England's 'new Nazareth' had been one of the country's main pilgrimage sites since the eleventh century. Here people had their sight miraculously restored while lunatics, lepers and those pursued by wicked spirits were all cured, or so the balladeers sang. Even the dead were raised again. Henry, like any self-respecting religious Englishman, loved it. He had just, in fact, had the windows glazed. 'When you look in you would say it is the abode of saints, so brilliantly does it shine on all sides with gems, gold and silver,' wrote Erasmus after he visited the shrine that same year. 'Our Lady stands in the dark at the right side of the altar . . . a little image, remarkable neither for its size, material or workmanship.' Destruction, however, awaited. Walsingham's future, like that of the English church itself, was intrinsically linked with Catherine's own later life.

Shortly after he pitched camp outside the walls of Tournai, news had reached Henry of the Flodden victory. The English army lit 'great fires' to celebrate. A special mass, with Henry's choristers – who had made the trip with him – singing a *Te Deum*, was celebrated in a luxurious pavilion tent of gold and purple. A few days later the prize of James IV's royal coat arrived. Henry was overjoyed.

Tournai fell, just as Thérouanne had a month earlier. That was enough for Henry. He only had three relatively modest victories under his belt, but the young king had blooded himself as a warrior. The campaigning season was now over. On 21 October, after three weeks of feasting, revels and celebratory tournaments, he sailed from Calais to Dover. He rushed eagerly home to Catherine, riding 'in post' to Richmond 'where was such a loving meeting that every creature rejoiced'. They were back together again, this time as a pair of young conquerors. There had been rumours that she was pregnant and had lost a child while Henry was away. Now was a good time to start again. A little more than six months later she was pregnant again.

Henry came home from his campaign a wiser man. Huge amounts of money had also been spent but his fellow princes now knew that he was capable of mounting military campaigns on mainland Europe. He fully intended to start again the following summer but knew he should never fully trust Catherine's father again. The latter had been genuinely ill, but was now wringing all he could out of what remained of his life, madly chasing stags through the woods. 'His appearance has changed, he does not have the same ease in listening, he does not have the same mildness,' explained Peter Martyr. 'Three things prevent him recovering his strength: his age, for he is in his sixty-second year; his wife' – he had married a second time, to Germaine de Foix, who was thirty-six years his junior – 'whom he never sends away from his side; and the hunting and desire to live outdoors, which keep him in the woods.' Ferdinand made a half-hearted attempt to win Henry back. A draft treaty was even signed in October in which Henry, Maximilian and Ferdinand (funded by Henry) again agreed to make war on France the following summer. None of the signatories were to make peace with France on their own. Ferdinand ratified the treaty in December. Within three weeks, however,he was already trying to strike a bargain with Louis XII of France that would benefit himself, the Emperor Maximilian and their mutual grandson, and heir, Charles Habsburg. The English, he claimed richly, could not be trusted.

The French campaign brought with it another major change. Thomas Wolsey, the man to whom Catherine wrote her letters during the campaign, emerged as Henry's right-hand man. The energetic and hard-working king's almoner had served, in effect, as a minister for war, proving himself to be a fine and loyal administrator. His ambitions, however, went much further. Although nominally an almoner, and so in charge of distributing alms for Henry, he was also a member of the king's council. He had judged Henry to perfection. 'The king was young and lusty, disposed all to mirth and pleasure and to follow his desire and appetite, not caring to toil in the busy affairs of this realm . . . He loved nothing worse than to be constrained to do anything contrary to his royal will and pleasure,' is how Wolsey's gentle-man usher, George Cavendish, summed up his master's assess-ment of Henry. While others urged him to take more interest in running his kingdom, Wolsey could see how this bored Henry. 'So busily did the almoner persuade him to the contrary: which delighted him much and caused him to have greater affection and love for the almoner,' Cavendish wrote. The almoner offered to take care of things, relieving Henry of the tedium of day-to-day rule. The young king was overjoyed. He could hunt, party, make music and plot wars without worrying about the annoy-ing details and 'troublesome business' of government. 'Who was now in high favour, but Master Almoner?' asked Cavendish. 'And who ruled all under the king, but Master Almoner?' Wol-sey's dizzying ascent saw him catapulted through the ranks of the church. In less than a year he would rise from being a mere dean to archbishop of York. In two years he was a cardinal. The chronicler Edward Hall in his entry for this, the fifth, year of Henry's reign observed that 'this man was born in Ipswich, and was a good philosopher, very eloquent and full of wit, but for pride, covetous[ness] and ambition he excelled all others, as you shall hear'. Or, as Cavendish himself put it: 'Fortune smiled so upon him, but to what end she brought him you shall hear after. Therefore let all men to whom fortune extends her grace, not trust too much to her fickle favour.' As Wolsey's influence grew, the power of the other key people around Henry diminished. That included Catherine. She could not know it, but this was a man whose actions would shape much of the rest of her life.

Catherine, her regency over, returned to her duties as queen consort. Amongst other things, she began to help prepare the wedding of Henry's seventeen-year-old sister, Mary Tudor. The headstrong Mary was engaged to marry Catherine's young nephew, fourteen-year-old Charles. He was the finest catch in Europe. As Juana la Loca's son, he was grandson and heir to both Ferdinand and the Emperor Maximilian. Impressed by her own future status, Mary sighed occasionally over the portrait of the youthful Charles that she now carried with her. They were due to marry at Calais by mid-May. There were wedding gowns and a rich trousseau to be fussed over. It was Catherine's task, too, to choose both a 'lady mistress' and the other ladies who would go with Mary to Flanders. There was nothing remarkable about Catherine shifting her attention so quickly from wars to weddings. They were, after all, two sides of the same coin.

England remained on a war footing over the winter to the immense irritation of that crotchety Dutchman Erasmus. 'Preparations for war are quickly changing the genius of the Island. Prices are rising every day and generosity is decreasing. It is only natural, that men so frequently taxed should be so sparing in their gifts. And not long ago,' he moaned, 'in consequence of the scarcity of wine, I was nearly killed by the Stone, contracted from the wretched liquor that I was forced to drink,' apparently attributing his kidney stones to drinking low-grade beer. 'Moreover, while every island is in some degree a place of banishment, we are now confined more closely than ever by war, so that it is difficult even to get a letter sent out.'

War fever grew as men and equipment were once more sent to Calais to prepare for the next season's campaign. The dream of a grand alliance against France finally crumbled, however, as Ferdinand and Maximilian turned their backs on Henry. Young Charles, meanwhile, had already been heard to grumble that his fiancée Mary was old enough to be his mother rather than his wife. Finally, and decisively, a new pope – Leo X – was intent on patching up the Vatican's differences with France. This removed the most important pretext under which Henry had fought his war the previous summer.

In March 1514 Ferdinand and Maximilian agreed a year-long truce with France, promising to persuade Henry to join them. Henry at first tried to carry forward his plans, this time with the help of the Swiss. Finally, and suddenly, he changed tack. Wolsey had, in Henry's own words, 'laboured and sweated' for a deal with France. A treaty was signed. Mary would not become a princess of Castile. She would marry the decrepit, gout-ridden King Louis and become queen of France instead. Rather than sending Mary off to marry her nephew, Catherine found herself at Greenwich witnessing her proxy marriage to the French king, with the duke of Longueville standing in for Louis XII. By early October the eighteen-year-old Mary – considered 'a nymph from heaven' by one Frenchman – was already in France and properly married. The about-turn was complete. Henry had played Ferdinand at his own duplicitous game. It was not a good moment to be, like Catherine, a Spaniard. 'The Spanish ambassador never appeared at these feasts, but remained at home,' a Venetian reported. 'Going through town strange words are said to him.'

Spain was now a dirty word. Henry's anger at Catherine's father's history of trickery was such that he dreamed of violent revenge. He even tried to push France into a joint war on Spain. One of the more bizarre excuses he presented for starting a war with his father-in-law was Catherine herself. He would conquer that part of Castile which, he suddenly claimed, belonged to his wife as a daughter of the previous queen, Isabel. This was clearly absurd but it reveals just how angry he was. Any excuse would do for getting even with Ferdinand. Fortunately, from Catherine's point of view, Henry's proposals came to nothing. It was clear, however, that her beloved Spain was the new enemy.

We cannot know for certain whether Catherine would have approved of a war fought in her name against her father and, ultimately, against her elder sister, Juana la Loca. Ferdinand, after all, governed Castile in Juana's name and few ideas, one assumes, could have been more painful to her. Catherine's disgust at her father's behaviour, however, had already wrought a major change in her. She was now more English than ever. By that December, as a heavily pregnant Catherine once more went into confinement, Ferdinand's ambassador Caroz complained that she was ignoring him completely. 'The queen of England greatly requires a discreet and able person who can take care not just of her soul but also of the government of her house and person, above all so that she can best serve our own king,' he wrote to Friar Juan de Eztuniga, provincial of Aragon. 'The reason the queen is behaving so strangely is that her confessor, Friar Diego, has told her to act as though she has forgotten Spain and everything Spanish in order to win the English king's love and the love of the English. She has become so accustomed to doing this that she will not change.'

Catherine's few remaining Spanish friends had also turned rabidly pro-English, especially her beloved María de Salinas (now Lady Willoughby), who had become her closest friend. 'María de Salinas has shown herself to be our enemy,' wrote Caroz, who suspected her of plotting with the family of Catherine's old lady mistress, Elvira Manuel. 'You can see how [little] use I can make of the queen in my negotiations.'

Henry also snubbed Caroz and saved his best insults for whenever Ferdinand was mentioned. The English now treated the Spanish ambassador like a 'bull at whom everyone throws darts', he complained. 'If God does not change Henry VIII's mind, he will carry out what he intends, which is to enrage and hurt our king as much as he can,' he warned Eztuniga. It was time for Ferdinand to 'give a good yank on this colt's reins' before he got completely out of control. Caroz was so depressed that he begged Ferdinand to relieve him. A mysterious letter from Catherine, he believed, prevented that from happening.

Although Catherine was again pregnant, Italian gossips were now claiming that Henry was thinking of divorcing her in order to marry a French wife. This was nonsense, but the rumour was a reminder of two truths. Catherine had yet to produce a living heir and her task of bringing Spain and England together had resulted in failure. Catherine herself was not to blame for this but, despite her new-found Englishness and the outstanding success of her regency, observers knew that the two main purposes of her marriage remained unrealised.

Hope, however, was in sight. This pregnancy was going well. In October Henry signed a warrant to the Great Wardrobe to deliver a cradle covered with scarlet 'for the use of our nursery, God willing'. The last proviso showed that he, too, knew there was no guarantee of success in childbirth. France's Louis XII wanted to be godfather, though only if it was a son. He was ready to 'send a good and honourable personage to be there against the queen's deliverance'. By mid-November she was readying to go into confinement.

Some time in December Catherine gave birth to a boy. Tragically, however, her misfortune at childbirth continued. The baby arrived a month early and, 'to the very great grief of the court', was either stillborn or died soon after birth. When the news reached Peter Martyr in Spain, he thought he knew why this had happened. 'The queen of England has miscarried, as a result of her upset at the quarrel between her father and her husband, the pain of which provoked her to give birth prematurely,' he said. 'Her husband was upbraiding the innocent queen with the desertion of her father, and held against her his anger and complaints.' Grief, he believed, had driven her to miscarry. This was not her fault but, once more, it was failure. As her twenty-ninth birthday went by that December, the lustre was beginning to come off Catherine's previously glittering marriage.

25 Daughters

Greenwich. Christmas Day 1514

The small troop of minstrels, drummer boys, torch-bearers and masked lords and ladies made their way to the far side of the courtyard of the waterside palace at Greenwich, heading towards the queen's chambers. It was Christmas Day, but Catherine had little to celebrate. Her stillborn son had just added another dose of tragedy to the already bleak experience of childbearing. Relations between Henry and her father were at their lowest point ever, trapping Catherine in the crossfire between two men she was meant both to love and unite.

With the seasonal celebrations now under way, however, her husband was bursting with playfulness. Henry's natural ebullience could not be kept down for long and Christmas was an excuse to indulge in many of his favourite pleasures. The partying, overseen by the Lord of Misrule, traditionally stretched through to Twelfth Night. There would be music, dancing and acting. Costumes had been sewn from the hundreds of yards of satin, silk and velvet ordered up for the mummers, minstrels and choir boys. Pageants had been built and dances rehearsed. The lists of seasonal gifts – to be exchanged, as usual, on New Year's Day – were ready. This year guests from Spain, France and Germany joined the throng of people at Greenwich as the court gathered in the elegant palace stretched along the south bank of the broad River Thames.

Henry had organised a surprise Christmas Day masquerade for his wife. Dressed in a blue velvet bonnet, he led the musicians and the seven other masked lords and ladies towards her chambers. Three years earlier, after the traditional Twelfth Night banquet at court, six masked men had appeared and required the ladies to dance. This 'thing not seen afore in England' had shocked some, who refused to indulge the masked gentlemen and play a game which was considered to be in 'the manner of Italy'. Masks had become all the rage since then and the mummers now accompanying Henry to the 'rich and goodly revels' in Catherine's chambers had covered their faces and necks with yellow 'visors' of soft sarcenet. Her husband loved dressing up – whether in gold and jewels for state occasions, in rustic green May Day outfits or shiny and colourful fantasy clothes for dancing, masques and mummery. The four masked lords were wearing sleeveless cloaks 'of cloth of silver, lined with blue velvet' and great capes. Their four ladies were in matching Savoy-style gowns of blue velvet, silver cloaks and 'bonnets of burned gold'. The strapping, six-foot-one-inch Henry must have been easy to spot, despite the disguise, but Catherine was delighted.

'This strange apparel pleased much every person, and in especial the queen,' Hall reported. 'These four lords and four ladies came into the queen's chamber with great light of torches, and danced a great season, and then put off their visors, and then they were well-known, and the queen heartily thanked the king's grace for her goodly pastime, and kissed him.'

One of Catherine's own ladies, Elizabeth Blount, a cultured, poetry-reading beauty who was talented in both dancing and music, was amongst those who removed their disguises. At the Twelfth Night celebrations, this time in the great hall, a pageant was brought in bearing four lords 'dressed in purple satin embroidered with gold wreaths and letters H and K'. The lords wearing Catherine's and Henry's letters then fought a fierce mock battle before the king and queen with a group of 'wild-men, all apparelled in green moss . . . with ugly weapons and terrible visages'. Children sang, minstrels played trombone-like sackbuts, reeded shawms and stringed viols, and there was dancing before the royal couple. Henry, unusually, chose to watch the show beside his wife rather than join it. There was no public sign of the king's wandering eye, or any dimming of his love for Catherine.

The queen seems to have cheered up quickly. A few weeks later at least one of Catherine's own yeomen was involved in organising a play for Candlemas, 2 February. Visitors to the court were beginning to comment that the queen was losing her youthful looks. For one she was, quite simply, 'rather ugly than otherwise' – especially beside her good-looking husband. (Though the Spaniards who visited her two years earlier went on to claim at the hearing in Zaragoza, no doubt fired by patriotic zeal, that she was 'as beautiful as a second Helen [of Troy]'.) Henry, in any case, remained a regular visitor to her bed, and soon she was pregnant again.

Developments inside Catherine's womb provoked interest and gossip well beyond the borders of England. In March 1515 an Italian in France started telling people he would wager his life on her giving birth to a baby boy within a year. Rumours that she was pregnant again were already spreading in May and by September there were several anxious enquiries as to whether this was true. The Emperor Maximilian twice asked whether she was pregnant and, in Tournai, authorities wanted to know whether it was time to start praying for her and the child. Experience had, however, made Catherine and Henry reticent about announcing pregnancies. She must have become pregnant in May but the news does not seem to have become common knowledge until October or November.

The changing seas of European politics swirled around Catherine's life, underlining just how important the matter of offspring was. King Louis XII of France died early in January 1515. His heir, Francis I, was twenty years old. He was not just younger than Henry but similarly energetic, ambitious and given to hot-headed dreams of military heroism. Catherine's sister-in-law Mary – who was said to have danced her elderly husband to death – was suddenly free from a marriage that had lasted just twelve weeks. It must have felt like a miraculous release to the eighteen-year-old. In an act of defiant (and apparently lust-driven) self-will, she secretly married Charles Brandon, the duke of Suffolk – the man Henry had sent to bring her home. Henry eventually forgave them this gross impertinence and the 'French queen', as she became known, joined the court, lodging with Catherine on 'the queen's side'. The Tudor sisters were as impulsive and obstinate as their brother. Margaret, queen of Scots, had also put personal desire above political expedience when she married the earl of Angus the previous year – thereby losing her right to remain regent for her son. She eventually fled the country and, as one Venetian merchant in London quipped in October 1515, that now meant there were three pregnant queens in England. The confusion of queens was such that, at one stage, the chronicler Hall felt it necessary to distinguish Catherine from Henry's sisters by referring to her as 'the queen his bedfellow'.

Catherine was, by now, stepping back from the world of political power. Wolsey had crowned his dizzying ascent to the top of both the ecclesiastical and administrative trees by becoming cardinal and lord chancellor in the second half of 1515. His hard version of power, based on real control of the mechanics of government, had eclipsed her own softer version as the voice in Henry's ear. Wolsey may also have been responsible for the sudden departure of Catherine's confessor, the friar Diego, who left under a cloud, his reputation in tatters after being accused and found guilty of fornication. Diplomats knew, however, that she could still influence the king. Ambassadors often arrived with direct instructions to seek her out. A visiting Venetian delighted her by addressing her in Spanish. This 'pleased her more than I can tell you; and she commenced talking to me about Spanish affairs and about her mother, making me all possible civil speeches', he said. Catherine, dressed in 'Spanish style' and accompanied by twenty-five ladies on white palfreys, then took the Venetians off into the woods near Greenwich to watch Henry enjoy his May Day entertainments. Her husband had managed to dress himself tip-to-toe in green, even donning green shoes. The woods had been filled with bowers full of singing birds. His men were dressed in green livery, carried bows and arrows and formed a procession – complete with pasteboard giant figures on carts – that reportedly drew a crowd of twenty-five thousand people.

The Venetian, who had recently been in Paris, soon realised that both Henry's vanity and traditional sense of rivalry with France had been piqued by the arrival of the young Francis on the throne. 'His majesty came into our arbour, and addressing me in French, said, "Talk with me awhile. The king of France, is he as tall as I am?"' he reported.

I told him there was but little difference. He continued, 'Is he as stout?' I said he was not; and he then enquired, 'What sort of legs has he?' I replied 'Spare.' Whereupon he opened the front of his doublet, and placing his hand on his thigh said, 'Look here; and I have also a good calf to my leg.'

Although Catherine was barely involved in politics, she keenly followed her husband's ambitious ship-building programme to provide England with a standing navy. On 29 October 1515, Catherine helped establish the long English tradition of royal women launching navy vessels with the mighty *Princess Mary* – a huge four-master that bristled with brass and iron guns. 'A galleass, of unusual magnitude, has been launched with such a number of heavy guns that we doubt whether any fortress, however strong, could resist their fire,' commented the Venetian ambassador. The vessel, carrying up to 207 artillery pieces and powered by 120 oars, was three times the size of Venice's best galleys.

The French were so worried by the ship that Wolsey eventually told their ambassador it had not been built to attack them but simply 'to give pleasure and pastime to the queen and the queen Mary his sister'. The two queens, Henry and his council had, he admitted, all 'dined on board, and made the greatest cheer and triumph that could be devised'. In this case the launch included not just a formal dinner but also a mass on the specially grav-elled deck. Catherine's husband was so delighted with this new toy that he dressed in a gold sailor's coat, cloth-of-gold breeches and scarlet hose for the occasion. A large, jewel-encrusted gold whistle hung from a thick gold chain around his neck. This he blew 'nearly as loud as a trumpet or clarionet'. The shared pas-sion for boats soon led Henry to order the construction of what might be considered England's first royal yacht. The barque, with cabins especially panelled and furnished for the royal cou-ple, was finished in 1518 and named – in his wife's honour – the *Katherine Pleasaunce*.

Catherine's father, meanwhile, tried to win back Henry's trust. He sent exquisite presents, including a jewelled collar, two handsome horses and a valuable sword. Their relationship had suffered, Ferdinand claimed, partly because of 'the common law of all earthly things, which deteriorate in the course of time, and partly a want of clearness in earlier treaties'. Henry's anger was not so easily assuaged. His initial reaction to the appearance of a new king in France early that year had even been to enquire whether he might help out with an invasion of Castile. He had finally, however, learned a few tricks from his father-in-law and so answered him in the same, silken-tongued, Machiavellian tones that Ferdinand liked to use. He now knew that Ferdinand's 'ardent love' was 'sincere' and, so, had 'wiped from his mind' all the disagreeable things that had passed between them. While privately expressing his mistrust of Ferdinand, he also signed a treaty of 'harmony and friendship' with him in October 1515 which stated that all 'injuries, offences' and losses were to be forgotten and forgiven.

Catherine, once more, found herself mediating between the two men. She obviously felt a need to explain to Ferdinand why the English reacted in such angry and emotional ways to what, for him, was the cold and calculating game of European power politics. The national stereotypes (inverted over time), of the English as excitable and prone to wild exaggeration while the Spanish were calm, serious and cold, were again present in Catherine's explanation. 'There is no people in the world more influenced by the good or bad fortunes of their enemies,' she said. 'A small amount of the one makes them overbearing while a small amount of the other casts them down.'

Catherine had been worried about her father's failing health and had, she said, been praying for him. Her prayers came to little. Signing the treaty with England was one of the last major things he did. On 23 January 1516 he died claiming that Spain was more powerful than she had been for seven centuries 'and all, after God, because of my work'. The English ambassador noted that he died 'with no manner of treasure' and 'wilfully shortened the days of his life, always in fair weather or foul labouring in hawking and hunting, following more the counsel of his falconers than of his physicians'. His successor was Charles Habsburg, Catherine's nephew. He was about to turn sixteen, already governed in the Netherlands and would go on to control much of Germanic central Europe and be elected Holy Roman Emperor after Maximilian died three years later. A generational change was now almost complete on the greatest thrones of Europe. The complex relationships between the three young, powerful and ambitious men now ruling Europe's most important lands would dominate the coming decades – and play a significant role in Catherine's future.

News of her father's death was kept from Catherine for a week or two. She, by now, was in confinement and no one wanted such a shock to upset the long-desired coming of a healthy child. At last, in mid-February, a healthy baby girl was born. 'The queen has given birth to a lively little daughter,' Ammonius wrote to Erasmus. She was named Mary and automatically became heiress to the crown. Both parents were delighted, though there was no hiding the fact that a boy would have been considerably better. The Venetian ambassador Sebastian Giustinian wrote home saying that, had the child been a boy, he would have rushed to congratulate Henry. As it was a girl, however, he would take his time about it and wait for the day she was christened. The birth of a girl, he reported, 'has proved vexatious, for never had this entire kingdom ever so anxiously desired anything as it did a prince, it appearing to every one that the state would be safe should his majesty leave an heir male, whereas, without a prince, they are of a contrary opinion'. Giustinian then bluntly told Henry himself that Venice would have been more pleased had it been a boy. Henry's reply was both elegant and optimistic. 'We are both young. If it was a daughter this time, by the grace of God the sons will follow,' he said. England had never had a proper queen regnant. A daughter was only a partial solution to the problem of succession. The job, in other words, was only half done.

26 A Match for Mary

The Queen's Great Chamber, Greenwich. 5 October 1518

The bride-to-be sat in front of Catherine, dressed in cloth of gold, a cap of black velvet perched on her tiny head. Her rich jewellery glittered in the velvet as the priest made his oration. She felt a pair of adult arms lift her up and hold her before the cardinal. He placed a small gold ring with a large diamond beside her tiny, two-year-old's fingers. Then the admiral of France reached out his hand, took the ring and passed it down over the second knuckle of her fourth finger. Catherine, visibly pregnant once more, looked on as her daughter Mary became engaged. Previously, the queen had been asked directly if she approved of her daughter's match. 'With great pleasure, we give our royal word,' she vowed, presumably through clenched teeth.

We do not know what little Mary made of the proceedings in Catherine's great chamber at Greenwich. The earliest reports of Catherine's daughter reveal a bright and vivacious child. A few months earlier a doting Henry had shown her off to some visiting ambassadors (one of whom thought more honour was accorded her 'than to the queen herself'). She had shouted 'Priest! Priest!' at Dionysius Memo, the organist from St Mark's in Venice whose musical brilliance so enchanted both Catherine and Henry that they listened to him play for hours at a time. On this occasion, however, little Mary had forced him to play. Her parents were delighted with their girl. Ambassadors were obliged to kiss her small hand while Henry boasted: *'ista puella nunquam plorat'*. 'This girl never cries.'

Catherine performed as expected during the engagement ceremony, pledging to do her utmost to make sure that the wedding took place, but she cannot have approved of her daughter's fiancé. This was none other than the dauphin of France, who was sometimes referred to as 'the dolphin' or 'dolphyn'. One report of the ceremony at Greenwich had little Mary firmly demanding to know whether the man who passed the ring over her knuckle, Lord Bonivet, the admiral of France, was himself the dauphin. 'Are you the dauphin of France? If you are, I wish to kiss you,' she reportedly said. In fact, her fiancé Francis was even younger than Mary herself. The heir to the French throne had been born just seven months previously. Their agreed wedding date was still fourteen years away. There was nothing surprising about the arrangement to Catherine. It almost exactly mirrored her own engagement to Prince Arthur.

Henry's determination to dazzle his French visitors with royal magnificence made this one of the most brilliant celebrations of his reign, stretching over days. Wolsey, who had negotiated the peace that came with the engagement, laid on much of the entertainment for the numerous French delegation at his York House residence on the River Thames, which would later be known as Whitehall Palace. 'We sat down to a most sumptuous supper, the like of which, I fancy, was never given by Cleopatra or Caligula,' observed one guest who was amazed by the huge silver and gold vases displayed by the increasingly wealthy Cardinal Wolsey. Catherine used her advanced state of pregnancy as an excuse for retiring early, while Henry and her sister-in-law Mary led the dancing. The Tudor siblings were amongst the three dozen masqueraders who, wearing green satin hooded outfits covered with cloth of gold, entertained the French at York House. Catherine's lively and cultured maid of honour Elizabeth Blount danced with them. No one would have noticed, but she, too, was probably pregnant by now – with Henry's child. Their affair seems to have been brief and this was her last recorded appearance at court.

Bonivet was impressed by their reception. The bill from Greenwich on 7 October shows that the party got through ten carcasses of beef, seventeen hogs, pigs and porkers, fifty-six carcasses of mutton and some five hundred chickens and capons as well as numerous swans, cranes, larks, geese, pigeons, peacocks and peachicks. They also consumed three thousand loaves of bread, three thousand pears, thirteen hundred apples, sixteen and a half gallons of cream, sixteen gallons of milk, seven gallons of curds and 367 dishes of butter. It was all washed down with three tuns and two pipes of wine and six tuns and seven hogsheads of ale – a thousand gallons of wine and almost twice as much ale. 'The ceremonial was too magnificent for description,' Bonivet wrote home.

The French admiral may, or may not, have realised that the match had a powerful enemy in Catherine. In bidding for England's alliance and her daughter's hand for his son, King Francis had an obvious rival in Catherine's new favourite – her nephew, now Charles of Spain. This contest also pitted Wolsey, usually keen to keep the peace with France, against the naturally pro-Spanish Catherine. The king's trusted adviser had won their undeclared battle this time, but Catherine had not given up.

Catherine had already shown her favouritism when, in 1517, Charles sent ambassadors to London. These were received in the queen's chamber, where the ambassador was paid 'as much honour as if he had been a sovereign, giving him amusements of every description'. These included a concert by the beloved Memo, who had been rapidly elevated to the rank of royal chaplain, 'which lasted during four consecutive hours, to the so great admiration of all the audience'. Catherine also had her ladies entertain her nephew's ambassador after one banquet when Henry took him 'into another hall where the damsels of the most serene queen were, and dancing went on there for two hours'. Her husband, as usual, joined in 'doing marvellous things, both in dancing and jumping, proving himself, as he in truth is, indefatigable'.

During the celebrations that followed Mary's engagement, a 'comedy' involving Pegasus the winged horse was enacted in front of the guests. Pegasus's rider, in a speech, explained to the guests the different symbols he had chosen for Europe's principal kings and why he had used a pomegranate tree for the king of Spain. 'To the king of Spain I have given the pomegranate, because it is round, and he in like manner is well-nigh lord of the whole world.' Earlier that year, indeed, Catherine had received a reminder of Spain's growing global presence. Exotic gifts arrived for her from the island of Hispaniola in the Caribbean – where Christopher Columbus had set up the first colony in the Americas twenty-six years earlier. They included a cloak and a chair used by an indigenous king and queen. The sender, who was her nephew Charles's treasurer general of the Indies, regretted being unable to send her a parrot as he thought it might not survive the English climate. Spain's power was growing and Charles, as Catherine would later discover for her own personal benefit, was a valuable ally for anyone who could win him over.

Something else was happening, almost imperceptibly, as Catherine came close to completing her first decade as the English queen. She was becoming popular. She spent part of the early summer of 1518 at Woodstock. On the evening of 5 July, Henry arrived home from a journey to be greeted by an exultant Catherine. 'The queen did meet with his grace at his chamber door, and showed unto him, for his welcome home, her belly something great, declaring openly that she was quick with child,' one of Henry's staff happily noted. She also visited nearby Oxford at around this time. On her entry into the city she was greeted by great demonstrations of popularity which inspired the archbishop of Canterbury to wax lyrical about how she was a shining example of all the greatest virtues of her sex.

After a decade as queen, Catherine had not lacked time to work her way into the hearts of ordinary English people. She had been their regent, sending Englishmen to death and glory in battle. She carried out her charitable duties with sufficient enthusiasm for her to be accused, later in her life, of deliberately setting about buying popularity. Catherine was a strict observer of Maundy Thursday, when she would have given alms and washed the feet of the poor. She gave away up to £200 a year, some five per cent of all her spending, in alms. Some of this, admittedly, went in meeting the duties she inherited with her lands – making regular payments to convents in Marlborough and Sheen, for example, or to the Greyfriars at Grantham. Given her own exaggerated dalliances with asceticism it is not surprising that Catherine felt drawn to England's solitary, severe and reclusive anchorites – adding at least two to her list of regular alms payments.

Presents and rewards accounted for another £1,000 or so a year – a quarter of all she spent. A further £100 went on thanking those who brought her gifts, great and small, as Catherine travelled the country. Presents, however humble, were a way to show respect and affection for the queen. No gift, it seems, was too small to accept. No one was too low to bring the queen a present. The gifts, as her late mother-in-law's accounts showed, could include such simple fare as cakes and quails or rabbits and bunches of roses. The rewards Catherine gave back allowed her, in turn, to display generosity and graciousness.

Catherine also looked after her own household in ways her mother would have approved of. She would have given away clothes and, if she followed her mother-in-law's example, copies of beautifully illuminated Books of Hours to her ladies. 'I think the prayers of a friend the most acceptable,' Catherine wrote inside one admirer's Book of Hours, 'and because I take you for one of mine . . . I pray you remember me in yours.' Not only did she pay salaries but she often helped household members obtain second incomes from her husband or gain valuable export licences for wool or ale. The steady drip of Catherine's munificence, to both friend and stranger, helped fill a growing lake of affection.

Her popularity, however, had received its most dramatic boost in May 1517 thanks to her key role in the turbulent events that came to be known as Evil May Day. In a sudden fit of xenophobia, London's apprentices rioted and turned on the capital's foreigners. Smouldering resentment at the wealth of foreign merchants had been whipped up by a preacher peddling the timeless libels suffered by successful immigrants. Foreigners scorned Londoners, he claimed. Not only did they steal their trade but they also 'took' their wives and daughters. 'From that day,' said the Venetian ambassador, Sebastian Giustinian, 'they commenced threatening the strangers that on the first of May they would cut them to pieces and sack their houses.' On the evening before May Day a mob of some two thousand men began to roam the city, attacking foreigners and closing the gates to keep troops from coming to their rescue. May Day – the day of pretty nosegays, maypoles and the kind of 'leaping and dancing' that would later make Puritans mutter about 'stinking idols' – turned into something ugly, violent and shameful. The rioters also 'overpowered the forces of the Lord Mayor and aldermen and compelled them to open the jails and release the prisoners'.

The rioting was quickly put down by Henry's nobles. The gates were forced open and the preacher, a dozen ringleaders and seventy others – some as young as thirteen – were detained. Roped together in pairs, they were led through the city to be tried. Gallows were erected. The hanging, drawing and quartering began as more than a dozen were executed. No foreigners had been killed, but the nobles set about their task as executioners with special sadism. The young rioters were 'executed in most rigorous manner', according to Hall. Their executioners 'showed no mercy but extreme cruelty to the poor younglings'. The mutilated remains of the dead rioters were left for all to see. 'At the city gates one sees nothing but gibbets and the quarters of these wretches so that it is horrible to pass near them,' reported one visitor.

Hundreds more were held in jail. Later that month, the remainder were brought before Henry as he sat on a high dais in Westminster Hall. It was a formal occasion and, along with numerous nobles and bishops, Catherine was there with both her sisters-in-law – Margaret, queen of Scots, and Mary, dowager queen of France. 'The king commanded that all the prisoners should be brought forth. Then came in the poor younglings and old false knaves, bound in ropes, all along one after another, in their shirts, and every one with a halter about his neck, to the number of four hundred men and eleven women.' Wolsey asked Henry to pardon them, but the king refused. 'Mercy!' they cried out loud, imagining they were all heading straight for the gallows.

Catherine then intervened. She dropped dramatically to her knees. Mary and Margaret, her sisters-in-law, followed suit. The three queens stayed on their knees before Henry for a long time, during which – according to one chronicler – they 'begged their pardon, which by persuasion of the Cardinal Wolsey . . . the king granted to them'. The papal nuncio, Francesco Chieregato, had no doubt about who had changed the king's mind. He reported that, with tears in her eyes and on bended knees, it was Catherine who obtained their pardon.

The prisoners cried with relief and happiness. 'It was a fine sight to see each man take the halter from his neck, and fling it into the air; and how they jumped for joy, making such signs of rejoicing as became people who had escaped from extreme peril,' observed one eyewitness. The gibbets around London were taken down, and calm returned to the city – though it would be a long time before foreigners felt safe on the streets on May Day. In all probability, this had been an elaborate piece of play-acting by Henry, Catherine and Wolsey – designed to defuse the rumbling discontent that continued in London. Ordinary Londoners, however, were not to know that. One shrewd observer decided that a 'very fine spectacle, and well arranged' had been put on for them. A huge crowd, deemed either 'innumerable' or of 'fifteen thousand', had gathered to watch the event. Catherine's standing amongst them can only have soared.

Londoners, and others, suffered badly that year and in 1518 as the sweating sickness spread through England with terrible virulence. It was as if God had sent a plague to punish them. Those Londoners (and, later, people in Oxford) who lived in infected houses were obliged to stay in, hang wisps of straw on their doors and, if they ventured out, to carry white sticks so others could keep away from them.

The generous belly with which Catherine had welcomed her husband to Woodstock in July 1518 sparked another round of prayers from great and small that this time, at last, her child would be a healthy boy. From the pope to the Venetian ambassador to the ordinary people of England, everyone hoped for a male heir. 'God grant she may give birth to a son, so that, having an heir male, the king may not be hindered from embarking, if necessary, on any great undertaking,' said the Venetian ambassador, Giustinian.

Catherine and Henry stayed away from London, fleeing the dreaded sweating sickness which, nevertheless, reached into the royal household and struck dead several pages. In November 1517 Catherine and Henry had started moving from country residence to country residence with a reduced court of just three gentlemen and their beloved Memo as they ran as far as they could from the infected areas. In the summer of 1518 both were

Catherine and Arthur were engaged before the age of four and, as young teenagers, wrote formal love letters to each other before marrying at St Paul's, London, in November 1501. They were both aged fifteen.

Parents and parents-in-law. Isabel of Castile and Ferdinand of Aragon turned Spain into a major European power, while Henry VII and Elizabeth of York finally brought an end to the Wars of the Roses between the houses of Lancaster and York. Catherine's marriage was meant to seal an alliance between the two royal families.

This portrait by Catherine's favourite court painter, Michel Sittow, was done while the young widow was still waiting to marry Henry, then Prince of Wales. Sittow also seems to have used Catherine as a model for his painting of Mary Magdalene with spectacular flowing locks.

The bust, believed to be of a very young Henry, is our best clue to the rumbustious ten-year-old child Catherine first met when she arrived to marry his brother Arthur. The portrait shows Henry at about the time of his own marriage to Catherine in 1509.

Friends and enemies. Cardinal Wolsey (top left) and Thomas Cromwell (top right) were both tasked with obtaining a divorce for Henry. Cromwell succeeded where Wolsey, who fell from grace, had failed. John Fisher, Bishop of Rochester (bottom left), bravely stood up for Catherine and paid with his life. Luis Vives (bottom right), the well-known Spanish humanist, was one of her closest friends.

An odd couple. Catherine's daughter Mary was, for a while, engaged to her powerful cousin, the Holy Roman Emperor, Charles V. She wears a badge with his title on it. Charles was Catherine's key ally as she fought the divorce from Henry.

Still together, still happy? The Latin on one of Catherine's portraits (top) refers to her as Henry's uxor, or wife, while his portrait is decorated with their joint symbol of H&K. Miniatures of Catherine and Henry by Lucas Horenbout.

Anne Boleyn won Henry's heart and eventually became his second wife. Soon after Catherine herself had died of natural causes, Boleyn was executed. She left a daughter – the future Queen Elizabeth I.

stricken by panic, with Henry especially worried once his wife was pregnant.

Catherine, in turn, refused to allow Henry to travel to London. She insisted that she was the best judge of how bad the epidemic there was and that, as one witness of their conversations reported, 'though she be no prophet, yet she would lose her finger if some inconvenient should not ensue unto the king's person if he should at this time repass towards London'. Henry was equally adamant that she should not be placed in danger. He wrote to Wolsey, telling him of the pregnancy, which was 'the chief cause why I am so loathe to repair London ward'. Too many pregnancies had already ended in disappointment and tears. Experience told him that Catherine was going through 'her dangerous times' and so 'I would remove her as little as I may now.' Both begged Wolsey, who was still at his post, to escape from London and seek the solace and protection of fresh air.

Catherine may have been afraid of the sweat, but pregnancy did not stop her pursuing her more vigorous pastimes. In July, for example, she set off without Henry for a day's hunting – presumably with her hawks – in Sir John Peachy's park. Henry himself admitted at this time that the pregnancy was not 'an ensured thing' but something of which he had 'great hope and likelihood'.

In November 1518 he, along with just about everyone else, was disappointed. A child was born, but it was another girl. As if to confirm Catherine's bad luck, the baby did not survive long. Henry's lack of a male heir played, ironically, against the French alliance which Catherine opposed. Had the birth taken place before Mary's engagement to the dauphin, Giustinian said, 'that event might not have come to pass: the sole fear of this kingdom being that it may pass into the power of the French through this marriage.' Catherine, however, was not the only woman bearing Henry's child. What would happen if her husband were to father a son, but with someone who was not his wife? That she would find out later. For the moment, however, her concern was for her daughter's future. Catherine's aim was still to unite England and Spain. Mary was now her most useful tool.

27 My Sister's Son

The Field of Cloth of Gold, Guisnes and Ardres. June 1520

Beauty was on Catherine's mind in the spring of 1520. It was not her own looks she was worried about. These, inevitably, were fading. Now in her mid-thirties, Catherine still possessed a 'very beautiful complexion' but was deemed 'not handsome'. Her younger husband cut a more dashing figure, though a Frenchman noted that he too was now getting 'a little bit fat'.

Catherine was engaged, however, in the great affairs of Europe. These occasionally required her to perform strange services for her adopted country. She was now preparing herself for one of the most extraordinary events of the time, a sumptuous seventeen-day encounter between the English and the French that would go down in history as the Field of Cloth of Gold. This was to be an elaborate display of national peacockery – a battle of ostentation and chivalry that both sides were determined to win. News had reached England that France's Queen Claude was scouring her country for beautiful maidens to accompany her to the event. Catherine was expected to recruit the cream of English beauty so that, in the words of one man for whom Englishwomen had no true rivals, Sir Richard Wingfield, Henry's ambassador, 'the visage of England, which have always had the prize' should triumph once more. Her retinue alone at the Field of Cloth of Gold – a dazzling array of luxurious pavilions, richly coloured tents and temporary wooden palaces straddling the English–French border on mainland Europe – was to number 1,175 people, with 778 horses.

While doing her bit to help England beat France in this competition of beauty and magnificence, Catherine was also busy undermining the very alliance it was supposed to strengthen. For if Henry – or, at least, Wolsey – wanted to meet King Francis, Catherine had other plans. She was desperate to see her nephew Charles, ruler by now of not just Spain, Sardinia, Sicily, Naples and the Netherlands but also of his grandfather Maximilian's lands and, to cap it all, recently elected Holy Roman Emperor.

This was not just a question of family sentimentality, even though Catherine had obviously reserved a special place in her heart for the young Charles. Both knew that a French alliance went against his, and Spain's, interests. They worked together to ambush the Field of Cloth of Gold by arranging for Charles to see Henry both before and after the meeting with Francis. Such was Catherine's determination to fight her nephew's corner that she emerged once again as a main player in English foreign policy, third only to Henry and Wolsey. As a result, Charles (and his aunt Margaret of Austria, Catherine's former sister-in-law and now regent of the Netherlands, once more, for her nephew) constantly turned to her for support. It was the beginning of a relationship that would prove of vital importance to her in the troubled years to come. The prize pushed before Charles's nose was Catherine's daughter, Mary, whose engagement to the dauphin could always be broken off so that she could marry him instead.

Catherine had not got involved in the contest between Charles and Francis to be elected emperor – but then, as the Venetian ambassador noted, Henry was already 'intrinsically . . . in favour of Spain' on that. 'The queen of England, as a Spaniard, is gratified at the success of her nephew,' he added.

Amongst those who spotted Catherine's obvious favouritism towards her nephew was the French king's feisty mother, Louise of Savoy. She put more than one English ambassador on the spot about it. Louise was particularly disturbed when Henry broke a pact between him and the dashing, youthful Francis not to shave their beards off before they met. 'I supposed it had been by the queen's desire,' the ambassador, Thomas Boleyn, explained. 'I have here afore time known when the king's grace hath worn long his beard, that the queen hath daily made him great instance, and desired him to put it off for her sake.'

'Is not the queen's grace aunt to the king of Spain?' Louise slyly enquired of Boleyn. 'Madame, he is her sister's son,' he replied. 'But the king of England has greater affection for your son than for any king living.' Louise was not convinced, but gave an elegant reply. 'Their love is not in the beards, but in the hearts,' she replied.

Louise remained suspicious that Catherine was trying to undermine the alliance that the forthcoming encounter was designed to affirm. She demanded of another English ambassador whether England's queen had 'any great devotion to the [Field of Cloth of Gold] assembly'. 'Whereunto I answered,' the ambassador said, 'I knew well that there could not be a more virtuous or wise princess anywhere than the queen my mistress was, having none other joy or comfort in this world but to do and follow all that she may think to stand with the king's pleasure.' Even he could not pretend that Catherine would be attending for any other reason than duty.

Catherine was reported, in fact, to have harangued her own council about the dangers of meeting the French king. 'There is no doubt that the French interview is against the will of the queen and of all the nobles,' one of Charles's envoys claimed. Chief amongst these was the mighty duke of Buckingham, a man who hated the low-born Wolsey with aristocratic intensity.

These reports reflect another trait in Catherine's character which endeared her to many Englishmen. She thought of France, as they did, as the enemy. Those same Englishmen were by no means all convinced that consorting with the French king was the right thing to do. 'The people here, to a man, detest the French interview,' the same, admittedly partial, envoy claimed. 'They say they are leaving their old friends for their old enemies.' More tellingly, one nobleman was overheard telling a friend: 'If I had a drop of French blood in me, I would cut myself open and get rid of it.' The response he got summed up many an Englishman's opinion on the matter. 'So would I,' said the friend.

Catherine had a tough rival in Wolsey. 'The cardinal is the man who rules both the king and the entire kingdom,' an Italian observed around this time. She was wise enough, however, to avoid confrontation. Wolsey, in any case, was not blind to the advantages of playing Europe's two great powers off against each other. Soon, indeed, he warmed to it. Henry may have been less powerful than either Francis or Charles, but his weight was enough to tilt the balance of power between the two great monarchs of continental Europe.

Catherine's campaign on her nephew's behalf paid off. A final decision was made at a meeting between Henry, Wolsey and Catherine in her chambers at Greenwich. Charles's ambassadors waited in the same room with baited breath. Finally, Henry turned and spoke to them. 'Well, I am very glad that affairs are in such good order, and I think all will go well,' he said. Then he turned back to Catherine and said: 'The emperor, my brother and your nephew, will come hither this time. I hope we shall see him before we visit the king of France; otherwise I shall be dissatisfied, although in that case I could not help it, for it is not my fault.'

'To give the emperor more time, I have written to the king of France to desire him to defer the time of our interview; but I have taken good care not to write to him the reason,' he added. 'He cannot yet know the state in which matters now stand between me and the emperor . . . the thing must be kept as secret as possible.'

Catherine was delighted. 'On this the queen, clasping her hands, and raising her eyes unto heaven, gave laud unto God . . . that she might behold her nephew, saying it was her greatest desire in the world,' Charles's envoys reported. 'So saying, she thanked the king, and made him a very low curtsey. The king, removing his bonnet, assured her that he would do all on his part that was possible.'

Henry's affectionate gallantry was proof to Catherine that she had won the day. 'You will speak to us another day,' she confidently told the ambassadors when they left her chambers.

The French, of course, eventually found out and complained. Wolsey, enjoying his role as Europe's power-broker, gave them a short reply.

To be plain with you, if the king of Castile should offer to descend at Sandwich or about those parts, as he hath done, to see and visit the king and queen, his uncle and aunt, the king being in journeying toward the sea and next thereunto, it were too marvellous ingratitude to refuse the same.

As it was, the awkward Atlantic winds meant that Catherine's nephew only just made it in time. While he sat stranded in port at La Coruña, he wrote begging Catherine to keep Henry in England until he arrived. 'We have been told of the effort and will that you have put into arranging these meetings,' he said. 'But as the sea is so changeable that men cannot always do what they want . . . we beg you, if there is some delay, that, as you have already done, you try to make our brother and uncle, the king of England, wait for as long as is possible.'

He finally landed at Dover on 26 May 1520, to what Sir Thomas More claimed was the delight of Henry, the nobles and, even, the common people. 'Great joy made the people of England to see the emperor,' agreed Hall. 'And more to see the benign manner and meekness of so high a prince'. Catherine and her husband were already heading towards the coast in order to cross the Channel for the Field of Cloth of Gold meeting but had only got as far as Canterbury. Henry immediately rode to Dover and, the next morning, brought Charles back. 'To see the queen of England, his aunt, was the intent of the emperor,' recorded Hall.

Catherine nervously awaited the nephew she had grown to love but had never met. He was greeted inside Canterbury cathedral with incense and a sprinkling of holy water by the censer-swinging archbishop and then taken to see his aunt at the archbishop's palace next door. A reception committee of 'handsome' ladies greeted him in the porch before he was taken down a corridor lined with yeoman pages in chequered gold brocade and crimson satin to the foot of the marble staircase where Catherine waited in her best regal attire. Her first glimpse of him would have been as he climbed the fifteen steps towards the landing where she stood in her ermine, cloth of gold and strings of beautiful pearls. The sight of her nephew was too much for the normally composed Catherine. 'She embraced him tenderly,' a witness recorded. Then she wept.

The pallid young man with the awkward, oversized features did not impress physically, but was mature beyond his twenty years. He was a careful, sober and clever monarch whose discreet style contrasted with the romantic flamboyance and occasional impetuousness of his two main rivals, Henry and Francis. 'A well-proportioned body, fine leg, and good arm with a somewhat aquiline nose; bright eyes, of serious aspect, but neither cruel nor severe,' was how one contemporary described Catherine's powerful young nephew.

The rest of his body cannot be criticised, except his chin and all the lower part of his face, which is so wide and long that it does not seem to properly belong to that body; rather it seems to have been stuck on in such a way that when he closes his mouth he cannot bring his upper and lower teeth together . . . This means that, when he talks, especially when finishing a phrase, he garbles the odd word, which you then cannot understand well.

But Charles also had 'much more in his head than appears in his face'.

For three days Catherine enjoyed the company of her lantern-jawed nephew. He had brought a huge retinue of Spaniards, including some two hundred ladies – deemed graceful rather than handsome by the Venetian ambassador – dressed in Spanish fashion. They must have evoked childhood memories in Catherine. She presumably spoke to her nephew in his recently acquired Spanish. He was a man who, with his vast territories bringing together so many separate parts of Europe, claimed to speak 'Spanish to God, Italian to women, French to men and German to my horse'.

Catherine's dress sense at this time tended towards the elegantly serious. She wore rich, dark fabrics of velvet and satin in black, purple, crimson, tawny or russet. At the banquets and masses she shared with her nephew, however, she wore exquisite, colourful gowns and dripped with precious jewellery. One cloth-of-gold gown – worn with a shiny silver 'lama' (similar to lamé) petticoat – was lined with violet velvet, the raised pile forming Tudor roses wrought in gold. Another petticoat was of cloth of gold with a black ground, laced with cords from which pearls and other jewels hung. Then there were the pieces of jewellery she wore: on one day a necklace of huge pearls and a valuable diamond cross below black velvet headwear powdered with jewels and pearls; then, on the following day, five strings of large pearls with a pendant made of diamonds depicting St George slaying the dragon. Charles, she was telling everyone through her clothes, was her favourite of Europe's princes – after her husband.

Her wardrobe had just been replenished, anyway, so she could impress the French. Over the previous six months dozens of yards of rich, sumptuous cloth had been ordered. There were

'13 yards of cloth of silver raised with damask gold' to make a single gown. Three yards of 'rich cloth of gold tissue', also raised with gold damask, were required to line another. That month alone there arrived more than sixteen yards of black tilsent (a costly silk, often woven through with sparkling gold or silver) decorated with Catherine wheels and a further eleven yards of black tilsent damask gold, probably for two more gowns. There had also been an order of crimson tissue 'pirled' with gold for one of the elaborately decorated V-shaped stomachers that were laced or pinned into place across her chest and stomach.

The games of courtly love played out during one four-hour banquet saw the Spanish gallants swarming around the ladies' tables in love-sick ecstasy. Some played the part so brilliantly that they 'could not have been bettered', according to a delighted Venetian witness. The count of Cabra swooned dramatically and fainted when overcome by the intoxicating powers of one lady. He had to be carried out of the banqueting chamber by his hands and feet in order to recover. That 'amorous' sexagenarian the duke of Alba led the dancing in his small tawny, tassled cap and was followed by the – now recovered – count of Cabra and his partner. Henry also danced during a party which went on until dawn. Catherine, it seems, contented herself with observing a display of Anglo-Spanish conviviality unmatched since her first wedding two decades earlier. She had good reason to feel deeply satisfied.

When the three days in Canterbury were over, they all headed for the south coast. At Dover Catherine and Henry boarded the freshly painted and gilded *Katherine Pleasaunce* for a calm, trouble-free crossing to Calais accompanied by a fleet of twenty-six ships. A specially panelled cabin had been built for Catherine with glazed windows bearing her arms and a set of 'a dozen joined stools' for her ladies and guests to perch on. Charles, meanwhile, sailed from Sandwich to his territory in nearby Flanders. Both he and Catherine knew that whatever had not been achieved at this first meeting could always be agreed on later, for they had arranged to meet again soon after the Field of Cloth of Gold.

The latter was, at least formally, centred on a tournament of jousting, tourneys and foot combats in which the 'field' was a tiltyard built on the border between the English town of Guisnes and the French town of Ardres. Here English and French knights could indulge in play combat while Catherine and France's Queen Claude watched from their specially glazed chambers. The meeting was, in many ways, a ritualistic playing out of the underlying historic conflict between the two neighbours. The codes of chivalry helped prevent any eruption of the real violence which lurked below the surface. That did not stop rumours spreading of French ambushes or mutual suspicion about whether the other side was sticking to the rules. As the concerns over the quality of national beauty showed, the contest was not just about the mock warfare in the tiltyard (where Henry and Francis sensibly teamed up together as brothers in arms to avoid confrontation, though an impromptu wrestling match between the two men turned awkward when Francis threw Henry). Magnificence was an even greater field of competition and the royal accounts show Catherine busily preparing her party in the months before the meeting.

Catherine personally oversaw the refitting of her fifty-five-strong guard of yeomen, her seven henchmen and sundry footmen, grooms, pages, littermen and chair-men who attended to her carriages, horses and litters. An early model of a green coat for her guard 'which she did not like' was rejected. When the new models were agreed on, cloth was ordered by the hundreds of yards – more than 440 yards of white satin and green velvet were needed for the yeomen's doublets and coats and there were vast quantities of rough woollen 'kersey' for their (presumably itchy) hose. Spanish 'feathers of arrows' were embroidered on the footmen's doublets. Catherine's henchmen were a riot of colour. They wore fancy orange boots, black velvet cloaks, doublets of yellow velvet, with green and russet velvet coats and soft, beret-shaped Milan caps. She had her saddles bordered with cloth of gold and silver and her 'close chair', or covered carriage, repainted. Catherine needed forty hackneys, six wagons and her own elaborately decorated litter just to move herself and her ladies around the site of the Field of Cloth of Gold.

Delicate silk and gold tapestries with intricate designs of foliage covered the walls of Catherine's chambers at the temporary wood, brick and canvas palace built at Guisnes. The oratories, one each for Catherine and Henry, were piled high with gold images, candlesticks, chalices and basins. Catherine, rather provocatively, had a large shield bearing the arms of England and Spain set in the centre of her oratory. Observers noticed, too, that she was wearing her head-dress in the 'Spanish fashion', with the tress of hair hanging down over her shoulders.

According to the plans set up in advance, Catherine's chambers were to be as big as, and connected to, Henry's. Much of the entertaining was her responsibility, so she was to have a great chamber bigger than that of the White Hall at Westminster and a second chamber bigger than any in the recently built palace at Bridewell (near Fleet Street, London). The third, and smallest, chamber still measured sixty by thirty-four feet, with a twenty-seven-foot-high ceiling. It was in these chambers that she entertained the French king, while her husband went to Ardres to dine with the French queen – whom she would meet at the jousts. These were elaborate displays not just of wealth and entertainment, but of courtesy and manners. Thus, when an open-air mass was held at the tiltyard, Catherine and Queen Claude both tried to insist that the other be the first to kiss the Gospel and, instead, ending up kissing each other. A twenty-four-foot-long firework dragon, launched by the English, sped across the sky above them – scaring some of those present. All was, at least in appearance, a great success. Peace was the subject of the sermon and the two monarchs pledged to build a chapel to Our Lady of Peace on the spot where they had met.

The Field of Cloth of Gold dazzled contemporary observers, who described it as the eighth wonder of the world. Hangers-on of all nationalities and classes had been drawn to it from miles away. Witnesses to its glory included the drunken 'vagabonds, ploughmen, labourers . . . wagoners and beggars' who, according to Hall, lay about in heaps and the 'knights and ladies' who were forced to sleep out on straw and hay.

It had been hoped that the seventeen days of sport and conviviality would produce real peace and friendship. When Charles visited his aunt Catherine and uncle Henry again at Calais and Gravelines a fortnight later, England's king did, indeed, hold out against his attempts to create a military alliance against France. For Catherine this meeting was, amongst other things, a chance to catch up with her former sister-in-law Margaret of Austria – who she had not seen since she left Spain after the death of Juan. Catherine and Margaret had two decades' worth of news to share when they finally sat down to supper together on a July night in Calais. The French looked on in concern. Anglo-French relations, despite Wolsey's best attempts, were already on a slippery slope. 'These sovereigns are not at peace,' a Venetian had already noticed. 'They hate each other cordially.' Indeed, by the summer of 1521, Mary's engagement to the dauphin of France was as good as dead. A secret treaty, hammered out by Wolsey and Margaret, was signed in Bruges that August. Soon Catherine's daughter had a new fiancé – Charles himself – bringing England together, once more, with Spain. Catherine had got what she wanted.

28 Infertility and Infidelity

Syon Monastery to Richmond. c. 1523

The boat slid across the surface of the Thames, leaving behind the riverside monastery of Syon and heading upstream the short distance to Richmond. Catherine was in a melancholy mood. The wealthy monastery, home to both nuns and priests, was known for its devotion and learning. Her visit there must have set her thinking. She was fortunate to have the brilliant Spanish humanist Juan Luis Vives with her as she travelled home. He was the one person she could turn to for intimate and intelligent conversation in her native tongue. There had been no fellow Spaniard to whom she could talk this way in the years since Fray Diego had left in disgrace. That day's conversation stuck in Vives's mind. 'I remember your mother, a most wise woman, said to me . . . that she preferred moderate and steady fortune to great ups and downs of rough and smooth,' he told her daughter Mary in a book written for her in 1524, a year after he arrived in England. 'But if she had to choose one or the other, she stated that she would elect the saddest of lots rather than the most flattering fortune, because in the midst of unhappiness consolation can be sought, whilst sound judgement often disappears from those who have the greatest prosperity.'

They were maudlin thoughts, perhaps explained by the new phase of life she had entered by the time Vives appeared in 1523. Catherine was now infertile. Her last pregnancy had been in 1518, when she had been only just in her mid-thirties, but so many failed pregnancies may have left lasting damage. She seems to have accepted her new state with equanimity, perhaps eased – given her painful experience of childbirth – by the thought that this was God's will. Catherine had borne children. God had taken all but one of them away. The confusing reports of the time seem to point to three live births and at least three stillbirths or miscarriages. The pregnancies proved that she had not shirked her responsibilities to her husband, parents or England. Her womb could no longer serve their, or her, ends. One child was left, an heiress. That was God's choice. It was also, at least in theory, enough.

Catherine's mother Isabel had been a queen regnant. This may have been rare for the age, but there was no convincing reason why her granddaughter should not also reign. It was true that England had never had a real queen regnant but, unlike in Catherine's father's kingdom of Aragon, there was no explicit rule against it. The Tudor name would be lost if Mary married. Henry's family, however, was not obsessed by its Welsh name. They preferred to cast themselves as the final and legitimate union of the rival royal families that fought the Wars of the Roses – Lancaster and York.

Catherine was an attentive mother. Like many a single child, indeed, Mary felt the weight of maternal expectation. It was certainly a close relationship, despite the long periods of time they would spend apart. The courage Mary displayed when siding with her mother in the face of danger later on in life shows a relationship strong enough to survive not just separation but also persecution.

Mary's education was one of Catherine's chief concerns from the start. She herself set about teaching her daughter the basics of Latin and delighted in Mary's precocious skills in dancing and, as a musician, at the keyboard of a spinet or plucking a lute.

Catherine had not forgotten her own humanist education in Spain and she turned to Vives for advice on educating her daughter. Vives came from a family that had been persecuted by the Inquisition and which may have practised crypto-

Judaism. He himself was a serious, thinking Christian, devoted both to religion and education. Catherine commissioned from him a groundbreaking and popular book called *The Education of a Christian Woman* which helped pave the way for the newly cultured women of later in the century. Although it contained its fair share of old-fashioned prejudices, Vives's book broke moulds by urging that girls be educated in more than just domestic skills and dancing. 'If the mother knows literature, she should teach her children when they are small,' Vives advised. 'As for her daughters, in addition to letters, she will instruct them in the skills proper to their sex: how to work wool, and flax, to spin, to weave, to sew and the care and administration of domestic affairs.' The aim, he said, should be to teach them the importance of 'justice, piety, fortitude, temperance, learning, clemency, mercy and love of humankind'.

With the help of Wolsey, Sir Thomas More and Oxford University, Catherine had attracted Vives to England – where he spent most of his time over five years. The Spaniard had been brought up by a harsh mother. 'She never lightly laughed upon me,' he said. 'There was nobody that I did more flee, or was more loath to come nigh, than my mother, when I was a child.' Given his experience, Vives might have been expected to suggest something different for Mary. Instead he heartily recommended more of the same. To spare the rod was to spoil the child. This was especially so if the child was a girl, given the potential magnitude of any (presumably sexual) disasters that could occur to her. 'Specially the daughter should be handled without any cherishing. For cherishing marreth sons, but it utterly destroyeth daughters.'

Catherine and Henry ignored this part of his advice. Where they did pay attention, however, was in his recommendations for Mary's studies. Here Vives was enlightened for the time, with his revolutionary idea that women deserved to be educated just as much as men. He even dared suggest, in fact, that women could often be intellectually more gifted than men. For Mary he recommended a mixture of reading that ranged from contemporary work by Erasmus or Thomas More's *Utopia* to daily sessions with the New Testament. Medieval romances, along with dolls, were discouraged. Both, he thought, could lead a girl astray by over-agitating the imagination. This was strict, possibly indigestible, fare – but at least a woman's education was being taken seriously. Catherine liked the idea so much that she produced money for a translation of *The Education of a Christian Woman* from Latin into English. The English version was reprinted eight times during the sixteenth century, suggesting it offered an idea that had found both its time and its place.

Catherine had, of course, already drunk at a fountain of learning that turned old-fashioned mores on their head. 'Our age has seen the four daughters of Queen Isabel . . . each of them well accomplished,' recalled Vives. Juana la Loca, he said, impressed her fellow Spaniards by replying in Latin to the speeches delivered whenever she entered a city or town. 'The English say the same of their queen Catherine,' he added. 'There have been no queens who were so loved and admired by their subjects.' Knowledge, then, was not a danger to women. It was a help, rather than the hindrance that some others saw, to virtue. This message was what Vives – a man who claimed not to know of a single learned woman who was evil – spelled out for Catherine and Mary on paper. In a world where ideas of women's inferiority had ruled so absolutely, it was a small revolution.

This apparently simple idea helped create an atmosphere of intellectual freedom to which women (and their men) were not accustomed. For Erasmus and others, indeed, the fact that Catherine and women like Sir Thomas More's clever daughters joined in debates 'afore the king's grace' was truly remarkable. This they put down, in part, to Catherine's own education under her mother Isabel. 'Who would not wish,' asked Erasmus, 'to live in such a court as hers?' Erasmus was no less fulsome in his praise of Catherine herself, for whom learning and religion necessarily went hand in hand. He called her 'a unique example in our age . . . who, with a distaste for the things of no account that women love, devotes a good part of her day to holy reading'. Serious, pious Catherine was a contrast to those women who 'waste the greatest part of their time in painting their faces or in games of chance and similar amusements', Erasmus said approvingly. Isabel would have been proud of the way Catherine passed the love of learning on to Mary. A visiting Frenchman found the girl 'thin, sparse and small' but 'admirable by reason of her great and uncommon mental endowments'.

Catherine believed that, educated or not, Mary's destiny was to marry one of Europe's great princes. This did not imply renouncing her rights as a queen regnant. Some worried, however, that a foreign husband might end up running her kingdom. Hence the dismay of certain Englishmen when they realised that a French match could mean that, one day, they would be ruled over by a French king. The new match with Charles, however, crowned Catherine's expectations. It was a way of fulfilling her own life's purpose. England and Spain could now come together through her daughter.

Catherine was so enamoured of this idea that she soon found ways to indulge her fantasy of Mary's perfect marriage – even though the little girl was still years away from being able to wed. A gold, jewelled brooch bearing the emperor's name was pinned to her six-year-old daughter's chest on Valentine's Day 1522. The emperor, her mother wished all to know, was the girl's valentine – even if he was sixteen years her senior. Catherine made sure the brooch was in place a fortnight later when Charles's ambassadors came visiting at Greenwich. There were sweet words, too, for her nephew. 'After we had saluted the princess, Catherine continued to question me no less sweetly and prudently about your majesty and there was much pleasant conversation,' one ambassador reported. This was 'especially about the beauty and the charms of the little princess, who, it should be noticed, wore on her bosom a golden brooch ornamented with jewels forming your majesty's name', he added. Catherine was all charm again when the ambassadors took their leave of her a few days later. 'She began to speak of you with such good and honest words that it was her greatest desire to see you here,' he reported.

She then said I should not leave without seeing how the princess, her daughter, could dance. Princess Mary did not have to be asked twice; she performed a *basse* dance, and twirled so prettily that no woman in the world could do better; afterwards, the queen commanded her again to dance a *gaillarde* and she acquitted herself so well that it was marvellous to see; then she played two or three songs on the spinet, and, indeed sire, it is hard to believe the grace and skill she shows, with such self-command as a woman of twenty might wish for. And, what is more, she is pretty and very tall for her age . . . and a very fine cousin indeed.

Catherine was wooing her nephew. Mary was her vehicle.

The seduction of Charles had its final act in the summer of 1522, when he visited again – this time for six weeks. On this occasion Catherine and Mary greeted him at the hall door at Greenwich where, Hall reported, 'he asked the queen's blessing . . . that is the fashion of Spain, between aunt and nephew'. Henry paraded the emperor through London and, as usual, put on a jousting tournament. Charles preferred to watch, standing in the gallery with Catherine as Henry hurled himself into the joust. At one stage a message arrived from France which provoked a ripple of warlike excitement amongst the onlookers. 'While the king and the emperor looked on the letter, a sudden noise arose amongst both their subjects that it was a letter of defiance, sent to them both by the French king.' The spectators, it seemed, were spoiling for a fight with the French. They feasted and danced.

Mary danced again, this time for her beau. The alliance against France was firmed up.

Mary's engagement to Charles was still in place three years later when she must have sat for a miniature portrait by the painter Lucas Horenbout, wearing a brooch boldly bearing her fiancé's title, 'The Emperour'. The brooch was pinned as close to her heart as it could be. A marriage day, however, was still years off and there was no guarantee that the stars in the political constellation of Europe would still be where Catherine wanted them when that day came.

The miniature of Mary showed a red-haired, ruddy-cheeked girl with pale blue eyes – more the English rose than a granddaughter of far-away Castile or Aragon. Catherine herself also sat for Horenbout at least twice about this time. She is noticeably more thick-set, with a heavier line to her jaw, than in earlier portraits – though the fine complexion noticed by some is still in place. She is, however, every bit a queen. In one she wears a gable head-dress and rich, spotted ermine over the sleeves of her black gown. A little silvery marmoset sits playfully on her arm, a small chain attached to its waist. In another she wears a red gown, the square neckline edged in jewels and a more discreet French hood revealing a generous amount of coppery hair.

Catherine had entered mid-life in a state of contentment. She may have lost the freshness of youth and the ability to bear children but she had produced an heir or, rather, an heiress, to the crown. Her husband was not sexually faithful, but he was loyal in other ways. The second Horenbout miniature – emblazoned with the Latin words 'Queen Catherine his wife' – was one of many signs of that. Vives, too, offered words of long-term encouragement for a good wife (and the perfectionist Catherine was nothing if not that) heading towards menopause. 'The truly good woman, through obedience to her husband, will hold sway, and she who always lived in obedience to her husband will command great authority over him,' he said. Most importantly for her happiness, perhaps, was the re-established link with Spain through her daughter. Catherine had played match-maker in more than one sense. It was not just Mary she was joining to Charles, but her husband too.

Henry showed genuine, if oscillating, passion for this arrangement. It was not so much Charles who interested him, but the grandiose plans they drew up. Together, Henry believed, they could tear France apart. This so-called 'Great Enterprise' would finally deliver England's old lands in France – lost during the Hundred Years War – back into Henry's hands. He even dreamed of asserting 'his ancient right and title to the crown of France'. It would be the greatest achievement in English history since Agincourt, with Henry as architect and the old enemy in France as victim.

Catherine spotted the danger immediately. She had seen Henry fooled and humiliated by her father. His boyish enthusiasm for glorious, over-ambitious projects was still easily aroused – even if it was often tempered by Wolsey. So, too, was his sense of bruised suspicion. Catherine had long ago warned that the English were given to excessive emotions, easily spurred to over-excited flights of fancy and just as easily cast down into the depths of resentment, hurt and wariness.

Her nephew, in other words, was playing with fire. He had offered Henry the moon. The English king had now reached out for it. If Charles did not deliver, Henry's anti-Spanish wrath would be aroused even more terribly than before. It was Charles's ambassador who felt the rough edge of Catherine's tongue when she first realised his master might have promised too much. 'She told us vehemently that the only way for you to retain the friendship of this king and of the English was to fulfil faithfully everything that you have promised,' he wrote back to Charles in January 1523. 'It was much better to promise little and perform faithfully than to promise much and fail in part.'

The Great Enterprise was an on–off affair from the start. Henry himself blew hot and cold and his frustration mounted whenever his own bouts of enthusiasm did not coincide with those of Charles. Wolsey, meanwhile, often sought ways to come to terms with the French. Catherine, for her part, began her own secret diplomacy. In March 1524 she warned Charles's ambassador Louis de Praet that Henry's patience was snapping. 'The king is very discontented,' de Praet wrote.

He has uttered loud complaints before his household, and matters have gone so far that the queen sent her confessor to me in secret to warn me of Henry's discontent and ask me to write to you and advise you to remedy matters. She is is very sorry that your majesty ever promised so much in this treaty, and she fears that it may one day be the cause of a weakening of the friendship between you two. I beg your majesty to keep this communication of the queen's secret; it would be regrettable if it came to the ears of certain English.

It soon became clear who those 'certain English' were. Wolsey was growing wary of Catherine. The woman who had done all she could to push Henry and Charles together – and had drawn Wolsey into the plan – began to feel the slow chill of suspicion. Wolsey watched her every move, seeing her as a danger to his own manoeuvrings. 'I would have communicated more frequently with the queen but I have been warned by some of her friends that it would not be discreet,' de Praet reported on 17 November 1524. 'Indeed, I have often noticed that the cardinal [Wolsey] was very restless whenever I talked to her, and often interrupted our conversation.'

By now, however, England had become something of a sideshow for Charles. He was busy fighting Francis in Italy and had little time, or money, for grandiose adventures with Henry. The latter's frustration was partially assuaged by Francis's problems in Italy. In November 1524 Henry gleefully read out aloud to Catherine the news that the French king, at the head of his own army, was getting into difficulties with Charles's troops there. 'He declared the news and every material point which upon the reading his grace well noted unto the queen's grace and all other about him who were marvellous glad to hear it,' wrote one of those present. 'The queen's grace said that she was glad the Spaniards had yet done somewhat [well] in Italy.' Henry speculated that Francis had pushed too far, and might be unable to fight his way home. 'The king's grace laughed and said he thinketh it will be very hard for him to get thence [i.e. back home].'

Their joy was still greater when Francis was captured at Pavia the following February and was taken off to Spain. Wine ran in the streets of London, bonfires were lit and trumpets blasted in celebration. Henry feasted and rode with Catherine in state to a celebratory mass in St Paul's – almost as if the victory had belonged to him rather than Charles. Catherine's joy, however, was tempered by the fact that Charles seemed to have forgotten her. She wrote to her nephew from Greenwich, begging him to explain his silence. Had the fickle sea swallowed up her letters? 'Nothing would be so painful to me as to think that you had forgotten me,' she wrote, adding that Henry had ordered solemn processions across the land to celebrate the victory over Francis. 'Love and consanguinity demand that we should write to each other more often.'

The joy was short-lived. Charles's victory shifted the balance of power in Europe dramatically in his favour. Henry – or, rather, Wolsey – no longer held the key and Charles was no longer interested in the Great Enterprise. The engagement with Mary was broken and, preferring an alliance closer to home, Charles soon agreed to marry a princess from Portugal. Anti-Spanish sentiment was quick to raise its head. Wolsey upset Charles by publicly calling him 'a liar, who observed no manner of faith or promise'. Charles's aunt Margaret, according to the plain-speaking English cardinal, was 'a ribald' while his brother Ferdinand was 'a child, and so governed'. Wolsey's undiplomatic outburst earned him a rebuke from his own ambassadors. 'Your grace's plainliness is not so well taken as it is worthy; wherefore it were as good to give them good words for good words, keeping secret your thoughts as they do,' they told him. The shifting sands soon saw Henry sign a peace treaty with France in August 1525.

Catherine's relationship with Wolsey followed the same downward spiral as the relationship with Spain. Until then it had survived the occasional competition over whether Henry should lean towards France or Spain. Catherine had sensibly avoided direct confrontation with Wolsey and was always politely solicitous as to his welfare. Early in 1525, for example, she 'very lovingly, both in words and countenance, did enquire of your . . . good health', according to one of Wolsey's regular correspondents at court. The time was nearly over, however, in which Henry could write to Wolsey saying that 'The queen my wife hath desired me to make her most hearty recommendations to you, as to him that she loveth very well . . .'

Something major, in fact, had changed. Wolsey was by now at the height of his power. He began to behave, for reasons Catherine herself could not understand, as though she had lost all influence over her husband. Such was his mysterious confidence, or arrogance, that he began to treat her with disdain.

Even her countryman Vives, whose learning both she and Wolsey had eagerly embraced, would eventually became a point of contention for them. In Catherine's mind, however, the kind of hardships Wolsey was beginning to subject her to were as much a gift from God as anything else. 'He knows what is expedient for all, and is often more propitious when he changes sweet for bitter,' Erasmus wrote to her later – echoing Catherine's conversation with Vives on the way back from Syon.

She had not expected, however, the sour pill she was forced to swallow in the chilly early summer of 1525.

29 Bastard

Summer 1525

Catherine had always turned a blind eye to Henry's sexual wandering. 'And not just during the period of these last indiscretions but also before,' the duke of Norfolk would say later, praising her forbearance, 'the king having continually been inclined to amorous intrigues.' An old-fashioned aristocrat like Norfolk (with a mistress of his own) appreciated a queen who knew when to close her eyes. Later rumours, only partly exaggerated, would talk of Henry bedding the mother and two daughters from one noble family. Now, however, forbearance had been replaced by fury. It was one thing for her husband to chase her ladies-in-waiting. It was quite another to flaunt his illegitimate offspring before the court and, worse still, to shower his bastard son with titles and honours. That, however, is what happened in the summer of 1525.

Six years earlier Elizabeth Blount had been sent off to an Essex priory to give birth to the child she was carrying. Where Catherine had failed, Blount succeeded. Her child was a boy – Henry Fitzroy. Blount disappeared from court, but Henry was quite happy to recognise the child as his and make sure that his former mistress was well looked after. Now the boy had emerged from semi-anonymity to be paraded as a potential heir to the throne.

In June 1525 Henry suddenly showered his son with some of the highest honours and titles in the land. The boy was made, in quick succession, knight of the Garter, earl of Nottingham, duke of both Richmond and Somerset, warden general of the Marches toward Scotland and, finally, lord admiral of England.

The six-year-old child rose, in the space of just six weeks, to become one of the highest-ranking and wealthiest people in the land. It marked him out, more importantly, as a rival for Catherine's daughter Mary. If Henry decided that he could not hand his crown on to a woman, then here was a potential male heir – ready and waiting.

Catherine's reaction was explosive. Henry was trampling on his own daughter and she let him know it. He was shocked by the sudden display of Castilian temper. Catherine rarely chose confrontation. The king, in turn, rarely encountered opposition. Henry had been a spoilt and adored child. Now he was a man surrounded by servants and sycophants. Few, if any, dared criticise his decisions. He could have and do almost anything he wanted. Yet here he was, being crossed by his wife.

Henry, as a result, was equally furious. His wife had no business telling him what to do. He directed most of his rage, however, against three of Catherine's Spanish ladies. They were deemed the instigators of such apparently unseemly anger. In fact, they were scapegoats. Turning his fury on them allowed Henry to avoid a more direct confrontation with a suddenly steely wife. He had the Spanish ladies expelled from court. That was a painful enough punishment for Catherine. Foreign ambassadors saw it as a harsh public reprimand to which she had no option but to 'suffer patiently'.

Henry Fitzroy bore the traditional surname of royal bastards. He had survived the perilous years of infancy in the Lincolnshire house of Gilbert Tailboys. His mother had been hurriedly, and uncomplainingly, married off to this son of a lunatic nobleman – who was also the king's ward. Henry's 'natural' son boasted Cardinal Wolsey as a godfather.. He would have been no secret to Catherine.

We do not know her initial reaction to the child's birth. Catherine had raged uselessly when her marriage was barely a year old and Henry first showed signs of a wandering eye. Jealousy was a sign of 'hearty love', Wolsey once claimed. It had a destructive history, however, in her own family. 'What torture and torment can be compared to it?' asked the same Juan Luis Vives who had set out the rules for Mary's education. Jealousy, he warned, was 'a relentless and uncontrollable tyranny'. It was better, he advised, to die than give way to it. If a woman allowed herself to suffer from it, she must do so in secret. Her jealousy must not be 'excessive and violent' or 'upset the peace of the home and become an intolerable burden for her husband'. 'If it is of that type,' Vives mused, 'I think she must be given medical treatment. Above all, a woman should bear in mind that her husband is master of the household, and not all things permitted to him are permitted to her; human laws do not require the same chastity of a man as they do of a woman.' A man as seriously devoted to his own pleasures as Henry was hardly likely to be an exception. Kings, anyway, were almost all philanderers. Envy of the sex of his bastard child may well have been a stronger emotion for Catherine than sexual jealousy.

Whatever she felt, Catherine had kept well hidden. With one of Henry's later, and more damaging, mistresses, she was praised for the fact that 'with wisdom and great patience [she] dissimulated the same'. That is how she behaved towards Elizabeth Blount, her former maid of honour. Royal bastards were not uncommon. Catherine had been used to seeing her own father's illegitimate children at court. Her sister-in-law Margaret encountered seven of James IV's illegitimate offspring already running around the royal nursery when she arrived to marry the Scottish king – who continued to see his mistress, Janet Kennedy. The important thing, then, was not whether the king had other children, but what he did with them. With Elizabeth Blount safely married and living far off in Lincolnshire with her son, Catherine had had little to worry about.

Her fury over Fitzroy's sudden rise was assuaged, at least partly, by Henry's decision to give nine-year-old Mary the task of governing Wales. This was the proper, traditional job of the heir to the throne. Her daughter was a child, so the task would be done by her council, but Mary was now treading in the footsteps of her uncle, Catherine's first husband Arthur. The old, grey castle in Ludlow was renovated for her.

The rivalry between Wolsey and Catherine resurfaced in the battle fought over two small children. The former had urged Henry to promote his bastard son, or so the child's own councillors obviously thought. They made the young duke write to Wolsey to thank him for a sudden change in status that had been, in great part, 'by the means and good favour of your grace'. Fitzroy, or whoever dictated letters to the seven-year-old, recognised that 'no creature living is more bound' to Wolsey's 'favour and goodness'. Being a young duke was hard work. The poor child hated the hours he now had to put into reading, writing and learning Latin. A deluge of letters from abbots and 'mean persons' arrived at his new home in Yorkshire. The task of answering them soon provoked, according to the schoolmaster he acquired as part of an ample new household, a 'dulling of his wits, spirits and memory, and no little hurt of his head, stomach and body'. In that respect, at least, he was no match for his clever and talented half-sister Mary.

Catherine's forthright objections to young Richmond's rise may have pushed her husband into sending Mary to govern Wales. This placed her daughter back on top of the pile, though her half-brother was now uncomfortably close behind. It was, however, a Pyrrhic victory. Catherine had already lost some of the last few precious strands still connecting her to her mother country when her Spanish ladies were expelled. Now she also lost a daughter.

In August 1525 Catherine waved goodbye to her only child.

With her servants in a brand new livery of blue and green damask, and her court of ladies and gentlemen in black velvet or damask, Mary set bravely off west towards the Welsh Marches. The train of wagons sent after her was piled high with everything a princess could need, from pots and pans to a 'chest with the irons for keeping the prisoners'. A trusted governess, Lady Salisbury (the same Margaret Pole who had been at Ludlow with Catherine), and a tutor, Richard Featherstone, were to oversee her continuing education. They were to prove two of Catherine's most loyal, diehard friends. The latter would, eventually, die for his devotion to the cause she espoused. The former languished in the Tower in her old age before her head, too, was clumsily hacked off – a victim of the terror that awaited many of Catherine's closest allies.

The golden sheen was beginning to rub off Henry's happy reign. Catherine was one of the first to feel the change and experience the creeping sense of mistrust and disquiet. She missed her little girl and her husband was also often away. 'The long absence of the king and you troubleth me,' she admitted to Mary. She fretted uselessly about her daughter's health and enquired anxiously about her Latin lessons. She grabbed at almost any token that might keep the chain that bound them from being broken. 'As for your writing in Latin I am glad that ye shall change from me to master Featherstone, for that shall do you much good, to learn by him to write right,' she wrote in a tender letter of regret disguised as encouragement. 'But yet sometimes I would be glad when ye do write to master Featherstone of your own inditing, when he hath read it, that I may see it,' she said. 'It shall be a great comfort to me to see you keep your Latin and fair writing and all.' Even second-hand Latin compositions, in other words, would do for a lonely mother.

Her empty-nest loneliness was soon compounded by something more sinister and isolating. The problem was not that

Catherine lacked company. It was that she was now under constant watch. Wolsey had begun to surround her with spies and
informants. A new world, coloured by suspicion and mistrust,
was beginning to encroach on the previously happy-go-lucky
regime of Henry's court. An early warning of what awaited had
come in May 1521 when, in a moment of suspicion that senior
nobles might be plotting against him, Henry had the testy, powerful and French-hating duke of Buckingham executed. With his
death, Catherine had lost a natural ally, but the execution had
seemed like a one-off event rather than a precursor of things to
come. Now pressure was being brought to bear on those closest
to her. They were to watch, listen and report back. Informants
were placed close to her. One of her ladies was so upset by the
change that she 'departed the court for no other reason than
that she would no longer betray her mistress'.

When Iñigo de Mendoza, an old family acquaintance, arrived
as Charles's new envoy to England at the end of 1526, he was
shocked to find that he could not see Catherine on her own. To
his surprise they communicated, instead, indirectly via Catherine's confessor – a timorous Spaniard called Jorge de Athequa,
who had become the bishop of Llandaff. He shuttled backwards
and forwards between them, with Catherine eventually telling
the astonished Mendoza that any formal interview would have
to be organised through Wolsey. Catherine told him to be careful
about how he made the request. He must pretend that his only
interest was to chat about old friends in Spain.

There were rumours that, with a marriage to Charles now
impossible, Henry and Wolsey planned to marry Mary to the
now-widowed French king. Catherine was not happy. There
were other reasons, apart from the shift away from Spain, for
worrying about Francis as a husband. His mother was a 'most
terrible woman' who would treat her daughter-in-law as a serving wench, or so one potential rival for the French king's hand

was told. The philandering Francis could not only be expected to drive her mad with jealousy but would probably give her the same lethal dose of pox that had killed his first wife, the terrified candidate was warned.

Whatever Catherine's concerns, Mendoza was not allowed to quiz her directly about them. When he finally saw her on a spring Sunday in 1527, Wolsey sat in on the interview. Catherine and Mendoza made small talk, swapping information about people they had known when they were at court together in Spain. Before any politically sensitive subjects could be touched on, Wolsey butted in. 'The king has many things to tell you. Her highness will perhaps excuse us if we take leave and go,' he said. 'You shall have audience another time.' Mendoza was shocked to find himself being deliberately bundled out of the room.

Catherine decided to avoid another meeting with her nephew's ambassador. This, Mendoza agreed, would only 'add further damage to what might be said about her'. Catherine had continued to write loving letters to her nephew, despite his apparent indifference to her, and Mendoza was sure 'would do anything in her power to preserve the old alliance between Spain and England'. She had, however, already been crushed as a political power by the omnipotent and ruthless Wolsey. 'But though her wishes are strong, her means of carrying them into effect are small,' observed Mendoza. Wolsey feared Catherine's influence but had, at last, succeeded in isolating her. 'Her suspicions are roused,' reported Mendoza. Only the cardinal and Henry now knew what was really going on. And that involved a lot more than just the swinging pendulum of England's continental alliances.

There was much to be suspicious about. On 17 May 1527, a secret tribunal had been called in Wolsey's York Place residence at Westminster. Those present were told that the king was racked by terrible and terrifying doubt. Someone had suggested that his marriage was illegal and that he and Catherine had been living in sin all this time. Now, eighteen years after their wedding, he doubted that it had ever been legal to marry his brother's widow. The Bible, he had been told, prohibited such a thing. It was a convenient excuse. Henry wanted to get rid of Catherine. Even he could not have suspected quite how difficult that would be, or what deep rifts it would provoke in England. Catherine was nothing if not obstinate. She was not going without a fight.

30 Divorce: the King's Secret Matter

York Place, Westminster. 17 May 1527

Catherine's name was uttered in reverential terms. She was '*serenissima domina Catherina*', the Most Serene Lady Catherine. The men talking about her, amid the luxury and ostentation of Cardinal Wolsey's town palace, must have been wearing their gravest semblances. The cardinal, as ever, was in control. The king sat on his right-hand side. Members of Wolsey's household, left on the other side of the door, might have felt tempted to listen in. Through the door, after all, had passed not just their master, the plump cardinal, together with the tall, broad and still impressive figure of the king. The archbishop of Canterbury, a registrar and several doctors of law had also entered the chamber. If any of Wolsey's servants did put their ear to the door, the Latin phrases drifting through would have shocked them to the core.

The king of England, no less, was being placed on trial. Such a thing, people agreed later, had never been heard of before. There was evidence that Henry had been committing a terrible sin. He had lived unlawfully, or so it was feared, with his brother's wife. His soul was in danger. Divine vengeance hung over him as a terrible threat. Was he prepared to accept trial, they asked, in this ecclesiastical court? Henry concurred. He read out, or handed over, a reply in writing. He was quite happy to admit the facts of the case. His proctor, Dr John Bell, would defend him from now on. The court was then adjourned, the day being Friday, until Monday.

The court was, of course, a farce. The king's proctor was not there to mount a real defence. The so-called defendant actually wanted the charges against him to be proven correct. Not only that, but the other defendant – Catherine – had not even been told of this secret gathering. The court was really meeting because Henry himself wanted to end his marriage. He claimed that this was because his conscience was troubled. A passage in the Old Testament Book of Leviticus said that: 'If a man shall take his brother's wife, it is an impurity: he hath uncovered his brother's nakedness; they shall be childless.' Was that why he had no male heir? Had God punished him for a crime committed in innocence? When he married Catherine, a pope used his authority to override this ancient law of scripture. He wrote, at the request of both sets of parents, a special papal bull to allow them to wed. What, though, if that pope had overstepped his authority or been fooled into signing the document? What if the prohibition was absolute, something that not even a pope could waive? Would that mean that he, the king, had been living in sin? Was he married at all?

The king's apparent attack of moral panic raised the question of who, or what, had stirred his suddenly troubled conscience. His wedding, after all, had taken place eighteen years ago – when he was half his current age.

A smokescreen explanation had already been devised. Officially it was Gabriel de Grammont, the French bishop of Tarbes, who first asked whether Henry's marriage was really valid. He had just left England after a visit to discuss a possible marriage between Mary and a member of the French royal family. If Henry's marriage was invalid, the logic went, then his daughter was both illegitimate and no longer heiress to the English crown. That would make her a far less valuable bride.

Henry was fully capable of convincing himself that the feelings now stirring inside him were dictated by his conscience rather than his own desires. There can be little doubt, however, that the latter burned with ferocious heat in his mind, heart and elsewhere. Henry longed passionately for two things, neither of which he could have. One was a male heir. The other was one of Catherine's young ladies. Her name was Anne Boleyn.

Catherine must have first noticed her some six years earlier, when Anne Boleyn returned from a long period abroad. The second daughter of Thomas Boleyn had spent her adolescence and early adult life in two of the most sophisticated courts of Europe – at Brussels with Margaret of Austria and in France with King Francis and the late Queen Claude. Catherine would have noticed, when Anne arrived back late in 1521 and took the role of Perseverance in the Shrove Tuesday pageant a few months later, that this was no run-of-the-mill English lord's daughter recently up from the country. She was clever, spoke French, could sing, play music and dance. More importantly, she brought with her the airs, graces and fashions of a French court that already missed her. She was, in other words, a sophisticate. 'No one would ever have taken her to be English by her manners, but a native-born Frenchwoman,' said one contemporary. Swan-necked, with striking dark hair and a long face, she was no spectacular beauty but was considered 'good-looking enough'. It was her style, not her looks, that Catherine would have noticed. She must also have seen how young men, like the unfortunate Lord Henry Percy, drifted 'into the queen's chamber and there would fall into dalliance among the queen's maidens, being at the last more conversant with Mistress Anne Boleyn than with any other, so that there grew such a secret love between them that at length they were engaged'. To the chagrin of the young lovers, their families (with Wolsey's encouragement) soon put a stop to the relationship.

By the time Henry and Wolsey met at the secret court in Westminster, the king was lost in his passion for Anne. He had already written, in one of a series of seventeen ardent letters, that he had 'been now above one whole year struck with the dart of love'. A year earlier, in 1526, Henry had appeared at the Shrove Tuesday jousts at Greenwich in the guise of a tortured lover. A flaming heart caught in a press was embroidered on the cloth of gold and silver of his horse's 'bard and base'. The mysterious words *declare ie nose* – 'declare I dare not' – were also embroidered. Who did the king not dare declare to? That he was playing the usually innocent game of courtly love was clear. Beyond the gossipy question of who the king was referring to (and spectators probably chatted more about fellow jouster Sir Francis Bryan, who lost an eye that day), few people would have seen much that was untoward in his display. The letters 'H' and 'K' that had adorned earlier jousting outfits were gone, but at the banquet that night – as if to reassure her and the world – Catherine was served by her husband himself.

Anne, more by accident than design, was discovering what later became an accepted way of winning Henry's vain heart. She turned his advances down. She had seen him use, and then cast aside, his last mistress – her own married elder sister Mary. Henry had been, in many ways, a spoilt child. As a man, too, he could have almost anything he wanted. Denial and frustration had an explosive impact on him. They fired his ardour. He threw his boundless energy and will-power into obtaining that which he had been told he could not have. Anne, having possibly hooked him by mistake, then played him long and slow until he was irretrievably enmeshed in her net – and she in his. It was marriage, she ultimately said, or nothing.

For that to happen, Henry had to dispose of Catherine. His quest for a way out of his marriage became known as 'the divorce', but that was never what Henry sought – at least not in the accepted modern sense of the word. His real aim, in fact, was to prove that he had never been properly married and that their marriage had been null and void from the very beginning.

Henry saw himself as a good man and an honest, orthodox Christian. The pope, after all, had given him the title of Defender of the Faith in 1521. He had written, admittedly with help, a best-selling treatise against that heretic Martin Luther, *The Defence of the Seven Sacraments*. He needed to convince himself that separation from Catherine would not compromise his standing, and self-image, as a virtuous Christian prince. It might have seemed obvious to almost everybody else that what he really wanted was to swap an old wife for a young one, but Henry's mind was both immensely self-centred and very supple. He quickly came to the conclusion that he was driven by far higher thoughts – the true 'scruples' of a thinking, religious man – about whether his marriage had ever been legal. Once he had decided that, there was no shifting him. The decision made the whole business of getting out of his marriage fraught with difficulties. It gave Catherine, at least in theory, a fighting chance of winning the argument. Henry's high opinion of himself, however, went even further than this. He not only believed he was high-minded, but also that he was right. Instead of finding a more direct or brutal way of getting rid of Catherine (as he did with later wives), he was sure that he could simply persuade everyone, including the pope, to agree with him.

It is possible that Wolsey, perhaps without meaning to, came up with the idea of challenging the initial validity of the marriage. This may be why he later warned that, with Henry, it was best to 'be well advised and assured what matter ye put in his head for ye shall never pull it out again'. Whether Wolsey planted the seed, or not, it would become his task to deliver what the king wanted. The all-powerful, arrogant and tough-talking cardinal was thus caught between two formidable women, Catherine and Anne.

Those who guessed the identity of the object of Henry's desire at the Shrove Tuesday jousts – assuming it was Anne Boleyn – would not have been scandalised. So what if the king pursued another of the Boleyn daughters? He had already been satisfying his sexual appetite with Anne's elder sister Mary. Catherine, indeed, initially took the relationship with Anne in her stride. When the French delegation led by the bishop of Tarbes visited in May 1527, the queen entertained him in her apartments at Greenwich. 'There was dancing and M. de Touraine, on the king's command, danced with Madame the princess, and the king with Mistress Boulan [Boleyn] who was brought up in France with the late queen,' the French commented afterwards. They suspected nothing. Did Catherine? Wolsey's servant and biographer George Cavendish claimed she not only knew but showed Anne special tenderness. 'There is no doubt that good Queen Catherine, having this gentlewoman daily attending upon her, both heard by report and perceived before her eyes,' he wrote.

Notwithstanding, she showed neither to Mistress Anne nor unto the king, any spark or kind of grudge or displeasure, but took and accepted all things in good part, and with wisdom and great patience dissimulated the same. She held Mistress Anne in more estimation for the king's sake than she had before.

Catherine was, he declared, 'a perfect Griselda' – the patient, obedient and suffering wife of medieval folklore who appears in both Boccaccio's *Decameron* and Chaucer's *Canterbury Tales*.

Perhaps Catherine realised early on that Anne was far more ambitious than Henry's former mistresses. One story, recounted years later, told of the two women playing a card game together in which Anne kept turning up the king. 'My lady Anne, you have good hap to stop at a king, but you are not like others, you will have all or none,' Catherine supposedly quipped. Having Anne close to hand at least made it easier to watch her.

The secret tribunal at York Place – which continued, on and off, for the next fortnight – changed everything. Henry had decided their marriage was over, but finding an acceptable way to terminate it, especially in the eyes of the church, would not be easy. Even someone as impetuous as the king felt the need to justify such a radical move. Leviticus, he was convinced, provided his excuse. But would the church agree? To do so, it would have to declare that an earlier pope, Julius II, had been wrong to legitimise his marriage. That was such a thorny question that Wolsey's court, which rose on 31 May, never did reach a conclusion. Wolsey, instead, said he wanted to consult expert lawyers and theologians. He would await their report. Henry had chosen a difficult path. Much would depend on how Catherine herself reacted. He may even have fooled himself into thinking that, in a final act of loyalty and obedience, she would understand his plight and meekly agree.

We cannot be sure about exactly when Catherine first discovered the truth about the earth-shattering events going on around her. The men who gathered at York Place on 17 May were intent on keeping the whole business secret. They spoke about it all in euphemisms. This was the king's 'secret matter' or his 'great and secret affair'.

Catherine, however, had been queen – and an increasingly popular one – for eighteen years. She had friends in many places. Over the previous year, as Wolsey tightened the stranglehold on her, she had developed secret lines of communication with men like Charles's ambassador, Mendoza. 'She sees that they do not tell her the truth in these and other matters,' Mendoza had already observed a few months earlier, talking about Wolsey's determination to keep her in the dark on diplomatic affairs. What she was not told, she could always glean from friends or – via her ladies – other people at court. 'Spanish ladies spy well,' commented the now one-eyed Francis Bryan on a later occasion. Catherine had to be careful because Wolsey had made sure that, even in her own chamber, she was also surrounded by spies.

It took Catherine less than twenty-four hours to discover

what had happened in that first meeting at York Place on 17 May. The remarkable speed with which she discovered Henry's 'secret' suggests, in fact, that she already suspected something was going on. The very next day, her ally, the Spanish ambassador Mendoza, had been fully informed. 'The "good" legate [Wolsey], to put the seal on his iniquities, is working on getting the queen unmarried and she is so fearful that she dare not speak to me about it,' he told the Emperor Charles in a letter written that day.

The king is so bent on this divorce that he has secretly assembled certain bishops and lawyers that they may sign a declaration to the effect that his marriage with the queen is null and void, on account of her having been his brother's wife. It is therefore to be feared that either the pope will be induced by some false statement to side against the queen – or that the cardinal, by virtue of his legatine authority, may take some step fatal to her marriage. I am perfectly aware, though the queen herself has not ventured, and does not venture, to speak to me on the subject, that all her hope rests, after God, on your imperial highness.

Mendoza's constant protestations that Catherine had not, directly or indirectly, spoken to him about the case read like the precautions of a man who knows his correspondence may be intercepted by spies. The speed with which he was able to inform Charles suggests Catherine had been watching her husband carefully, perhaps waiting for something like this to happen. Mendoza and, presumably, Catherine, wanted the pope warned. He must not be pushed by the English into suddenly acting against her marriage. In the meantime, Mendoza suggested, it would be good if the pope prevented Wolsey from deciding the matter on his own account. The affair, should Henry choose to continue, had to be decided in Rome.

'Should the king see that he cannot succeed, he will not run the risk of any preliminary steps being known. But should he persist on pursuing the course he has begun, some great popular disturbance must ensue; for the queen is much beloved in this kingdom,' Mendoza wrote. Catherine, however, knew her husband. She did not want him forced to publicly defend what he was doing, for that would push an obstinate man into a corner from which he could not budge. 'The queen desires perfect secrecy to be kept in this matter, at least for the present,' said Mendoza, as their cloak-and-dagger contacts continued. 'The above wish of hers has been communicated by a third person, who pretended not to come from her, though I suspect he came with her consent.'

Within a day of Henry formally starting proceedings to have his marriage declared null and void, Catherine had already begun tracing out a strategy for defeating him. On the one hand, he obviously feared her popularity. On the other hand, she knew that the final decision on her marriage could not be left to Wolsey, as cardinal, or any of his appointees. If she was to save her marriage, she must take the battle to Rome. Her nephew, the powerful emperor, was her best ally. The first round of a bitter and complex battle that would stretch over the next six years had, in effect, already been won by Catherine. Henry thought she knew nothing. His ignorance, and desire for secrecy, worked to her advantage. He was giving her time to prepare her defence.

31 Virginity

Windsor. 22 June 1527

Catherine wept hot, angry tears. Her husband stood before her, presumably both anxious and relieved now that he had finally plucked up the courage to tell her in person what her future held. He phrased it in the same way that he had persuaded himself to view the 'great and secret matter'. It was a grave question of conscience, he said. They had been living in mortal sin all these years. He now knew this, because canonists and theologians had told him so. For the good of both their souls, they must separate *a mensa et thoro*, from both bed and board. She must, therefore, choose a place of retirement. His wife's answer was to burst into tears. Words failed her. Henry tried to console the woman with whom he had lived for the past eighteen years. She had, after all, borne his children – both living and dead – and been at his side since he was an inexperienced and youthful king. It was 'for the best', he insisted. In the meantime, though, he was still officially her husband and, so, her master. He begged her to keep the matter a secret. Her tears were an eloquent form of silence. She had shown him no opposition. Nor, however, had she acquiesced.

We do not know where this scene took place, though it was probably at Windsor – where Henry, who also spent time at Westminster that day, conducted business on 22 June 1527. His insistence on secrecy was, by this stage, absurd and suggests that he may already have feared the steel that lay below his wife's pleasant, subservient facade. Catherine's husband was in strange ignorance of the scandal he had already caused. His 'secret' was already known in Spain. In London and other places it was the subject of outraged gossip. 'Not that the people of England are ignorant of the king's intentions, for the affair is as notorious as if it had been proclaimed by the town crier,' Mendoza observed. 'They cannot believe that he will ever carry so wicked a project into effect.'

There was, indeed, another reason for Henry to be afraid of Catherine. She was popular. Mendoza saw trouble brewing for the king, 'so great is the attachment of the English people to the queen.' The divorce, he predicted, would create a 'scandal'. One of Henry's own ambassadors later agreed, telling an Italian in Paris that 'the queen was as beloved as if she had been of the blood royal of England'. Catherine was also mother to the heiress to the crown. If her marriage was declared null and void then her daughter, Princess Mary, would not just lose her rights to the crown but would also bear the stigma of bastardy. 'Everyone feels so strongly about what is being said about setting the queen aside, both for her sake and because the princess would end up as a bastard,' said Mendoza. 'Should it really happen and six or seven thousand men landed on the coast of Cornwall to espouse the cause of both mother and daughter, then forty thousand Englishmen would join them.' He admitted, though, that 'popular favour often fails them when put to the test'. With no obvious leader to turn to, the people might content themselves with mere 'grumbling' – especially against the unpopular Cardinal Wolsey, who many thought was behind the divorce.

Henry's determination to get rid of Catherine, in fact, created all sorts of problems for Wolsey – not least because, as a cardinal, he also owed special obedience to the pope. That explains why he counselled Henry to treat Catherine 'gently and doulcely [sweetly]' while the manoeuvring to dispose of her was being carried out. After all, Wolsey knew that in the past popes had often been indulgent to kingly whims.

It was too late, however, for sweetness and gentility. Catherine was seething, albeit quietly. To be an obedient wife was one thing, but to be a passive onlooker at her own downfall was something quite different. She did not declare loud, outright rebellion, but she would not bend. She had long ago found it easier to deal with men if they thought she was witless, pliable and naïve. While Henry had been slowly assuming the role of a silently tortured soul, he had given her time to think. That, he soon discovered, was a dangerous thing to do.

Catherine's first blow was simple but devastating. Henry claimed they were sinners because she had 'carnally known' his elder brother. Henry, she declared, was wrong. She and Arthur, despite their very public bedding on the wedding night, had never had sex.

The truth about Catherine's virginity will never be known. Whatever the case, she must already have worked out that no one could disprove what she said. It was clear, too, from the murky affair of her first pregnancy that she had no qualms about lying when she thought it necessary. The evidence on her virginity that was presented later, both in London and Zaragoza, is contradictory. She now claimed, however, that Henry had always known she was a virgin when he first went to her bed. Wolsey was beside himself when he heard that Catherine had been, as he put it to Henry, 'affirming that your brother did never know her carnally'. If true, this sank a large part of Henry's argument. She had also demanded her husband allow her to take on foreign counsellors to advise her what to do. All this was proof, Wolsey decided, that she was receiving secret advice. 'This device could never come of her [own] head,' he said. Wolsey was seriously underestimating his opponent. Perhaps she had always encouraged him to think – as she once did with Henry VII and his counsellors – that 'I have no more in me than what appears outwardly, and that I shall not be able to fathom his designs'.

Catherine had just destroyed Henry's chances of an easy, discreet separation. 'These were the worst points [against the divorce] that could be imagined,' Wolsey admitted. Seeing the problems that lay ahead, he tried to persuade Henry not to insist on the part of his argument that required Catherine and Arthur to have had sex. It was enough, he said, that Arthur and she had been married. Henry ignored him.

Some in Henry's council had already pointed out one major problem in his argument for nullity. Another Old Testament book, Deuteronomy, contradicted the passage in Leviticus on which his claim was based. This stated that it was actually a man's duty to marry his brother's widow if the first marriage had failed to produce a son. 'Her husband's brother shall go in unto her, and take her to him to wife,' it said.

Wolsey had fallen into the trap of thinking that Catherine could not mount a defence for herself. Her secret advisers, he suspected, were the ones who had made her become so 'stiff and obstinate'. He soon began to accuse her of being unreasonable. He told some of the country's senior bishops that Catherine had now 'broken with your grace [Henry] thereof, after a very displeasant manner, saying, that by my procurement and setting forth a divorce was purposed between her and your highness'.

Both he and Henry became suspicious. They began to realise that Catherine must have found out about the 'secret and great matter' long before Henry himself broke it to her. Henry wanted to find her informant. He suspected, too, that she was broadcasting the news, thereby spoiling his plans for the whole matter to be carried out in secret. 'By her manner, behaviour, words, and messages, [she] hath published, divulged and opened the same,' said Wolsey. The cardinal, meanwhile, began to bully the country's bishops into backing their king against the queen. Henry was being perfectly reasonable, he told them, while Catherine was 'being suspicious, and casting further doubts than was meant or intended'. Even the elderly, fair-minded and incorruptible John Fisher, bishop of Rochester, initially allowed himself to be pushed into agreeing that the queen was behaving in a 'perilous and dangerous' fashion. The aim was to turn things on their head: Catherine, the victim, was to be cast as the troublemaker; Henry, who had started it all, was to be turned into the victim who needed saving from the 'pensive and dolorous life' into which he had been enslaved by the revelation that his marriage was invalid. Catherine's irresponsible, rumour-mongering attitude, they claimed, threatened both the stability of the kingdom and the chance of a European peace. She should remain silent, obey her husband (even though he claimed that he was no such thing) and await the decisions of important men.

Wolsey, meanwhile, also wanted to find out whether she had been secretly lobbying for support. His visit to Fisher confirmed his worst fears. A messenger had come from her, Fisher said. Catherine had simply told him 'she would be glad to have his counsel' in an affair between her and the king. The messenger had not said exactly why she needed his help but, as his brother had already passed on the divorce gossip circulating in London, the bishop had worked it out. Even Fisher, however, told Wolsey that he would not respond to her plea without the king's permission. Catherine, in other words, was alone. Any help she wanted would have to be found in secret and, if necessary, by subterfuge and deceit.

Wolsey had another problem. The king was beginning to doubt the man on whom he had become so dependent. His enemies at court, who were close to the Boleyn family, had started whispering to Henry that the cardinal's heart was not in the divorce. Wolsey was shocked when Henry sent a message suggesting he might actually be trying to hinder the 'secret matter'. 'I take God to record that there is nothing earthly that I covet so much as the advancing thereof,' he replied. Wolsey's own future, whether he liked it or not, now depended on his ability to deliver. He had become – along with Catherine, Henry, Princess Mary and Anne Boleyn – an interested party to the Great Matter. The stakes, for him, were just as high as – if not higher than – for the others. Henry was not a man to forgive anything that smelt of betrayal.

Wolsey's other great difficulty was that Catherine had a potential ally who out-muscled not just the cardinal but the king himself. Her nephew, the Emperor Charles, had been enjoying military victories in Italy. While Henry and Wolsey had been secretly working out their divorce strategy, Charles's troops had – unknown to them – taken and sacked Rome itself on 6 May 1527. Pope Clement VII was now at the emperor's mercy. The task of persuading him to ease Henry elegantly out of his marriage had suddenly become hugely complex.

Catherine knew that her salvation lay in Rome and she wanted the pope to accept that only he could override the decisions of a predecessor. She also knew that the best person to persuade him of that was her nephew. Mendoza's letters to Charles show that, far from needing someone to point this out to her, Catherine was the one pushing hardest to get both Rome and her nephew involved. But how could she, a woman under almost constant vigilance, get a letter out to Charles? She was fortunate that, early in July, Wolsey temporarily left the country to negotiate with King Francis in France. Her husband was far easier to fox than the cardinal.

In Wolsey's absence, Henry had to fend for himself. He was not used to keeping an eye on the minutiae of business but he spotted, or so he thought, Catherine's attempts at smuggling a message out to her nephew. One of Catherine's closest confidants was Francisco Felipez, her Spanish sewer – the man whose formal task was to oversee her service at meal-times. He was typical of Catherine's more faithful friends – an intellectual and friend of Erasmus. He was deeply loyal and would stay by her side to the end. Henry himself believed that Felipez 'is and hath been always privy unto the queen's affairs and secrets'. This was the man she chose to be her messenger. An elaborate game of double bluff ensued.

In July Felipez began to say that he urgently needed to travel home to visit his sick mother. Catherine pretended to be against his going and asked Henry to deny him permission. Henry thought that she was trying to fool him and decided to outwit her. 'The king's highness does perceive that the queen is the only cause of the man's going to Spain,' Henry's secretary, William Knight, wrote to Wolsey. 'Knowing great collusion and dissimulation between them, [the king] doth also dissemble, feigning that Philip's [Felipez's] desire is made upon ground and consideration, and easily hath persuaded the queen to be content with his going.' Henry even pledged to ensure his release if, as was a danger, he was kidnapped along the way. 'The king hath said that in case Philip [Felipez] be taken by his enemies his highness will redeem him and pay his ransom,' said Knight. What he really wanted, however, was for Wolsey or the French king to arrange for Felipez to be 'detained in some corner of France'. To round the trick off, Wolsey was to make sure that no one discovered this had been done at the king's orders. By this clever ruse, Henry thought, he could not only stop the messenger, but discover the message. So it was that Felipez set off to see his mother.

Catherine had, in the meantime, reached what onlookers took to be some sort of peace with Henry. Shortly after Felipez left, Catherine, Henry and Mary went together from Hunsdon, in Hertfordshire, to Beaulieu, in Essex. Catherine's bad humour had, to the relief of everyone, disappeared. 'The merry visage is returned,' the dean of Henry's royal chapel, Richard Sampson, told Wolsey. There was also 'good countenance, much better than was, in my opinion, less suspicion, or little'. Catherine obviously had not forgotten the art of dissimulation.

Sampson concluded that things were going well. 'The *great matter* is in very good train,' he reported excitedly. Henry was doing his part to treat Catherine 'gently and sweetly' and, so, keep her tame. The normally impatient king had even waited, at length, for Catherine to finish getting ready at Hunsdon so they could ride off together for Beaulieu. Both, in fact, were playing charades. Anne Boleyn was either with them or joined them at Beaulieu. There she received, as part of a deluge of gifts that seems to have followed her decision to accept Henry's offer of marriage, an emerald ring.

Henry had put his trust in Wolsey. Catherine had placed hers in Felipez. It was she, once more, who triumphed. Felipez, rather than go via France, ignored Henry's pointed warnings about the dangers of the sea and got on a ship. Having thus evaded the trap, he arrived at Charles's court in Valladolid, in the north of Castile, before the end of July. Charles immediately ordered his people in Rome into action. He wrote to the pope demanding that Wolsey be barred from deciding the case. This, he said, should not be heard in England – where Catherine could not get a fair trial – but in Rome. 'You can imagine how much it weighs on our spirit to see something so scandalous and with such bad consequences, that will bring such infinite evils . . . We cannot desert the queen, our good aunt, in her troubles, and intend doing all we can in her favour,' Charles wrote to Mendoza as he sent Felipez back with a letter to his aunt. 'It is not to be presumed that his serenity [Henry] would consent to have her [Mary] or her mother so dishonoured, a thing so monstrous of itself and wholly without precedent in ancient or modern history.'

His other aunt, Margaret of Austria, had found out for herself about the affair and tried, from her base in the Netherlands (where she still governed on Charles's behalf), to get Wolsey to explain what was going on. The last remaining scraps of secrecy had been torn from Henry's 'great matter'. The great powers of Europe were becoming involved and the pope was under pressure to prevent anyone declaring Catherine's marriage null and void. Like the fabled emperor with the invisible new clothes, Henry now stood naked – but unaware – before the world.

32 Disease

London. 6 December 1527

The queen was diseased. The writer of the letter making this claim was too much of a gentleman – or so he pretended – to give explicit details of Catherine's terrible condition. He thought, however, that Pope Clement VII should know why her husband now found her so physically repulsive. 'There are secret reasons, which cannot be committed to writing,' he confided. 'Certain diseases in the queen defying all remedy, for which, as well as for other causes, the king will never again live with her as a wife.' The writer left the exact nature of this disease, apparently too terrible to mention and only visible to the man who shared her bed, a mystery. The clear implication was that Catherine's disease had to do with her sexual organs. Any man, the writer implied, would be repelled by such a thing.

This, at least, is what Cardinal Wolsey – the author of this letter – wanted his representative in Rome, Gregorio Casale, to tell Clement. Both the pope and Catherine herself must also realise that the queen's body was something that Henry – as the king later instructed his ambassadors to tell Clement – 'is utterly resolved and determined never to use'. He needed to understand, therefore, 'the danger that may ensue to the king's person by continuing in the queen's chamber'. It is not entirely clear what Henry meant by this. Either he was suggesting that an angry Catherine could try to do him physical harm (as he would later claim) or he was worried that she might place him in moral danger by tempting him sexually when his new-found 'scruple' obliged him to stay away from her bed. Either way, he wanted the pope to know that he would never go to her chamber again. She had lost what Italian observers called the *persona del re* – the king's person – for ever.

Wolsey's line of argument went even further. Catherine, he later suggested, could not do without her king. Libidinous desire, that most dangerous and frightening of female things, controlled and betrayed her. It was what drove her frenzied need to keep hold of Henry. This was immoral and disgraceful, Wolsey argued. Her desire to indulge in carnal pleasure with her ex-husband's brother was soon expected to be exposed as a mortal sin. He now regretted ever seeing 'perfection' and 'virtue' in a woman of such 'ungodly purposes' – especially as she denied having slept with her first husband, when he, Wolsey, knew that Ferdinand's envoys had sent the blood-spotted wedding sheets back to Spain. Catherine, in short, was guilty of doing 'nothing but declare her own *sensual affection*'. What she desired had already been shown to be 'both by God's law and man's law . . . justly condemned'.

Wolsey was desperate. The queen was not diseased. No blood-spotted sheets had been sent back to Spain. Nor was Catherine's defence of her marriage driven by sexual desire or despair. She did not lust uncontrollably over the king's magnificent body. It would not be long, in fact, before she was also being accused of not making herself available to him in bed (while confusing reports would also emerge that Henry had been knocking on her chamber door again). The cardinal, however, was fighting for his future. He had been made rudely aware that there was no turning back from the divorce and needed to grasp any tool, real or invented, to use against her. Unlike Henry himself, he realised that the task of winning the pope's support was difficult, if not impossible. He was also beginning to realise that, if he failed to deliver what the king desired, his enemies would destroy him.

Wolsey discovered all this abruptly on his return from his trip to France in September 1527. While he was away, Henry sent his own embassy to Rome. Wolsey was not consulted. Such a move would have been unthinkable at any stage over much of the previous decade but at Beaulieu and elsewhere that summer, Henry had surrounded himself with people close to Anne Boleyn. The embassy was proof that power was slipping from Wolsey's hands. Already he had found himself writing apologetic, ingratiating letters to Henry from France. 'There was never lover more desirous of the sight of his lady than I am of your most noble and royal person,' he wrote. It was an unfortunate simile. The king, by now infatuated with Anne Boleyn, was only too aware of how much a frustrated lover could burn with desire.

The greatest humiliation came soon after Wolsey landed at Dover. He had expected a warm, lavish reception – perhaps with the king and, certainly, other noblemen present. Instead, Wolsey had to make his way to the king at Richmond. Once there, he immediately sent a servant to ask exactly where and when they should meet. The custom, Mendoza noted, was that 'whenever the legate [Wolsey] has affairs of state to communicate, for the king to retire with him to a private closet'. This time, however, Anne Boleyn was present when Wolsey's messenger arrived. 'Before his majesty could reply,' Mendoza reported, 'she exclaimed: "Where else should the cardinal come? Tell him to come here, where the king is."'

It was an extraordinary moment. The great cardinal was, in effect, being summoned by the king's girlfriend. Catherine had never been so high-handed. Wolsey had no option but to obey. 'Though extremely annoyed,' Mendoza noted, '[Wolsey] concealed his resentment.' There could be no more telling a sign of how power was shifting. Mendoza shrewdly drew two conclusions: first, that the king's new love 'seems to entertain no great affection for the cardinal'; second, that this treatment was 'indicative of the king's displeasure'. Catherine, too, must have heard of the episode. It can only have increased her anxiety.

Rumours circulated, in fact, that Wolsey had been trying to find a French bride for Henry. The cardinal almost certainly feared that, with Anne Boleyn as queen, he would be in trouble even if he did deliver the divorce. His enemies were her allies. There was, however, no longer any choice. Anne, as determined as Catherine herself, was by then secretly engaged to marry Henry.

The story of how Anne Boleyn became the 'so great folly' of Catherine's husband can be traced through the series of remarkable love letters mysteriously conserved in the Vatican archives. The seventeen letters, frustratingly, are not dated but appear to belong to the period – some time between 1526 and 1528 – that started with her still refusing his advances and ended with them well and truly betrothed.

In his first letters, Henry teased her – sending a buck he had killed the previous evening and telling her that he 'wishes you [were here] instead of your brother'. He was playing the game of courtly love, but also making it clear he wanted something more. At this stage he probably just wanted to get into her bed. Anne turned him down, but then gave confusing signals. 'I have put myself in great distress, not knowing how to interpret them, whether to my disadvantage, as in some places is shown, or to advantage,' he complained.

If it shall please you to do me the office of a true, loyal mistress and friend and to give yourself up, body and soul, to me . . . I promise you that not only shall the name be given you, but that also I will take you for my only mistress, rejecting from thought and affection all others save yourself.

Though he wanted her 'body and soul', he was not offering marriage.

A clumsy Henry then pushed Anne Boleyn too far. Perhaps he was too brazen and made a crude attempt at getting her into his bed – expecting acquiescence. It took a strong-willed woman to turn down the king. Anne Boleyn was just that. One report of her reply, apparently delivered on bended knee, was that she thought Henry 'speaketh these words in mirth to prove [test] me, without intent of defiling your princely self, who I find thinks nothing less than of such wickedness which would justly procure the hatred of God and of your good queen against us'. The same report had Anne insisting she was still a virgin – the proper role for a damsel in the courtly love game – holding out for a husband to whom she could make the gift of 'my maidenhead'. Catherine was her mistress, she added, and not a woman to be crossed. Was sophisticated Anne, already in her mid-twenties and from a family not known for its sexual morals, really a virgin? She may well have been. It does not really matter, from Catherine's perspective, whether Anne was gallantly holding out against an insistent king or whether she was a teasing schemer with her eyes set on something far greater. The point is that refusal wound Henry up, driving him into a frenzy of mad, uncontrollable passion. 'Wishing myself (specially an evening) in my sweetheart's arms, whose pretty *duckies* [breasts] I trust shortly to kiss,' is how he signed off one of his letters. Perhaps he was permitted that much, but no more. Whatever the truth, Henry was determined to get all that he desired. If marriage was the only way, it would have to be marriage. If she could bear him a son, then even better. So it was that, in secret, Catherine's husband became betrothed to someone else.

Does that mean that a manipulative Anne drove Henry to leave his wife of eighteen years, or did his decision to abandon Catherine come first, opening the door for the ambitious Boleyn girl? The question is impossible to answer with absolute confidence. The evidence is confusing and scholars disagree. It may well be, indeed, that the urge to separate and the urge to marry developed in parallel, alternately driving each other on.

Whatever the case, the two things became so rapidly scrambled together – not least in Henry's head – that, as the evenings shortened and the summer of 1527 drew to a close, they had become one and the same thing. This was the alarming new world that was developing around Catherine and which caught Wolsey by surprise when he stepped off the boat at Dover that September. Most importantly, Henry – a man whose spine sometimes needed stiffening – had found another strong-willed woman. Once committed, she would keep his nose to the grindstone of divorce. Catherine had a formidable rival.

Henry could be a chronic optimist. He felt sure the pope would see the wisdom of his arguments and annul his marriage almost immediately. No doubt he told Anne Boleyn this when he proposed. Neither counted on Catherine's obstinacy or her skill at mustering the weapons she had to hand. The battle that Henry expected to win in months took another six years. His final victory, if that is what it can be called, eventually required drastic measures that changed the course of English history. That, in the end, was the only way to defeat his wife.

33 Never with the Mother

England and Rome. 1527–1528

Sir George Throckmorton was a plain-speaking man. He was worried about his king's plans to remarry and did not mind telling him so. His concern was not about Henry leaving Catherine, but about him marrying Anne Boleyn. He had heard rumours that Henry had slept with all the women in the Boleyn family and, in his blundering fashion, was prepared to ask the king straight.

'It is thought ye have meddled with both the mother and the sister,' he told Henry. The king's answer was both abrupt and revelatory. 'Never with the mother,' he said.

Throckmorton had hit on another major problem with Henry's plan to swap Catherine for Anne Boleyn. Henry may have not touched Anne's mother, but he admitted his affair with her sister, Mary. Throckmorton was concerned, indeed, that 'your conscience would be more troubled at the length' by marrying Anne. What if, just as Leviticus said it was wrong to marry your brother's wife, it was equally wrong to marry your mistress's sister? In both cases, after all, 'carnal knowledge' existed.

Henry was also worried. In this respect extramarital sex was, indeed, legally considered as important as marriage itself. It meant that Anne was related to Henry 'by affinity'. Henry's ambassadors in Rome, then, were given a double task. Not only did he want his and Catherine's marriage annulled, he also needed to clear the way for her rival. That would require a papal dispensation allowing him to marry Anne, despite his previous sexual relationship with her sister. The dispensation, it was suggested, should allow him to marry a woman who might 'be related . . . in the first degree of affinity, arising from whatever licit or illicit intercourse'. The double standard was remarkable. On the one hand the pope was being told it had been wrong for Catherine to win a dispensation to marry her former husband's brother. On the other hand, he was being asked to write a dispensation for Henry to marry his former lover's sister.

Many, including the pope, would have preferred him to declare himself a bachelor unilaterally, marrying Anne first and then waiting for Catherine to challenge him. The king had a prodigious ability, however, to persuade himself both that he was in the right and that everyone else would inevitably agree with him. Henry's line of argument was best summed up by Wolsey, when the latter applied, in February 1528, both for the dispensation Henry wanted in order to marry Anne and for the commission to allow him – preferably alone, but otherwise accompanied by another cardinal – to hear the divorce case in London. The ambassadors going to Rome were to persuade the pope that the king was not acting 'out of vain affection or undue love to a gentlewoman of not so excellent qualities' but because of his noble, now troubled, conscience. 'The king's desire is founded upon justice, and does not spring from any grudge or displeasure to the queen whom the king honours and loves and minds to love and to treat as his sister, with all manner of kindness.' Catherine, after all, was 'the relict of his dearest brother'. Anne Boleyn, however, was no less a lady.

On the other side the approved, excellent virtuous [qualities] of the said gentlewoman, the purity of her life, her constant virginity, her maidenly and womanly pudicity, her soberness, chasteness, meekness, humility, wisdom, descent of right noble and high through regal blood, education in all good and laudable qualities and manners, apparent aptness to procreation of children . . . be the grounds on which the king's desire is founded.

Wolsey did not really share Henry's confidence. He saw not just the weakness of his arguments, but the power that Catherine's nephew Charles exerted over the pope. His attempts at persuasion were, therefore, not just limited to painting Catherine as diseased, sex-crazed and selfish. He also warned the pope that if he thwarted Henry, England might turn its back on the papacy. Luther's heresy would spread, he added, and Wolsey's own life would be in danger.

In the meantime, Catherine had another sort of a problem to deal with. For Henry not only wanted to marry Anne Boleyn, he also wanted to have her as close at hand as possible while he waited for permission to divorce. As a result there were times when all three lived together, if not under the same roof then, at least, under the same complex of roofs in the rambling royal palaces near London. Thus in May 1528 Anne Boleyn enjoyed her own rooms in the splendid Tiltyard Gallery at Greenwich, where Henry sent a recently returned ambassador from Rome to give her his news. She had been sent there to keep her away from a smallpox outbreak amongst the queen's maidens.

Catherine dissimulated bravely, hoping that her husband would either get bored of her rival or return to his senses so that Anne Boleyn could become just another name on the list of royal mistresses. It was a hope she clung to blindly, in the face of growing evidence that it would not be. Her life took on a strange duality. There were moments of relative normality, when Anne Boleyn was not at court, as well as moments of strange and, presumably, painful abnormality, when she was there. To confuse things further, both she and Henry still felt obliged to behave in public as if nothing untoward was happening. When the sweat broke out in and around London once more in June 1528, Henry and Catherine fled together. The panic was widespread, and notaries found themselves inundated with people making wills. Anne Boleyn went to her father's home at Hever, where she eventually came down with – but survived – the disease. Henry sent her a doctor and said that he would willingly give up his own health to cure hers, especially as he now feared 'still longer being harassed by enemy, Absence'.

If the sweat failed to eradicate Catherine's rival, it did at least bring a momentary return to something familiar. They had run from the sweat before and, this time, also kept their household as small as possible to avoid infection. Henry continued to hear mass with Catherine in the morning. 'Every morning as soon as he cometh from the queen he asketh whether I hear anything from your grace,' Sir Thomas Heneage wrote to Wolsey after the latter had retired to his magnificent new palace at Hampton Court. Henry popped his purgative pills of Rasis every week and recommended sweet Manus Christi powder to ward off illness. They both also confessed daily, just in case the sweat should get them. Late that summer, however, Anne Boleyn was back. 'The king is in so deeply that God alone can get him out of it,' commented the French ambassador.

Catherine's legal strategy was clear from the very start. The case had to be heard in Rome. She could not expect a fair trial from English judges, who would inevitably bend to the king's will. This would be even more so if Wolsey, the king's right-hand man, was the judge. In that case, she would simply refuse to appear before the court. In the meantime she wanted to bring over lawyers from Spain and Flanders, as English lawyers could not be trusted. It was a frustrating time. She had no direct contact with the imperial ambassador in Rome, so news of how her case was going there came only second-hand, via Mendoza, and with a considerable time lag.

She felt alone and unprotected. Some of her own councillors worked against her, while some supporters began to abandon her – tempted by Henrician favours or simply terrified of what might happen to their court careers if they stuck by Catherine.

To Catherine's evident chagrin, Clement eventually agreed that Wolsey could hear the case in London, though only in the company of another cardinal sent from Rome, Lorenzo Campeggio. This was better for her than leaving it up to Wolsey on his own, or in the company of other English bishops, but – as the gouty and grumpy Campeggio got closer to England in September 1528 – Catherine panicked. She thought he was bringing instructions from the pope to give Henry all that he wanted and told Mendoza that the pope had been fooled into thinking not only that the people of England were in favour of the divorce, but that both she and her nephew were too. Campeggio's impending arrival meant, it seemed to almost everybody, that the final showdown was about to happen. Henry and Anne Boleyn were fully convinced that their betrothal would soon turn into marriage.

Catherine was beside herself with anxiety. She felt herself a foreigner once more, abandoned and friendless in a distant land. She was still, however, England's queen and told Mendoza that she would just have to place her trust in three things: in God; in her nephew Charles; and in a group that was genuinely unhappy about the way she was being treated – the people of England.

34 God and My Nephew

Bath Place, London. 26 October 1528

Catherine's barge would have picked her up in the chilly October morning, its two dozen oarsmen rowing her along the River Thames past the great houses of Westminster. By nine o'clock in the morning it must have docked at the nearest landing stage to Bath Place. It was here that the irritable, pain-racked Cardinal Lorenzo Campeggio had taken to his bed, resisting – as best he could – the sudden, sharp and excruciating stabs of gout that felt like hot needles piercing his knee.

The Italian cardinal had added reasons for feeling cantankerous that morning. Not only was he tormented by physical pain, but he had been woken at dawn by Wolsey. His fellow legate had come to bombard him with still more information about the troublesome case they were to hear together. Wolsey had told him about a recent encounter between Henry and Catherine, when she had been informed that the only Spanish counsellor she was allowed would be her friend, Juan Luis Vives. Various English bishops, including John Fisher and William Warham, the archbishop of Canterbury, had also been appointed to advise her, the cardinal said. Then Wolsey told him that Catherine herself was on her way. She wanted to confess.

If Catherine was going to put her faith in God, then Campeggio – with his direct line of communication to the pope's most intimate advisers – was the closest thing to Him that she could commune with. They had already had an uncomfortable encounter ten days earlier, when the recently arrived Campeggio went to see her accompanied by his fellow cardinal Wolsey.

On that occasion, she discovered to her horror that both men thought the whole affair could be easily solved if she took a vow of perpetual chastity, became a nun and moved into a convent. This solution suited Henry, though only if it allowed him to marry again. More importantly, it provided a quick and painless fix for a pope who was terrified of being trapped in the middle of a bitter – and potentially violent – dispute between the English king and the Emperor Charles. The pope, Campeggio told Catherine, 'counselled her, confiding much in her prudence, that, rather than press it to trial, she should of herself take some other course, which would give general satisfaction, and greatly benefit herself'. He had slyly left it at that, avoiding explicit mention of nuns and convents, to see what she would say.

Catherine, however, was a step ahead and had managed, once again, to find out what was going on behind closed doors. 'She had heard we were to persuade her to enter some religion,' Campeggio wrote back to Rome. She told him forthrightly that 'she knew the sincerity of her own conscience and that she was resolved to die in the Faith and in obedience to God and his Holy Church'.

Campeggio had then tried his powers of persuasion. If she retired honourably then she would be losing little more than her right to use the *persona del re*. Henry had already told him that he had stopped sleeping with her two years earlier and Campeggio himself told her this was something 'which I knew she would never recover'. Surely, then, it would be better to 'yield to his displeasure than submit her cause to the hazard of sentence'? If he and Wolsey decided against her, the Italian warned, her reputation would be ruined for ever, her dower forfeited and a huge scandal would ensue. 'On the other hand, if she complied, she would retain her dower, the guardianship of the princess [Mary], her rank and whatever else she chose to demand; and would neither offend God nor her conscience,' he reported. 'I enforced these arguments by example of a queen of France who did the same and is still honoured by God and that kingdom.'

He got no further than that. 'She concluded the conference,' he wrote, 'by saying that she was a lone woman and a stranger, without friend or adviser, and intended to ask the king for counsellors, when she would give us audience.' Her stubbornness, and Henry's determination, were already getting him down. 'Imagine my condition when, besides indisposition of the body, I suffer from such infinite agitation of the mind,' he wrote.

Now she was returning to agitate him further. He could be forgiven for hoping that, at the very least, the queen might prove easier to deal with than her husband. Henry had visited Campeggio himself a few days earlier, excitably and irascibly demanding that the court came to a prompt decision.

He did not know that Henry and Catherine had rowed a few days earlier, the controlled stand-off between them breaking under the weight of Campeggio's presence in London. Henry had tried to bully her, claiming that Campeggio was there with strict instructions to nullify their marriage. The pope was angry with the emperor after his troops had sacked Rome, he had said, and would punish her to spite her nephew. By appealing to her nephew and encouraging him to meddle, he added, she had dug her own grave. She should go into a convent now, or he would find ways to force her. 'How can the pope condemn me without a hearing?' she had cried. 'I know very well that if the judges are impartial, and I am granted a hearing, my cause is gained, for no judge will be found unjust enough to condemn me.' This encounter, combined with the stream of English bishops sent by Henry to pressure Catherine into becoming a nun, had hardened her. She was now ready to give Campeggio his reply.

Catherine insisted that they talk under the seal of confession. Their conversation had to remain secret from Wolsey, the king and almost everyone else. She explicitly waived that secrecy, however, with respect to the pope. It was to him that her words were really directed.

'Her discourse ranged from her first arrival in England to the present time,' Campeggio wrote afterwards.

First, she affirmed on her conscience that from her marriage with Prince Arthur, on 14 November, until his death on 2 April, she had not slept in the same bed with him more than seven nights and that she remained as intact and uncorrupted as the day she left her mother's womb. Secondly, after I had exhorted her at great length to remove all these difficulties, and to content herself with making a profession of chastity, setting before her all the reasons which could be urged on that head, she assured me she would never comply; that she intended to live and die in the state of matrimony, to which God had called her: that she would always remain of that opinion, and that she would never change it.

Given Catherine's normally demure and cheerful disposition, Campeggio may have been surprised by what came next. They could tear her 'limb from limb', Catherine said, and she would stay firm. If she was then brought back to life, she 'would prefer to die over again, rather than change'. These were no idle threats. Catherine's obstinacy was cast out of solid iron. If she had to die for her beliefs and in order to maintain her honour, then she was quite prepared to do so. Her words were a warning to the pope about just how high she was ready to raise the stakes.

What she really wanted Pope Clement to do was persuade Henry to turn back the clock, accept his marriage and behave as if nothing had happened. Her request hid a small promise of reward. If Henry recapitulated, she would then use her influence with her emperor nephew 'to conclude a universal peace'.

God, she had told Mendoza, was one of her three great hopes – along with her nephew and the people of England. God, via

Campeggio, did not yet seem to be fully on her side. It was her nephew who now came to her rescue. Or, rather, it was that poor, mistreated ambassador with the Jewish blood, De Puebla, who reached out from the grave to offer a final piece of loyal sustenance. A key, and previously unknown, document had been found by his sons amongst his papers. It was a papal brief, dating back to the time of Catherine's marriage with Henry, which added extra strength to the original papal bull that allowed them to marry. A brief was a slightly less formal document, but nevertheless valid. Not even Catherine had heard of this brief, which was dated on the same day as the bull that cleared her to marry her former husband's brother. It was, apparently, the document that had been sent by the pope to Queen Isabel on her deathbed so that she could die knowing that her daughter's future had been settled.

The brief was handed to Charles by De Puebla's sons at the end of 1527. Catherine had known about it since at least May 1528. Once she had a properly notarised copy, she sprung it on an unsuspecting and furious Henry towards the end of 1528.

Catherine's brief was dynamite, as it widened the justifications for allowing her marriage to Henry so far as to make them almost impossible to argue against. The brief's arrival threatened to blow the entire divorce case apart. 'In it consists the whole of the queen's right,' Mendoza reported excitedly. The court case had not even started and, to her husband's profound annoyance, she had already landed a lethal blow.

35 The People's Queen

Bridewell, London. November 1528

Catherine walked across the long, raised gallery connecting the new royal residence at Bridewell, just south of Fleet Street, to the neighbouring friary of the Dominicans, Blackfriars. The gallery rose over the stinking, sewer-like River Fleet and penetrated the city walls, stretching a full 240 feet to the friary. For the people of London it was one of those places where they might snatch a rare glimpse of the king or the queen themselves – for, unusually, the recently completed, brick-built palace at Bridewell had no chapel of its own where they could observe the daily rituals of their religion. Catherine walked along the gallery, as she would have done most days, heading for the chapel run by the Dominican friars with their customary black mantles over white habits. A large crowd of Londoners watched their queen as she walked above them. Suddenly protocol and decorum were broken. The crowd called out words of encouragement. May she win her case, they shouted. She must have victory, they called out, otherwise England itself would go to ruin.

Henry was shocked and furious. These were his subjects. They were meant to support him. He issued orders banning anyone from going near the gallery. Above all, he was angry with Catherine. She had been deliberately 'showing herself' to the people, he claimed. He suspected her of trying to steal their support and stir their anger. Henry remained a popular king, but times were bad. Rainless summers, winter frosts, cattle disease and the drying up of trade with Charles's empire had all combined to create an atmosphere in which popular displeasure could fester. England's new alliance with France, which was to blame for the lack of trade, rankled. On a Sunday the previous May, an angry miller from Goudhurst, Robert Bailey, had told a group of disgruntled Kentishmen how he and a group of conspirators planned to kidnap and drown Wolsey. 'We will bring him to the seaside, and there will put him into a boat, in the which shall be bored four great holes, and the holes shall be stopped with pins,' he said. The boat would be towed out to sea where 'the pins shall be pulled out, and so sink him'.

Public opposition to the 'divorce' may not have been quite as rabid as Mendoza made out, but there was a strong groundswell of popular anger. It was simply easier, and safer, for people to blame Wolsey than the real culprit – their still beloved king. One of the first intellectuals to change sides and offer his support to Henry over the divorce, Robert Wakefield, admitted he was taking a risk. 'If the people should know that I, which began to defend the queen's cause . . . should now write against it, surely I should be stoned of them to death, or else have such a slander and obloquy raised upon me, that I had rather to die a thousand times,' he said. Even in far-off Flanders, one Englishman reported, the 'great matter' was considered 'sufficient to cause the stones to come out of the streets to cry vengeance upon us'.

Campeggio's arrival had incited popular grumbling in the streets of London. 'The common people . . . and in especial women and others that favoured the queen talked largely and said that the king would for his own pleasure have another wife,' said Hall. 'Whoever spoke against the marriage was of the common people abhorred and reproved.'

It was these 'rumours and foolish communications' that, again according to Hall, drove Henry to embark on a disastrous public relations exercise. Like a politician attached to unpopular ideas, he believed the matter simply had not been explained properly. Who better to put the people right than the king himself?

On the afternoon of 8 November 1528, he called together

the lord mayor and aldermen of London along with nobles, judges and other assembled dignitaries, to the great chamber at Bridewell. He was driven, he told them, by a conscience that had been torturing him 'ever since a bishop of France [Tarbes], a great personage and learned man, then being ambassador here, had spoken of it to his council in terribly expressive terms'. His great wishes were 'to assure the succession of his kingdom, the peace and tranquillity of his subjects, to understand what was right and reasonable, and whatever was reasonable he would implicitly adopt'. He feared, however, that he and Catherine 'live together abominably and detestably in open adultery'.

Hall, who was present, claimed the king even told them he would be delighted if his marriage to Catherine were proven valid. 'There was never thing more pleasant nor more acceptable to me in my life . . . for I assure you all, that besides her noble parentage, of the which she is descended (as you all know), she is a woman of most gentleness, of most humility and buxomness.' It would hurt him deeply to have to separate from the woman he had assumed to be his lawful wife for the previous twenty years, he assured them gravely. Such was his love of Catherine, he claimed, that: 'If I were to marry again, if the marriage might be good, I would surely choose her above all other women.'

These fine words were, according to a different report, matched by a sinister threat. 'If, not withstanding, he found anyone, whoever he was, who spoke in other terms than he ought to do of his prince [i.e. himself], he would let him know that he was his master,' reported the French ambassador Du Bellay. 'I think he used these terms: "That there was never a head so dignified but that he would make it fly".' It would take courage, from now on, to side publicly with Catherine.

For Henry to convince himself of his own elevated morality was one thing, but to convince his people was quite another. The speech did not go down well and it showed on the listeners' faces. 'It was a strange sight,' reported Hall. 'Some sighed and said nothing. Others were sorry to the hear the king so troubled in his conscience. Others that favoured the queen [were] much sorrowed that this matter was now opened.'

Henry left London to see Anne, while Catherine was sent back to Greenwich. Some thought he was so upset by the reaction to his speech that he would stay away until the trial started. Anne Boleyn, however, persuaded him to return to London a few days later having, presumably, found ways to stiffen his spine. She followed soon afterwards, probably to stop Henry from wavering. The charade set up for Campeggio – that she and Henry lived apart and rarely saw each other – was dropped and Wolsey found her some 'very fine lodging' close to Henry.

In October the French ambassador had been so fooled by Catherine's brave face that he reported she and Henry must still be sharing not just meals but also beds: 'The queen makes such cheer as she always has done in her greatest triumph,' he reported. 'Nor, to see them together, could anyone have told there was anything the matter. To this hour they have the same bed and the same table.'

By early December, however, the same man reported that Anne Boleyn had become the focus of both court life and of the grumbling of the common people.

Greater court is paid to her every day than has been for a long time paid to the queen. I believe that they wish to accustom the people by degrees to endure her, so that when the *grand coup* comes, it may not appear strange. Notwithstanding, the people always remain hardened against her, and I think that they would do more than they do if they had more power; but strict order is everywhere kept daily . . . a search has also been made for hackbuts and crossbows, and wherever they have been found in the town they have been taken, and no other weapon now remains except the tongue. In the country, also, a great and continual watch is kept up.

Catherine's ability to thwart Henry's moves, while maintaining such outward calm, provoked rising paranoia in the king. He suspected that Charles planned to follow Mendoza's advice and, using Catherine, encourage the English to rebel against him. The appearance of the brief drove him to a still greater frenzy. He eventually became enraged by Catherine's combination of good humour and bold blows to his strategy. How could she continue to smile and be cheery? He, after all, was suffering. She must, he concluded, be playing to the gallery – trying to turn the people of England against him. A fierce reprimand was written out. It may not have been delivered in its exact form, but the text shows just how scared Henry was becoming of his wife. She had dealt a terrible blow to his legal arguments by producing the new brief. She also had the people on her side. Now, he suspected, she might be planning to lead a rebellion and have him murdered. Conspirators and 'ill-disposed personages' were, the text said, plotting to murder Henry and Wolsey 'for your grace's [Catherine's] sake, or for your grace's occasion'. Should anything happen to either of them, she would pay – even if she was not involved. The result would be 'your grace's utter undoing and destruction'.

Catherine, in short, was being accused of fanning the flames of treason and regicide – crimes punishable by death. Henry had heard rumours that members of Charles's privy council were saying a trial would spark war, with the king's own subjects rising against him. 'This has made the king very fierce,' Mendoza reported. 'But, believe me, his fear is greater than his rage, however great that is.'

The text went on to accuse Catherine of a random slate of misdeeds ranging from denying Henry access to her bed to smiling too much.

The king's highness taketh this very earnestly, and much the more doubteth in this behalf because you do not show such love to his noble grace, neither in nor yet out of bed, (and specially to such a noble and loving prince as he is) as a woman ought to do to her husband. What was done in bed between both your graces we pass over, but openly your grace does not bemean yourself accordingly . . .

Given that Campeggio had recently been informed that Henry had refused to sleep with her for the previous two years and that Wolsey had insinuated to the pope that she suffered some terrible disease, this was rich stuff indeed.

If her private behaviour was deemed wrong, her public demeanour was denounced as either frivolous or downright provocative. 'For whereas the king's highness is in great pensiveness . . . ye [appear] not so to be,' the document said. This was apparent 'in your countenance, in your apparel, yea and all your other behaviour'. Catherine was accused, indeed, of 'exhorting other ladies and gentlemen of the court to dance and pastime, and make other assemblies of [pleasure]'. She should, the writers said, have been encouraging them to pray.

Worst of all was her behaviour outside the court. There she was deemed to be encouraging protests just by smiling at people.

Your grace do show yourself too much to the people, rejoicing greatly in their exclamations and ill obloquy. And by beckoning with your head and smiling . . . your grace have rather comforted [encouraged] them in their doing [so rather] than rebuked or refrained them therefrom as your grace's duty had been to do.

The real reasons for this outrageous list of accusations seem two-fold. On the one hand, she had kept the existence of the brief secret for several months when she 'should have advertised [advised] the king's highness thereof'. On the other hand, Henry was looking for excuses to separate even before a divorce had been granted. 'The king's highness cannot persuade himself that your grace do bear unto his grace such love as your grace ought to do, but that your grace rather do hate him.'

His council, as a result, had said it was no longer safe for him 'to be conversant with your grace, neither at bed nor at board, specially after the beginning of the process [trial]'. Catherine, they suggested, might be tempted to murder him. Henry was within his right to withdraw from her company 'for there is neither law nor reason that will enforce a man to be in the presence of such persons by whom he have just suspicion to be in great danger of [his] life'.

Henry, or whoever wrote the draft for him, was feeling especially vindictive. The final lines were designed to sap Catherine's morale and sink her, so far indomitable, spirit. The king 'will not suffer hereafter the lady princess [Mary] to come in your grace's company', they threatened. Her daughter Mary, who was now at an age when she needed her mother to oversee her education, would be kept away. 'Which should be a thing to your grace very grievous,' the authors added with needless malice.

Even if these exact words were never delivered to Catherine, she certainly heard something similar when visited by members of her own council – probably acting on Wolsey's commands – who wanted to know if she really had been plotting to murder her husband. Catherine was outraged that Henry should make such an accusation. She valued his life, she told them, above her own. She would not, therefore, deign even to answer the question. Then Henry himself confronted her with the allegations. He was not scared of her, he said, but was not so sure about her servants – especially the Spaniards.

If Henry wished to wipe the smile off Catherine's face, he had managed it. In public he showed her courtesy. In private he made her life impossible. It was not a happy Christmas for Catherine. She and Henry retired with the court to Greenwich. Anne Boleyn was also there with her own establishment. The two women seem to have maintained their strange stand-off by studiously ignoring each other. Earls, dukes and familiar court figures arrived to join in the merriment. There were jousts, tourneys, masks and huge banquets, with Campeggio as one of the special guests. Catherine, however, remained steadfastly glum. 'The queen showed to them no manner of countenance and made no great joy of nothing, her mind was so troubled,' said Hall.

By January 1529 even Campeggio could not avoid noticing the increasingly public presence of Anne Boleyn. 'The king persists more than ever in his desire to marry this lady, kissing her and treating her in public as though she were his wife,' he noted. He also saw that Henry and Anne were holding out on 'any further [sexual] conjunction' until they got approval from a pope 'from whom he fully expects to obtain some remedy whereby to gratify his desire'. It was up to the pope, in other words, to release Henry's sexual and amorous tension. That was what Henry and Anne Boleyn fully expected him to do. It was also what Catherine feared that Campeggio had been sent to achieve.

36 Spies and Disguises

Greenwich. 23 November 1528

Mendoza disguised himself as best he could. Catherine had sent a message that she needed to speak to him urgently and in the utmost secrecy. No one must recognise him. She had secret information to impart – gleaned from her own informants around the king. He must appear 'in disguise and as secretly as possible'. They met, somehow, at Greenwich. Quite how the Spanish ambassador sneaked through into her chamber, if that is what he did, we do not know. Or perhaps they met in the gardens, or Catherine simply took a wintry walk along the River Thames.

These were difficult times. The net that had begun to close around Catherine before the divorce process started had been tightened to the point of asphyxiation. She was, for the moment, trapped inside the same royal court that her husband planned to expel her from. Mendoza was her only contact with the outside world. It was he who passed on information, forwarded letters and listened to her anxious explanations of the goings-on and rumours at court.

Her anxiety this time centred on the brief, the document that had been originally sent to her mother and which had recently been found amongst the deceased De Puebla's things. She had called the clandestine meeting with Mendoza to tell him that Henry was desperate to get his hands on the only existing copy of the brief. Charles must be warned, she said, that her husband would destroy or hide it at the first opportunity.

Mendoza did not see the urgency. If Henry sent an ambassador to request the brief, there would be plenty of time to warn Charles. He calmed her fears but, nevertheless, sat down that afternoon to write to the emperor. 'The queen has been warned that the king wants to send someone to your majesty because he has been told you have the original brief in your possession,' he said. 'The person will try by fair words to see it and, once he has got hold of it, place it where it cannot be found again.' He repeated the message a few days later. 'She warns your majesty never to let the original leave your hands, because she knows these people will work hard and try anything to get hold of it.'

In fact, Mendoza almost certainly found another piece of news more intriguing. Henry had been visiting Catherine's bedchamber again when he was in Greenwich. 'They eat and sleep together,' he said. This, he thought, was because Henry's lawyers had advised him not to deny the queen her conjugal rights. Perhaps Catherine and Henry were simply maintaining a sexless, but comfortably familiar, form of cohabitation born from the habits of twenty years of marriage. Henry may have been passionate and energetic in the tiltyard or on the dance floor but – at least later in life – he was not always such an ardent lover, suffering occasional impotence. Or perhaps Henry, who may have dreamed about Anne's 'duckies' but was not sharing her bed, was seeking something more from his wife. The reports are contradictory and may be based on rumour.

Even without sex, though, the implied intimacy is surprising. Henry's belief in his own virtue certainly forced him to behave, at least in public, in a polite fashion to Catherine. Perhaps, just occasionally or even out of sentimental nostalgia, Henry was capable of believing the words he himself had delivered at Bridewell and which Hall summed up when he said: 'Surely he loved her as well as any prince might love his wife, and she him again, and therefore it was a great pity that their marriage was not good.' Whatever the reasons for Henry being in his wife's bedroom, Mendoza thought it important enough to communicate the fact to the emperor. Certainly it meant that the threats of him retiring completely from her had not been carried out. Perhaps the French ambassador, too, had been right about them sharing a bedroom over the summer. Catherine may be excused, if that was the case, for thinking that she still had a chance of winning her husband back.

Henry and his council, meanwhile, became increasingly obsessed by the brief – a copy of which had already been presented in Rome. Henry's representative there, Gregorio Casale, confirmed that it seemed to close any loopholes left by the original bull. It widened the reasons Julius gave for allowing her to marry Henry, adding to the primary cause of fostering peace the words '*certain other reasons*'. As these last reasons were not explicit, they were impossible to argue against – even if, confusingly, the document also stated that she and Arthur had consummated their marriage.

Henry suspected a forgery. He was increasingly willing to see conspiracies and now issued detailed instructions about how the original, should his men get hold of it, should be subjected to minute scrutiny. It had to be examined in sunlight for signs of rubbings out or rewriting, checked to see whether additional pieces of paper had been craftily pasted over parts of it, scoured for blemishes and the seals double-checked. Was it all in the same handwriting? Had the last line been finished? Did it have the proper wax seal with the imprint of the pope's ring, with St Peter fishing from a boat, on it? Linguistic experts were to study it for style and the type of Latin used.

The pressure on Catherine to obtain the original and show it to Henry became unbearable. 'They are trying by every means to get it into their hands,' Mendoza reported. Her counsellors were afraid of Henry and some acted at his behest. A stern, threatening script of what they were to say to her about the brief was even written out for them. If she did not diligently set about the 'attaining [obtaining] of the said original' then, her counsellors were to say, it deserved to be invalidated as a piece of evidence. It was her duty to get hold of the original, not just so justice could be done but to show 'the continuance of love' that she still professed for her husband. She must show the brief within three months and pledge before a notary to do all in her power to get it. The counsellors were told to add a subtle threat. Her daughter Mary, they must say, might lose her inheritance if she failed to get it.

A frightened Catherine did as she was told. Mendoza wrote hurriedly to Charles, warning him to ignore the letter when it arrived. 'The king has made the queen swear that she will do all she can to procure it, for which purpose she has been made to write a letter and protestation against her will,' he explained.

He need not have worried. Catherine, once more, had selected her messengers carefully. They were men who could be trusted both to deliver the letter and to tell her nephew to take no notice of it. Her servant Francisco Felipez, the man who had first slipped past Wolsey and Henry to warn her nephew about the 'great matter', was sent via France. This time, however, he did not get far, mysteriously falling and dislocating his shoulder at Abbeville.

A second copy went by sea across the treacherous Bay of Biscay with her English chaplain, Thomas Abel. Catherine did not yet trust Abel, who seems to have been with her a short time, and so sent another Spanish servant, Juan de Montoya, with him. Abel turned out to be one of those brave, if rare, Englishmen who were prepared to stand up to Henry's bullying. It was he who told the real story to a shocked Emperor Charles. What Catherine really wanted, he explained, was the exact opposite to what she had written in the letter he was delivering. 'The first thing we beg your majesty is that you do not give us the brief even though the queen implores you to in her letter,' he said. Catherine was, he explained, effectively a prisoner to her husband. 'She neither says, nor writes, nor signs anything but what the king commands her,' he told Charles. 'To this she is compelled by solemn oath.'

Charles eventually had the document read out aloud to Henry's own ambassadors in April 1529 and gave them a copy. Abel stood mutely to one side. Charles wrote back to Catherine assuring her he would take the case to Rome. 'Your highness can be certain that I am taking as good care of this business of yours, as of any other that I deal with, and that I will continue to do so,' he said.

The fuss over the brief served, above all, to buy time. Campeggio had been in England since the end of September 1528, but arguments over the brief and other matters were still going on the following April. The pope's secret orders to Campeggio were, anyway, to drag things out as long as possible. This gave Catherine time to seek a way to escape Henry's vigilance and write directly to the pope. With the help of Mendoza, this was done by April. So it was that, more or less at the same time Henry's ambassadors were being handed a copy of the brief in Madrid, letters written in Catherine's own hand were being delivered to the pope in person.

It was a crucial move for, although the pope was deeply unhappy about the situation, he could not now ignore Catherine's protestations. Not even Clement could fail to be moved by the letters Catherine wrote to him. They were sad and eloquent enough 'to make rocks crack', said Miçer Mai, Charles's ambassador to the pope. Cardinal Giovanni Salviati, who was present when the letters were delivered, was not so moved. He responded by warning that, if she did not enter a convent, Henry might simply arrange to have her murdered. She should take the vow of chastity, he said, because of 'the danger [that exists] to her health'. Even if Henry did not order her secretly assassinated she should 'beware of herbs', as his servants might poison her anyway.

Mai left him in no doubt about Catherine's determination. 'I said that the queen was ready to incur this danger rather than be a bad wife, and prejudice her daughter,' he said. 'And that if they should resort to poison, the emperor was the sort of person who would seek to avenge it.' The pope agreed that if she formally presented a petition in her own name, the case would be recalled to Rome. It was, perhaps, surprising that Catherine had so far declined – despite Mendoza's urging – to send powers of attorney to Mai so that he could present the petition in her name. The fact that she was being so closely watched only partially explains this. To send powers would have been an act of open defiance of her husband. There were several reasons why she was not ready to do that. The most important of all was that, in her heart of hearts, she clung to the hope that Henry would suddenly tire of Anne Boleyn and return to her.

When the English ambassadors saw the pope early in May they began to realise that the wind was now blowing against them. They seemed unaware, however, that Catherine was in direct contact with Clement. The pope, who had been fuelling Henry's false hopes, now admitted that things were looking grim for the English king. That did not mean Clement was on Catherine's side. He told the English, in fact, that he wished she had died. 'He would, for the wealth of Christendom, the queen were in her grave,' Henry's ambassadors reported. Clement was beginning to realise, just as Wolsey had warned him, that Rome's future control of the church in England was at risk. Just as the emperor's troops had sacked Rome and destroyed much of the material wealth of the church so, he feared, Catherine's obstinacy would 'be the cause of the destruction of the spiritualities'.

Henry's sudden fear that Catherine might actually succeed in getting the case 'revoked' to Rome meant there was now pressure for the long-postponed case to be started in London – and finished as soon as possible. Eight months had gone by since

Campeggio first set foot on English soil, far longer than Henry had expected to wait. On 31 May 1529, as temperatures in London remained obstinately at wintry levels (and southern Europeans like Campeggio grumbled about needing fires to keep them warm), the formal trial process started. Two bishops were appointed to visit both Catherine and Henry, citing them in court at Blackfriars on 18 June, between 9 and 10 a.m.

As the trial date approached, a frightened Catherine finally signed powers of attorney for Miçer Mai to appeal in Rome in her own name – rather than that of her nephew – against the court in London. Margaret of Austria, who had received panicked letters from Catherine asking for help as soon as the trial date was announced, secretly sent her a notary from Brussels. Mendoza, waiting in Brussels and mightily relieved that she had finally taken the step, arranged the rest. By 16 June, two days before she was due to appear in court, the paperwork had been drawn up and at least some of it was already on its way.

The scene was now set for a trial which was extraordinary by the standards of this, or any, period. 'This was the strangest and newest sight and device that ever was read or heard of in any history or chronicle in any region,' said Wolsey's gentleman usher, George Cavendish. 'That a king and queen should . . . appear in court like common persons.'

The promising Tudor period would have to wait many years for a piece of theatre to match the trial that ensued at Blackfriars. The leading man was not just a king, but famously handsome and genuinely popular. The supporting roles were taken by imposing and colourful characters like Wolsey, Campeggio and, as the off-stage villain, Anne Boleyn. The austere John Fisher, bishop of Rochester, was inspired to a cameo performance that would be remembered for years. Even the bit parts, played by plain-speaking, elderly country squires who came up from their rural seats to recall their metropolitan youth and speculate bawdily on the queen's teenage sex life, were guaranteed to enthral the audience. But it was the leading lady, Catherine of Aragon, who stole the show.

37 Defiance

Blackfriars, London. 21 June 1529

'King Harry of England, come into the court!' The crier's words rang through the great chamber at Blackfriars. This had been specially converted into a solemn court. Wolsey and Campeggio presided over it from their elegant, cushioned, cloth-of-gold chairs on a raised tribune covered in carpets and tapestries and set with tables, benches and bars.

'Here, my lords!' answered Henry, who already sat on the right side of the courtroom in a chair of rich tissue set under a gold canopy. Across the court from him, on the other side of the benches where England's bishops perched, sat Catherine herself. 'Catherine, queen of England, come into the court!' said the crier.

With these words the most exciting and eventful day of one of the most remarkable trials ever seen in England began. That a king and queen should be called into court – to be tried by two cardinals representing the pope – was unprecedented. Men scratched their heads and attempted in vain to recall anything similar from the past. It was not just unprecedented in England, they decided, but in the Christian world. The great courts and centres of learning of Europe looked on from afar with bemused fascination at the unique event unfolding at Blackfriars.

It was as if three of the principal powers of Europe, via proxy or in person, were facing one another in the courtroom. On the right was the king of England. On the left, in the form of Catherine, was the mighty Emperor Charles himself. Stuck in between, like a man being squeezed in a slowly closing vice, was the pope – represented by Campeggio and, to a lesser extent, by

Wolsey. Although his cardinals were nominally there to resolve the dilemma, the pope mainly saw himself as a victim. The mutual intransigence of both Catherine and Henry, he felt, was to blame for his plight. Clement, one of Charles's more experienced diplomats had sniffed, may have come from the great Medici family, but he was a timid man surrounded by mediocrity. In Rome, when asked about the divorce, he sometimes gave way to bouts of weeping or simply declared that he wished he were dead.

England's bishops were front-row onlookers at this strange spectacle involving their two masters – the king and the pope. The common people were also present at the Blackfriars court, crowding into the chamber to witness the unprecedented show. Catherine was cheered as she entered the court. She probably came with the same grandeur as when, three days earlier, she had appeared unexpectedly to lodge a formal protest against the court and its judges. On that occasion she was accompanied by the four bishops and other members of her council with a 'great company of ladies and gentlewomen' following her. The show of solidarity from her ladies was echoed by the women waiting in the crowd outside the court. 'If the matter were to be decided by the women, the king would lose the battle, for they did not fail to encourage the queen at her entrance and departure by their cries, telling her to care for nothing, with similar expressions,' noted the French ambassador, Du Bellay. 'She recommended herself to their good prayers, with other Spanish tricks.'

Some confusion exists about the exact order of events after Catherine, Henry and all the others had walked into the court. Henry seems to have been one of the first to speak. He repeated his, by now worn, argument that he loved his wife but had become sorely troubled by his conscience about being married to his brother's widow. Wolsey, meanwhile, asked for public recognition from Henry that he, Wolsey, had not instigated the divorce. This, bizarrely, was the judge asking the defendant to defend him against Catherine's allegations that he was not impartial. 'I can well excuse you,' replied Henry. 'Indeed ye have been rather against me.'

Catherine's response to the court was what stuck in the minds of all those present. She rose from her chair in silence as all eyes fixed upon her. She then walked deliberately across the room and past the bishops to where her husband sat on his luxurious, cushioned chair. Catherine knelt at his feet. It was a posture of absolute submission. No one present could doubt that this was a woman showing respect and love for her husband. In this position she began her dramatic act of defiance. She started to speak, not just to her husband, but to the entire court. Such was the tension of the moment that her English occasionally failed her, and her phrases were broken and, presumably, accented in Spanish.

'Sir, I beseech you for all the love that hath been between us, and for the love of God, let me have justice,' she began, as Cavendish later recalled. "Take of me some pity and compassion, for I am a poor woman and a stranger born out of your dominion. I have here no assured friends, and much less impartial counsel.'

He was, she reminded him, England's 'head of justice'. It was his responsibility to make sure she was treated fairly. He was also, of course, her husband and the person whom she had done all in her power to please for two decades. 'Alas! Sir, wherein have I offended you, or what occasion of displeasure have I deserved?' she asked.

I have been to you a true, humble and obedient wife, ever conformable to your will and pleasure, that never said or did any thing to the contrary thereof, being always well pleased and contented with all things wherein you had any delight or dalliance, whether it were in little or much. I never grudged in word or countenance, or showed a visage or spark of discontent.

Her next comment may have been a dig at Wolsey, who sat listening from the tribune, though she could just as easily have been referring to Anne Boleyn. 'I loved all those whom ye loved, only for your sake,' she told Henry, 'whether I had cause or no, and whether they were my friends or my enemies.'

Was it really her fault they had no son to inherit his crown? 'This twenty years or more I have been your true wife and by me ye have had divers children, although it hath pleased God to call them out of this world, which hath been no default in me,' she said.

Her reward for the years of loyalty and love was, she could now see, to have her word doubted and her affairs dragged through this court. The best, and only, witness to the truth about her virginity was Henry himself, she insisted. This, he well knew, had been given to him.

'When ye had me at the first, I take God to be my judge, I was a true maid without touch of man. And whether it be true or no, I put it to your conscience,' she said.

If there be any just cause by the law that ye can allege against me, either of dishonesty or any other impediment to banish and put me from you, I am well content to depart to my great shame and dishonour. And if there be none, then here, I most lowly beseech you, let me remain in my former estate.

The court, she said, was being asked to pass judgement not just on her, but also on her father Ferdinand and her father-in-law, Henry VII. After all, they had been the promoters of this marriage. 'The king your father was in the time of his reign of such estimation throughout the world for his excellent wisdom, that he was accounted and called of all men "The Second Solomon",' she reminded him. The two old kings had 'wise counsellors about them . . . of as good judgement as there are at this present time in both realms, who thought then the marriage between you and me good and lawful'.

'Therefore it is a wonder to me to hear what new inventions are now invented against me – who never intended anything but honesty – that cause me to stand to the order and judgement of this new court,' Catherine said. 'Herein ye may do me much wrong, if ye intend any cruelty.'

The men whose task it was to defend her in court owed their first loyalty to the king, she reminded him. 'They are your subjects, and taken out of your own council beforehand, and dare not, for your displeasure, disobey your will and intent,' she said, still unaware of just how brave some of them would be.

Therefore I most humbly require you, in the way of charity and for the love of God – who is the just judge – to spare me the extremity of this new court, until I may be advised what way and order my friends in Spain will advise me to take. And if ye will not extend to me so much impartial favour, your pleasure then be fulfilled, and to God I commit my cause!

Catherine had stayed on her knees. Henry had tried to raise her up twice, but she had remained stubbornly down. She was his wife, her posture said, and entirely subject to his whims and decisions. Now she asked him for one last thing. Would he give his permission, as her husband and master, for her to write directly to the pope to defend her honour and conscience? Henry raised her up and told her that, yes, she had his permission. It was a brilliant coup. She had backed an unsuspecting Henry into a corner. Unable to resist either the force of her petition or the gaze of the massed onlookers, he had cleared Catherine to do the one thing that might save her – appeal directly for the case to be revoked to Rome. In fact Henry may have been giving permission for something she had already done. Catherine was capable of both lying and trickery. The power of attorney and appeal were already signed and may have been on their way to Rome already. Would Catherine have sent them even if Henry had refused her permission? It would have been foolish, at this stage, not to. With his permission granted so publicly, however, Henry could not now accuse her of going behind his back. That was something she would never let him forget.

Catherine had said what she came to say and had got what she needed. She made a low curtsey to her husband. Those watching expected her to return to her seat. To their astonishment, however, she walked straight towards the door. She sought the arm of Griffin Richards, her receiver general, and proceeded in a stately fashion past the aghast onlookers.

The crier tried to call her back. 'Catherine, queen of England, come into the court!' he bellowed.

'Madame, ye be called again,' said Richards.

Her reply was audible to those in the hall. 'On, on,' she said. 'It makes no matter, for it is no impartial court for me, therefore I will not tarry. Go on.' And so she strode out, never to return.

38 Ghostly Advice

Blackfriars, London. June–July 1529

Catherine's dramatic walk-out did not bring the trial to an end, though Henry must have thought it put paid to her chances of victory. She ignored all future summonses to the court and so was declared contumacious. Lorenzo Campeggio was the only unknown quantity in the courtroom. The other judge, Wolsey, was Henry's. Even Catherine's defence team, the councillors who she had left to argue her case, owed their allegiance, and often their livelihoods, to Henry. He and Wolsey had already felt free to give them orders in the run-up to the hearings, sending them to bully her about the brief, causing Catherine to complain that she could not get trustworthy advice. A sham trial, with a single possible outcome, looked assured.

Henry, however, was in for some more surprises, during the dozen or so court sessions held over the following month. He soon discovered that not all Englishmen were as supine as he might have hoped. The first hint of opposition came when Henry grandly informed the court that all the bishops who were currently sat in the Blackfriars' chamber agreed on the need to put his marriage on trial.

According to Wolsey's gentleman usher George Cavendish, Henry claimed that he had first taken his worries about the marriage to his 'ghostly father', or confessor, the bishop of Lincoln. Then he had asked the archbishop of Canterbury and all the bishops present in the court whether the matter should go to trial. 'To the which ye have all agreed by writing under all your seals, which I have here to be shown,' he said, brandishing a document weighed down by the heavy wax seals of England's bishops.

'That is the truth,' agreed Warham, the archbishop. 'I doubt not but all my brethren here present will affirm the same.'

Unfortunately for Henry, the bishops did not then all nod their heads in assent. One of them, the ascetic and incorruptible bishop of Rochester, John Fisher, protested that Warham was wrong. 'No sir, not I,' he interrupted. 'Ye have not my consent.'

Henry waved the document with the seals at him. 'Have I not?' he demanded. 'Look here upon this. Is this not your hand and seal?'

'No forsooth, sire,' an indignant Fisher replied. 'It is not my hand nor seal!' The archbishop of Canterbury, he said, had come to ask him to sign the document, but he had refused. Then he accused Warham of both forging his signature and abusing his seal. 'I said to you that I would never consent to any such act,' he told the archbishop, 'for it were against my conscience.'

Warham admitted that he had falsified the signature but claimed that Fisher had given him permission. 'You say truth,' the archbishop replied. 'But at last ye were fully persuaded that I should subscribe your name for you, and put the seal myself, and that you would allow the same.'

Fisher refused, however, to sanction the fraud. 'There is nothing more untrue,' he retorted.

Henry brushed the complaint aside, thinking that the elderly Fisher alone could not put up much opposition. 'Well, well. It shall make no matter,' he said. 'We will not stand in argument with you herein, for you are but one man.'

The king's legal advisers had not done their research very well if they thought Fisher would be a pushover at the trial. He had previously offered a double-edged welcome to the case. 'Kings usually think that they are permitted to do whatever pleases them, because of the magnitude of their power,' he said in a letter to a friend. 'Therefore it is good for these kings, in my opinion, to submit themselves to the decrees of the church . . .

lest otherwise they kick over the traces and do what they please.'
In the same letter he observed that not everybody had been bullied into taking the king's side, though it was clearly dangerous
to oppose him openly.

Catherine's virginity became the centre of debate at the fifth
session of the court, when Fisher once again leapt to her defence.
Henry was determined to press this point and brought in more
than a dozen witnesses to back his line of argument. 'The king's
counsel alleged the marriage not good from the beginning,
because of the carnal knowledge committed between Prince
Arthur her first husband, the king's brother, and her,' reported
Cavendish. 'To prove the same carnal copulation they alleged
many coloured reasons and similitudes of truth.'

The witnesses paraded in court that day as Henry tried to
prove that Catherine had slept with his brother were mostly
former members of Arthur's household, many of whom had
long since retired to the shires. They were asked to think back to
events of more than quarter of a century before. Some struggled
to recall their own ages. Sir William Thomas, one of Arthur's
grooms of the privy chamber, said he thought he must be fifty 'or
thereabouts'. He claimed to remember, however, often accompanying Arthur in his nightgown to Catherine's bedroom door
and picking him up again in the morning. The fifty-nine-year-
old earl of Shrewsbury, meanwhile, recalled how he himself had
consummated his own marriage when he was fifteen and a half.
Surely, he suggested, Arthur must have done the same. The marquess of Dorset remembered seeing the teenage Spanish princess lying under a coverlet on her wedding night at the bishop's
palace 'as the manner is of queens in that behalf'. He felt sure,
he added, that Arthur later had sex with his wife. Some of the
witnesses, like the widowed duchess of Norfolk, were too frail to
travel and commissioners were sent out to grill them. She confirmed that she, too, had seen Catherine lying in her wedding

bed. Some witnesses also remembered Arthur's calling for ale and boasting about the thirsty work of having been 'in the midst of Spain' that night.

Against all this weighed Catherine's own signed protestations of her virginity. The witnesses who might have backed her version of events, like those who gave evidence at the hearing in Zaragoza, were not called. Even Henry's counsel eventually suggested that the absolute truth of the matter might never be known. That provoked an angry riposte from Fisher. '*Ego nosco veritatem*,' he said. 'I know the truth.'

'How know ye the truth?' asked an angry Wolsey.

'I know that God is truth itself,' Fisher replied. Then he threw a quotation from the New Testament Book of Matthew at Wolsey.

Quos Deus conjunxit, homo non separet. 'What therefore God had joined together, let not man put asunder.' And, for as much as this marriage was made and joined by God to a good intent, I say that I know the truth; which is that it cannot be broken or loosed by the power of man.

Fisher's next line of argument sent shock waves through the court. So convinced was he of Catherine's cause, he said, that he would lay down his life for it. John the Baptist had said it was impossible to die more gloriously than in the cause of marriage. That was even more so now, after Christ's death, than it had been then.

It was both an act of defiance and a challenge. It was also an unsubtle reference to the story of John the Baptist's own death, with Henry cast as Herod – the king who had John's head chopped off after the latter questioned his decision to change wives. Henry knew his Bible and was furious with Fisher. 'What is the meaning of that comparison of his, in which he endeavours to assimilate his own cause to that of John the Baptist, unless he held the opinion that I was acting like Herod, or attempting some outrage like that of Herod?'

It was, however, an impressive speech. Campeggio's secretary was convinced that Fisher had won the day. 'As this man is a man of good fame, the king can no longer persist in dissolving the marriage; for this man being adverse to it, the entire kingdom will not permit the queen to suffer wrong,' he wrote in gushing Italian.

The French ambassador rated Fisher 'one of the best and most holy divines in England'. Not only had he remonstrated with the judges but also presented 'a book', or report, 'enlarging upon the queen's cause with many wise words'.

Even the tired and gouty Campeggio was impressed. 'Rochester made his appearance,' he reported back to Rome, 'to say, affirm, and with forcible reasons demonstrate to them that this marriage of the king and queen can be dissolved by no power, human or Divine, and for this opinion he declared he would even lay down his life.'

'This affair of Rochester was unexpected and unforeseen, and consequently has kept everybody in wonder,' the Italian cardinal went on. He was sure Fisher had the mettle for martyrdom. 'What he will do we shall see when the day comes. You already know what sort of a man he is, and may imagine what is likely to happen.'

The speech was a gauntlet thrown down to Henry. Fisher had destroyed Henry's argument that Catherine was alone in maintaining the validity of their marriage. He had also taken the trial to freshly dramatic heights. How far was the king prepared to go in his quest to exchange Catherine for Anne Boleyn? Would he draw blood?

Catherine was not there to witness this eloquent act of bravery, though she too had been flirting with the idea of death before dishonour so Fisher's stance must have seemed entirely coherent to her. Between them, she and Fisher had increased the stakes by raising the flag of defiance to the point of martyrdom. The

Roman Catholic church had not produced martyrs in considerable numbers for a long time. It was Catherine's cause, and the principles it represented, that provided the first major outpouring of fresh martyr's blood for centuries. Fisher did not know it, but he was signalling the start of a new era, where martyrdom would stop being theoretical and become real once more.

All that, however, lay in the still dim future. For the moment, Catherine was worried about other things. She had publicly turned her back on the court and had done so in a way guaranteed to be gossiped about everywhere from the taverns of London to the corridors of Rome. She had sent her appeal to the pope. She had even forced Henry to give his approval for that.

Now she was in a hurry. She needed the pope to suspend the court before it passed a sentence that might prove impossible to undo. All now depended on Lorenzo Campeggio. A few days before the trial started she had visited the feverish, gout-ridden Italian as, once more, he lay in bed. He had made a final, unsuccessful attempt to push her into a convent. Her future was now in his, and Wolsey's hands.

39 Carnal Copulation

Blackfriars, London. 22 June–23 July 1529

Lorenzo Campeggio went wearily to court for two or three days a week over the early summer. His sense of impending doom increased as each trial day went past. Unlike Wolsey (who, nevertheless, had two illegitimate children by a Mistress Lark), he knew something about matrimony. He had been married – had, in fact, five children of his own – and only began a church career after his wife died in 1509. As a judge and diplomat he first met Henry and Wolsey on a mission to England in 1518. He then became cardinal protector of England and Henry, as a gift, added the bishopric of Salisbury to his various job titles. He would not have been expected to visit his diocese. The gift, instead, provided added income to an already influential and prosperous cardinal – who then lost all when Charles's troops sacked Rome in 1527.

Campeggio was a long-term recipient of English favours and Henry had expected the Italian to repay his generosity by backing the divorce. In fact, Campeggio's secret instructions all along had been either to change Henry's mind or persuade Catherine into a convent. If those failed, he was to do nothing. He was urged to delay the whole process as much as he could and above all, as constant letters from Rome implored, to avoid passing sentence.

Catherine must have heard this version of Campeggio's mission early on. The Spanish ambassador, her great ally Mendoza, had guessed from the start that these were Campeggio's instructions. He would certainly have shared his guess with Catherine. It was, however, just one of many rumours about Campeggio's real mission that were circulating around London. Catherine, like Henry, did not believe it. She lived, instead, in constant dread of the Italian. Given that he was so often in Wolsey's company, and spent so much energy trying to get her to take a nun's vows, this was understandable.

While Catherine's formal protest against the Blackfriars proceedings travelled on its express route to Rome, the weather changed rapidly from chilly to sweltering. As the temperature rose outside the courtroom, so the tension mounted amongst all those involved in the proceedings within.

On one especially hot and humid day, Henry called Wolsey to see him at Bridewell. It was a bruising encounter, born of Henry's impatience and frustration. The battered cardinal gave the bishop of Carlisle a lift back to Westminster on his barge afterwards.

'Sir, it is a very hot day,' said the bishop, wiping sweat from his face as they endured the scorching July heat on the open, exposed river.

'Yes,' replied Wolsey. 'If you had been as well chafed as I have been within this hour, you would say it were very hot.'

The chafed and exhausted Wolsey took straight to his bed at York Place in Westminster only to be woken two hours later by Anne Boleyn's father. The king, he said, had decided it was time for a final try at bullying Catherine into submission. He and Campeggio were to visit her immediately. 'They should advise her to surrender the whole matter into the king's hands by her own will and consent.' It was an order that could not be ignored. Wolsey cursed the king's councillors in his most colourful language and got back out of bed. The barge was got ready once more and, after picking up Campeggio – who must have been muttering similar curses in Italian – made its way back to Bridewell.

The two cardinals, with Cavendish and others in attendance, went straight to Catherine's presence chamber and asked an usher to inform the queen of their arrival. Catherine had been sewing and came out of her privy chamber with a skein of white thread still around her neck. She could, of course, have set her sewing aside if she had wanted to, but Catherine obviously preferred to appear a model of innocent, womanly domesticity. She had long sewed Henry's shirts for him and continued to do so (to Anne Boleyn's evident fury) for at least another year. She might no longer be 'using' the king's body, but she was certainly dressing it. That, after all, was part of a wife's duty. It was a subtle form of possession and Anne Boleyn knew it.

'Alack, my lords, I am sorry to cause you to attend upon me. What is your pleasure with me?' she asked as her ladies and servants looked on.

Wolsey said that, if she did not mind, they would rather talk privately in her privy chamber.

'My lord, if you have anything to say, speak it openly before all these folks,' replied Catherine. 'For I fear nothing that you can say or allege against me, but I would that all the world should both hear and see it. Therefore, I pray you, speak your minds openly.'

Wolsey started talking to her in Latin but Catherine interrupted him. She wanted the witnesses to understand what he was saying. 'Speak to me in English I beseech you, although I understand Latin,' she said.

'Madam, if it please your grace,' said Wolsey, 'we come both to know your mind, how you be disposed to do in this matter between the king and you, and also to declare secretly our opinions and our counsel unto you.'

Catherine decided to use a tactic she had employed on powerful men before. She played naïve and dumb. 'I cannot make so sudden an answer to your request. For I was set among my maidens at work, thinking little of any such matter,' she said. 'There is need of a longer deliberation, and a better head than mine, to make answer to so noble wise men as ye be.'

She used the opportunity to complain, once more, about her lack of independent advice. 'Will any Englishmen counsel or be friendly unto me against the king's pleasure, they being his grace's subjects?' she asked, obviously forgetting Fisher.

Those in whom I do intend to put my trust are not here. They are in Spain, in my native country. Alas, my lords! I am a poor woman, lacking both wit and understanding sufficiently to answer such approved wise men as ye be both, in so weighty a matter. I pray you to extend your good and impartial minds in your authority unto me, for I am a simple woman, destitute and barren of friendship and counsel here in a foreign region. And as for your counsel, I will not refuse but be glad to hear.

Then she took Wolsey by the hand, led the two cardinals into her privy chamber and added to Wolsey's dose of chafing for the day. Cavendish recalled her voice carrying through doors and walls. 'We, in the other chamber, might sometimes hear the queen speak very loud, but what it was [she said] we could not understand,' he said. 'The cardinals departed and went directly to the king, making to him relation of their talk with the queen; and afterwards they resorted home to their houses to supper.'

Campeggio had wanted the trial to proceed at a slow trot. Soon, however, he found it galloping forward at such a pace that he could hardly draw breath. Henry's legal team rushed it forward, spurred by fear of Catherine winning her appeal to have the case moved to Rome. Catherine, having declined to have anything more to do with the Blackfriars tribunal, could do nothing to slow things down. There was now a danger, however, that she had not acted fast enough. A favourable judgement from Campeggio and Wolsey might, after all, allow Henry to remarry instantly. It would then be difficult (if not impossible) to turn the clock back, even if Rome did accept her appeal and declare the Blackfriars court invalid.

Her direct appeal to the pope and the powers of attorney for

Miçer Mai reached Rome on 5 July. A weeping Pope Clement told the English ambassadors in Rome the following day that he could not deny her request. They begged him to wait, hoping the Blackfriars case might reach sentence before the pope's instructions got to London. The acrimony amongst those doing the arguing in Rome was already such that one tipstaff bearing a message from Charles's ambassadors to Henry's was deemed fortunate to have escaped without a broken head. When letters arrived from Campeggio, however, explaining how fast the case was going, the pope had no choice but to approve the appeal. This he did on 13 July. Six days later, after the appeal had been passed at a meeting of the congregation of cardinals, he wrote an apologetic explanation to Wolsey. Clement knew he had condemned him to personal ruin and, possibly, death.

Catherine knew none of this. Messengers were taking a fortnight or more from Rome. She began to despair. As July drew to a close, and the court looked ready to pass sentence, she grew tearful and sad. By appealing in person to the pope she had both defied her husband and pushed him further away. Yet there was still no sign of the court having the case taken out of its hands, and sentence was nearly upon her. 'The queen is miserable because, despite having taken all the medicines prescribed for her as a patient, she sees no relief at hand,' Mendoza reported. 'It pains her to see that, by these actions, she has irritated her husband still more while seeing no improvement in her condition.'

She was not the only one who feared Henry might succeed in forcing the court to pass sentence. Campeggio had admitted that it could become unavoidable. If sentence had to be passed, he said, it would be done thinking of God and the good of the Holy See. That sentence was due to be delivered on Friday 23 July. All the arguing had been done and the facts presented to the court. Expectation was such that Henry himself came into one of the galleries overlooking the great chamber at Blackfriars to watch from above. Would he, at last, get his divorce? It is not difficult to imagine Catherine's state of mind when she awoke that Friday. Her future, and that of her daughter, now depended on the words that Wolsey and Campeggio were due to pronounce later that day. She must have been beside herself with fear.

Campeggio, however, seems to have had a flash of inspiration some time over the previous week. In Rome, he told the court, the 'reaping and harvesting' holidays had begun. It was a time when the courts there did not sit. As this was, in effect, a Roman court, it too was going on holiday. 'I will adjourn this court for this time, according to the order of the court in Rome,' he told the chamber. He would see them all again at the beginning of October. Henry and his followers were furious. Both Cavendish and Hall recalled the duke of Suffolk stepping forward at the king's command in a menacing fashion. 'Now I see that the old said saw is true, that there was never legate nor cardinal that did good in England,' he said, slamming his hand down on the table. It was a dart aimed not just at Campeggio and Wolsey but against anyone exercising the pope's power in England. Soon after the court was suspended, news came from Rome that Catherine had won her right to an appeal. The case was being transferred there. The Blackfriars court would never sit again. Catherine, for the time being, had been saved.

40 The Lull

Greenwich. 30 November 1529

Catherine and Henry dined together. This formed part of the merry-go-round of their now schizophrenic relationship. Sometimes Catherine saw her husband. Other times he was away, often with Anne Boleyn. For the most part, however, all three moved together with the court, the two women dancing around each other's shadows. In this confusing world, the king not only had a queen. He also had, depending on whose opinion you listened to, a queen-in-waiting, a mistress, a concubine or a whore. The three members of this *ménage* were each, in their own way, strong figures, with the king sometimes seeming the weakest. The court looked on, unsure how to react but always ready for gossip. A tense, false patina of normality was maintained. When they were together, Henry and Catherine behaved with exaggerated cordiality. Catherine hid her anguish and tried to maintain queenly serenity. Henry also remained outwardly calm. He wanted to be viewed as a fair and noble king, not as a cruel man intent on imposing his will at all cost. Sometimes, however, the facade of amiability slipped.

The feast of St Andrew, late in November, was one such day. Henry had spent increasing time with Anne Boleyn ever since Campeggio adjourned the Blackfriars court. With the case then being recalled to Rome, and Campeggio also returning home, the king no longer felt the need to be discreet. He obviously thought it was proper, however, to dine with his wife on a feast day. After the dinner at Greenwich on 30 November, Catherine found she could no longer hold back. The dam of self-control burst, her anguish and anger pouring out. She was in purgatory, she told him, because he shunned her. They had not dined together for days. He did not visit her apartments, or her bed. Why not? Henry began to give a feeble excuse, something about work keeping him busy. Then he, too, became angry. Catherine had no reason for complaint, he insisted. She was mistress of her own household and could do whatever she wanted. 'As to his visiting her in her apartments and partaking of her bed, [he said] she ought to know that he was not her legitimate husband,' her nephew's new ambassador, Eustace Chapuys, reported after seeing Catherine.

Henry boasted to her that he had been scouring Europe's universities for support, gathering opinions from the most learned men of the continent. He omitted to say that many had been paid for. The illustrious theologians of Paris, he crowed, were now on his side. He would present their opinions to the pope and if Clement did not 'declare their marriage null and void' then he would simply 'denounce the pope as a heretic'. After that he would marry whoever he liked.

The threat to the pope was momentous. It came just a dozen years after Luther had also challenged the pope – and sounded the start of the Protestant Reformation – by pinning his ninety-five theses to the doors of the castle church at Wittenberg. Other princes in northern Europe were already discovering radical ways of shaking off papal authority. Pope Clement had been warned that he might lose not just Henry, but England as well.

This, however, was a marital row. It was the smaller details and the lies that niggled them both. There was plenty to pick over. Catherine wanted to argue about her virginity. Henry knew full well that he had 'found her a maiden' on their wedding night, she insisted. He had admitted so more than once. (Or had that all been, as he later claimed, just a young man's joke?) The opinions of those who claimed his marriage was no good were worthless, she added. 'I care not a straw,' she said. 'If you give me permission to procure counsel's opinion in this matter, I do not hesitate to say that for each doctor or lawyer who might decide in your favour and against me, I shall find one thousand to declare that the marriage is good and indissoluble.' Catherine and Henry had both become experts in the nuances of canon law over the previous few years. Catherine, indeed, had spent a small fortune on legal advice. Then, as now, divorce lawyers were not cheap. They accounted for the equivalent of ten to fifteen per cent of her household expenses over two years. She had listened to them carefully, however, and learned enough to beat off her husband whenever they argued. Eventually Henry gave up, turned around and stormed off.

His supper, which he shared with Anne Boleyn, was no easier. Henry had jumped from the frying pan into the fire. 'Did I not tell you that whenever you disputed with the queen she was sure to have the upper hand?' barked Boleyn. 'I see that some fine morning you will succumb to her reasoning and that you will cast me off.' She, too, could play the victim. 'I have been waiting long and might in the meanwhile have contracted some advantageous marriage, out of which I might have had issue, which is the greatest consolation in this world,' she stormed. 'But alas! Farewell to my time and youth spent to no purpose at all.'

The king went to bed that night well and truly roasted. Catherine's fiery behaviour was driven by inner dread that Henry might be irretrievably lost. Anne Boleyn's frank response (at least as reported by an admittedly partial Chapuys) revealed her own deepest fear. She had already spent more than two years waiting for Henry, but here she was – childless, unmarried, nearly thirty years old and worried she might never be his wife. That, in turn, coincided with Catherine's last, desperate hope. If only she could wrestle Henry away from Boleyn for a few weeks, Catherine thought, she might win him back for good.

'My plea is not against the king, my Lord, but against the

abettors and inventors of this case,' Catherine wrote to the pope a year later as she awaited a decision now that the case had been transferred to Rome.

I have such faith in the natural goodness and virtues of the king that if I could only have him two months with me, as I used to, I alone would be enough to make him forget what has happened. And, as they know this is true, they do not let him be with me.

This was the hope she clung to in the year and a half after her victory at Blackfriars.

It would seem a remarkable piece of self-delusion, were it not for Anne Boleyn's reaction on St Andrew's Day. Catherine thought she could still pull Henry back from divorce. Her rival worried that she was right. Most other people considered Henry ready to do absolutely anything to obtain the divorce. Chapuys, who was to become Catherine's greatest ally over the next few years, sensed this almost as soon as he arrived in August 1529. He saw that Henry was in so deep that he could think of little else. 'He is so blinded by his love for the lady that he sees nothing else but the means of having her,' Chapuys commented. The duke of Norfolk, now one of Henry's chief councillors, confirmed as much. 'The king is so much bent upon it that I do not think anyone but God could turn him aside,' he said.

As if to prove just that, Henry ended 1529 with an effusive homage to the woman who had, by now, been waiting so long to marry him. On 8 December he solemnly raised her father from the rank of viscount to earl, granting him the earldoms of both Wiltshire and Ormond. The following day Henry gave a huge banquet at which Anne Boleyn was treated as though she was already the queen. She sat on the king's right, occupying the spot that belonged to Catherine who – according to Chapuys – was weeping seven miles away. Henry's sister Mary, the 'White Queen', and the wife and mother of the duke of Norfolk (three of the most senior women in the land) suddenly found themselves placed below her. Chapuys declared that he had never seen such a thing. There was dancing and carousing. 'Nothing was wanting to the feast except for a priest to give the nuptial ring and pronounce the benediction,' he said.

The relationship, however, was tempestuous. Henry was alternately excited and appalled by Anne's fiery, haughty manner. At moments, indeed, Catherine's civil, if steely, serenity may still have seemed preferable. The pendulum swung briefly the other way over Christmas 1529, when Catherine welcomed Henry back to Greenwich. The seasonal celebrations were done 'in great triumph' – but seem to have been boycotted by Anne. Henry, apparently desperate, sent her an expensive present on New Year's Eve and was soon spending most of his time with her. A few months later, riding back from Windsor, Henry shocked onlookers by sitting Anne on a pillion behind him. Two men were reported to have been slapped in jail for the crime of 'commenting' on it.

Anne Boleyn had begun to wield her new-found political influence, sometimes with vindictive glee, soon after the Blackfriars trial ended in fiasco. Catherine had put many sticks in the wheels of the divorce and Anne was bitter at being made to wait. Much of her bile was saved for Wolsey, who called her 'the night-crow'. Failure to deliver a divorce spelled, as he himself had predicted, the demise of the greatest man – after the king – in England.

Catherine had warned Chapuys on his arrival to steer clear of Wolsey. He already bore the aura of a doomed man. She had heard his enemies sharpening their knives during the aborted Blackfriars trial. Now, she knew, they would plunge them in. 'The cardinal's affairs are at this moment rather embroiled,' she whispered to Chapuys during a hurried meeting at Grafton, Northamptonshire, where she and Henry had stopped during the summer progress of 1529. Even the courtiers in the room could not have seen her lips move, a startled Chapuys reported after this first meeting with the woman whose cause he would fight with passion and tenacity. Chapuys was getting his introduction to Catherine's by now customary cloak-and-dagger methods. 'There are, however, matters upon which I dare not, surrounded as I am, speak to you in detail,' she confided. 'I will send you one of my servants to explain the remainder.' It was the start of a secretive but intense relationship conducted, more often than not, through intermediaries – with ciphers and clandestine encounters included. It was the only way Catherine could operate, surrounded as she now was by spies. Chapuys's more formal attempts to see her at court could, anyway, be frustrated by officials who simply pretended she was not there.

Anne Boleyn, egged on by her father and their ally the duke of Norfolk, pressed for Wolsey's complete destruction. The cardinal was eventually accused of *praemunire* – abusing his legatine powers to place the law of Rome above that of England – and, to limit the damage, he pleaded guilty in October 1529. 'Wolsey has just been put out of his house, and all his goods taken into the king's hands,' a breathless Du Bellay, the French ambassador, reported on 22 October. 'He is quite undone.' Mademoiselle Anne, he added, had engineered everything. She was now 'above everyone'. 'All the rest have no influence except what it pleases the lady to allow them,' added Du Bellay. Crowds gathered on the banks of the Thames, expecting the disgraced Wolsey to be taken to the Tower of London. Instead he was allowed to go to his house at Esher and, on the way, received a ring from Henry as a gift. The disgraced cardinal fell to his knees in the mud out of relief at this sign of hope. He sent his fool, Patch Williams, to the king as a thank-you present, ignoring the protests of the fool himself.

Anne's faction was continually afraid that the cardinal would wheedle his way back into Henry's affection. Catherine, however, had begun to feel some sympathy for Wolsey. Perhaps it was having a mutual enemy in Anne Boleyn that softened her. It was not until November 1530 that Wolsey's enemies managed to ensure treason charges were brought against him. Catherine was central to these charges. Chapuys reported that Wolsey was being accused by some of plotting to have the pope excommunicate Henry if he did not treat his wife with proper respect and dismiss Anne Boleyn from court. Henry later declared that Wolsey had intrigued 'both in and out of the kingdom'. There had been, it was claimed, signs of 'sinister practices made to the court of Rome'. Wolsey had, indeed, been advising Chapuys about how best to advance Catherine's cause. At one stage he had even urged Chapuys on to 'bold and immediate action' in reply to Henry's own manoeuvres.

Wolsey was arrested and, though he had been ill for a long time, refused to eat. He died of natural causes as he was being taken to the Tower of London on 29 November 1530. He thus saved himself the ignominy of long-term imprisonment, execution or both. He went to his death fully aware that the titanic clash of wills between Catherine and Henry had caused his downfall. 'This is the just reward that I must receive for my worldly diligence and the pains that I have taken to do the king service and satisfy his vain pleasures,' he said as, with his final words, he regretted having served Henry more loyally than God. Wolsey's parting message to Henry was that he should study his own conscience 'in the weighty matter yet depending . . . [to decide] whether I have offended him or no'. That 'weighty' business, Cavendish confirmed, was none other than 'the matter newly begun between him and good Queen Catherine'. The once all-powerful cardinal thus became the first major casualty in the battle between Henry and Catherine. Anne Boleyn's supporters were delighted. Her father celebrated in the cruellest of fashions – by putting on a farce about Wolsey's descent into hell for some visiting Frenchmen.

Catherine's softening towards Wolsey in his final days suggests that, amidst the turmoil of the divorce case, she had decided it was better to deal with a devil she knew. Who, after all, would fill the void he left behind? She would have been right to worry. Sir Thomas More, a friend, replaced him as lord chancellor. Unknown to her, however, a Wolsey protégé called Thomas Cromwell lurked dangerously in the wings – ready to prove what true ruthlessness could achieve. The vast list of luxurious goods found in Wolsey's houses, and confiscated by Henry with a gleeful Anne looking on, included reminders that Catherine and Wolsey's relationship went back many years. The Spanish coat of arms was emblazoned on the borders of some of his gorgeous Flemish tapestries and a set of bowls, almost certainly a gift from Catherine, were decorated with both her arms and cardinals' hats.

Boleyn's anger now turned against more than just Wolsey and his sympathisers. Her feisty, hard-talking style led to clashes with senior nobles who began to store up resentment for later revenge. She rowed with the duchess of Norfolk – her own aunt – about wedding plans for the latter's daughter. She used the sort of 'high words' that the most senior ladies in the land could never recall coming out of Catherine's mouth. The falling out between aunt and niece explains why the duchess later sent Catherine a gift of some poultry together with a secret message hidden inside an orange – a rare token of support – and then pledged allegiance to her. The duke of Norfolk's own public dalliance with one of Boleyn's ladies, Bessie Holland, may also have prompted his wife's outspokenness on Catherine's behalf. The duchess was eventually expelled from court at Anne's request. Henry's brother-in-law, the duke of Suffolk, was also growing to hate her. He spread colourful stories about her and stayed away from court – possibly piqued by her assumption of precedence over his wife, the 'White Queen'.

By June 1530 Catherine herself had become Anne Boleyn's direct target. The queen, it seems, was too formidable a rival to leave for Henry to deal with on his own. His attempts at arguing with Catherine had already proved that to Anne. It was now that she threw a fit about Catherine's shirt-making for Henry. 'Recently he sent the queen some cloth begging her to have it made into shirts for him,' Chapuys reported.

The lady [Anne Boleyn], hearing of this, called before the king the person who had taken the cloth – one of the principal gentlemen of the bedchamber. Although the king himself acknowledged that this had been done by his order, she said many things to the bearer in the king's presence, vowing that she would have him punished severely.

It was, perhaps, no coincidence that this happened at one of those moments when Chapuys agreed with Catherine that, if she could get Henry on his own, she might win him back. Henry, the ambassador observed, did not seem to bear her 'ill-will' even though, when they talked, she was given to making him listen to her vigorous defence of their marriage. Anne obviously felt insecure. Perhaps she worried that he would weaken in the face of popular discontent and the prospect of a fight with the pope. She began to exert pressure on Catherine's ladies as well. The young wife of the marquess of Dorset (another senior lady-in-waiting and close friend) left the court and two of Catherine's most intimate friends had already been sent home on Anne's command.

Anne also began to realise just how well informed Catherine had been all along about Henry's moves in the divorce case. In September 1530 she had Catherine's regular gentleman courtier visitors – who were, undoubtedly, her informers – banned from seeing her. She also introduced ladies loyal to her into Catherine's entourage to spy and report back. These were effective tactics. Catherine soon complained that she was no longer up to date with what was going on.

Later in the year, Chapuys found himself at the centre of a bizarre charade enacted purely for Anne's benefit. He was called in to speak to Henry during one of his regular visits to the court. The king both manoeuvred him towards a small window in a gallery and constantly tried to turn the subject of conversation to Catherine and the divorce. Chapuys was perplexed by his unusual vehemence and determination to return, again and again, to the same subject. Then he glimpsed Anne spying on them. 'The lady was at a little window in the king's chamber that looked onto the gallery where we were, from where she could see and listen to us,' he said. Henry, in other words, wanted to show Anne that he was working hard to wear down opposition to their intended marriage.

That Anne felt it necessary to spy on Catherine, and that Henry allowed her to, had much to do with the queen's continuing successes in Rome. This was now the main legal battle-front for the divorce case. Following the closure of the Blackfriars court the pope was the only person who could decide whether Catherine was in the right. She was insistent that he should do so as fast as possible. Henry, to the contrary, did all he could to slow it down while an acquiescent Pope Clement was delighted to postpone any decision-making for as long as he could.

Catherine kept up the pressure on her representatives in Rome, on her nephew and on the pope himself. She became obsessed by both detail and rumour. Some of the latter suggested that popular anger at the divorce was occasionally bubbling to the surface. She asked Chapuys, for example, to check some of the wilder rumours, especially of trouble at the universities in both Oxford and Cambridge after they had been bullied into supporting Henry. Could the king explain the reports that women in Oxford hurled stones at his representatives or that in Cambridge seven people had died? Henry denied there had been either violence or coercion.

Catherine had still not given up on her husband and plotted ways of getting him to herself. She begged the pope, for example, to order him to leave her rival until judgement was passed. She despaired over the delays – which would, nevertheless, drag on for several years more. Her moods swung violently. A little bit of good news from her nephew or from Rome lifted her. Another university decision against her, a petition from some of England's more acquiescent nobles to the pope or an upcoming meeting of parliament – where she imagined the divorce might be pushed through anyway – sent her into tearful paroxysms of anxiety.

As the pope timidly began to issue briefs on her behalf, Henry grew increasingly suspicious about how his wife was organising her defence. He blamed her for scandalous rumours going around Italy (which, presumably, painted Anne Boleyn as a sexual predator). These, he claimed, could only have originated in Catherine's letters to the pope and the emperor. Henry carefully studied the offending phrases which had been written down and sent back to him from Italy. He even claimed to recognise 'by the words with which it had been written . . . that it was of the style and language of the queen'.

Henry had good reasons to worry. Catherine worked hard at her defence. One moment she wrote to her nephew or insisted that Chapuys send Charles a new 'book' from Fisher in her defence. The next she chivvied her attorneys in Rome, appealed directly to the pope or secretly encouraged an unnamed ally to preach her cause in the courts of the German princes.

Many powerful people around Europe were interested in her case. Catherine's marriage was, after all, now a key factor in European politics. Both Henry and Charles feared they might be forced to go to war over her. Charles told his brother Ferdinand to avoid a war in Germany early on in 1530 because they might have to fight one with England over their aunt.

Henry, meanwhile, fretted about calling Charles's bluff. 'Should the king . . . marry this woman, what will the emperor do?' the duke of Norfolk asked Chapuys. 'Will he make war on us?' The French, meanwhile, looked on with unashamed glee at the difficulties Henry and Charles were getting themselves into. They stirred the pot of trouble as vigorously as they could, seeing an opportunity for themselves as arbiters.

One of Catherine's greatest fears had always been that Henry would come up with an excuse for bypassing the Rome process and marrying Anne anyway. In the early stages of the divorce some of the pope's advisers had suggested, indeed, that the simplest solution was for him to marry Anne first and then wait for Catherine to challenge the move at Rome. In September 1530, the pope himself even wondered out loud whether it might not be best for Henry to take two wives. 'Some days ago the pope in private offer'd to me this proposal,' reported Henry's representative in Rome, Gregorio Casale, 'that your majesty might have a dispensation to have two wives.' It was not an idea that went any further. Fear of the reaction in England seems to have put Henry off the idea of jumping before he had formal permission, which might, anyway, never have come. Catherine's popularity was something he always had to take into account – which was one reason why he still insisted on seeking a legal way out of his marriage.

In the meantime, both sides continued to bombard Rome with evidence, opinions and arguments. The latter ranged from the obscure to the banal. Catherine's virginity, for example, remained an obsession for both sides. In one of his more absurd sets of instructions, Henry told one of his ambassadors to explain that Arthur had been a red-blooded, virile and highly sexed prince. His brother had constantly demanded that women be brought to him, he said. Arthur had also displayed his 'erect and inflamed member' to his friends and complained that, although he and Catherine were having sex, he was not getting nearly enough.

The king, however, never provided Clement with a direct answer to his observation that Catherine had vowed to accept his word on the question of her virginity, if only he was prepared to swear under oath. Catherine was calling Henry's bluff. The fact that he never provided the necessary sworn statement is the strongest evidence of all that she was telling the truth. Was he too scared for his soul to lie? Or did he simply not know? His own side argued that Henry had been so young and inexperienced when he married that he had been incapable of telling whether she was a virgin or not. 'The king said he was such a young lad that he had not known how to ascertain the truth of it,' Gregorio Casale told one of the emperor's ambassadors. Catherine, perhaps, understood that Henry's sense of nobility would, in any case, not allow him to lie outright – especially on oath. She had by no means lost all faith in the decency of the man she had loved 'much more than myself' when they married two decades earlier.

Catherine and Chapuys, meanwhile, sought witnesses to prove her virginity. The latter eventually found four witnesses in England alone, though their testimonies were later deemed not to have been sworn in the correct manner. Orders went out to scour Spain for those who had travelled with her almost three decades earlier to England, whatever their rank. María de Rojas, the girl who shared her bed after Arthur's death, was now the wife of the wealthy Álvaro de Mendoza and was thought to be living in Nájera, Vitoria or Madrid. Catalina, the slave girl who cleaned her chamber and changed her sheets, had married a crossbow-maker called Oviedo from the town run by the family of Elvira (the lady mistress). Then she had moved south to her home town of Motril with two daughters. Other ladies, and even the servants of Catherine's servants, were sought out in nunneries and cities across Spain. Even Fray Diego, the young confessor who had been the object of Catherine's youthful passion and had left England in disgrace, was to be tracked down.

The questionnaire they had to answer ranged from the biologically precise to the absurd. Was it true that there had been no blood on the marital sheets ? Had Henry bragged that it was he, not his brother, who took her virginity? Did Arthur look impotent? Was it generally accepted, and commented on, that they had never had sex? Had a group of doctors who diagnosed the long-running illness of Catherine's widowhood declared that 'the cause of her sickness was that she was still a virgin'? Did they really say it could be cured by marrying 'a man who had *skills* with women'? The answers were to be secretly sent back to the Spanish royal court. Records show that witnesses were interrogated across Spain. With the exception of the hearing at Zaragoza, however, their answers are mostly lost.

Above all, though, what Catherine wanted was for the pope – or the cardinals – to reach a decision on whether Henry could divorce her. Further delay would be a disaster, she warned Clement at the end of 1530. In the meanwhile, she claimed, the pope himself was torturing her by letting it all drag on.

Catherine was remarkably perceptive about the terrible struggle into which she and her husband were about to plunge England. At stake, she could already see, was not just her own future but the form of Christianity that had been dominant in England for nine centuries. 'Those who make war on me', she warned Clement, were also planning to destroy the church in England and grab its property. 'You must put a bit on them,' she insisted. 'This can only be done by passing sentence . . . If you wait any longer you will find that you have created a new hell that will be worse to mend than the one they have managed to create so far.'

Cowardly Clement was fast becoming a hate figure for her. 'My only consolation is the idea that God wishes to punish me for my sins in this world,' she wrote to him. 'And that therefore your holiness, His vicar on earth, will not forgive me'. If the pope failed to administer justice, she threatened, he would never free himself from her. Even from the bottom of hell she would shout so loud that God could not fail to hear her complaints against him.

41 Poison

John Fisher was not hungry. A stern ascetic, the sixty-two-year-old bishop liked to fast and scourge his own body. The broth prepared by his cook that day was rejected. He was, anyway, not feeling well. Some put this down to his disgust at the ease with which Henry – in an act of rebellion against a pope who was failing to give him his divorce – had bullied the country's bishops into recognising him as 'Supreme Head' of the English church. They had added a get-out clause saying that this was only 'as far as the law of Christ allows', but the damage was done. Henry was on his way to becoming not just England's king but, as one commentator noted, its pope as well.

Fisher's household ate the broth instead, with the leftovers given to the beggars who came to the gates of his London home, Rochester House. None of his servants noticed the strange 'powders' that a mysterious person had persuaded the cook, Richard Roose, to sprinkle into that day's fare. Soon all were ill. At least two people, a gentleman servant called Bennet Curwen and a poor widow called Alice Tryppytt, died – tormented by pain as the poison slowly did its work. The startled cook was arrested and – with some painful encouragement from the rack – admitted adding the powder. Roose had been told it would make people a little ill, without killing them. He had simply thought it was a powerful laxative. It had seemed like a good joke.

Who wanted to kill Catherine's most important ally in the English clergy? Fingers were immediately pointed at Fisher's most obvious enemies, the untouchable Boleyn family. Poisoning was considered a specially horrific crime and, though the mighty of the land had people taste their food for them, it was the stuff of nightmares. Henry made sure no suspicion came his way by ensuring the cook suffered the most horrible of punishments. He was boiled alive in a brass cauldron. Strangely, and despite the torture inflicted, the identity of the person who handed him the poison was never disclosed.

This attempt to murder John Fisher was another sign of how high the stakes had been raised after his dramatic intervention on Catherine's behalf at the collapsed Blackfriars trial. Fisher had declared himself ready to die for her. Now someone had shown themselves ready to kill – if not for Henry, then, at least, for Anne Boleyn. Catherine began to feel real fear. '*Ira principis mors est*' ('the wrath of the king is death'), the archbishop of Canterbury, William Warham, replied when she sought his help against Henry. Wolsey, too, had used almost exactly the same phrase when he began to feel the sting of Henry's displeasure.

Anne Boleyn had been so openly delighted with Henry's victory after he had bullied the bishops into accepting him as a 'supreme head' that, according to Chapuys, she behaved as though she had gained paradise. Catherine was so worried by the euphoria displayed by both Henry and Anne Boleyn that she fretted they would be emboldened into striking directly against her. The bishops, threatened with *praemunire* charges similar to those brought against Wolsey, had also pledged to give Henry £100,000. It was only the beginning of a long, sustained campaign against the church – often with Catherine as the excuse. The future of the church itself was now in play, just as she and Wolsey had predicted.

Catherine was certainly right that Henry was building towards something momentous. He and Anne had started the year 1531 feeling bolder about their position. Anne had ordered that her servants' livery coats be embroidered with a version of Margaret of Austria's proud and boastful motto: '*Ainsi sera, groigne qui*

groigne.' 'Let them grumble! That is how it will be!' She soon
withdrew this arrogant put-down to her critics, but Chapuys
observed she was now 'braver than a lioness'. Boleyn even told
one shocked lady-in-waiting that she wished 'all the Spaniards
in the world would drown in the sea'. As for Catherine, well,
she 'would rather the queen was hanged than recognise her as
her mistress'. Catherine saw them both so bold that she thought
Henry was either planning to marry Anne without waiting for
a decision from Rome or was plotting to bully parliament into
granting him permission that January.

Whenever Anne Boleyn and Henry were feeling up, however, Catherine seemed to find a way to slap them down. The
papal orders may only have trickled slowly out of Rome, but
they almost always went her way. Not only was there now a ban
on Henry remarrying before a decision was reached, but there
was also a papal prohibition on English courts, or parliament
itself, from trying the case. Henry, not without reason, blamed
Catherine and her nephew for every blow that crashed down
from Rome. Catherine, he felt, was emasculating his kingship.
He fretted and lost sleep as each papal order wounded his kingly
pride. Anne, meanwhile, was worried and furious in equal parts.
Henry, as was becoming usual, was the victim of her rages and
well-filed tongue. A tearful king even begged her relatives to
intervene and calm her down – a story that provoked hearty
laughter and joky asides from the pope. 'If he has shed tears in
consequence of a quarrel with his lady-love,' quipped one of
those present when the pope told the story, provoking another
round of laughter, 'it might be that his divines had counselled
him to cry for the relief of his conscience.'

A love-struck king being verbally lashed by a woman who
was not even his wife was, indeed, a curious thing. Henry's royal
might, so proudly and extravagantly defended elsewhere, crumbled under Anne's waspish onslaught. In fact, as the perceptive

Mai observed, the dynamic of heated rowing and tearful making up seemed to add both strength and passion to the relationship. Henry, for his part, had been busy erecting a defensive shield against his wife and her successes in Rome. He had already, for example, issued orders preventing anyone from executing mandates from the Holy See that might damage him or his authority. Ancient law, he began to claim, meant an Englishman could never be cited by a court abroad. Henry was not just an Englishman, however, he was England's king. As such, he was 'not only prince and king, but set on such a pinnacle of dignity that we know no superior on earth' and was doubly protected from the Roman courts. His desire to be recognised as Supreme Head of the church fitted perfectly with this idea of his superiority. He was, in words used by the Boleyn faction, on his way to becoming 'absolute emperor and pope in his kingdom'. A revolution, backed by a new theory of English kingship, was under way. These were momentous times. The English Reformation – the split from the Roman Catholic church – was beginning. Other factors were at work in Henry's mind and in England as a whole, but his collision with Catherine was like striking two hard pieces of flint together. It produced the sparks that lit the revolutionary fire.

Catherine girded herself for further battle. She made plans with Chapuys to fight any moves that might be made against her in parliament and even considered appearing herself to defend her rights. Henry did not try to get the divorce debated there until March 1531, however, and then his attempt flopped. The debate was started with the excuse of denying a popular rumour that Anne Boleyn, rather than Henry's famous scruple, was the cause of the divorce. Catherine's closest supporters were either absent or deliberately kept away as the king's men led the verbal attack, but the bishops of Bath and St Asaph both stood up to defend her. The duke of Norfolk, apparently fearing the king's side might lose the debate, brought it to a halt. England, it seems, was not yet ready.

The fact that two bishops were prepared to stand and support Catherine was a sign that, while the king got bolder, so too did some of her allies – as if everyone had suddenly realised they were no longer playing a game. The Boleyns were suspected by some of being secret Lutherans and Anne had already pressed on Henry the banned, heretical writings of the exiled reformist William Tyndale – whose translation of the New Testament, complete with Lutheran prologues, was circulating widely and surreptitiously. Tyndale stated that it was 'a shame above all shames' for kings to bow to the authority of the church. 'This is a book for me, and all kings to read,' Henry declared after she gave him a copy of Tyndale's *The Obedience of The Christian Man*. Her father was amongst a group of senior councillors who told the papal nuncio, according to Chapuys, that 'they cared neither for the pope or for popes in this kingdom'.

One of the first to raise his head over both pulpit and parapet was Thomas Abel, the chaplain who had been sent to Spain to tell Charles not to hand over the magic brief. Henry had already expelled Abel from court for declaring that anyone helping in the divorce was 'a traitor to God and the king'. Henry had demanded Catherine punish him for his cheek. She simply replied that her chaplain was right. Now Thomas Cranmer, a priest and gifted writer who would play a key role in Catherine's future, had helped Henry produce what became known as *The King's Book* or *The Determinations*. This was a widely distributed propaganda pamphlet designed to win popular support. It contained all Henry's arguments, along with those from universities in France and Italy, as to why his marriage was invalid. Abel had replied with another book, *The Unconquered Truth*, in which he lashed out at the 'false persons and false sayings' behind the king's cause. The book was considered dangerous enough to warrant official replies against Abel's 'babbling'.

Abel was by no means the only person now babbling against the divorce. A country girl called Elizabeth Barton, whose strange fits, prophecies and religious pronouncements had won her the nickname of Holy Maid of Kent, was warning that terrible things would happen if the king divorced Catherine and remarried. Henry, she said, would 'not be king of this realm' within a month of divorcing. In God's eyes, she said, he would cease to be king the moment he abandoned her. These were superstitious times and the Maid – who had had more than one audience with Henry himself – had a wide following. Some major churchmen also listened carefully to what she had to say.

Popular prophecies about the king's love life swirled around England. One predicted that a woman was set to destroy the kingdom. Another, which reached Anne Boleyn, said that a queen would soon be burnt. About this time an anonymous poison-pen drawing was sent to Anne. It showed herself, Catherine and Henry, each marked with the initial of their first name. The female figure marked with the letter 'A' was, however, missing her head. 'Come hither Nan, see here a book of prophecy,' she said, calling to her lady-in-waiting Anne Gainsford. 'This, he saith, is the king, this the queen and this is myself with my head off.' Her lady said that, if true, it was a warning against marrying Henry. 'I am resolved to have him whatsoever might become of me,' Boleyn replied.

The long-running battle over who would get more of Henry, his wife or his fiancée, reached one of its many climaxes in the late spring of 1531. Wolsey's former house at York Place – soon to be called Whitehall – was being refurbished and extended. Neighbouring houses were being pulled down, to the dismay of their owners, so that a long, covered gallery could give direct access to a new park. This was Anne's favourite royal residence, not least because Catherine had no apartments there. Anne was becoming increasingly possessive. That April she had fallen out with Henry over Princess Mary. Catherine's daughter, by then a young woman of fifteen, had fallen ill with stomach pains and wrote asking to be with her mother and father at Greenwich. At Anne's insistence, the request was turned down. When Henry praised Mary in front of Anne, the latter apparently reacted with one of her more venomous outbursts. The duchess of Norfolk, by now an implacable Boleyn enemy, passed on the gossip. Henry had even complained to her husband about Boleyn's abrasiveness, she said, adding that Catherine had never spoken to him like that.

This explains why, a few days later, Henry was unexpectedly considerate when Catherine and he dined together on 3 May, Holy Rood Day – observing, still, the formality of the king and queen sharing feast days. Freshly bawled out by Anne, he suddenly found Catherine's gentler ways a relief. The queen, seeing her husband soften, asked the following day whether Mary might really come to them at Greenwich. This was a mother's love talking. It was also, surely, an attempt to score against Anne. Henry's brusque, rude reply suggests he was thinking of how Anne would treat him if he assented. If she wanted to see her daughter, he said, she could do so elsewhere – and on her own. Catherine bit her tongue and replied that she would never abandon her husband for her daughter.

Catherine continued to hold her head high. Senior courtiers marvelled at her courage and resilience. The queen seemed to show neither care nor anxiety, the duke of Norfolk commented as he watched her step out of her chamber one day. This, the marquess of Dorset replied, was because she was so sure of the righteousness of her cause. Norfolk, who was meant to be one of the king's staunchest supporters, nodded agreement. 'It must be owned that the devil and no other must have been the originator and promoter of this wretched scheme,' he said.

Things then began to go downhill again for Catherine. Renewed threats from Pope Clement to cite Henry to appear at a tribunal in Rome enraged him further. It was, he felt, insulting to his newly rediscovered English customs and his royal status. 'I shall never consent to his being the judge,' Henry told the papal nuncio angrily, threatening to lead an army to Rome. 'I care not a fig for all his excommunications. Let him follow his own at Rome. I will do here what I think best.'

First, however, Henry wanted his councillors to make yet another attempt at bullying Catherine into submission. His privy council took days to work out how they might carry out Henry's instructions to talk Catherine into surrender. Some were nervous. Others were plain embarrassed. Others, still, were on her side. Catherine, once more, was ahead of the game. Someone had told her, in advance, what was due to happen. On 31 May 1531, therefore, she fortified herself by having several masses said. The impressive delegation, led by the highest men in the land, did not arrive at her Greenwich quarters until late that evening. The dukes of Suffolk and Norfolk headed the group, which included the marquess of Dorset, three earls and some twenty-five others. It was one woman, the queen, against the senior nobility – and some of the bishops – of England.

Norfolk spoke first. The king had sent them, he said, to express his displeasure and hurt at the 'contempt and vituperation with which he had been treated on her account by the pope, summoned as he had been by public proclamation to appear personally at Rome: a strange measure never before enforced by the popes against the kings of England'. She could never make the king leave his kingdom, he said, and should accept his invitation to have the case heard elsewhere. Otherwise she might be 'the cause of great troubles and scandals throughout the kingdom, by which all those present, their children, and the rest of their posterity might be thrown into great danger and confusion'. He seemed to be suggesting that popular unrest, perhaps even civil war, was in the air.

Catherine had been treated honourably as queen of England, Norfolk insisted. She had to realise that Henry was now recognised as 'supreme chief and sovereign in his own kingdom both temporally and spiritually'. As such she must know that he could not go to Rome and should consent that the court be moved somewhere else.

Catherine could not be bullied. She reminded them how the whole affair had started, with Wolsey's secret ecclesiastical court at Westminster – to which Henry had willingly submitted himself. 'The king himself did in the first instance appeal to His Holiness [as all ecclesiastical courts belonged, ultimately, to the pope],' she said. If he had started it, all she had done was carry it to a logical conclusion by seeking justice. The rest was up to the pope – who seemed to her, with his constant delays, remarkably partial to Henry. The pope's prompt sentence was necessary, she said, 'for the repose and example not only of this kingdom, but also of Christendom at large'. Henry, she was quite willing to recognise, was her chief and master. He also ruled the temporal affairs of England. The church, however, had only one true sovereign. That was the pope. If any of them wished to argue the king's case, she invited them to pack their bags and set off for Rome.

Had her husband not given her permission to appeal to Rome in front of everyone at Blackfriars? 'It was in pursuance of the said royal permission that the cause was advoked to Rome, and on it I found my right,' she said.

When they accused her of trying to rush the pope into passing sentence, Catherine appealed to their hearts. 'Had you experienced one half of the hard days and nights I have passed since the commencement of this wretched business you would not consider it too hasty or precipitate on my part to wish for, and try to procure, the sentence,' she said.

The bishop of Lincoln then tried to play tough. He called her a concubine, saying God had punished her unlawful marriage by making her sterile. Her virginity, he added, was a lie that they could easily disprove. Catherine simply referred him back to the oath she had sworn to Campeggio.

The councillors retired defeated. Norfolk and even Anne Boleyn's father nervously insisted before they left that they had not been the promoters of the divorce. The bishop of London, invited to speak, lost his tongue. Many had no heart for bullying the queen. Some, in fact, so enjoyed her replies that they dug elbows into their neighbours' sides at each rebuttal offered to Henry's more aggressive advocates. Catherine played the innocent until the very end. She had been astonished, she told them, to be surrounded by so many powerful men.

It had been a shameful episode. Some of those present felt it deeply. The king's comptroller, Henry Guildford, even suggested that all Henry's lawyers and backers should be strapped together and carted off to Rome to argue the case. Anne was so angry with Guildford that she told him he would be sacked the moment she became queen. He stormed straight off to see Henry and tendered his resignation. Henry turned him down, but Guildford still went off to his country house in a huff. Henry's nobles were getting increasingly uneasy about the divorce and where it might take the country. About this time the marquess of Dorset was also temporarily banished from court, for allegedly creating trouble in Cornwall – though Catherine suspected his banishment was really due to his support for her.

The two dukes, Norfolk and Suffolk, reported back to Henry after the meeting. The whole sorry affair, and Catherine's response, could be summed up with the names of the two things she would always obey above Henry, said Suffolk. Henry guessed the names. Were they Charles and the pope? No, said Suffolk, they were 'God' and 'her soul and conscience'.

'I feared it would be so,' said Henry as he digested the failure of their mission. 'It is now necessary to provide the whole affair by other means.'

Henry did not say what those 'other means' might be, but that June he increasingly rode off with Anne and just a handful of others to go hunting, leaving Catherine behind. The triple menage eventually moved to Windsor with Henry, Catherine and Anne, once more, under the same collection of roofs.

On 14 July Henry and Anne rode off together towards Chertsey Abbey and more hunting. Henry did not forewarn Catherine so that she could be there to wish him a safe journey. Nor did he seek her out to say his own goodbyes. He just left a message to say where they were going.

Few people would have guessed it, and perhaps even Henry himself did not realise, but Catherine's husband had left her. 'After this the king and she never saw [one another] together,' Hall recorded. 'Wherefore the common people daily murmured and spake their foolish fantasies. But the affairs of princes be not ordered by the common people, nor it were not convenient that all things were opened to them.'

Catherine's situation was dramatic. She was forty-five years old. Almost two-thirds of her life had been spent in England. She had been married to Henry for twenty-two years. Now she was alone and, definitively, without a husband.

42 Alone

Windsor Castle. Late July 1531

Catherine was alone, or as alone as one could be in a castle with thirty ladies-in-waiting and 170 servants. Henry had gone, but she did not know he had gone for good. Nor, perhaps, did he. His cowardly, surreptitious exit offered hope. Anne Boleyn may have been the only corner of the triangle with a clear picture of the future in her mind.

Henry saw what he was doing as a form of punishment. If the pope was threatening to call him to Rome, it was because his wife had asked him to. Catherine, in other words, was the one challenging his new-found idea of England's traditional kingship and, in Henry's mind, that meant he could now hit back without remorse. The queen, Henry informed the papal nuncio later on, was rude and disobedient. 'Since his holiness (Pope Clement) chooses to consider her my legitimate wife, it is evident that the right of punishing her for the rudeness with which she has treated – and is daily treating – me belongs exclusively to me,' he said. If Catherine was going to play the submissive, loyal wife then he would scrape back the gloss of husbandly gallantry and reveal a basic truth of their marriage. While she was his, she was his to punish.

Catherine was not sure how long he planned to punish her for. Nor was her friend Chapuys, who spent a further four months speculating about when, or whether, she would be called back to court. Perhaps, to begin with, Catherine did not even mind that much. Henry had, after all, been absent before. There were advantages that came with Anne's departure. Princess Mary, for example, could come to Windsor Castle. Catherine, at last, spent precious time with her daughter. 'She will make her forget the pain of the king's absence,' said Chapuys. They rode and hunted through the fine, long summer days. They also talked. There were serious matters to be discussed. One of them faced divorce. The other faced being tarred with the brush of bastardy.

The habits of matrimony proved difficult to destroy. For more than two decades Catherine and Henry had followed a regular system of communicating when apart. Every three days they sent a messenger who carried a token, a counter-sign, as proof of identity. A few days after Henry had left Windsor Catherine gave her messenger a letter and the token (perhaps a jewel).

In her message, Catherine asked after Henry's health and told him that she wished he had let her say adieu. She was sad without him, but knew it was for him to order and for her to obey. Henry treated the messenger with gravity. He would consult his councillors. Then he called the messenger back and unleashed his anger. He cared not for her adieux or enquiries after his health. He had no wish to console her as she had annoyed him in a thousand ways, humiliating him with the call to Rome and refusing the advice of his councillors. He poured scorn on her nephew, the emperor, and ordered her to stop sending him messengers.

Catherine defied his ban and sent a message back. Forget my nephew, she said. God will decide who is right. Henry found defiance confusing when it was masked, as it had been earlier, as subservience. The latter stroked his kingliness, his sense of chivalry and his manliness. That is why it had worked so well these past four years. Catherine's outright defiance, however, enraged and emboldened him. He knew he was right, he replied, because so many people had told him so. His own expertise on canon law was now universally recognised, or so, in a moment of revelatory hubris, he proclaimed. Then he sent another messenger. He planned to go hunting around Windsor and did not want to see her. She must leave.

Catherine was sent to The More, one of Wolsey's former houses in Hertfordshire. This was insult added to injury. First her husband had gone off without her, now she was being turned out of her house by Anne Boleyn. Her daughter, to make things worse, was sent away to Richmond. Their days together were over. Henry wanted Catherine to suffer, and soften. Her 'purgatory', as she liked to call it, was just beginning. Catherine would never see her daughter again.

Even then, she could not bring herself to criticise her husband directly, at least not in writing. That would have been too dangerous. He was a good and virtuous man at heart, she insisted in one of the deluge of letters she began sending to her nephew Charles. The pope, by delaying judgement, had allowed her enemies in the Boleyn camp 'to take him prisoner'. Henry was like a Spanish bull, she explained, pricked and goaded into action by their lances. Catherine's own supporters, meanwhile, were terrified. 'They have scared them so much that they no longer dare speak,' she complained. She had already noticed how the waverers were being drawn over by royal offerings 'like hawks to the lure'. Catherine felt humiliated. She struggled to hold back the hyperbole. Surely no Christian had ever suffered more than she. It was enough to kill ten people, she insisted.

Mario Savorgnano, a Venetian who saw her at The More, noted that, although the king made sure she had few visitors, there were still more than two hundred people in her court. 'In the morning we saw her majesty dine: she had some thirty maids of honour standing round the table, and about fifty who performed its service,' he reported. 'Her majesty is not of tall stature, rather small. If not handsome, she is not ugly; she is somewhat stout and has always a smile on her countenance.'

Wolsey's building programme had turned The More into a grand, modern country house with long galleries and bridges extending over the moat into the privy gardens. The broad moat that now surrounded her, however, must have felt as if it were there to keep her prisoner. She told Chapuys that she would rather be publicly locked up in the Tower of London and planned to tell the king as much. There, at least, 'her misfortune would be immediately notorious to all the world'.

Three months after abandoning his wife, Henry decided to test Catherine's will. Had Catherine's Spanish stubbornness finally weakened? He sent four of his most loyal and strong-willed men to find out. It was, in its way, a repeat of the visit by the thirty councillors though his men had obviously decided they needed to vary their strategy if they were to have any chance of success. She had defeated the thirty visitors to Greenwich with her womanly protestations of innocence and subservience to both the king and God. This time she told them just as sweetly that she was defending not just herself but her daughter. She had also finally realised, to her great sadness, that the king was not ruled by his conscience but by passion. Henry too, she implied, needed saving – from himself. Then, as Catherine's court of ladies and gentlemen looked on in astonishment, Henry's envoys threw themselves down on their knees before her. This was their new tactic. They would be the supplicants this time. The peace of the kingdom and the king's honour, not to mention her daughter's welfare and her own comfort, depended on her decision, they told her. This was not just begging. It was also, with its unsubtle threat to Mary, menace.

Few people, however, could outdo Catherine when it came to supplication. The queen sank dramatically to her own knees and raised her voice. They had spoken quietly to her, but she wanted to make absolutely sure that everyone could hear what she had to say. Her ladies and gentlemen listened avidly. She began pleading with Henry's envoys. For God's sake and out of respect for Christ's blood and suffering, could they please persuade Henry to return to his lawful wife, she begged them. If he refused, could he not allow God, through the pope, to decide what must be done? So she went on, the wronged woman begging her husband's councillors to put him back on the right track. By the time she had finished there was barely a dry eye in the room.

Her visitors recovered their tongues, and their malice, shortly before they left. If she hated The More, the king had told them, he could always move her to a smaller house or to an abbey. Catherine's reply contained its own, not so veiled threat. She would go wherever the king, her master, sent her. If he ordered her to be burnt at the stake, she would obey. This was the ultimate defiance. If Henry wanted to make England's queen a martyr, then he could go ahead. She was ready to burn.

Catherine had crossed a line. She would be queen or they could kill her. It was very clear and very simple. Only God could take away her title and He, obviously, was on her side. For Catherine, this was both dangerous and liberating. In some ways she was returning to the dramatic, obstinate misery of her youth, when she had proclaimed that she would rather die than leave England unwed. She was, however, no longer an immature young girl. Age had made her more, not less, determined. Not even the threats to Mary would move her from now on. If her daughter had to become a martyr too, that would be God's will – and her husband's.

Catherine's outward security hid her inner pain. Writing to her nephew Charles shortly before Christmas 1531, she signed her letter: 'At The More, without my husband, without having offended him in any way'.

That Christmas was sombre for Henry as well. Even Edward Hall, his loyal chronicler, admitted that Christmas and the New Year gift-giving that marked the arrival of 1532 were the worst for years. 'All men said there was no mirth in that Christmas because the queen and the ladies were absent,' he reported. To make things worse, Henry suddenly found himself presented, on New Year's Day, with a beautifully crafted gold cup – a present from his banished wife. It was a piece of deliberate provocation on Catherine's part. He had renewed his ban on messages but forgotten to tell her not to observe the custom of giving New Year's presents. Catherine saw an opportunity to publicly reassert her matrimonial status. She was still his wife, so he would get a wife's gift. Henry narrowly avoided the embarrassment of having it presented to him in front of Anne and the rest of the court. He angrily ordered it taken away. For the first time, Henry did not buy New Year's presents for Catherine or her ladies (while Anne got a room full of tapestries and a bed covered in cloth of gold and silver, crimson satin and embroidery). Catherine's own haul of gifts was the worst for two decades, as Henry had also banned his gentlemen from sending her anything.

John Fisher, Anne Boleyn's bête noire, remained steadfast, despite further threats against his life. He vowed that, even if he met a hundred thousand deaths, he would still defend Catherine. These were dangerous times, however, and a certain amount of subterfuge was needed if he was to help Catherine. He told Chapuys, with whom he was in regular contact, never to acknowledge in public that they knew one another. Chapuys was not to be offended if he ignored him when they were in the same room. He obviously did not want to be arrested and accused of fraternising with Henry's enemies, as Wolsey had been. Another senior clergyman, Henry's cousin Reginald Pole, turned down the archbishopric of York because of Catherine. He asked, instead, to be allowed to go abroad – warning Henry that, if he stayed, he would be obliged to defend the queen in parliament.

The church, increasingly squeezed by Henry, began to protest. One preacher at St Paul's openly denounced the divorce in March 1532, and was arrested afterwards. Henry apparently then issued orders for preachers to come out in his defence.

When one did so in the diocese of Salisbury, however, he was booed and hissed by the women. The forces of law and order were required to restrain them from attacking him.

Even Hall, a natural Henry supporter, had to admit that popular opinion was on Catherine's side. 'The Lady Anne Boleyn was so much in the king's favour that the common people which knew not the king's true intent said and thought that the absence of the queen was only for her sake, which was not true,' he said.

Henry even discovered that a handful of people were ready to defy him to his face. On Easter Day in 1532 the provincial of the Observant Friars, William Peto, preached in front of Henry at the chapel that this order of largely incorruptible Franciscans had beside the palace at Greenwich. The friars were Catherine's favourite men of the cloth, and her relationship with those at Greenwich was specially close. Unbounded affection and false counsel, Peto warned in his sermon, were bad for kings. These were unsubtle references to Henry's 'unbounded' desire for Anne Boleyn and to those who encouraged him to believe he deserved a divorce. When Henry asked afterwards what he had meant, Peto did not shrink from explaining. The divorce, he said, was endangering the crown. All of England, he added, was against it. Henry tried to counter Peto by putting up his own preacher in their church soon afterwards, while the former was out of the country. The other friars reacted angrily and the preacher's claim that all theologians backed Henry was greeted with an outraged rebuttal, there and then, by their warden. The friars privately told Chapuys that they, too, were willing to die for Catherine. A serious rift in the church, which would have bloody consequences, was beginning to appear.

Henry began to employ a heavy hand. His increasingly influential new councillor Thomas Cromwell was already keeping an eye out for dissenters. He kept a close watch on the Observant Friars, and even had a spy amongst them. Two friars were banished to far-off monasteries. Thomas Abel was locked up in the Tower of London for the next eight months. Orders reportedly went out to find all copies of his book rebutting Henry's arguments.

Some in the church began to sense that Henry might one day start suppressing monasteries. The ever-vigilant Cromwell discovered that the prior of one London friary had already claimed that Henry might eventually be known not as *defensor fidei*, Defender of the Faith, but as *destructor fidei*, Destroyer of the Faith. The loose-tongued prior also claimed that the next time the king's fool performed one of his favorite tricks by falling off the back of his horse, he should explain that Henry, too, was set for a fall.

Peto was right that the country was, generally, against the divorce – though few seemed ready to stir themselves to action. Already, in late 1531, the Venetian envoy Ludovico Falier had returned home to declare: 'The queen being so loved and respected, the people already commence murmuring; and were the faction to produce a leader . . . it is certain that the nation would take up arms for the queen.' Savorgnano, for his part, came away with the firm impression that the people of England were on Catherine's side. 'There is now living with him [Henry] a young woman of noble birth, though many say of bad character, whose will is law to him,' he said.

He is expected to marry her, should the divorce take place, which it is supposed will not be effected, as the peers of the realm, both spiritual and temporal, and the people are opposed to it; nor during the present queen's life will they have any other queen in the kingdom.

In May 1532, as if to prove Savorgnano right, two members of parliament stood up to complain about the king asking for money to fortify the Scottish border. The Scots, they said, never did anything without a foreign ally. If the king just took back his wife and treated her properly, thereby pacifying the emperor, there would be nothing to worry about – and the danger that Englishmen would start fighting amongst themselves over the divorce would also be averted. A member of the Commons called Temse called on the house to demand that Henry 'take the queen again into his company' in order to avoid 'bastard-ising the Lady Mary, the king's only child, and diverse other inconveniences'.

Then Sir Thomas More, unable to bear the moral conflict of obeying Henry while the latter pursued the divorce and asserted his supremacy over the church, resigned as chancellor in May 1532. 'There has never been, nor ever will be such a fine man in the position,' observed Chapuys. Even Dr Benet, one of Henry's team in Rome, privately let Catherine know of his shame at what he was being asked to do. He was not alone. Other English ambassadors also privately recognised that justice was on Catherine's side. The senior nobles, a generally conserv-ative group who were offended by the upstart Anne, watched nervously. Henry's sister Mary, who had been Catherine's com-panion at many of the great events of her father-in-law's court, was amongst those who most disliked her brother's fiancée. Her husband, the duke of Suffolk, had already been heard saying it was time the king was persuaded to drop his marriage plans. Remarks that Mary made against Anne then sparked a sudden burst of violence at the Sanctuary in Westminster. One of the Suffolk family's principal gentlemen died in the fracas. Her hus-band had to promise to restrain his people, though these later plotted revenge on the killers.

The marchioness of Exeter, Gertrude Courtenay, also began to pass information to Chapuys on the moves against Catherine at court. When the young marquess of Dorset had been tempo-rarily banished from court in 1531, Catherine saw Anne's secret hand at work. She was sure that her friendship with him was to blame. Given that the duke of Norfolk's wife had also expressed concern, it was clear that the greatest families of England were increasingly disturbed by Boleyn's ascendancy. Chapuys was soon claiming that several high people had secretly told him that, should the pope pass sentence declaring Catherine's marriage valid, they would ensure (presumably by force of arms) that the sentence was obeyed. Chapuys delightedly passed each item of anti-Boleyn gossip on to the emperor.

As the king rode north with Anne Boleyn on an extended hunting trip in July 1532, the royal entourage was reportedly hooted and hissed at. Women's voices called out insults against Anne, Chapuys reported. After several days Henry ordered the party to turn back. This may well have been because he and Boleyn were preparing to meet the king of France in an attempt to win his support for their plans. Henry could have had little doubt by then, however, that Catherine's support ran deep. When he returned south, perhaps to assuage Anne, he called in the officials involved in coronation protocol. It was time, he said, to begin preparations for Anne's big day.

43 The Queen's Jewels

The Queen's House. Late September 1532

The coffer had written on it the words 'The Queen's Jewels'. This was where the glittering collection of unset gemstones, pearls, bracelets, strings of beads, rings, aglets, chains, clasps, crosses, jewelled buttons, collets, carcanets, partlets and decorated girdles of the English queen lived. The jewels in the collection now belonged to Catherine. They may not yet have entered the special jewel coffer that was first described by a court official in 1547, but she certainly kept them with her.

Some had come to England with her from Spain in her dowry. Others she had picked out from the selection offered to her by Henry VII to cure her homesickness. Still more had been inherited shortly after her second marriage when Henry's grandmother, Margaret Beaufort, died. While many items had probably long been part of the royal collection, the contents of the jewel box also increased over the years with gifts from Henry. Many of these arrived – and some later departed – as part of the traditional exchange of gifts at court every New Year.

Whatever their origin, Catherine's jewel-edged formal clothes and the heavy, elaborate chains and crosses she wore around her neck for portraits were evidence of status. They allowed her to show off her royal magnificence. They were, in short, proof that she was queen.

In late September 1532, a messenger from the duke of Norfolk arrived at her house to deliver the news that Henry wanted her jewels. This was not an attempt to increase his own, already abundant, collection of personal jewellery. He was preparing to meet the French king, the messenger said, and needed the jewels for the woman accompanying him, Anne Boleyn.

Catherine refused to hand over the jewels to her rival. 'I cannot present the king with my jewels as he desires, inasmuch as when, on a late occasion, I, according to the custom of this kingdom, presented him with a New Year's gift he warned me to refrain from such presents in future,' she said, alluding to the gold cup he had so angrily rejected. 'Besides which it is very annoying and offensive to me, and I would consider it a sin and a load upon my conscience if I were persuaded to give up my jewels for such a wicked purpose as that of ornamenting a person who is the scandal of Christendom.' Anne Boleyn, she said, was turning Henry into a laughing stock by flaunting herself beside a man who was not her husband. Catherine blamed the woman who was stealing her husband away for 'bringing vituperation and infamy upon the king, through his taking her with him to such a meeting across the Channel'.

If the king wanted the jewels, she said, he would have to order her to hand them over. 'I am ready to obey his commands in that as in all other matters,' she said. A gentleman of the king's chamber duly arrived with the order. Catherine had no choice. She handed over all the jewellery she possessed, according to Chapuys. The one thing she held on to was a small, plain gold cross on a gold necklace. This contained something she considered far more valuable than any shiny gem – a sliver of the cross on which Jesus Christ died.

Catherine watched Anne's progress from a distance, kept up to date by her ladies and their contacts at court, as her rival grew in confidence and pressed home her advantage. Anne had started the year by taking over Catherine's own quarters at Greenwich and surrounding herself with a queen-sized entourage of ladies-in-waiting. The trip across the Channel to meet King Francis was designed to be a moment of crowning glory. Before they sailed for Calais in October 1532, Henry gave Anne the title of marchioness of Pembroke. This made her, in her own right, one of the senior people in the land. It also ensured her a hefty income. Unusually, though, the terms of the patent allowed her to pass the title on to any illegitimate children – a sign, perhaps, that Henry was still not fully confident about being granted a legitimate divorce.

Anne kept her own suspicious, watchful eye not just on Catherine and her supporters but on Princess Mary as well. When Henry and Mary, apparently by accident, met while out hunting that autumn, Anne sent two of her ladies to listen in to their conversation. A cowed Henry confined himself to swapping pleasantries with his own daughter.

For the trip to see the French king, Henry ordered up a queen's wardrobe of magnificent gowns for Anne. The English let it be known that Henry would rather not meet Francis's Spanish wife Eleanor, who was Charles's sister and Catherine's niece, as 'he hates Spanish dress, since it makes him see a devil'. Catherine wondered if the confiscation of her jewellery meant, as was strongly rumoured, that Henry planned to marry Anne while they were on the continent. Chapuys reported, however, that Anne had said she would not do that. 'She wants it done here, in the place where other queens have customarily been married and crowned,' he reported.

Catherine's husband and her rival returned from the continent in mid-November. They lingered for a while in Kent and the south-east. This may be where Anne, after more than five years, finally allowed Henry into her bed. Or perhaps it was in the English port of Calais, where rain, wind and fog kept them huddling in the town's handsome Exchequer, that they took advantage of two bedrooms connected by a single door. Wherever it was, it was a momentous decision on Anne's part. It meant, apart from anything else, that she felt absolutely secure that she would be queen.

Neither Catherine nor anyone else, except for those sworn to secrecy, knew about the change in Henry and Anne's relationship – which may have involved some kind of binding exchange of vows in front of witnesses. There was no escaping, however, the changes that were happening to England's government and church – and which gave Anne the confidence to take Henry into her bed.

Henry had been struggling to find a way both to achieve a legal divorce and to impose his new vision of an English kingship. Catherine beat him continually in Rome – where his main achievement was, to his wife's continual frustration, to slow things down to a snail's pace. His ideas developed incrementally. His actions were piecemeal. Each shift moved him closer to the idea that, with no ifs or buts, it was he, not the pope, who ruled the English church and clergy. Henry had always had a flamboyant sense of himself.

He was not, however, surrounded by great revolutionaries. Henry himself had the charisma, and power, to lead but he needed others to help him provide ideology and enthusiasm and, above all, to enforce change. The nobles who Henry had turned to after Wolsey's departure were, however much they coveted the church's wealth, conservative men. So, too, were the bishops. Even those, like Archbishop Warham, who were scared of Henry's wrath or who, like Stephen Gardiner, bishop of Winchester, had helped him pursue the divorce, could suddenly dig in their heels if the pope's, and their own, authority was challenged.

Men such as the scholar Edward Fox and Thomas Cranmer were helping Henry gather ideological arguments for his revolution. Anne, too, helped by pushing the works of William Tyndale into his hands. Hers was a formidable voice within Henry's circle, but she could not be seen to be leading change. Wherever Henry's ideas came from, there can be no doubt that the engine driving him forward was primed, first and foremost, by his need to overcome Catherine's resistance to a divorce.

What the revolution needed most of all was an enforcer – someone with the talent, determination and, above all, discipline to drive through the changes. Thomas Cromwell began to fill the role. He was nothing if not disciplined. He was also hardworking, clever, ambitious and ruthless. And he was a believer. Increasingly, he oversaw Henry's assault on the church of Rome.

Cromwell's expertise lay both in the law and in the implacable pursuit of money. He had been Wolsey's agent when the cardinal suppressed a series of minor monasteries in order to use their resources to fund his colleges at Oxford and Ipswich. At the fall of Wolsey, Cavendish found a teary-eyed Cromwell reciting his matins to himself in the latter's house at Esher. 'Which would since have been a very strange sight,' he observed ironically some years after Cromwell had taken a key role in Henry's attacks on the Roman Catholic church. Cromwell explained that he was feeling sorry for himself. What would he do without Wolsey? Then he pulled himself together and declared that he would seek his luck at Henry's court. 'I do intend (God willing), this afternoon, when my lord hath dined, to ride to London and so to the court, where I will either make or mar,' he said.

Cromwell's original success stemmed from his overseeing of Wolsey's largess, when the cardinal suddenly had to start buying support. Wolsey began to spread his money as widely as possible, giving out generous annuities to, amongst others, Anne Boleyn's brother, George. Cromwell organised this for him, reaping the gratitude of those who benefited from the cardinal's sudden munificence. After Wolsey's death he proved just as formidable at helping the king administer the cardinal's former estate. He also began to prove himself in parliament. In 1529 he had heard, perhaps even joined in, the cries of 'Down with the church!' that echoed around the chamber during a debate which showed that not only Henry was tiring of corrupt, over-fed priests. Years of clerical abuse had left the field well manured. He also seems to have helped persuade the clergy to accept Henry as their Supreme Head – albeit with that caveat of only 'as far as the law of Christ allows'. By the end of autumn 1531 he had become Henry's man in parliament. He soon acquired a new skill – that of turning parliament against the church and the clergy.

In March 1532 parliament denounced the abuses of the church and its courts in the so-called 'Supplication against the Ordinaries'. This explicitly described Henry as the 'only head, sovereign lord, protector and defender' of the church. It removed the ifs and buts the clergy had included when they had previously insisted that this was only so 'as far as the law of Christ allows'. The clergy fought the changes, but lost. It was the moment Sir Thomas More, ever faithful to his own view of the church, decided he could no longer serve the king and resigned as lord chancellor.

Catherine, meanwhile, saw the tide washing away from her. The pope was feeble. He offered only mealy-mouthed admonitions to Henry and avoided, at all costs, reaching a sentence. She would lodge her complaints against Clement to God after her death, she told her nephew. Charles continued to support her, but he had more important business elsewhere. In November 1532 she wrote to congratulate him on a victory over the Turkish army in Hungary. She urged him, also, to tell the pope 'to kill the second Turk, which is the business of my lord the king and I'.

She despaired, but kept her hand on the tiller. Chapuys and, occasionally, even the papal nuncio in England awaited her instructions – as did a team of people in Rome. There was no holding back the tide, however. In August 1532 William Warham died. Old age, rather than the king's rage, eventually killed the man who, as archbishop of Canterbury, Catherine had found so spineless. Warham had, however, refused to disobey the pope and try the case himself. All Henry needed to do now was place someone in Canterbury who would not shrink from delivering a divorce – whatever Rome said. That man, much to his own alarm, was Cranmer. His own secret marriage may have weighed on his conscience. 'There was never man came more unwillingly to a bishoprick than I did to that,' he claimed later.

Almost everything was now in place to defy Rome. Cromwell could be counted on, when necessary, to deliver the final parliamentary acts. Cranmer would do the rest.

Little surprise, perhaps, that Anne Boleyn now felt confident she would finally get what she had been promised five long years before. Her sluggish lover, though, still needed pushing. Soon events moved to the point of no return. By Christmas 1532, Anne was pregnant. It was a final, calculated move to bind Henry to her. In January 1533, in absolute secrecy, they were married. Catherine's husband was now a bigamist.

44 Secrets and Lies

London. 23 February 1533

One late February morning Chapuys came across 'a worthy man', whom he dared not name in writing. The man was setting off to see Catherine at The More in a state of nervous excitement. He had heard a terrible secret. Henry had married Anne Boleyn. The ceremony had been performed by none other than Thomas Cranmer, the archbishop elect of Canterbury, in front of her parents, brother and two intimate friends – or so he had been told. The queen, he insisted, must be informed.

Chapuys, a man with a fine ear for rumour, especially if it went against Anne, only partially believed this piece of gossip. Cranmer may not have married them yet, he said, but he surely would. Henry was just waiting for the pope to confirm the future archbishop's appointment and send the necessary papers. Then, Chapuys was convinced, he would act.

The 'worthy man' was, indeed, only partly wrong. A wedding had taken place, but in such secrecy that even today it is hard to tell where, when and by whom Henry and Anne were married. Perhaps the most plausible tale is of a handful of people gathering, before dawn, in a chamber above the Holbein Gate at Whitehall.

Cranmer was not at the wedding, but he was no stranger to secrets himself. How many people knew that, defying church norms, he himself had married the niece of a Lutheran pastor while in the German city of Nuremberg the previous year? He was certainly a believer in reform, but was it the knowledge of this secret that gave Henry such tremendous power over a man who so obligingly did what he was asked? Late that March there was another short ceremony. At this one Cranmer swore that his archbishop's oath to the pope would not bind him to do anything against the king's prerogative or to refrain from reforming the church in England. With that done, he was consecrated archbishop of Canterbury.

The one secret that had already slipped out concerned Anne Boleyn's womb. One day in February, she had emerged from her chamber in an excitable, skittish mood. Bumping into a former suitor, probably the poet Thomas Wyatt, she exclaimed that 'for the last three days she had had such an incredibly ferocious desire to eat apples, as she had never felt before, and that the king had said to her that it was a sign that she was with child'. She then laughed hysterically and rushed back into her chamber. Henry confirmed her state in April when, quite needlessly, he offered an overexcited reply to Chapuys' insinuation that remarrying might still not bring him a male heir. 'Am I not a man like other men? Am I not? Am I not?' he retorted. Henry challenged the ambassador to answer the question twice more before adding that he was not going to prove it by letting Chapuys 'into my secrets' (which the ambassador, correctly, took to mean that Anne was pregnant). Anne probably wanted people to know about her condition. Nothing, after all, was more likely to cement her position than bearing Henry a male child. Henry's reply to Chapuys, however, seems to have revealed deep-seated fears about his own fertility and, perhaps, impotence.

Catherine had all the London gossip passed on to her by Chapuys. It was not, however, until Cranmer received the papal paperwork that allowed him to be consecrated archbishop, and Cromwell drove through a parliamentary bill banning future appeals to Rome, that Henry dared tell her that he had married. Even then he did not do it himself. He despatched, instead, four of the most senior men in the land to her country house on 9 April. It was one of several errands that – to his great shame and embarrassment – her brother-in-law, the duke of Suffolk, had to run on Henry's behalf. They wearily set about the latest round of bullying. 'She was to renounce her title of queen, and allow her case to be decided here in England,' they said. 'If she did, she would confer a great boon on the kingdom and prevent much effusion of blood, and besides the king would treat her much better than she could possibly expect.' English blood would run, they implied, if she did not accept. It was only when, predictably, she refused to comply that the four men turned to the next part of their instructions. Resistance was useless, they said. The king had married more than two months previously in front of witnesses. None of them, they added guiltily and unnecessarily, had actually been present at the wedding. Then, with much apologising, bowing and muttering about disagreeable duties, they left. The blow had been delivered.

Now it was the turn of Lord Mountjoy, the former chamberlain who had been married to her friend and former lady-in-waiting Inés de Vanegas, to drive the knife in further. He had been sent back to watch over her the previous week. The king, he informed her, had ordered that she no longer be addressed as queen. A month after Easter he planned to stop her money, fire her servants and send her off to a small house with a vastly reduced income. An indignant Catherine replied that he could do as he liked, but she was not about to learn how to keep her own house. If she could not live properly as a queen she would happily go out and become a beggar. But she would always call herself 'Queen Catherine'.

Henry and his new wife now felt so confident of themselves that at Easter Anne – who had yet to be crowned – turned out in all the trappings of a queen. 'The Marchioness Anne went to high mass with the king, as queen, and with all the pomp of a queen, clad in cloth of gold, and laden with the richest jewels,' an Italian in London reported. Anne glittered with Catherine's best diamonds and other royal jewels, setting people muttering about how they had been snatched from the true queen. She was followed into church by a large retinue of ladies, one of whom carried her train. Preachers, at least those who did not want trouble, began to call her 'queen' in their sermons and prayers – even if it made the congregation walk out. Anne's servants obviously took all this as a sign that their mistress's long battle was won. They excitedly tore Catherine's arms off her royal barge. The barge, they had decided, now belonged to Anne – though Henry later told them off for jumping the gun. Catherine's arms also disappeared from the great gate of the hall at Westminster. The whole thing, said Chapuys, was turning into a nightmare.

People did not know what to do or, especially, what to say. Some feared that Catherine's mighty nephew would appear on the horizon with a huge fleet and put them all to the sword. Others thought that Charles would shut down the ports of Flanders to English traders. They would be ruined. Cromwell, now recognised by Chapuys as Henry's right hand, was rumoured to have locked all his personal goods up in the Tower of London. Perhaps he had already heard the rumour, which circulated through Flanders later that year, that the emperor was plotting war with some of the great men of England. These would 'have Queen Catherine with them, and to assist her from field to field as they shall march forwards, with her crown upon her head'. Even Henry and his councillors wanted to know. Would Charles, they asked Chapuys, now make war?

Henry may have married Anne Boleyn and displayed her to the world as queen but he had not yet divorced Catherine. He was still a man with two wives. The pope, clearly, was not going to grant Henry his divorce, but the king now had Cranmer at hand to do so instead. Henry wanted Anne crowned by early June. That gave Cranmer, who had been consecrated archbishop on 30 March, only a few weeks to set up a court and deliver a verdict. The goings-on in Rome, which a frustrated Catherine cared about passionately and which her husband still watched with a concerned eye, were proceeding at the usual sluggish pace. The pope could not – would not, in fact – get in the way. The English court's decision would be final, too, since appeals to Rome had now been banned by act of parliament. On 11 April, Cranmer wrote to Henry 'most humbly' requesting permission to finish what had started six years previously. The 'rude and ignorant common people', he claimed, wanted the matter settled. Henry graciously conceded, congratulating Cranmer on his zeal for justice and concern for the people. Then he added, just in case there was still any doubt, that he himself no longer recognised any 'superior on the earth'.

The court was set up at Dunstable Priory, in Bedfordshire, far enough from London for people not to interfere or to cause trouble in the streets. 'They fear that if the affair were managed here, the people would not refrain from speaking of it, and perhaps from rioting,' said Chapuys. It was also near to Catherine's new home at Ampthill, where she seems to have been hurriedly moved at the beginning of March. When the orders arrived for her to appear at the court on 1 May, Catherine was frozen with fear and doubt about what she should do. Chapuys advised her to do nothing. Her appeal was already lodged at Rome. Anything that might make it look as though she recognised the English court could be used against her there. Catherine followed his advice. Cranmer was relieved. The last thing he wanted was for the queen to actually appear in court and start slowing things down by defending herself. It would be best, he said, if she heard no news at all from Dunstable, in case she suddenly decided to appear. 'Speak as little of this matter as ye may,' he begged Cromwell. The trial opened on 10 May and, with Catherine absent, Cranmer passed sentence thirteen days later. There was no surprise. Catherine, in the eyes of the new English church, had never been properly married to the king. Henry's church was claiming that she had spent half of her life, as she herself indignantly phrased it, as the king's concubine.

Five days later Cranmer validated Henry and Anne's marriage. Four days after that he oversaw the coronation of a six-months-pregnant Anne – and was a guest of honour at the banquets afterwards. Reaction to the coronation was, when compared to the reception Londoners had given Catherine, muted. A handful of important people, including Henry's sister Mary and Sir Thomas More, stayed away. A new order had, however, now been firmly established in England. Both Henry and Anne were determined to make Catherine – and the rest of the country – bow to it.

45 That Whore

Leigh, Lancashire. Autumn–Winter 1533

'Who the devil made Nan Bullen [Anne Boleyn], that whore, the queen?' raged James Harrison. The loose-tongued priest from Leigh, Lancashire, was indignant and did not mind people knowing it. 'I will take none for queen but Queen Catherine!' he insisted to the group of men gathered in a neighbour's house. Then he uttered words of treason. 'The king,' he said, 'should not be king.'

It was a belligerent outburst of the kind that Eustace Chapuys was increasingly hearing. Popular anger over Catherine's mistreatment could easily be marshalled into rebellion, he thought. If the people did not accept Anne Boleyn, then they should be encouraged to rise against their king. All it would take, Chapuys believed, was a move by her nephew, the Emperor Charles. If he invaded, or simply appeared ready to invade, the English would do the rest.

Chapuys did all he could to encourage Charles, saying the people of England would welcome him with open arms. The place was a tinderbox, he assured the emperor. Those pushing for rebellion had started reminding him of how Richard III had been dethroned. The Tudor claim to the throne was, anyway, not that good, they argued. Some even stated that Charles himself, or Catherine's sister Juana la Loca, had a better claim.

The final decision about whether Henry's divorce should be answered with a declaration of war lay with two people. One, of course, was the emperor. The other was Catherine. She had to decide whether she wanted her country of birth to challenge the country where she had now lived for almost two-thirds of her life. In fact, Catherine had always been clear that she did not want war. 'She thinks that she would be irredeemably damned if she took any path that led to war,' Chapuys reported. In April 1533, as Anne flaunted her jewels and Cranmer prepared a quick divorce, she briefly wobbled and began to consider the possibility of 'another remedy' but soon decided against. A few months later she wrote to Chapuys about whether the pope should urge others to go to war on her behalf. 'What I ask for from his holiness is not war,' she said. 'I would rather die than be the cause of it.' That was a relief to Charles. The emperor, to his ambassador's chagrin, also had no appetite for an English war – though many Englishmen found that hard to believe.

The fear spreading through England was not, however, just of Charles and his armies. Cromwell watched out for dissidence as a new sort of terror slowly took hold. Fisher was arrested. Spies tracked potential subversives amongst the communities of monks, nuns or friars. A close eye was kept on exiles such as the Observant Friar Peto in Antwerp. Catherine's chaplain Thomas Abel was again on the wanted list – though he seems to have been successfully hidden away. 'I perceive that there is secret confederacies,' one of Cromwell's allies wrote when Abel disappeared out of sight. The Observant Friars were a particular concern. Two who had sneaked in to visit Catherine were tracked on their way to London, where they were detained. Cromwell suggested that torture might produce an interesting confession from them. A month later Cromwell's ally, the new lord chancellor Sir Thomas Audley, duly reported that two friars accused of uttering seditious words had, indeed, confessed.

Catherine's messengers were being watched. Each letter and each present was carefully logged to see who was in contact with her. Few dared write to her. Her beloved María de Salinas, who had made the journey to England with her and become Lady Willoughby, was one of them. So, too, were the marchioness of

Exeter (who had been a stepdaughter to another of her former Spanish ladies, the deceased Inés de Vanegas) and Margaret Pole, Lady Salisbury, her daughter's governess. The latter was Catherine's oldest English friend, having accompanied her to Ludlow all those years ago. She was also mother of the man who had refused to become archbishop of York, Reginald Pole.

Cromwell's growing body of spies and informers were fully aware of the upset caused by the divorce. One of his clerks wrote around this time:

There be, I think, [people] in this realm that be not in their minds full pleased and contented that our sovereign hath married as he hath done, some bearing their favour to the lady Catherine princess dowager, some to the lady Mary [her daughter], some because the pope's authority was not therein. And though they forbear to speak at large for fear of punishment, yet they mutter together secretly; which muttering and secret grudge within this realm, I think, doth not a little embolden the king's adversaries without the realm.

When the prior of the Austin Friars called on people to pray for Anne at Easter, part of the congregation stood up and left. Henry took his anger out on London's mayor, who called together the city guilds and told them to stop all grumbling about the divorce. They were to make sure their journeymen and servants kept their mouths closed. They were also to stop their wives talking disparagingly about Anne – though this was recognised to be the most difficult command to enforce.

Women were a particular concern. One London chronicler recorded a clumsy and brutal attempt at keeping them quiet. 'On the 23rd day of August two women were beaten about the Cheap, naked from the waist upward, and their ears nailed to the Standard . . . because they said Queen Catherine was the true queen of England and not Queen Anne. And one of them was big with child,' the chronicler wrote. The punishment, however, did not seem to work. 'When these women had thus been punished, they fortified their saying still, to die in the quarrel [arguing] for Queen Catherine's sake.'

Even the mad wife of the king's former jeweller, Mrs Amadas, came under scrutiny. Her ramblings about dragons, burning stars, white towers, the banishment of Cadwallader and the prophecies of Mouldwarp suggest either advanced dementia or drunken hallucination. Anne Boleyn, she declared, was a harlot who would be burnt to death. Her father was pimp not just to Anne, but to her sister and mother as well – and had given all three over to the king. 'Tush the straw. I care not for the king a *reshe* [rush] under my foot,' she proclaimed. 'It is the king of heaven that rules all.' Catherine's nephew Charles, she thought, would come to the rescue of all good English wives and Henry would be destroyed amid a mighty battle of priests. She was just one of those who latched on to the doom-laden prophecies that began to circulate. The abbot of Garendon also thought the Emperor Charles would come and eject Henry. 'And the king shall come in [back] again . . . and be slain,' he said. Violence would rack the kingdom from 1535 to 1539, he predicted. 'When the Tower [of London] is white and another place green, then shall be burned two or three bishops and a queen; and after all this be passed we shall have a merry world.'

His words were written down as Cromwell's men gathered up all the evidence of dissent. 'Lewd and naughty' priests like the abbot and James Harrison of Leigh were the new enemy within.

46 A 'Bastard' Daughter

Ampthill. 4 July 1533

Catherine looked at the report Mountjoy had brought her and reached angrily for her pen and ink. She was already in a black mood. A harsh cough had been troubling her. and, to make things worse, she had stepped on a pin. The wound meant she could not stand and was forced to lie on a pallet bed. A delegation had come the day before to threaten her once again. Some, like Griffin Richards and Mountjoy, had been friends or servants – on and off – for years. They did not like doing the king's dirty work, but they did not refuse either. They were duty bound to obey.

Mountjoy had brought her the report they had prepared so she could see it before it was sent off. She scribbled out the words 'Princess Dowager' wherever she found them. The previous day she had interrupted them almost as soon as they began to read their instructions out loud. 'At the first she made exception to that name, saying that she was not princess dowager, but queen and the king's true wife,' Mountjoy explained. 'She firmly persisted in the contrary, protesting . . . how she came to the King a clean maid, for [without] any bodily knowledge of Prince Arthur and thereupon was crowned and anointed queen and had by the king lawful issue and no bastard.'

Whatever Henry said or did, nothing had changed that, she argued. Only the pope – the man she would complain loudly about if she ended up in hell – could say that she was not queen. Never mind that Henry, via Cromwell, had ordered these men to tell her that their marriage was now deemed 'detestable, abominable, execrable, and directly against the laws of God and nature'. Never mind that they threatened to keep Mary from her. She could not damn her own soul, even for her daughter. She would not slander herself, either, by confessing that, in effect, she had been the king's harlot for twenty-four years. '*Maledictus homo qui negligit famam suam*,' she said. 'Cursed be the person who neglects their own reputation'. Her Spanish pride shone through. When Henry's men accused her of grasping on to her title out of vanity, she told them that being the daughter of Isabel of Castile and Ferdinand of Aragon was more than enough for her. Mountjoy, in his covering letter, explained that the crossings out were Catherine's work.

Henry was incandescent. He immediately sent for Mountjoy, who must have caught the full royal ire. Cromwell, in his cold and detached way, was impressed by Catherine's determined resistance. 'God and nature wronged [Catherine] in not making her a man,' he observed. Her courage, he said, meant 'she would have surpassed in glory and fame' all the great princes. That did not make Catherine a saint in his view. It simply made her a challenge.

Catherine received new marching orders towards the end of July. This time she was to go from Ampthill to Buckden, in Cambridgeshire. Henry was upset by news that the pope had already effectively declared his new marriage illegal and, worse still, was threatening to excommunicate him if he did not leave Anne Boleyn and return to Catherine by October. He was still worried, however, about provoking Catherine's nephew, so Chapuys was informed that her household, for the moment, was only being 'moderately' reduced. 'The reform which the king, my master, contemplates . . . will be such that all parties will know that in so doing he has had due regard not only to her quality and birth, but likewise to the emperor,' Cromwell said. It was expensive to have two women living like queens, he explained, and she was costing Henry forty thousand ducats a year. Crucially, however, she was to have no train or royal estate. This, Henry knew, was something Catherine cared about. Eliminating the trappings of a queen was another way to sap her morale.

If her morale was low, however, her trip to Buckden must have helped restore it. At Ampthill the neighbourhood came out to wave her off, show their support and wish her luck at her new home. Some wept. Others loudly desired the worst to her enemies. It was by now forbidden, on pain of death, to call Catherine queen but that did not stop some people who shouted it out at the top of their voices. Others effectively offered to take up arms, tearfully crying out that they were ready to die for her – or so Chapuys claimed. This happened, he said, all along the twenty-mile route to Buckden. Clearly it would take more than a remarriage and a coronation to bend Catherine – or to quieten those who, despite the evident danger of speaking out against the king, so spontaneously showed their support. The reports that reached Henry and Cromwell can have left them in little doubt. People still loved Catherine.

Henry's threats to take his anger out on their daughter Mary worried her mother. Catherine had replied bravely to them, but she did not want the seventeen-year-old girl punished for standing by her mother. Mary was the greatest living menace to Anne Boleyn and her future offspring – who she might one day challenge for the crown. But was she now illegitimate? Anne readily referred to her as 'a cursed bastard'. Both the French ambassador and gossips in Flanders also thought Henry's intention was that she should be 'reputed for a bastard'. The law, however, suggested otherwise. Mary had been born in a marriage considered legitimate at the time and, so, was technically legitimate herself, making her even more dangerous.

Already there were reports that – like her mother – young Mary was being cheered when she went out. Anne was furious. 'She has complained to the king that in the villages through which the princess passed the other day as much rejoicing went on as if God Almighty had come down from heaven,' Chapuys reported, adding that Anne wanted the villagers punished. It was all further proof of her 'perversity and wickedness', he wrote to Charles.

Catherine's daughter was, then, her most powerful weapon, but she was also the weakest link in her maternal armour. If a stubborn Catherine was going to be forced to bend, her daughter could be the key to breaking down her resistance. Their strength was in unity.

The campaign against Mary did not get fully under way until the event that Henry and much of the country had been waiting for took place. Anne Boleyn took to her birthing chamber at Greenwich in August 1533. Henry had hidden from her the pope's declaration that, at least in the eyes of Roman Catholic Europe, her future children would be considered illegitimate. On 7 September 1533, the child was born. It was not the son that Henry and his astrologers had been convinced would come. It was a baby girl who, three days later, was christened Elizabeth. One of the ironies of Henry's life was that a man so desperate for a male heir should end up fathering two of England's few queens regnant. Mary and Elizabeth would rule, consecutively, for half a century. His reaction, apart from ordering a herald to announce the birth of a 'legitimate' princess and forcing many of Catherine's closest allies to take part in the christening, was to cancel the jousts he had been preparing. They were only fit for a son. Catherine had already signalled her own disgust at the whole affair by refusing to hand over an elaborate christening cloth that she had brought with her from Spain. She did not mince her words. 'God forbid that I should ever be so badly advised as to give help, assistance, or favour, directly or indirectly, in a case so horrible and abominable as this,' she said.

Mary soon felt the fallout from the birth of her half-sister. A herald publicly proclaimed that she was no longer to be considered a princess. Her servants had the badges torn off their livery and replaced with Henry's own scutcheon. Mary's reaction to the birth of a challenger was, according to Chapuys, extremely cool-headed. She wrote a kind, consoling letter to her mother and waited to see what would happen.

Catherine feared the worst. Her daughter had already suffered during the long-protracted divorce, often falling ill. Catherine realised that things were about to get much worse. She had heard, it seems, that Mary was to be ordered to accept her new condition as mere 'lady' rather than princess. Mary needed both strength and comfort, so Catherine sat down and wrote to her daughter, revealing just how close mother and daughter had become in their mutual hardship. It was one of her most tender letters, but it was also a call to resist.

'Daughter, I heard such tidings today that I do perceive, if it be true, the time is come that Almighty God will prove [test] you; and I am very glad of it, for I trust He doth handle you with a good love,' Catherine wrote. If instructions came from Henry – presumably to stop using the title of princess – Mary was to reply with the same mix of obedience and rebellion that Catherine herself used. 'Answer you with few words, obeying the king your father in everything, save only that you will not offend God and lose your own soul; and go no further with learning and disputation in the matter,' she said. If Mary was to avoid offending God, of course, she would have to stand by the decisions of Rome and act as though her parents were still married.

To fortify her resistance, Catherine suggested a diet of prayer, reading and, for light entertainment, playing on the lute or virginals. Mary's virginity, above all, should remain protected and her body kept 'from all ill and wanton company'. She should repel, likewise, any attempts to marry her off. Catherine sent her daughter two books in Latin which reveal how she herself was preparing for the trials ahead. *De Vita Christi*, by Ludolph of Saxony, suggested a route for mental escape – by imagining the scenes of Christ's own life as intensely and vividly as possible. The Letters of St Jerome, especially the more dramatic ones to the tenacious Paula and her daughter Eustochium, were there to strengthen her moral fibre. These contained not just references to 'the drawbacks of marriage, such as . . . the torture caused by a rival' but to the paradise that greeted those who stuck to their principles. Jerome also reminded them that God was uncompromising. 'The Saviour likes nothing that is half and half, and, while he welcomes the hot and does not shun the cold, he tells us in the Apocalypse that he will spew the lukewarm out of his mouth.' It was, in other words, a moment for all or nothing.

Catherine was confident that her daughter would pass the test but she also wanted to reassure Mary that, though her mother could not be with her, she would continue loving her from a distance. 'I would God, good daughter, that you did know with how good a heart I do write this letter unto you. I never did [write] one with a better,' she said.

Although Henry insisted on keeping them apart, she told her daughter that they would be sharing the same painful ordeal and, if things came to that extreme, might next meet in paradise. 'You shall begin, and by likelihood I shall follow. I set not a rush by it; for when they have done the uttermost they can, then I am sure of the amendment.' Even her signature contained a call to resistance. 'By your loving mother . . . The Queen,' it read. Catherine was not going to stop signing with her proper title.

Mary had inherited such a strong dose of obstinacy from both her parents that she was capable of outdoing even them. She refused to obey a command to stop calling herself princess. She even wrote to Henry complaining that his officials now called her 'the lady Mary, the king's daughter'. She would not accept that his marriage to her mother was invalid. 'If I agreed to the contrary, I should offend God,' she said, repeating Catherine's exact words. Henry was outraged. Officers were despatched to Beaulieu, where Mary was staying. They were to warn her that she was trying 'arrogantly to usurp the title of princess, pretending to be heir apparent'. If she did not change, her father would punish her. He would cut her expenses and get rid of some of her staff. She followed her mother's example, again, by insisting that all this was said in front of her household. 'All those present wept hot tears,' reported Chapuys.

Mary did not have Catherine's experience of Henry's mercurial anger. It was one thing for him to have a defiant wife, and quite another to have a disobedient daughter. His response was to give her house to Anne Boleyn's brother and move her somewhere smaller. Catherine had been worried for some time that Henry would either marry Mary off forcibly to some inferior suitor or make her enter a nunnery. In November, however, a furious Henry decided to inflict the ultimate humiliation on her. She was to be made a lady-in-waiting to her baby half-sister, Elizabeth. Her staff and ladies were to be sacked. Chapuys wrote instructions for her about what to do and say when they came for her. She should protest but, if necessary, allow herself to be taken. Mary was told to learn her lines of protest by heart, repeating them daily to others, so that no one would think she had gone of her own free will.

They did not come for her until mid-December, by which time little Elizabeth had been sent to Hatfield, in Hertfordshire, and given her own household. The duke of Norfolk was deputised to deal with Catherine's defiant seventeen-year-old daughter. She replied angrily when told that she must go into the princess of Wales's service, 'That is the title which belongs to me by right, and to no one else.' Norfolk, however, was not in the mood for debate, so she asked for half an hour to get ready. That gave her time to write out the protestations that Chapuys had prepared for her. She was allowed to keep just two ladies-in-waiting, even though her governess, Lady Salisbury, offered to pay the upkeep of Mary's full household herself.

After they had arrived at Elizabeth's house, Norfolk asked if she wished to pay her respects to the baby princess. Mary boldly replied that, as far as she was concerned, 'the daughter of the marchioness of Pembroke' had no right to that title. She might, however, manage to call her 'sister'. Norfolk then asked if she had any message for her father. 'None, except that the princess of Wales, his daughter, asked for his blessing,' she said. Norfolk shook his head. He was not going to say that to the king. 'Then go away, and leave me alone,' she retorted. Mary went off to weep in her room, something she then did almost daily. That was not enough, however, for Henry. He scolded Norfolk for being too soft and punished her further by taking away her last ladies, leaving her with just one chambermaid.

Mary's treatment hit Catherine hard. She was largely responsible for her daughter's obstinacy. It was she, after all, who had advised her to defy Henry in those things which 'offend God' – meaning the divorce and her own status as princess. Catherine became increasingly convinced that martyrdom awaited them both. 'This next [meeting of] parliament, I am told, is to decide whether my daughter and I are to suffer martyrdom,' she wrote to Chapuys as they waited for Mary to be forced into Elizabeth's service. 'Which I hope to God will be for her and me a meritorious act as we shall suffer for the sake of truth, trusting that – even if the whole world abandons us – we shall not lose the joy and pleasures of the other.' Catherine, in other words, was preparing herself for death and was ready to take her daughter with her. They could be martyrs together.

It was in this state of anxiety and religious fervour that Catherine confronted her final trial of 1533. Her most loyal staff still refused to call her anything but queen and even Henry's servants bridled at having to bully and spy on them. 'It shall not lie in me to accomplish the king's pleasure herein,' Lord Mountjoy had retorted in October when asked to name those of Catherine's servants who still called her queen. 'It shall not well be possible for me to be a reformer of other folks' tongues, and for me to be a complainer and accuser of them,' he said, begging to be relieved from his job.

It is not for me to vex or unquiet her . . . and if it be thought by the king's highness that any other can serve him in this room better than I have done, and I doubt not but there be many, I heartily require . . . that I may, without his grace's displeasure, be discharged from the post of chamberlain [to Catherine].

Mountjoy was echoing the earlier words of Lord Vaulx. He had said he would 'rather die' performing some other service for the king, than remain in Catherine's house.

What Henry saw as Catherine's arrogance was to be punished with yet another change of house. This time she was to go even further away from London − either to Fotheringay, in North-amptonshire, or to Somersham, in the damp and unhealthy Cambridgeshire Fens. The latter, she had been told, was 'a house surrounded by water and marshes . . . the most insalubri-ous and pestilential residence in all England'. Chapuys thought that Henry and Anne, who were already spreading rumours that Catherine was close to death's door, planned to make out that Catherine needed locking away because she had gone mad. The court rumour-mill spun out other theories. Anne wanted Cath-erine discreetly murdered, some said. Others warned that she should lock her door carefully at night because Henry and Anne wanted to plant evidence − of anything from adultery to plotting rebellion − that they could use to accuse her of treason.

Suffolk, once more, was deputed to inform her of the move. Suffolk's wife Mary, who was Henry's sister but Catherine's loyal friend, had died in June. He had remarried, with indecent haste, to the fourteen-year-old daughter of the now widowed Lady Willoughby, María de Salinas. Her former lady-in-waiting remained one of Catherine's diehard supporters. Salinas told Chapuys that, before setting out in mid-December, Suffolk had taken mass and prayed that some accident would happen to prevent him reaching Buckden.

But reach it he did. It was an even worse experience than he had imagined. He found not just Catherine but her entire household in a state of rebellion. Once more, she gathered her servants around her in the great chamber so that they could bear witness to the encounter. Suffolk was as rough as he knew how. He used his worst language, but his bravado simply stiffened Catherine's resolve. She would rather be hacked to pieces than accept the divorce, she told him. Then she refused point blank to go to Somersham. Suffolk and those with him wrote back saying that she had answered them by 'utterly refusing not only the name of princess dowager, and her moving to Somersham, because of her health; but, also, refusing utterly to move to any other place'. A move to Somersham would be tantamount to committing suicide, she protested, for she would surely die in that pestilential house surrounded by marshes and bog water. And suicide was a sin, so she would not go unless by force.

What was more, Catherine added, she would not accept into her service anyone who addressed her as 'princess dowager'. One of Suffolk's tasks, however, was to exact an oath from her servants to call her exactly that. Having failed with her, he bullied them. They, too, refused. It would be committing perjury, they argued, as they had already sworn allegiance to her as queen. That was what her English chaplains, led by Thomas Abel (who had not only avoided arrest but was now publicly back at Catherine's side), had told them. Suffolk locked Abel up in the porter's lodge, forced some servants to swear the oath and sacked others. Then, in desperation, he wrote back to Henry begging for fresh instructions. If he wanted to move Catherine, he would have to 'bind her with ropes', he said. 'We find her the most obstinate woman that may be.' His deepest fear was that she might simply refuse to put her clothes on and that he might have to force her, bound and half-naked, onto a litter and transport her across the country roads of Cambridgeshire. He wrote back to Henry, asking him exactly what they should do next.

The stand-off lasted a week. By the end of it Catherine was left with just a handful of ladies-in-waiting and her Spanish confessor, physician and apothecary. Those servants who had now taken the oath, she declared, had become her jailers. Suffolk had her luggage packed onto wagons. A menacing crowd of Cambridgeshire villagers looked on, 'weeping and cursing to see such cruelty'. Catherine, however, simply shut herself up in her room and locked the door. When Suffolk tried to talk to her, he found himself addressing her through a hole in the wall. 'If you wish to take me with you,' the Spanish voice at the other end of the hole said, 'you must break down the door.' Suffolk did not dare. One of his party admitted they were too scared that, if they tried to drag her out, they 'would be set upon . . . by the crowd'.

If Henry ever needed proof that his wife outmatched him in obstinacy, he now had it. Anne had already observed that Catherine always won their arguments. There was, however, a price to pay for this moral victory. Catherine was now a prisoner.

47 Hang, Draw, Quarter

Rome and London. 23 March 1534

Cardinal Campeggio was fed up. After his return to Rome, he had found himself immersed again in the arguments over Catherine and Henry's divorce. By March 1534, he and his fellow cardinals had already spent almost a year deliberating on the matter, while the pope continued to procrastinate. But Henry's marriage to Anne had changed everything and Campeggio was amongst those who resisted attempts to delay the decision further. The cardinals unanimously flung out Henry's old divorce request, declaring the marriage 'valid and canonical'. They did not even bother to pronounce themselves on the question of Catherine's virginity or the validity of the surprise brief found in Spain. Pope Julius II had given her permission to marry Henry and had been within his right to do so, they said. There was nothing else to argue over.

It should have been a monumental victory. In practice, however, it was almost worthless. Justice arrived late and, by doing so, became injustice. Five years had passed since Catherine lodged her appeal. Henry had used that time to wrench the English church away from Rome and place it in his own pocket. For Catherine, however, the moral and ideological victory was as important as the practical one. God was the real judge. In his eyes, the cardinals had said, her marriage had always been good. She had not sinned. Her daughter was not just legitimate but the true heiress to the English crown. Never mind that many now worried the sentence might drive Henry to have her killed. Her status as a martyr, should that happen, was guaranteed. Even the pope was concerned. 'I am afraid that I have committed a great sin, for the queen may suffer death by it,' he declared after the sentence was finally passed.

The cardinals had swept aside Henry's supposedly encyclopaedic knowledge of canon law. They had proved, once more, that Catherine always won their arguments. England's parliament, however, was already busy burying all hope that she might win anything but that. The House of Lords finished its readings of the Act of Succession, declaring her marriage 'utterly void and annulled', on the very day that she won her victory in Rome. Catherine, it added, 'shall be from henceforth called and reputed only dowager to Prince Arthur, and not queen'. Within a week, the act had Henry's royal consent. Mary was now a bastard. His marriage to Anne was declared – in one of parliament's worst predictions – 'true, sincere and perfect ever hereafter'. Anne's children were to inherit the crown. Catherine had not even heard of her own victory in Rome yet and already she was facing an even fuller defeat.

Worse was to come. Cromwell, the great manipulator, was using parliament to rubber-stamp Henry's revolution. This gave a veneer of benevolence to the king's more radical changes – as if he were magnanimously bowing to parliament's pleas rather than thrusting his own self-centred, divorce-driven agenda onto the country. Never mind that Catherine's supporters in parliament were encouraged, even ordered, to stay away or that Cromwell carefully selected many of the new members himself. Chapuys's request to go there himself and defend Catherine was turned down. Parliament was Cromwell's tool. It was an accident – and a magnificent piece of irony – that he was also laying down the foundations of future parliamentary control of the monarchy.

The act carried both a sharp-clawed introduction and a venomous sting in its tail. The preamble stated that the pope could not encroach on 'the great and inviolable' God-given rights of kings. The sting was an oath that the entire country was meant to swear to observe the act. It placed Catherine, her supporters and all whose hearts remained loyal to Rome in mortal danger. Either they swore, or they could be convicted of 'high treason'. The ghastly punishments of death by burning or by being hanged, drawn and quartered awaited those who refused. It was Cromwell's masterstroke. He now had the means to spread terror into every English household.

Cromwell wasted little time in proving that he meant to enforce obedience with violence. One of his first victims was Elizabeth Barton, the mystical, charismatic and dangerously outspoken Holy Maid of Kent. Barton's trances, visions, prophecies and fits had brought a constant flow of people to her door. Nobles, priests, bishops and even King Henry had wanted to meet her and seek her advice. Her predictions that Henry would lose his crown if he divorced, however, had brought the full wrath of the king. On 20 April 1534, the former country girl was strapped to a hurdle and dragged behind a horse over the bumpy streets from the Tower to Tyburn – London's favourite spot for executions. These were public spectacles and this particular execution, designed to instil fear, would have been well publicised.

Barton was hanged first and then beheaded. Her head was stuck on a pike above London Bridge at the spot where Catherine had made her grand entry into the city as a teenage bride. Five of her followers died with her, their heads distributed around the city's gates. Although the Holy Maid had succumbed to the pressure of captivity and admitted inventing her prophecies, her true crime was to support Catherine. The price of doing that was now clear.

Barton's crime had been explicitly spelled out earlier during a public sermon at Paul's Cross where she had been displayed alongside those who would hang with her. 'Under this manner, by false visions and revelations of the nun, hath grown the great sticking, staying, and delaying of this the king's grace's [new] marriage,' the preacher declared. Martyrdom was now a real possibility for Catherine and her fellow dissenters, especially as they were now obliged to swear the oath that accompanied the Act of Succession. Some, indeed, began to see it as a probability. Catherine was never going to swear an oath declaring her own marriage invalid. Mary, pressed by her mother, could also be expected to deny she was a bastard. Both were mentally prepared for martyrdom. Catherine would herself feel the spiritual draw of the martyr's pyre. It was certainly preferable, in her view, to a sinner's death.

It was reasonable to think, then, that Catherine's blood would join that of others. She had long dwelt on this. One reason why she had her food cooked in front of her was that she was worried someone wanted her poisoned. Henry, she also believed, had tried to put her amongst the damp Fens in order to accelerate her end. Excess humidity, it was thought, could provoke dropsy. To Chapuys's consternation, Henry had already been claiming she suffered from the disease. 'He told the French ambassador that she could not possibly live long, as she had dropsy,' the ambassador reported. 'One wonders whether [they plan] . . . to give her an artificial form of dropsy.' Rumours were also circulated that she was going slowly mad. 'No one doubts that some terrible act will befall the queen given the rude and strange treatment to which she is subjected,' wrote Chapuys. What they really wanted, he said, was 'the death of the queen'.

As the atmosphere of fear thickened in May 1534, Catherine received yet another bullying visit from Henry's emissaries, this time led by the archbishop of York, Edward Lee. The sentence from Rome, they said, was meaningless. They made her the usual offers of a life of elegant retirement if, this time, she accepted the Act of Succession. Catherine, they complained afterwards, reacted 'in great choler and agony and always interrupting our words'. She was not Henry's subject, she retorted scornfully, but his wife. Cranmer, she told them, was a mere 'shadow'. The bill did not concern her. She may have been small and famous for her cheerful public temperament, but Catherine's 'loud voice' delivered a full broadside of what the assembled bishops deemed to be 'unseeming words'. They had come armed, however, with a new threat. 'They threatened her expressly with the punishments contained in the act, making it clear that this included death,' an indignant Chapuys reported.

The threat may have been less naked than Chapuys thought, but it was still there. Catherine hurled it back in their faces. If any one of them wished to be her executioner, she said, they should step forward and perform the act there and then. Her only regret would be that, when execution time came, she had always wished 'it might be in public, and not in a room or at some secret spot'. Like many a martyr, Catherine wanted her death to be a final show – one which proved her right, showed her courage and exposed the cowardliness of her killers. Henry's envoys, once again, beat a cowardly retreat. Death was no threat to a woman already preparing herself for both the pain and the glory of martyrdom.

Cromwell rounded up suspects. The various orders of friars, especially Catherine's much-loved Observants, were increasingly viewed as dangerous subversives. They were both popular preachers and men with little to lose. Unlike the rest of a clergy widely corrupted by wealth, they had no personal property that could be taken away. Cromwell's informers amongst them offered evidence and named names. Those in exile, like Father Peto in Antwerp, were still being watched closely. Others were tailed. In June 1534, two cartloads of friars could be seen entering the Tower of London.

Years after her death, copies of letters supposedly exchanged at this time between Catherine and an old Observant friend from Greenwich, Friar John Forrest, appeared in Roman Catholic literature. He was one of a number of friars who had continued to visit Catherine and her ladies over the previous six years. Often they pretended that they were merely stopping off on the way from one Observant friary to another. They visited on feast days and heard confessions. Their preaching hardened the resolve of Catherine and those around her.

Forrest was one of the imprisoned friars and, so, amongst the first of Catherine's friends to be threatened with execution. The letters between them are almost certainly fictitious but they reflect well both Friar Forrest's character and the way Catherine might have reacted. 'Learn to suffer for Christ's truth, and to die for his spouse,' one of Forrest's pseudo-letters said. 'Do not try to lead me away from these torments, by which I hope to achieve eternal happiness.'

Catherine was said to be consumed with anguish at what appeared to be his certain death. Catholic writers later claimed that, by now, she spent much of her time in prayer, kneeling on bare stones that she flooded with tears 'as though it had rained upon them'. Men like Forrest were Catherine's real heroes. They were steadfast, courageous and ready for death. The fictitious letters between them show her writing admiringly back, urging him to be brave and stay firm. 'If your family is noble, disgrace it not by yielding to the king's request,' she said. 'You will receive an eternal reward.' Several years earlier, when it had not seemed so likely, she had already mused to the pope that 'it would be a pleasure to suffer [martyrdom] for the truth'. Now it seemed close and real.

This was not a question of simple masochism or proof of a suicidal nature. Martyrdom was, and is, seen as an expression of love. Jesus had been the greatest martyr – dying to save everyone's souls. His suffering was his 'passion'. Meditating on this passion was a central part of Catherine's devotions. Martyrdom required not just rock-solid belief, obstinacy and courage but also the sort of exceptional, intensely 'passionate' character that Catherine – and few others – possessed. 'I shall not fail [in this task] until death, as otherwise I should imperil my soul, and I hope to God the princess will do the same, as a good daughter should do,' she told her nephew. Martyrdom held out the promise of an afterlife filled with eternal happiness. Better this, surely, than a sinner's death followed by eternal damnation.

In fact, Forrest survived this spell in the Tower and was released. The psychosis of persecution, however, was founded on brutal reality and in August 1534 Chapuys reported that the Observants had been expelled *en masse* from their monasteries. Some 143 friars were locked up with, according to the Catholic literature, a quarter of them dying in captivity. Even those sent to monasteries of other orders were treated brutally. 'They are locked up, chained and treated as if they were in jail,' Chapuys wrote that August. Most of London had sworn the oath to the Act of Succession on the same April day that, in order to concentrate their minds better, the Holy Maid of Kent and her friends were executed. John Fisher, bishop of Rochester, and Sir Thomas More had been amongst the first to refuse. Both now sat wasting away in what was to be their last home, the Tower of London. John Forrest himself was rearrested, hung above a fire and burned to death four years later. A similar fate awaited Thomas Abel.

Catherine was bitter at the way others had abandoned her. The pope had declared her to be in the right. He had also failed her by waiting so long and then not even carrying through her husband's excommunication immediately – in the eternal, and vain, hope that he might somehow win Henry back. Even her nephew Charles, she now realised, put politics before principle. When the sentence had been passed in Rome, Charles's ambassador there, the count of Cifuentes, had rejoiced that it did not include a demand that the emperor enforce it. That would almost

certainly have required war. Although Chapuys constantly conspired with Catherine's many secret supporters amongst the
nobility to start an uprising in England, the emperor himself did
not want to open a new military front. He was already stretched
in other parts of the empire. The sentence was a toothless – and
useless – piece of paper without Charles's might behind it. Catherine had already fired off an angry letter to him in February,
complaining that he was shirking his duty by not forcing the
pope to act. The tone of polite reverence that she normally used
to address the most powerful man in Europe changed to that of
a stern aunt lecturing a wayward nephew. Charles 'might have
done more', she said. He had been 'somewhat cold' to his aunt
and had slackly passed over 'a good opportunity for persuading
his holiness to do me justice'. She demanded he study his conscience, change his attitude and be more affectionate to his aunt
and her daughter.

'Other remedies are now needed,' was the message she passed
on via Chapuys in May 1534, once the sentence was received.
Charles knew full well what needed to be done, she said. This was
too dangerous a thing, however, to explain in a letter that could
be intercepted and used against her. 'She dare not spell them [the
remedies] out,' Chapuys explained. It was an enigmatic message. If she meant, finally, that it was time for war then it was a
momentary aberration. Catherine preferred martyrs to soldiers.

As Catherine hardened, she also increased the pressure on
Mary. Their fate was, at least in Catherine's mind, inseparable.
She wanted more, not less, defiance. The princess, she decided,
was 'to show her teeth' to Henry. Her daughter needed little
encouragement. When Henry had visited little Elizabeth in
January 1534, Anne had bullied him into refusing to see Mary,
who forthrightly refused to accept her new, inferior rank. As
her father mounted his horse to leave, however, he sighted the
figure of a young woman on a terrace high up in the house,

her hands clasped together in supplication. It was his daughter. Even Henry could not avoid touching his hat to her. His relieved courtiers, who had been studiously looking away, immediately did the same. The next time Henry visited, Anne made sure that Mary did not leave her room.

Anne constantly urged Henry to be tougher on his daughter. She vowed to 'bring down the pride of this unruly Spanish blood-line'. Soon Mary had her jewels and ornaments confiscated. Catherine's daughter, however, remained unbroken. On one occasion she had to be manhandled into a litter after she refused to go, as part of Elizabeth's entourage, from one house to another.

The court rumour was that Anne wanted to poison Mary. Chapuys fretted constantly that the new queen would, indeed, 'carry out her wicked will'. In the meantime, he said, Anne had ordered her aunt Anne Shelton (Elizabeth's governess) to 'box her ears like the cursed bastard that she is'. Mary was also prevented from going to mass at a nearby church in case, like her mother, she aroused the support of the country folk who still enthusiastically greeted her as princess.

Things came to a head during a row with Anne's aunt, when the latter said she would happily 'have kicked her out of the king's house for her disobedience'. She reminded Mary that she was now, thanks to the Act of Succession, a bastard. If Mary refused to swear the oath, she added, the king had said he would chop her head off.

Catherine's daughter, however, was quick and resourceful. She asked to be allowed to speak privately to the house physician, who seems to have been her old Latin teacher Richard Featherstone. She was only allowed to see him in public but cleverly managed to get her message through. Her Latin, she told him with feigned regret, had gone rusty. Featherstone invited her to try. Knowing that no one else would understand them, Mary told him the king had said that 'as she was breaking the laws of the kingdom he would make her lose her head'. The shocked physician immediately told Chapuys. It may be assumed that Catherine found out soon afterwards.

The ambassador, however, had heard enough. This was all Henry's fault but Catherine was pushing her daughter too far. It was one thing for Mary to declare obediently that she was not just ready but willing for martyrdom and the paradise that followed. It was quite another to provoke an unnecessary death. Christian martyrs, after all, were not meant to seek death actively. He insisted that Mary be allowed to soften her line.

Chapuys made sure Mary signed some new written protests that Catherine had previously been unable to get through to her. She could still speak her mind, he said, but it would be better to avoid extreme confrontation. The protests made it clear that she did not accept her new status. They also freed her to obey her father without it looking as though she was renouncing her rights. It was quite reasonable to do things under duress, Chapuys told her, as long as she made clear this was her only reason. The one thing she had to avoid at all costs, however, was to swear the Act of Succession, despite the ferocious punishments contemplated by the law. Henry, seeing his daughter less fierce, now softened. He put her earlier obstinacy down to her mother's 'Spanish blood'. He seemed happier, in his changeable and sentimental way, if he could treat her better. Catherine's Spanish doctor was even allowed to visit when Mary suffered bouts of illness in September 1534, bringing back first-hand news of a daughter she had not seen for several years. On one visit to Henry's court at The More, almost all the courtiers went to visit Mary, much to Anne's annoyance. Once, as Mary travelled by barge down the Thames that August, Chapuys stuck to a promise and stood by the river bank in disguise. 'It was a pleasure to see such excellent beauty accompanied by heroic bearing,' he reported. They repeated the trick two months later. This time Mary arranged everything, including the bank that the barge-master was to steer along. She had the barge uncovered and stood on the deck, 'never moving from the place she had taken up to look at me'. She was 'handsome and plump'. The same terms, most probably, were used in describing her state to Catherine.

Henry refused now to hear an ill word against Mary, to Anne's great chagrin. She was doubly furious because the king, by late 1534, was busily courting a new love interest. They had already rowed about this, with Henry reportedly telling Anne to put up with it and remember how high he had raised her up. The girl Henry had started pursuing was said to be one of Mary's supporters. When the barge episode became public, however, Anne counter-attacked and Mary's conditions worsened again. She claimed not to care. Her mother had indoctrinated her to expect death and its golden rewards. 'She says she is quite ready for paradise, expects this and is not bothered,' Chapuys had already observed that summer.

Catherine, then, was gathering her troops. She wanted 'action', but not war. Her soldiers were to be of an entirely different kind. They would be holy martyrs and she herself, if God required, would lead them. Her daughter would come too. It was an extraordinary situation. England had produced few martyrs over the previous centuries. Christendom itself had been relatively short on them for a long while. Not a single martyr had been created a saint between 1254 and 1481. Two-thirds of the principal saints in Voragine's hugely popular *The Golden Legend* had been martyrs, but they had almost all died centuries before. England, alone, was about to buck the trend. 'I hope that I shall see you not very long hence,' is the sentiment attributed to her by the author of the Forrest letters, 'when the storms of this life shall be over, and I shall be taken to the calm life of the blessed.'

48 Prisoner

London. 17 July 1534

Eustace Chapuys must have eyed his sixty horsemen with satisfaction. Here he had enough men to make a proper spectacle. The clack of hooves, the snorting, whinnying and braying of horses and mules, the sharply shouted commands, the bright colours and rich textures of the riders' livery would all draw curious looks as the cavalcade clattered through London's narrow streets. They were a motley bunch, dressed up to look like something better. His own servants were here, as were some friendly Spanish merchants who had put together their own small retinues. That did not matter. Chapuys wanted bulk, noise and colour. He wanted every tradesman, apprentice or washerwoman in London to know that the emperor's ambassador was on his way to visit their banished and incarcerated queen.

This show was, he had second-guessed, what Catherine herself had envisaged when – without ever explaining why – she repeatedly begged him to visit. She wanted to be London's main subject of gossip for that day and, if possible, for the days, weeks and months to come. If Chapuys was let in through the tightly guarded doors of her house, then she would have the comfort of her chief friend and ally. If he was stopped at the gates then that, too, would serve its purpose. It would prove that she really was a prisoner. People would know almost immediately that their only true queen, as she still saw herself, was her husband's captive. Catherine had an instinctive understanding of publicity. She also knew how to play popular heart-strings. Chapuys's cavalcade set off as loudly as it could on a route which he described, with mock ingenuousness, as taking them 'by necessity, the full length of this city'. That would ensure they were seen by as many people as possible. It was, he admitted, 'the desired effect'.

The house that Chapuys's troop headed for was neither at waterlogged Somersham, which Catherine had successfully vetoed by challenging Suffolk to knock her door down, nor at Buckden. By May 1534 she had moved a short distance to the fortified manor house at Kimbolton, in Huntingdonshire. It was only half a dozen miles to the west of Buckden but, though rather gloomy and old-fashioned, it was further from the dreaded Fens. Catherine had already been suffering from a terrible cough. Her physician would have explained that her humours were out of balance and that she had an excess of the one humoral fluid, phlegm, that could only have got worse in the dampness of the Fens. What had not changed, however, were the conditions under which she was held. Catherine had no control over her own household. This, by now, was made up of northerners who Chapuys – with typical metropolitan prejudice – thought more suited to grubby warfare than sophisticated serving. Many of her goods had disappeared since she left Buckden and she had little or no access to money. She had even been prohibited from distributing Maundy alms by Anne Boleyn – who both recognised and feared her rival's skill at winning ordinary people over.

Imprisonment was made worse by Catherine's own, self-imposed strictures. At Buckden, she had stayed bolted inside her room even after Suffolk had given up his attempts to carry her away. 'The queen has not been out . . . except to hear mass in a gallery. She will not eat or drink what the new servants provide,' Chapuys reported a month later. 'The little she eats in her anguish is prepared by her chamberwomen, and her room is used as a kitchen for lack of a proper place.' At Kimbolton she followed the same practice, retiring to her room with a handful of servants, some ladies and her trio of faithful Spanish men – the confessor, the doctor and the apothecary. The rest of the household served, in her mind, a non-existent woman called the princess dowager. That made them her jailers.

Catherine had first been drawn to the delights and dangers of virtuous suffering during the exaggerated fasting sessions of her youth. Her decision to lock herself away was not, however, simply a return to her youthful penchant for self-punishment. Henry had erected around her a facade of opulent, honourable living – as if she had simply retired to a comfortable country retreat. This charade cost him the considerable sum of £4,000 a year in household expenses but Catherine would not allow him to fool himself, or anybody else, into thinking that this meant he was treating her well. Her only recourse was to make her conditions worse. If Catherine was going to be treated as a prisoner, she was determined to live like one – and make sure people knew about it. Her room could serve as her cell, even if she had the key. This, being the person she was, still required the aid of a staff of up to a dozen people. Her requests for Chapuys to provide almonds and 'old' wine rather than the 'new', unpalatable stuff bought by the men Henry had appointed to run her house show that the hardship was decidedly relative. A decent wine, she thought, was simply better for her health.

Chapuys's cavalcade had set out, in part, as a response to Henry's refusal to answer his formal request to visit Catherine. The king was a notorious procrastinator. He hated difficult decisions. Henry did not wish to refuse the emperor's ambassador, but nor did he want him to see Catherine. Even the all-powerful Cromwell, who promised to produce an answer, failed to wring one out of the king. He tried, instead, to put Chapuys off with a cheap joke about how 'women cannot be trusted'.

Chapuys was, however, not easy to ignore. The Savoyard, who was in his early forties, combined the humanist learning and Italian pragmatism picked up at Turin university with vigorous, energetic enthusiasm. He was also devoted to both Catherine and Mary. While Catherine remained bolted inside her room, he served as her eyes and ears. They were in regular contact, via messengers and servants who carried notes or memorised their messages. In a country where no one else could openly declare their support for her, Chapuys would argue endlessly with almost anyone – including Henry himself – about the unjust treatment meted out to Catherine. His meetings with Henry brought the king's councillors out in a sweat. 'For God's sake, monsieur, I beg and entreat you on this day to use all your discretion and prudence, and so moderate your language that you may not fall into trouble or inconvenience,' he was told before one interview in which he planned to defend the two women. 'You are about to enter on matters so odious and unpleasing that not all the sugar or sauces in the world would render them palatable. That is why I again pray and entreat you for God's sake to be careful and guarded in your speech.'

Chapuys schemed and conspired on Catherine and Mary's behalf. Occasionally, indeed, he appeared to be directing their small ensemble. First and foremost, however, he remained his master's faithful servant. When Charles's interests came into conflict with those of his aunt, as they increasingly did, Chapuys looked after the former first. The emperor kept his ambassador reined in, rapping his knuckles whenever his passion for Catherine's cause and his enthusiasm for action clashed with his master's broader pragmatism. Chapuys found Henry, by turns, amusing, irascible, temperamental and simply incomprehensible. He much preferred Cromwell, a fellow meritocrat whose cold, calculating, unemotional logic he could, at least, understand. 'He is a man of wit who understands affairs [of state],' he observed. Chapuys knew, however, not to trust him. 'Cromwell's words are good, but his deeds are bad, and his will and intent incomparably worse,' he remarked in one of his regular despatches to the emperor.

After his flamboyant passage through London, Chapuys set out on the road north. The noisy, colourful outing became legend amongst the Spanish merchant class in London. 'All along the road they went with much gaiety and merry-making, for they took with them their minstrels and trumpeters, and in every place they entered it seemed as though a prince was arriving,' a Spanish chronicler recalled more than a decade later. Chapuys wanted the king, above all, to know he was on his way. He sought confrontation, not subterfuge.

Chapuys deliberately set a slow pace to give Henry time to react. Sure enough, one of the king's men galloped past on the second day and returned with a messenger from the steward and chamberlain in charge of Catherine at Kimbolton. 'They had received orders from his majesty the king not to allow me to enter or be [with] the queen or speak to her,' he reported. The king, they said, had ordered them not to let him in. Chapuys refused to acknowledge the order, saying he needed it in writing. That, he must have thought, was the sort of evidence he could show to the world. He was now just five miles from Kimbolton but said he would rest and continue the following day. Early the next morning yet another messenger arrived, warning that he would provoke Henry's rage if he appeared at either the manor house or the village. The king specifically did not want local villagers, who at Buckden had shown themselves so openly on Catherine's side, to know that Chapuys had been refused entry. Henry was afraid of what Chapuys called a 'scandal' or, in other words, another angry mob. A game of cat and mouse ensued. Catherine let it be known that she already considered the outing a success. 'That night the blessed lady sent the ambassador a great deal of game and venison, and many bottles of wine of all sorts, and begged him to make good cheer,' the Spanish chronicler recalled later. They had already backed Henry into a corner and proved their point. She would be even more delighted, she suggested, if some of his troop just happened to ride past the house as they continued on their way.

So it was that this particular piece of early Renaissance theatre reached its dramatic peak. Chapuys despatched a group of his men to Kimbolton. 'The next morning about thirty horsemen started, all in very good order, and they took with them a very funny young fellow who had been brought by the ambassador, and who was dressed as a fool, and had a padlock dangling from his hood,' said the chronicler. The padlock was a witty, and not so subtle, reference to Catherine's imprisonment.

They were greeted by Catherine's ladies, who leant exultantly out of windows and hung over the battlements. A loud exchange of joyous Spanish split the East Anglian air. The fool led what became a corrosively funny bit of slapstick. 'The fool, as soon as he saw the ladies at the windows, alighted from his horse, and made as if to get into the moat of the castle, crying out that he wanted to get to them,' the same chronicler explained in what may have been an exaggerated version of the trip. 'He got himself in as far as his waist and everybody who was looking on thought that he was silly and cried out that he would drown.' Three of the party dragged the fool theatrically back. He eventually hurled his padlock across the moat. 'Take this,' he shouted. 'Next time I will bring the key.' His fellow Spaniards fell about laughing while the locals looked on in slack-jawed amazement. 'It seemed to the local peasants that the Messiah himself had come,' said Chapuys. Word of what happened must have blown across the gently undulating countryside like a northerly wind gusting down from the Wash.

The party was shadowed by one of Cromwell's loyal henchmen, Stephen Vaughan. Like Catherine herself, Vaughan must have witnessed the small Spanish fiesta outside Kimbolton's solid, moated walls. He eventually presented himself to Chapuys just before the latter got back to London (having deliberately taken an alternative route home so that even more people could see them). Vaughan tried to argue that it had been the house officials, not Henry, who had stopped Catherine seeing him. Chapuys was not fooled. Nor, one may assume, were those who heard the story as it spread across Huntingdonshire, down the Old North Road and into the rest of England.

49 The Terror

Tyburn and Tower Hill. 4 May–6 July 1535

Margaret Chancellor later claimed to have been drunk. She had, perhaps, quaffed an excess of Suffolk ale. Drunk or not, she did not like what the king was doing to Queen Catherine. 'Goggle-eyed whore!' she spat out at the mention of Anne Boleyn's name. 'God save Queen Catherine!' When challenged in court later the spinster from Bradfield St Clare, by then sober, claimed she had only called Boleyn 'a *naughty* whore'. She also admitted having hoped out loud that the future children of the 'whore' would, like the one she miscarried in August 1534, be stillborn. It must have been the alcohol talking, or the devil, she told the abbot of Bury and other judges who listened to her explanations.

On the other side of the country, eighty-year-old husbandman Edmund Brocke trudged home through the rain from Worcester market, cursing as he went. 'We shall never have better weather whilst the king reigneth,' he told his companions. An ideal solution, the octogenarian added, would be 'if he were knocked . . . on the head'. They were a madman's words, he admitted later. The drink, once more, was to blame.

Similar sentiments were being expressed across England, though it often took dangerously strong ales with names like 'huffcap', 'mad dog', 'Father Whoreson', 'go-by-the-wall', 'stride wide' or 'lift leg' to give someone the courage – or foolhardiness – to say them in public. The people, ambassadors observed, sided with Catherine against Anne Boleyn. Many were also disturbed by the changes forced onto their religion. They knew it had been done, principally, so that the king could abandon the old queen and marry the new one. Now the weather had turned foul, spoiling crops and stopping the corn harvest. God, they thought, was unhappy. So were they. It was treasonous, however, to say why. The new state listened in wherever it could and hauled those with treacherous, or merely forgetful, mouths into courts and jails.

The state repeated its message wherever it could. Preachers in their pulpits, even schoolteachers in the classroom, were forced to intone the monotonous litany of the new order. The king was supreme over the church. Catherine was not, and never had been, his true wife. The new queen must be respected. Her children, not Mary, would inherit the crown. The orders poured out: erase the pope's name from the mass books; remember, too, that the king's titles now include that of Supreme Head of the Anglican Church; and, finally, preach, teach and make the people swear their oaths. Everyone had to be tested. Those who did not bow to the new order were to be punished. Executions would concentrate their minds.

Priests who only covered up the pope's name with glued-on slips of paper in their missals or who, out of habit or old age, got confused about the name of the current queen found themselves in trouble. Some exacted revenge by denouncing their enemies to Cromwell's people, claiming they had maligned the new queen or praised Catherine and the pope. Did Richard Boord really say he 'would rather be torn with wild horses' than consent to the pope's authority being diminished? Did an Irish hooperman, David Leonard, exclaim 'God save King Henry and Queen Catherine!' while predicting that all 'England shall rue' the coming of Anne Boleyn? The accusations were enough to land them in trouble, whatever they really said.

But people did voice, or at least whisper, their support for Catherine and the pope and, as a result, Henry did not want her seen in public. When she insisted that she was going to perform the traditional Maundy rites of washing the feet of the poor at Kimbolton church in March 1535, Henry refused her permission. She could do it in her chambers, if she liked, but only as princess dowager – not as queen. He did not want her stirring up the people. The Maundy plea was a small and ineffectual attempt at rebellion, probably provoked by the fact that Henry was still, slowly and maliciously, turning the screw on his first wife. The previous month he had sacked her most loyal, and longest-lasting, servant – Francisco Felipez, the man who had bravely carried messages to her nephew – though he later seems to have been reinstated. She worried that Mary might be poisoned or would crack under the pressure. If her daughter was to die, Catherine wanted to be at her side. Her requests to be allowed to nurse Mary, who frequently fell ill as the strain and fear grew, were turned down. 'Speak to the king and beg him on my behalf to be so charitable to me as to send his daughter and mine to where I am,' she urged Chapuys in February 1535. 'Because if I care for her with my own hands by the advice of my and other physicians and God wished to take her from this world my heart will be at peace, otherwise at pain.'

'I myself will be her nurse,' Catherine added in this desperate plea to see the eighteen-year-old girl she had not set eyes on for almost four years. 'She can come . . . to the bed where I sleep and I will watch over her when necessary.' Henry was not moved. Her mother merely fuelled Mary's obstinacy, he said.

Catherine's desperation was such that she pledged not to visit her daughter, if only she could be moved close enough to be in regular contact. A letter in which she promised not to see Mary even if she was just a mile away reveals how little control she had left of her life. 'The times do not permit me to go about making visits and, even if I wanted to, I do not have the means,' she wrote. Henry was, with reason, worried that someone might be plotting to smuggle Mary out of the country. 'From now on I offer my own person as surety,' Catherine said. 'So that if such a thing was attempted [Henry] may mete out justice to me as if I was the most treacherous woman ever born.' Perhaps Catherine really did not know that Chapuys and Mary had been talking about ways for her to flee, or perhaps she was fully prepared to pay the price of her daughter's freedom.

Support for Catherine and Mary was by no means confined to drunken farmers. 'The king thinks he has got his subjects more under his command by making them swear to maintain the laws made against the queen and princess in favour of this second marriage, but it only irritates them the more,' Chapuys had observed. 'They are at present in such fear that there is neither small nor great who dare speak or grumble in any way. But when the time comes everyone will declare himself.'

Some had, indeed, begun to declare themselves to Chapuys. His New Year's present from Lord Darcy was a sword. It was time, Chapuys understood, 'to play at swords'. Those who surreptitiously let Chapuys know that they would rise, if only the emperor would make war, included some of Henry's closest aides and best military leaders. They were men of the old order, or people so appalled by Anne Boleyn's high-handedness and sharp tongue that they could stand her no longer. Even her uncle, the duke of Norfolk, was heard calling her 'a great whore' after one bruising encounter. Henry and Cromwell looked on anxiously. They worried more about an imperial fleet coming over the horizon, though, than plotters at home, given the efficiency of the terror in England.

A prophecy said that Henry would start his reign as a lamb and finish it as a raging lion, executing all those in the Tower of London – and many others too. That, Henry was overheard saying later, was exactly how he intended to be. In April 1535 he ordered more arrests of those suspected of sedition. Some men of the cloth were not bending. Amongst the first to face execution were the Carthusian monks of London. They refused to accept the king's supremacy over the pope, so three of their priors were condemned to be executed alongside the scholarly Brigittine monk Richard Reynolds and the vicar of Isleworth, John Hale. 'In all this kingdom, though the smaller part holds with you, I am sure the larger part is at heart of our opinion,' Reynolds told their inquisitors at the end of April. 'Although outwardly, partly from fear, partly from hope, they profess to be of yours.' Asked exactly who supported him, Reynolds defiantly replied: 'All good men of the kingdom.'

Hale, meanwhile, had claimed that three-quarters of England was against the king. He was also reportedly given to discussing the morals of the Boleyn women. Anne was 'his wife of fornication', he had said, while the king was thought to have 'had meddling with the queen's [Anne's] mother'. He had also been told that Henry was the mother of Mary Boleyn's child, had 'violated' most women at court and had a bevy 'of maidens over one of his chambers at Farnham while he was with the old lord of Winchester'.

The five were tied upside down onto wooden hurdles and dragged by horses along the bumpy route from the Tower of London to Tyburn on 4 May 1535. They were each hung for a while on a short rope, slowly choking until almost dead. They were still alive, however, when the executioner took them down and started cutting out their bowels and their hearts. These were burned. Then their heads were chopped off, the rest of their bodies butchered and quartered and their body parts displayed on long spears. The last ones to die probably had to watch the others' gruesome deaths. A document that ended up in the Vatican archives claims they died calmly, exhorting the onlookers to defy Henry when he acted against the honour of God and the Roman church. 'In their modesty, look, colour and speech no sign of human weakness was observed,' it says. Their final defiance may have encouraged Henry to repeat the exercise with three more Carthusians seven weeks later.

Catherine's husband behaved increasingly like the angry lion of the prophecy. The day after the executions of Hale and the first Carthusians, Chapuys reported that John Fisher, Sir Thomas More, Catherine's faithful priest Thomas Abel and her daughter's old Latin teacher, Richard Featherstone, had all been given a six-week deadline to swear the oaths or pay the consequences.

One of the most poignant, and pathetic, descriptions of the times came from More. 'I am the king's true subject . . . and pray for his highness and all [of] his [people] and all the realm,' he wrote to his daughter, one of the new generation of learned and well-read women to which Catherine herself belonged. 'I do nobody harm, I say no harm, I think no harm, but wish everybody good. And if this be not enough to keep a man alive in good faith I [have] not long to live.'

Catherine's physician, the main go-between with Chapuys, reported that she was now in a state of 'limitless consternation'. News reached her Kimbolton hideaway with surprising ease. These executions touched her far more directly than those of the Holy Maid of Kent and her friends. Catherine knew her husband would not have needed to claim supremacy over the church had it not been for her own determination to fight the divorce. That, ultimately, was why these men had died. The question of whether she was to blame for these heresies and their bloody consequences played on her conscience. She worried more about the heresies than the dead. The martyrs had suffered torment on earth but were, after all, heading for paradise. She expected to follow soon. Already Catherine and Mary were being told they might be the next ones told to swear or die. 'The queen, in the midst of her continual suffering, is sending martyrs ahead to precede her,' said one of the imperial ambassadors in Rome, Dr Ortiz, who had long been urging the emperor's wife, Isabella, to collect her aunt's letters as future relics of a holy martyr.

The shock provoked by the Carthusians' deaths was nothing compared to what followed. Both John Fisher and Thomas More refused to swear the oath. The offer of the oath was like 'a sword with two edges', said More. One edge, refusal, would kill his body. The other, to swear, would slay his soul. He preferred the former. A new and stronger-willed pope in Rome, Paul III, acted to bolster Fisher's position. He made the sixty-five-year-old Fisher, all 'skin and bare bones' after his fourteen months in the Tower, a cardinal on 21 May. Henry was furious. He reportedly threatened to 'send the bishop's head to Rome' in order to have the cardinal's red hat placed on it. Fisher turned down a last offer for him to swear the king's oath as he mounted the executioner's scaffold on 22 June 1535. More followed him on 6 July. 'I know well that the reason why you have condemned me is because I have never been willing to consent to the king's second marriage,' he said when sentence was passed. Both were allowed the cleaner, less painful death of beheading. It was a small token of respect.

Catherine felt sure that she and her daughter would be next. That they would be guilty of the same treasons if they refused a direct order to swear to either the king's supremacy over the church or the Act of Succession was obvious. Cromwell's interrogators looked carefully for ammunition to use against Catherine. They had grilled Fisher, for example, about how much Catherine knew about a letter found in his study from one of her supporters in Germany. Another letter, apparently written to Catherine in Fisher's own hand, suggested that she had 'despaired of the Mercy of God'. The interrogators jumped on this. For Catherine, of all people, to start doubting God was a sure sign of a guilty conscience. Or so they thought. Was this, they asked Fisher, because she had committed perjury by claiming she never slept with Arthur? Had she admitted as much?

Rumours circulated that Catherine and Mary faced imminent arrest and execution. Cromwell even insinuated to Chapuys that things would be much easier for everyone, including the emperor, if they just died. 'What harm or danger could there be in the princess dying just now . . . would the emperor have reason to regret her death?' he asked at one stage. Henry and Anne's most loyal servants thought day and night about ways of ridding themselves of Catherine and Mary, Chapuys reported. Catherine was not, however, going to run. 'I am determined, without doubt, to die in this kingdom,' she had said when making her offer to stand as surety for Mary.

Charles did little to help. Early in 1535 he was busy preparing to take on a mighty Turkish fleet which the corsair Barbarossa had gathered off Tunisia. In February he spelt out exactly why he would not do anything yet, listing the main obstacles as his Tunis campaign and the war-like noises coming from France. The willingness of certain English nobles to rise against Henry was not enough. 'Notwithstanding the good-will of the said personages and others in England, we do not see how it is possible for the present to remedy the mischief by force as, in truth, we have more than just cause to do,' he said. 'We think it best still to temporise, entertaining the said personages and others in hope . . . and waiting to see whether God will inspire the said king of England to bow or some good opportunity may arise to compel him by force.'

Henry's executions appalled Europe. He was seen as increasingly temperamental, cruel and unreliable – a prisoner to his own changeable passions. He was, however, still a highly prized ally. The dominant rivalry in Europe was, as ever, between France and the emperor. Both were wary of Henry joining one side or the other. The French king reluctantly put up with Henry's increasingly erratic ways. 'The king of England is the hardest friend in the world to bear: sometimes so unstable . . . other times so obstinate and fiercely proud that it is almost impossible to bear with him,' was King Francis's verdict. 'At other times he is so high and mighty that he treats me like a subject.' Francis, however, had little choice. 'He is the strangest man in the world,' he added. 'But I must put up with him, it is no time to lose friends.'

Charles, too, played safe with Henry despite his obvious disgust. 'The ill-will of the king of England to the queen and princess is cruel and horrible,' he said. The new pope, Paul III, wanted him to back moves to have Henry punished for refusing to bow to the divorce sentence. He even wanted to declare him to have forfeited his kingdom. But Charles stalled. This did not fit the big picture. All courses of action against Henry were deemed dangerous. Not even his victory in Tunis persuaded Charles that the time was right.

Catherine wrote two letters on 10 October 1535, to the two men who still had it in their power to do something for her. She told Charles that he and the pope must together devise a cure for her, and England's, problems. 'If it be delayed . . . they will do with me and my daughter what they have done with many holy martyrs,' she warned him. Her only consolation was that it would be a martyr's death. 'I do not say so out of fear of death for, as I already wrote, I am comforted to think that I would follow in the same kind of death those who, sadly for me, I could not imitate in life, as their lives were religious and mine worldly.' To Pope Paul III she wrote that 'if your holiness does not apply a remedy to these matters with all speed , there will be no end to the damnation of souls or the making of martyrs'. Death, she added dramatically, beckoned. 'I write to your holiness frankly to discharge my conscience as one who expects death along with my daughter.'

Conditions were right for a rebellion against Henry. Even the French ambassador, the bishop of Tarbes, said so. He found the English worried about the weather, the threat of war and the emperor's ability to close their markets for cloth, woollen kerseys, hides, tin and lead. 'The English people are marvellously discontented. They will join any prince who takes their [Catherine and Mary's] side,' he wrote in October. 'Most are upset over Catherine and Mary, others over the ruining of their religion or fearing war . . . They have not harvested half the grain crops they need . . . Lower people are exasperated against the queen, saying terrible things . . . If there is war, people will rebel.'

In the meantime Catherine and Mary's situation became increasingly dangerous. The marchioness of Exeter, an old ally of Catherine's, sent panicked messages from court, saying that Henry planned to use the next sitting of parliament to rid himself of her. He had been 'swearing most obstinately that he would wait no longer', Chapuys reported. The marchioness even turned up at Chapuys's house in disguise to confirm the awful news. 'The king, seeing some of those to whom he used this language shed tears, said that tears and wry faces were of no avail,' she told him. 'Even if he lost his crown, he would not forbear to carry his purpose into effect.'

Chapuys now believed that Henry would ask parliament to order the executions of Catherine and her daughter. 'The concubine [as Chapuys called Anne], who long ago conspired the death of the said ladies, is the person who governs everything,' he reported. 'And the king is unable to contradict her.'

50 Death and Conscience

Kimbolton. December 1535–January 1536

No one knows when Catherine gained a taste for Welsh beer. Almost four decades earlier Henry's grandmother had told her to start getting used to drinking wine before she left Spain, as English water was undrinkable. Perhaps she turned to beer to avoid the young wines that so disgusted her at Kimbolton. Whatever the reason, she drank a draught of Welsh beer during a prolonged illness in December 1535 and soon felt worse. Chapuys thought afterwards that it may have contained a slow-acting poison, but that is highly improbable.

The illness had been of no special concern. Cromwell at first told Chapuys that she was very sick, but this seems to have been wishful thinking. Catherine's doctor told Chapuys, who was worried enough to be preparing to travel to Kimbolton, not to bother. She was getting better and the doctor said he would let Chapuys know if she took a turn for the worse. 'She has recovered and is now well,' Chapuys wrote on 13 December. She was, indeed, well enough that day to write a last pleading letter to her nephew Charles and another to Dr Ortiz, her ardent admirer in Rome. She warned the latter that if the pope did not act now against Henry, he would be handing England to 'the devil, who, till now, is half-tied'.

'I am forced to write again by the need to remedy what I am daily told by friends and others who feel scandalised, they will attempt in this [coming] parliament against God, the church and our own persons,' Catherine told her nephew. She begged Chapuys, when he sent the letter on, to add words that would 'move a stone to compassion'. The ambassador admitted, however, that he had already exhausted his repertory. If no one listened now, it was not for want of trying.

Anne Boleyn, meanwhile, was pregnant again. There was, as yet, little reason to suspect that Henry would soon stop speaking to his second wife or that one of Catherine's former gentlewomen, Jane Seymour, would catch his eye and – partly thanks to the coaching of Catherine's old friends – successfully play Anne's own game by insisting on marriage and nothing else. Catherine certainly could not have imagined that Anne herself was to fall victim to the executioner's sword within just six months.

On 29 December, her doctor sent Chapuys an urgent message. Catherine had had a serious relapse and he should get permission to come to Kimbolton immediately. The following day Henry received him in the lists at Greenwich, where he rode his jousting horses. A few weeks later Henry would have a serious fall here, but right now he was in a good mood. He slung an arm around Chapuys's neck, walked him off to his rooms and began to talk politics. Catherine would not live long, he said with evident relief. That would clear the way for an alliance with the emperor. As if to confirm his optimism, news arrived that Catherine really was now very badly ill. This time Chapuys set out for Kimbolton, though he was still not sure how serious it was and did not get there for three days, during which time he organised a suitably large suite of people to go with him. Cromwell again sent Stephen Vaughan to keep an eye on him. Even on her deathbed, he was not going to allow Catherine to escape his all-encompassing scrutiny. Henry, meanwhile, turned down a request for Mary to go to her mother's bedside.

They were beaten to Kimbolton by a surprise visitor. Early on the evening of New Year's Day 1536 a bedraggled-looking lady knocked at the gates of the house, explaining that she had fallen from her horse less than a mile away and needed shelter to recover. This was María de Salinas, the faithful Lady

Willoughby, who had rushed up from her London property of
Bas Court. News of Catherine's illness had travelled swiftly and
Salinas 'thought never to see the princess again'. They had survived the terrifying sea journey to England together as young
girls all those years earlier. Since then she had proved to be her
closest and most loyal friend. 'In all my suffering, she is the only
one who gives me consolation,' Catherine had said two decades
earlier. Now Salinas was determined to be back at her mistress's
side during her final hours. She acted out an elaborate charade
to force her way into the house, claiming the letter licensing her
to enter was on its way and begging them not to turn away a
woman who had been thrown from her horse on a cold winter's
night. The men running the household had no answer to that.
Salinas went straight up to Catherine's rooms and slammed the
door behind her. 'And since that time we never saw her, neither
any letters of her licence [to come here],' reported the house's
befuddled steward, Sir Edmund Bedingfield.

Salinas found Catherine very sick. She had just turned fifty.
She could barely sit up, let alone stand. She had been unable to
eat, or hold food down, for several days. The pain in her stomach had stopped her sleeping for more than two hours in total
over the previous six nights. She was still alert enough, however,
to suggest to Chapuys – when he arrived the following day –
that their first meeting should be in front of witnesses. She did
not want a suspicious Henry claiming they were plotting against
him. Vaughan was invited in. So, too, were the senior officers
of the house – Bedingfield and Sir Edward Chamberlain. They
must have been astounded. True to her word, Catherine had
refused to deal with those officials who called her 'princess dowager'. They had not seen the woman whose house they were
running for more than a year.

Catherine and Chapuys had not seen each other often, but
they shared an intense friendship forged in adversity. They were

both too worldly, however, to let emotions run away with them while the king's men watched. Even under such extreme conditions, they knew how to observe the niceties of what was Catherine's first formal reception of a visitor for several years. There was bowing, hand-kissing and elaborate words of greeting. They had agreed in advance a list of things that must be said – loudly and slowly enough to be understood by those listening in – so that Henry would hear them afterwards. The steward and chamberlain stood by, unable to understand, while Vaughan translated for himself and took mental note. Catherine thanked Chapuys for coming. 'She said . . . that it was a relief to her that she could now die in my arms, and not disappear like a beast,' he recalled afterwards. Chapuys urged her to cling on to life. The peace of Christendom depended on it, he said. After a short while she sent them all away, claiming to be tired.

At five that afternoon she called Chapuys back, this time without witnesses. The conversation lasted a full two hours. 'For fear of over-tiring her, I made several attempts to get up and leave the room,' he said. 'She would not hear of it.' Bedingfield worried that he did not know what was being said behind Catherine's doors. The trusty old women who cleaned her chamber did not speak Spanish either. They were his only source of information about what happened inside that mysterious chamber into which Catherine had disappeared so long before.

Chapuys went to Catherine's rooms for two hours each afternoon for four days. She was worried about her daughter Mary's trials. Catherine complained, once more, about the inaction of the pope and the emperor. Chapuys stretched the truth to calm a sick woman's worries, claiming that the pope was now so enraged by the executions that he was determined to act against Henry.

Catherine's sharp mind was probably not fooled. She admitted, instead, that her conscience was troubled by the thought that England's problems, or at least the 'heresies' and 'scandals' let in during the divorce battle, might be her fault. Had her obstinacy in choosing to fight her husband pushed her adopted country away from Rome and brought the unnecessary deaths of good men? It was an uncomfortable question. The honest answer was that it had – even if the ultimate blame lay with Henry's overarching selfishness. Chapuys, however, reassured her. She might have 'doubts and scruples' but, he said, she could have done nothing else. Perhaps Catherine, seeing her life's mission of binding England and Spain in tatters, secretly deposited her hopes for the future in her daughter.

His visits, and the loving care of María de Salinas, restored her morale and improved her health. Catherine began to eat and hold down her food. On the fourth day she was so much better that they decided Chapuys should leave. Henry might think, otherwise, that he was abusing his licence to visit a woman supposed to be at death's door. 'That same evening I saw her laugh two or three times and half an hour after I left her, she wanted to amuse herself with one of my people, who entertained her,' he said. She slept well the following morning and Chapuys set off at a leisurely pace. The doctor had said he would send a rider after him if anything happened. No one appeared, however, and he pushed on to London.

Catherine's health continued to improve over the next two days. On 6 January she sat up in bed, tied up her own hair and dressed her head. That night, however, she began to get fidgety. After midnight she started asking what time it was. She wanted to take communion and worried she might not last until daylight. Her confessor, the nervous old Spanish bishop of Lland-aff, Jorge de Athequa, offered to break the rules and give her communion then and there. The circumstances, he saw, were extreme enough to warrant it. A growing sense of panic spread through her small band of faithful servants. Catherine waited until dawn. She took communion and confessed, though Lland-aff forgot he had promised Chapuys that he would extract a deathbed vow to settle for posterity the issue which had dominated much of her final years – whether she had remained a virgin while married to Arthur.

Catherine, anyway, had more practical things to do. She knew she was dying and did not expect to see the day out. She signed a request to Henry specifying what she wanted done with her goods and saying that she wished to be buried in a chapel belonging to her beloved Observant Friars.

Some years after her death the text of a letter she supposedly dictated to her husband as she lay on her deathbed began to circulate amongst Roman Catholic writers. As with her letters to Friar Forrest, this is almost certainly fictitious. It is not unreasonable, however, to imagine that the words reflect something of Catherine's state of mind as she lay in her bed that morning.

My most dear Lord, King, and Husband, The hour of my death now approaching, I cannot choose but, out of the love I bear you, to advise you of your soul's health, which you ought to prefer before all considerations of the world or flesh whatsoever. For which yet you have cast me into many calamities, and yourself into many troubles. But I forgive you all, and pray God to do so likewise. For the rest, I commend unto you Mary, our daughter, beseeching you to be a good father to her. I must entreat you also to look after my maids, and give them in marriage, which is not much, they being but three, and to all my other servants, a year's pay besides their due, lest otherwise they should be unprovided for until they find new employment. Lastly, I want only one true thing, to make this vow: that, in this life, mine eyes desire you alone. May God protect you.

Catherine fell to prayer. She begged God to set Henry back on the right path and forgive him for wronging her. She asked pardon for her own soul. Death was now clearly in sight. The bishop of Llandaff administered extreme unction. Catherine answered him bravely, in a clear and audible voice. She continued to mutter prayers to herself. They were her final consolation. Then, shortly before two o'clock on the afternoon of 7 January 1536, she drew her last breath. Henry's Spanish queen had died, her mind still troubled by whether she had been good to a country which, in the end, had been bad to her.

Afterword

Many people suspected foul play. There were rumours of a special poison imported from Italy and slipped into Catherine's food or drink. In fact, she almost certainly died of cancer. The embalmer charged with preparing her corpse 'found all the internal organs as healthy and normal as possible, with the exception of the heart, which was quite black and hideous to look at'. The embalmer, actually a chandler whose real expertise was with wax, sliced the heart in half and washed it through several times, but it remained stubbornly dark. Another strange black body was attached to it. A secondary melanotic sarcoma was almost certainly to blame.

Reactions to her death varied. An indignant Chapuys reported that Henry dressed in yellow, stuck a white feather in his cap and went dancing with Anne Boleyn's ladies. 'Thank God, we are now free from any fear of war,' Henry reportedly proclaimed. Popular reaction, Chapuys said, was quite different. The sadness and anger that her death provoked in some failed, however, to produce the sort of instant, violent rebellion against Henry that Chapuys would like to have seen.

Catherine's death did not close wounds. It simply confirmed the end of the first act in England's murderous Reformation drama. The bloody separation from Rome that she had foreseen proved, despite her daughter's later efforts, to be unstoppable. The death toll would only grow. Few would have predicted, however, that the most famous head to roll would belong to Anne Boleyn, or that it would go so quickly.

Catherine was laid to rest at Peterborough Abbey on 29

January. Anne miscarried that same day. If there was one lesson to be learnt from Catherine's own fall, it was that Henry's
great obsession was the fathering of a male heir. Anne's failure
weighed heavily against her. Catherine's death, ironically, also
freed Henry from what now felt like the yoke of Anne. The same
sharp, fiery character that had been so alluring became rapidly
unbearable to him now that both the challenge of the chase and
the immense task of divorcing Catherine were over.

Anne's many enemies were quick to act, encouraging Henry
to see treason while dangling the young Jane Seymour in front
of his eyes. Cromwell, cold and efficient as ever, did the rest.
Charges of treason and adultery sealed Anne's fate. She met the
kind of death that Catherine had feared for herself. She was despatched by an executioner brought specially from Calais, who
sliced her head off with a sword on a scaffold at Tower Green
on 19 May 1536. Henry's second queen outlived Catherine by
only nineteen weeks.

The craven and obedient Cranmer had already pronounced
Henry's second marriage to be null and void. The day after
Anne's execution, Henry and Jane Seymour were betrothed. Ten
days later they married. The king got his son and heir, the future
Edward VI, seventeen months later. But Henry's only long-
lasting marriage was to Catherine. Jane Seymour died a few days
after giving birth. Her successors – Anne of Cleves, Catherine
Howard and Catherine Parr – would each spend less than four
years by Henry's side. Catherine of Aragon had lasted more than
twice as long as Henry's queen as the other five put together.

Her most important legacy to England was her daughter.
Mary eventually made her peace with her father and, soon
after her half-brother Edward VI (who had succeeded Henry
on his death in 1547) died in 1553, she won what was clearly
her rightful crown. To all intents and purposes, Mary was England's first queen regnant. It is deeply ironic that this was one of

the things Henry was trying to avoid when he divorced Catherine. His daughter gained the nickname of 'Bloody Mary' by trying to turn back the clock of Reformation, creating a swathe of Protestant martyrs (including Cranmer) along the way. Anne Boleyn's daughter, Elizabeth I, succeeded Mary on her death in 1558, and the religious pendulum swung back the other way.

Catherine's body was taken to the abbey at Peterborough, which later became a cathedral. Her request to be buried at a monastery belonging to her beloved Franciscan Observant Friars had been turned down because, as Cromwell observed, the friars' convents no longer existed. The funeral ceremony, inevitably, was for a dowager princess rather than for a queen. Later in the century another unfortunate queen, Mary queen of Scots, was buried in the same building.

Even at rest, Catherine aroused passions. Catholic literature soon turned her into a shining example of pious womanhood, in contrast to her cruel husband. Shakespeare, inevitably, made her a key character in his play *Henry VIII*. The first Globe Theatre burned down during a performance of the play in 1613 when a stage cannon set the thatch roof on fire. In 1643 Oliver Cromwell's troops ransacked the cathedral and despoiled her tomb. Two centuries later, an appeal to Englishwomen also named Catherine (or its variants, such as Katharine) raised enough money to put a new stone on their namesake's tomb. A wooden plaque there today calls her: 'A queen cherished by the English people for her loyalty, piety, courage and compassion'.

That commentary is not far off the assessment of Chapuys, the person outside the tight circle of her close servants who had come to know her best. He thought that she had been excessively compassionate. Later on in his life he described her as 'the most virtuous woman I have ever known and the highest hearted, but too quick to trust that others were like herself, and too slow to do a little ill that much good might come of it'.

Debate over Catherine's character and her place in history usually concentrates on the twin questions of whether she was really a virgin when she married Henry and whether England would have remained Roman Catholic had she chosen to go quietly into a convent. Chapuys reminds us, in his way, of another choice, the impact of which cannot be measured but which was possibly as important as any other she made. Given the chance of promoting war between England and the mighty empire of her nephew Charles in order to re-establish her marital rights, Catherine chose peace. Charles may have been unwilling, but Chapuys seemed convinced he could be pushed into it if Catherine encouraged her English supporters to rise against Henry. We can only speculate about the bloodshed prevented by her decision and the radically different course that Europe's history might have taken had Catherine opted for war.

Acknowledgements

Of the many people who have helped with this book, first mention must go to Dr Glyn Redworth of Manchester University – who offered his help spontaneously and then stuck with it to the very end. He is one of several people who have read through the manuscript. I am, of course, responsible for any errors that might remain.

Ruth Miguel Franco of Università degli Studi di Padova, Italy, translated (into Spanish) or checked many of the other translations done by myself or others from the original Latin, Italian and French. I am specially grateful for her translation from the original Latin of the Zaragoza tribunal manuscript held in the archives of the Real Academia de la Historia. I am responsible for all translations from Spanish and Catalan. I am grateful to Dominic Pearce for his translations from Latin into English and to Alison Adams of Glasgow University for pointing me towards Randle Cotgrave's 1611 French–English dictionary.

My thanks go also to the staff at the Biblioteca Nacional in Madrid, the library of the Real Academia de la Historia in Madrid, the Archivo de la Diputación de Zaragoza, the British Library and the National Archives in London. The Spanish government deserves special gratitude for its openness and generosity in making so many original documents from the Archivo General de Simancas available for study online through its *pares* web service. This edition of the book does not carry footnotes, but these will be posted at www.faber.co.uk/catherineofaragon with links to original source material available online, where possible.

Thom Richardson at the Royal Armouries in Leeds, Maria Hayward of Southampton University, Luis Garrido González of the University of Jaen, Salvador Salort-Pons of the Detroit Institute of Arts and author Robert Hutchinson have all responded kindly to petitions for help. I would also like to thank staff at Catherine of Aragon's former homes at Ludlow Castle, Kimbolton and Buckden as well as at her final resting place in Peterborough Cathedral.

I owe much, as ever, to Walter Donohue at Faber and Faber in London and George Gibson at Walker and Company in New York for their faith and hard work when reviewing and commenting on the manuscript. Georgina Capel and Abi Fellows at literary agency Capel and Land have been stalwart supporters and readers. Samuel Tremlett and Lucas Tremlett have gamely put up with the appearance of another Catherine in their lives. The greatest thanks go to the other Katharine (Blanca Scott) – for her mix of support, intelligence, criticism and *cariño*.

Giles Tremlett

Madrid

23 March 2010

Bibliography

The following bibliography contains most, but not all, of the sources consulted. For a full bibliography and for footnotes to the text – with links to some online source material – please go to the following website: www.faber.co.uk/catherineofaragon.

Manuscript collections

Biblioteca Nacional, Madrid.
Real Academia de la Historia, Madrid.
Archivo General de Simancas (largely at www.pares.mcu.es).
Archivo de la Diputación de Zaragoza, Zaragoza.
The National Archives, London.
British Library, London.

Calendars and document collections

Calendar of Letters, Despatches and State Papers relating to the negotiations between England and Spain preserved in the archives of Simancas and elsewhere, vols 1–5, Supplement and Further Supplement to vols 1 and 2, G. A. Bergenroth, Pascual de Gayangos and Garrett Mattingly, eds, London: Longman, Green, Longman and Roberts (1862).

Letters and Papers, Foreign and Domestic, Henry VIII, vols 1–14, J. S. Brewer, James Gairdner and R. H. Brodie, eds, London: Longman, Green, Longman and Roberts (1864).

Calendar of State Papers Relating to English Affairs in the Archives and Collections of Venice and in other libraries of northern Italy, vols 1–5, Rawdon Brown, ed., London: Longman, Green, Longman and Roberts (1864).

Calendar of State Papers and Manuscripts in the Archives and Collections of Milan 1385–1618, Allen B. Hinds, ed., London: Longman, Green, Longman and Roberts (1912).

Letters and papers illustrative of the reigns of Richard III and Henry VII, 2 vols, James Gairdner, ed., London: Longman, Green, Longman and Roberts (1861).

Monumenta Habsburgica. Sammlung von Actenstücken und Briefen sur Geschichte des Hauses Habsburg dem Zeitraume von 1473 bis 1576, Vienna (1863).

Journal articles

'Original documents relating to Queen Katharine of Aragon', *The Gentleman's Magazine*, new series 42 (Dec. 1854), p. 572.

Robert Barrington, 'A Venetian Secretary in England: an unpublished diplomatic report in the Biblioteca Marciana, Venice', Institute of Historical Research 1997. *Historical Research* vol. 70, no. 172 (June 1997).

Álvaro Fernández de Córdova Miralles, 'Imagen de los Reyes Católicos en la Roma pontificia', *España Medieval* 28 (2005), pp. 259–354.

José Ramón Fernández Suárez, 'Luis Vives: Educador de los jóvenes ingleses', *ES: Revista de filología inglesa* no. 17 (1993), pp. 141–50.

Manuel Fernando Ladero Quesada, 'Recibir princesas y enterrar reinas (Zamora 1501 y 1504)', *Espacio, tiempo y forma* Series 3, *Historia medieval* no. 13 (2000), pp. 119–38.

Manuel Gómez-Moreno, 'Joyas arabes de la Reina Catolica', *Al Andalus* vol. 8, Madrid–Granada (1943), pp. 473–5.

Frances A. Mace, 'Devonshire Ports in the Fourteenth and Fifteenth Centuries', *Transactions of the Royal Historical Society* 4th Series, vol. 8 (1925), pp. 98–126.

Ricardo Marín Ibáñez, 'Juan Luis Vives. (1492?–1540)', *Prospects: the quarterly review of comparative education* vol. 24, nos 3/4 (1994), pp. 743–59.

Garrett Mattingly, 'A humanist ambassador', *Journal of Modern History* vol. 4 (June 1932), pp. 175–85.

——, 'The reputation of Doctor De Puebla', *English Historical Review* vol. 55, no. 217 (1940), pp. 27–46.

Richard Rex, 'The Execution of the Holy Maid of Kent', *Historical Research* 64 (1991).

Ernest L. Sabine, 'City Cleaning in Mediaeval London', *Speculum* vol. 12, no. 1 (Jan. 1937), pp. 19–43.

Cristina Segura Graiño, 'Derechos sucesorios al trono de la mujeres en la Corona de Aragón', *Mayurqa: revista del Departament de Ciències Històriques i Teoria de les Arts*, no. 22, 2 (1989), pp. 591–600.

David Starkey, 'Henry VI's Old Blue Gown. The English court under the Lancastrians and Yorkists', *The Court Historian* vol. 4, no. 1 (1999), pp. 1–28.

Antonio de la Torre y del Cerro, 'Maestros de los hijos de los Reyes Católicos', *Hispania* (Madrid), vol. 63 (1956), Supplement.

Books in Spanish

Continuación de la Crónica de Pulgar por un autor anónimo, C. Cayetano Rosell, ed., Madrid: Biblioteca de Autores Españoles (1953).

Crónica anónima de Enrique IV de Castilla, 1454–1474 (Crónica castellana), M. P. Sánchez Parra, ed., Madrid: Ediciones de la Torre (1991).

Alfredo Alvar Ezquerra, *Isabel la Católica*, Madrid: Temas de Hoy (2002).

Tarsicio de Azcona, *Isabel la Católica. Estudio crítico de su vida y su reinado*, Madrid: Biblioteca de Autores Cristianos (1964); Edition de La Esfera de los Libros, Madrid (2002).

Andrés Bernáldez, *Memorias del reinado de los Reyes Católicos*, edición de Manuel Gómez-Moreno y Juan de Mata Carriazo, Madrid (1962).

Carmen Bernis, *Trajes y modas en la España de los reyes Católicos*, Madrid: CSIC (1978).

Berwick y de Alba, Duque de, *Correspondencia de Gutierre Gómez de Fuensalida. Embajador en Alemania, Flandes e Inglaterra (1496–1509)*, Madrid: Imprenta Alemana (1907).

José Maria Doussinague, *La política internacional de Fernando el Católico*, Madrid: Espasa-Calpe (1944).

Francesc Eiximenis, *Carro de las donas: Valladolid, 1542 / adaptación del Llibre de les dones de Francesc Eiximenis O. F. M. realizada por el P. Carmona O. F. M.*, Carmen Clausell Nácher, ed., Madrid: Fundación Universitaria Española (2007).

Diego Enríquez del Castillo, *Crónica del rey don Enrique el Quarto de este nombre*, A. Sánchez Martín, ed., Valladolid: Universidad de Valladolid (1994).

Álvaro Fernández de Córdova Miralles, *La Corte de Isabel I. Ritos y ceremonias de una reina (1474–1504)*, Madrid: Dykinson (2002).

G. Fernández de Oviedo, *Libro de la Cámara Real del Príncipe don Juan e offiçios de su casa e seruiçio ordinario*, Madrid: Sociedad de Bibliófilos Españoles (1870).

Lorenzo Galíndez de Carvajal, *Crónica de Enrique IV*, Juan Torres Fontes, ed., Murcia: CSIC (1946).

José Antonio García Luján, *El Generalife. Jardin del paraiso*, Granada (2006).

Félix de Llanos y Torriglia, *Catalina de Aragón, Reina de Inglaterra (conferencia leída en la Unión de Damas Españolas . . .)*, Madrid: Imprentas Helénicas (1914).

——, *En el hogar de los Reyes Católicos y cosas de sus tiempos*, Madrid: Ediciones Fax (1946).

Vicenta María Márquez de la Plata y Ferrándiz, *Mujeres renacentistas de la corte de Isabel La Catolica*, Madrid: Editorial Castalia (2005).

José-Luis Martín, *Isabel la Católica: sus hijas y las damas de su corte, modelos de doncellas, casadas y viudas, en el Carro de las donas (1542)*, Avila (2001).

Pedro Mártir de Anglería, *Epistolario*, J. López de Toro, ed. and trans., in *Documentos inéditos para la Historia de España*, vols 9–12, Madrid (1953).

Molins, Marqués de (ed.), *Crónica del Rey Enrico Otavo de Inglaterra escrita por un autor coetáneo y ahora por primera vez impresa é ilustrada con introducción, notas y apéndices por El Marqués de Molins*, Madrid: Librería de los Bibliófilos (1874).

Hieronymus Münzer, *Viaje por España y Portugal (1494–1495)*, Madrid: Polifemo (1991).

Alonso de Palencia, *Crónica de Enrique IV*, 3 vols, A. Paz y Melia, ed., Madrid: Biblioteca de Autores Españoles (1973).

Antonio Rumeu de Armas, *Itinerario de los Reyes Católicos (1474–1516)*, Madrid: Consejo Superior de Investigaciones Cientificas (1974).

BIBLIOGRAPHY

María Jesús Pérez Martín, *María Tudor. La gran reina desconocida*, Madrid: Ediciones Rialp (2008).

Joseph Pérez, *La España de los Reyes Católicos*, Madrid: Arlanza (2004).

Fernando del Pulgar, *Crónica de los Reyes Católicos: versión inédita*, Juan de Mata Carriazo, ed., Madrid: Espasa-Calpe (1943).

Francisco Javier Sánchez Cantón, *Libros, tapices y cuadros que coleccionó Isabel la Católica*, Madrid: CSIC (1950).

Alonso de Santa Cruz, *Crónica de los Reyes Católicos*, Juan de Mata Carriazo, ed., Seville (1951).

Miguel Sobrino, *Catedrales. Las biografías desconocidas de los Grandes Templos de España*, Madrid: La Esfera de los Libros (2009).

Luis Suárez Fernández, *El Camino hacia Europa*, Madrid: Rialp. (1990).

——, *Los Reyes Católicos*, Barcelona: RBA (2005).

Antonio de la Torre y del Cerro, *La Casa de Isabel la Católica*, Madrid: CSIC (1954).

——, *Cuentas de Gonzalo de Baeza, tesorero de Isabel la Católica*, 2 vols, Madrid: CSIC (1955).

Luis Ulargui, *Catalina de Aragón*, Barcelona: Plaza Janés (2004).

Diego de Valera, Mosén., *Crónica de los Reyes Católicos*, Madrid: Juan de Mata Carriazo (1927).

——, *Memorial de diversas hazañas, crónica de Enrique IV*, Juan de Mata Carriazo, ed., Madrid: Espasa-Calpe (1941).

——, *Epístolas*, Madrid: Sociedad de Bibliófilos (1878).

Jerónimo Zurita, *Anales de Aragón*, Ángel Canellas López et al., eds, Zaragoza: Institución Fernando el Católico at http://ifc.dpz.es/publicaciones/ver/id/2448.

——, *Historia del rey Don Fernando el Católico. De las empresas, y ligas de Italia. Zaragoza, en 1580*, Oficina de Domingo de Portonariis, y Ursino impresor de la Sacra, Real, y Católica Majestad, y del reino de Aragón. José Javier Iso et al, eds, Zaragoza: at http://ifc.dpz.es/publicaciones/ver/id/2423.

Books in English and other languages except Spanish

A collection of Ordinances and regulations for the government of the royal household, made in divers reigns from King Edward III to King William and Queen Mary, London: Society of Antiquaries (1790).

A litil boke for the Pestilence . . . (1485?), Manchester: Manchester University Press, John Rylands facsimiles (1910).

An inventory of the wardrobe etc. . . . *of Katharine of Arragon, at Baynard's Castle* in *The Camden Miscellany*, vol. 3, London: Camden Society (1855).

Peter Ackroyd, *The Life of Thomas More*, London: Vintage (1999).

——, *London: The Biography*, London: Vintage (2001).

Eugenio Albèri, *Relazioni degli ambasciatori veneti al Senato*, vol 8, pp. 1–28 for 'Relazione d'Inghilterra di Ludovico Falier', Florence: Societa Editrice Fiorentina (1853).

Bethany Aram, *Juana the Mad. Sovereignty and Dynasty in Renaissance Europe*, Baltimore: Johns Hopkins University Press (2005).

William Benham, *Old St. Paul's Cathedral*, London: Seeley and Co. (1902).

Samuel Bentley, ed., *Excerpta Historica, or illustrations of English History*, London (1881).

G. W. Bernard, *The King's Reformation. Henry VIII and the remaking of the English Church*, New Haven: Yale University Press (2007 (2005)).

J. S. Brewer, *The Reign of Henry VIII from His Accession to the Death of Wolsey*, 2 vols, J. Gairdner, ed. (1884).

——, ed., *Monumenta franciscana*, London: Longman, Brown, Green, Longman and Roberts (1858).

Dom Bede Camm, *Lives of the English Martyrs declared blessed by Pope Leo XIII in 1886 and 1895. Martyrs under Henry VIII*, vol. 1, London: Longmans, Green and Co. (1914).

James P. Carley, *The Books of King Henry VIII and His Wives*, London: British Library (2004).

George Cavendish, *The Life and Death of Cardinal Wolsey*, Roger Lockyer, ed., London: Folio Society (1962).

Francesca Claremont, *Catherine of Aragon*, London: R. Hale (1939).

Charles Henry Cooper, *Memorials of Cambridge*, Cambridge: William Metcalfe (1861).

Randle Cotgrave, *A Dictionarie of the French and English Tongues*, London: Adam Islip (1611). Assembled from two scans in the French

National Library by Greg Lindahl and currently available at http://www.pbm.com/~lindahl/cotgrave.

Thomas Cranmer, *Miscellaneous Writings and Letters of Thomas Cranmer, Archbishop of Canterbury, Martyr*, Cambridge: Parker Society/CUP (1846).

Sean Cunningham, *Henry VII*, London: Routledge (2007).

F. H. Dickinson, *Missale ad usum insignis et praeclarae ecclesiae Sarum; labore ac studio Francisci Henrici Dickinson*, Farnborough: Gregg (1969 reprint of 1861–3 original).

Janette Dillon, *Performance and Spectacle in Hall's Chronicle*, London: Society for Theatre Research (2002).

Maria Dowling, *Fisher of Men, A life of John Fisher, 1469–1535*, Basingstoke: Macmillan (1999).

Eamon Duffy, *The Stripping of the Altars: traditional religion in England, c. 1400–c. 1580*, New Haven: Yale University Press (2nd edn 2005).

——, *Marking the Hours. English people and their prayers 1240–1570*, New Haven: Yale University Press (2006).

Theresa Earenfight, *Queenship and Political Power in Medieval and Early Modern Spain*, Aldershot: Ashgate (2005).

Stephan Ehses, ed., *Römische Dokumente zur Geschichte der Ehescheidung Heinrichs VIII*, Paderborn (1893).

J. H. Elliott, *Imperial Spain 1469–1716*, London: Pelican (1970).

Henry Ellis, ed., *Original Letters Illustrative of English History*, 1st series, 3 vols, 2nd series, 4 vols, 3rd series, 4 vols, London: Harding, Triphook and Lepard (1824).

G. R. Elton, *England under the Tudors*, Abingdon: Routledge (3rd edn 1991).

Desiderius Erasmus, *Opus epistolarum Des. Erasmi Roterodami*, 12 vols, P. S. Allen et al., eds, (1906–58).

——, *Correspondance d'Érasme. Édition intégrale traduite et annotée d'après l'Opus epistolarum de P. S. Allen, H. M. Allen, et H. W. Garrod*, vols 4–8, Aloïs Gerlo and Paul Foriers, eds, Paris: Gallimard (1968).

Carolly Erickson, *Great Harry. The Extravagant Life of Henry VIII*, London: Robson Books (2004).

Felipe Fernández-Armesto, *Ferdinand and Isabella*, New York: Dorset Press (1991).

Richard Fiddes, *The Life of Cardinal Wolsey*, London: Knapton and others (2nd edn 1726).

William Forrest, *The History of Grisild the Second: A narrative, in verse, of the divorce of Queen Katharine of Arragon*, Revd W. D. Macray, ed., London: Whittingham and Wilkins (1875).

John Foxe, *A History of the Lives, Suffering, and Triumphant Deaths of the Primitive as well as the Protestant Martyrs*, Philadelphia (1845).

James A. Froude, *The Divorce of Catherine of Aragon: The Story as told by the Imperial ambassadors resident at the court of Henry VIII*, Honolulu: University Press of the Pacific (2003 reprint).

James Gairdner, *Henry VII*, London: Macmillan and Co. (1889).

John Galt, *The Life and Administration of Cardinal Wolsey*, Edinburgh: Oliver and Boyd (3rd edn 1824).

Henry Gee and William John Hardy, *Documents Illustrative of English Church History*, London: Macmillan (1921).

Sebastian Giustinian, *Four Years at the Court of Henry VIII. Selection of despatches written by the Venetian ambassador, Sebastian Giustinian, and addressed to the signory of Venice, January 12th 1515, to July 26th 1519*, Rawdon Brown, trans., London: Smith, Elder and Co. (1854).

Edmund Marsden Goldsmid, *A collection of 18 rare and curious historical tracts and pamphlets*, Edinburgh: Privately printed (1884).

Brad S. Gregory, *Salvation at Stake. Christian martyrdom in Early Modern Europe*, Cambridge, Mass.: Harvard University Press (1999).

Francis Grose, *The Antiquarian Repertory*, 4 vols, London: E. Jeffery (1807–9).

John Guy, *Tudor England*, Oxford: OUP (1988).

Peter Gwyn, *The King's Cardinal: the rise and fall of Thomas Wolsey*, London: Pimlico (2002).

Edward Hall, *Hall's Chronicle – The union of the two noble and illustre famelies of Lancastre and Yorke (1548)*, London: J. Johnson (1809).

James Orchard Halliwell, *Letters of the Kings of England*, 2 vols, London: Henry Colburn (1846).

Nicholas Harpsfield, *A Treatise on the Pretended Divorce between Henry VIII and Catharine of Aragon*, Nicholas Pocock, ed., London: Camden Society (1878).

William Harrison. Elizabethan England: from 'A description of England' by William Harrison (in 'Holinshed's Chronicles'). London: Walter Scott. Undated.

Maria Hayward, *Dress at the Court of King Henry VIII*, Leeds: Maney (2007).

Henry VIII, *The Love Letters of Henry VIII to Anne Boleyn*, Boston: John W. Luce (1906).

Edward Lord Herbert, *Autobiography of Edward Lord Herbert of Cherbury. The History of England under Henry VIII*, London: Alexander Murray (1870)

Martin A. Sharp Hume (ed. and trans.), *Chronicle of King Henry VIII of England. Being a contemporary record of some of the principal events of the reigns of Henry VIII and Edward VI. Written in Spanish by an unknown hand*, London: Bell and Sons (1889).

Robert Hutchinson, *The Last Days of Henry VIII*, London: Weidenfeld and Nicolson (2005).

——, *Thomas Cromwell. The rise and fall of Henry VIII's most notorious minister*, London: Weidenfeld and Nicolson (2007).

The Huth Library, *A catalogue of the printed books, manuscripts, autograph letters, and engravings collected by Henry Huth.* Vol .V, London: Ellis and White (1880).

Robert Irwin, *The Alhambra*, London: Profile Books (2004).

Eric Ives, *The Life and Death of Anne Boleyn*, Oxford: Blackwell (2005).

Michael K. Jones and Malcolm G. Underwood, *The King's Mother. Lady Margaret Beaufort, countess of Richmond and Derby*, Cambridge: CUP (1992).

Henry Ansgar Kelly, *The matrimonial trials of Henry VIII*, Eugene, Oregon: Wipf and Stock (2004).

Gordon Kipling, ed., *The Receyt of The Lady Kateryne*, Oxford: Oxford University Press for The Early English Text Society (1990).

Hugo Laemmer, *Monumenta Vaticana historiam Ecclesiasticam saeculi XVI illustrantia*, Freiburg (1861).

J. L. Laynesmith, *The Last Medieval Queens*, Oxford: OUP (2004).

Henry Charles Lea, *History of the Inquisition of Spain*, vol. 1 at the Library of Iberian Resources Online: http://libro.uca.edu/lea1/1lea.htm (original edn Macmillan 1906–7).

John Leland, *Joannis Lelandi antiquarii de rebus britannicis collectanea*, London: Richardson (1770).

—— and Lucy Toulmin Smith, *The Itinerary of John Leland in or about the years 1535–1543*, parts 4 and 5 with an appendix of extracts from Leland's collectanea, London: George Bell and Son (1908).

John Lewis, *The Life of Dr John Fisher, Bishop of Rochester in the reign of King Henry VIII with an appendix of illustrative documents and papers*, London: Joseph Lilly (1855).

Robert Lindesay of Pitscottie, *The Historie and Cronicles of Scotland*, vol. 2, Edinburgh: William Blackwood and Sons (1899).

Karen Lindsey, *Divorced, Beheaded, Survived – A Feminist Reinterpretation of the Wives of Henry VIII*, Da Capo Press (1995).

John Lingard, *A History of England*, vol. 4, London: J. Mawman (1820).

David Loades, *The Tudor Court*, Bangor: Headstart History (1992).

——, *The Politics of Marriage: Henry VIII and his queens*, Stroud: Alan Sutton Publishing (1994).

——, *Mary Tudor. The tragical history of the first queen of England*, London: National Archives (2006).

——, *Henry VIII. Court, church and conflict*, London: National Archives (2007).

Mary M. Luke, *Catherine, the Queen*, New York: Paperback Library (1967).

Frederick Madden, Privy Purse Expenses of the Princess Mary, Daughter of King Henry the Eighth, London: William Pickering (1831).

William Maskell, *Monumenta ritualia ecclesiae anglicanae or occasional offices of the church of England according to the ancient use of Salisbury the prymer in English and other prayers and forms with dissertations and notes*, London: William Pickering (1847).

Garrett Mattingly, *Catherine of Aragon*, London: Jonathan Cape (1942).

St Thomas More, *The Yale Edition of the Complete Works of St Thomas More*, 15 vols, New Haven: Yale University Press (1963).

——, *The Correspondence of Sir Thomas More*, Elizabeth Frances Rogers, ed., Princeton: Princeton University Press (1947).

——, *St Thomas More: selected letters*, Elizabeth Frances Rogers, ed., New Haven: Yale University Press (1961).

Alfred Hamy, *Entrevue de François Premier avec Henry VIII*, Auxerre (1898).

Nicholas Harris Nicolas, *Privy Purse Expenses of King Henry the Eighth*, London: William Pickering (1827).

——, *Privy Purse Expenses of Elizabeth of York: Wardrobe accounts of Edward the Fourth*, London: William Pickering (1830).

Francis Morgan Nichols, *The Epistles of Erasmus . . . English translations*, London: Longmans, Green and Co. (1901).

John E. Paul, *Catherine of Aragon and Her Friends*, London: Burns and Oates (1966).

Fernán Pérez de Guzmán, *Pen Portraits of Illustrious Castilians*, Washington, D.C.: CUA Press (2003).

Maria Perry, *Sisters to the King*, London: Andre Deutsch (2002).

Hazel Pierce, *Margaret Pole Countess of Salisbury 1473–1541*, Cardiff: University of Wales Press (2009).

Nicholas Pocock, ed., *Records of the Reformation: the divorce, 1527–33*, 2 vols, Oxford: Clarendon Press (1870).

A. F. Pollard, *The Reign of Henry VII from Contemporary Sources*, vol. 1, *Narrative extracts*, London: Longmans, Green and Co. (1913).

H. F. M. Prescott, *Mary Tudor*, London: Phoenix (2nd edn 2003).

Glyn Redworth, *The She-Apostle. The extraordinary life and death of Luisa de Carvajal*, Oxford: OUP (2008).

Jessica Erin Riddell, *'A Mirror of Men': Sovereignty, Performance, and Textuality in Tudor England, 1501–1559*, PhD thesis submitted to the Department of English, Queen's University, Kingston, Ontario, Canada (2009).

Hastings Robinson, ed., *Original Letters relative to the English Reformation*, Cambridge: Parker Society/CUP (1846).

Nancy Rubin, *Isabella of Castile. The First Renaissance Queen*, Lincoln, NE: ASJA Press (2004).

Thomas Rymer, *Foedera*, Vol. 13, Jean Maulme (1739).

Nicolas Sander, *Rise and Growth of the Anglican Schism*, D. Lewis, ed., London: Burns and Oates (1877).

Marino Sanuto, *I Diarii di Marino Sanuto*, vols 14–17, 39, 54, Venice: Fratelli Visentini Tipografi Editori (1886).

J. J. Scarisbrick, *Henry the Eighth*, London: Eyre Methuen (1981).

John Sephton, *A Handbook of Lancashire Place-names*, Liverpool: Henry Young and Son (1913).

William Shakespeare and John Fletcher, *King Henry VIII (All is True)*, Gordon McMullan, ed., London: Arden Shakespeare/Thomson Learning (2000).

Ron Shoesmith and Andy Johnson, eds, *Ludlow Castle: Its History and Buildings*, Almeley: Logaston Press (2000).

David Starkey, *Rivals in Power: Lives and Letters of the Great Tudor Dynasties*, London: Macmillan (1990).

——, ed., *A European Court in England*, London: Collins and Brown (1991).

——, *Six Wives: The queens of Henry VIII*, London: Vintage (2004).

——, *The Reign of Henry VIII: personalities and politics*, London: Vintage (2002).

——, *Henry: Virtuous Prince*, London: Harper Press (2008).

—— and Susan Doran, *Henry VIII. Man and monarch*, London: British Library (2009).

Agnes Strickland, *Lives of the Queens of Scotland*, 2 vols, New York: Harper and Brothers (1851).

——, *Lives of the Queens of England*, Philadelphia: Blanchard and Lea (1852).

Agustín Theiner, *Vetera Monumenta Hibernorum et Scotorum historiam illustrantia quae ex Vaticani, Neapolis ac Florentiae tabulariis deprompsit et ordine chronologico disposuit A. Theiner*, Rome (1864).

A. H. Thomas and I. D. Thornley, eds, *The Great Chronicle of London*, Gloucester: Alan Sutton Publishing, 1983.

Simon Thurley, *The Royal Palaces of Tudor England*, New Haven: Yale University Press (1993).

William Tyndale, *Expositions and notes on Sundry Portions of the Holy Scriptures: together with the practise of prelates* (1528), H. Walker, ed., London: Parker Society, 33 (1849).

Juan Luis Vives, *The Education of a Christian Woman. A sixteenth century manual*, Charles Fantazzi, ed. and trans., Chicago: University of Chicago Press (2000).

—— and Foster Watson, *Vives: On Education. A translation of the tradendis disciplinis of Juan Luis Vives together with an introduction by Foster Watson*, Cambridge: CUP (1913).

Peter G. Wallace, *The Long European Reformation*, Basingstoke: Palgrave Macmillan (2004).

Foster Watson, *Luis Vives. El gran valenciano*, Oxford: OUP (1922).

Alison Weir, *The Six Wives of Henry VIII*, London: Pimlico (1991).

——, *Henry VIII. King and Court*, London: Pimlico (2002).

Anna Whitelock, *Mary Tudor, England's First Queen*, London: Bloomsbury (2009).

Neville Williams, *Henry VIII and His Court*, London: Cardinal (1973).

Mary Anne Everett Wood, *Letters of Royal and Illustrious Ladies of Great Britain*, 3 vols, London: Henry Colburn (1846).

C. M. Woolgar, *The Senses in Late Medieval England*, New Haven: Yale University Press (2006).

Ann Wroe, *Perkin, A Story of Deception*, London: Jonathan Cape (2003).

Index

13–20; heir, 16–19; civil war, 16; Guisando agreement, 13–14, 17–18; death, 19, 20

Erasmus, Desiderius, on Catherine's education, 47–8, 241–2; on London, 82; correspondence, 154, 216; on winter in England, 205; letter to Catherine, 248

Erkenwald, St, 84

Esquivel, Alfonso de, 97

Estrada, Hernán, 105–6, 108, 114

Estúñiga, Diego López de, 15

Exeter, Gertrude Courtenay, marchioness of, 359, 375–6, 416

Eztuniga, Friar Juan de, 207

Falier, Ludovico, 358

Featherstone, Richard, 253, 397–8, 412

Felipe, Salvador, 1, 2, 3

Felipez, Francisco, 271–2, 273, 302, 409

Ferdinand V of Aragon: appearance, 19; character, 19, 163; marriage, 18–19; relationship with Isabel, 20–1, 24–5, 30, 120; campaigns, 24, 25–6, 60, 68; accession to throne of Aragon, 30; government, 163; children, 2, 27, 38, 53; birth of daughter Catherine, 27–8; daughters' marriages, 25, 38–9; relationship with daughter Catherine, 60–1; daughter Catherine's marriage, 10, 60–1, 62, 105–8, 111; daughter Catherine's dowry, 106, 118, 128, 138, 140, 144–5, 157; negotiations with Henry VII, 106, 116, 120, 138, 144–5; papal dispensation for Catherine, 111–12; Catherine's financial affairs, 117–18, 141; Isabel's death, 119–20; daughter Juana's rule of Castile, 120, 125, 131, 132, 141, 206; correspondence with Catherine, 119–21, 129, 141, 142–3, 147, 156–7; appointment of Catherine as ambassador, 140–1; daughter Catherine's role as ambassador, 141–5; daughter Catherine's marriage, 156–8, 310; relationship with son-in-law Henry, 158, 182–6, 190–1,

203, 205–8, 209, 214–15; daughter Catherine's pregnancy, 169–70; English alliance, 182–4; African project, 184–5; French campaign plans, 185, 190–1; conquest of Navarre, 185–6, 194; truce with France, 191; illness, 203, 215; remarriage, 203; treaty negotiations, 203, 205; truce with France, 205–6; treaty with Henry VIII, 214–15; heir, 54, 215; death, 2, 215

Ferdinand, archduke of Austria, 247, 335

Ferrara, duke of, 199

Field of the Cloth of Gold (1520), 227–9, 235–7

Fisher, John, bishop of Rochester: character, 270, 340; on Catherine and Arthur's wedding, 87; Catherine's appeal to, 270; appointed to advise Catherine, 286; performance at Blackfriars hearings, 305, 314–18; Catherine's defence, 314–18, 335, 356; attempted murder of, 340–1; arrested, 375; imprisonment in Tower, 395; interrogation, 413–14; deadline to swear oath, 412; execution, 413

Flandes, Juan de, 38, 122

Flodden, battle (1513), 198, 200, 201, 202

Foix, count of, 143

Forrest, Friar John, 394, 395, 399, 422

Fox, Edward, 364

Francis, dauphin, 218, 228

Francis I of France: appearance, 213; character, 211; accession, 211, 213; Henry's rivalry with, 213, 235; son's betrothal, 219, 228; court, 259; Field of the Cloth of Gold, 228–9, 235; defeat by emperor, 246–7; marriages, 254–5, 363; Wolsey's negotiations, 271; Henry and Anne's visit, 362–3; view of Henry, 414–15

Fuensalida, Gutierre Gómez de, 135, 136–7, 144–6, 153, 155, 157

Gainsford, Anne, 345

Galíndez de Carvajal, Lorenzo, 16

Galindo, Beatriz, 47